POLITY AND

The Edinburgh/Glasgow Law and Society Series
Series Editors: Professor Emilios A. Christodoulidis and Dr Sharon Cowan

Titles in the Series

Polity and Crisis
Reflections on the European Odyssey

Edited by

MASSIMO FICHERA
University of Helsinki, Finland

SAKARI HÄNNINEN
National Institute for Health and Welfare (THL), Finland

KAARLO TUORI
University of Helsinki, Finland

Routledge
Taylor & Francis Group

LONDON AND NEW YORK

First published 2014 by Ashgate Publishing

Published 2016 by Routledge
2 Park Square, Milton Park, Abingdon, Oxfordshire OX14 4RN
711 Third Avenue, New York, NY 10017, USA

First issued in paperback 2016

Routledge is an imprint of the Taylor & Francis Group, an informa business

British Library Cataloguing in Publication Data
A catalogue record for this book is available from the British Library

The Library of Congress has cataloged the printed edition as follows:
Polity and crisis : reflections on the European odyssey / by Massimo Fichera, Sakari
Hänninen and Kaarlo Tuori.
    pages cm.—(Edinburgh/Glasgow law and society series)
  Includes bibliographical references and index.
    ISBN 978-1-4724-1291-1 (hardback)
1. Law—European Union countries. 2. European Union countries—Politics and
government. I. Fichera, Massimo, editor of compilation. II. Hänninen, Sakari, 1948- editor
of compilation. III. Tuori, Kaarlo, editor of compilation.
  KJE958.P65 2014
  341.242'2—dc23
                                                                                          2014006818

ISBN 13: 978-1-138-63692-7 (pbk)
ISBN 13: 978-1-4724-1291-1 (hbk)

Contents

List of Figures and Tables

Figures

Tables

List of Abbreviations and Acronyms

ECT	European Constitutional Treaty
CJEU or ECJ	Court of Justice of the European Union
ECB	European Central Bank
ECI	European Citizens' Initiative
ECtHR	European Court of Human Rights
EFSF	European Financial Stability Facility
EFSM	European Financial Stabilisation Mechanism
EMU	European Monetary Union
ESM	European Stability Mechanism
EU	European Union
FATF	Financial Action Task Force
FSB	Financial Stability Board
FSF	Financial Stability Forum
ICANN	Internet Corporation for Assigned Names and Numbers
ICAO	International Civil Aviation Organization
ILO	International Labour Organization
ISO	International Organization for Standardization
IMF	International Monetary Fund
NATO	North Atlantic Treaty Organization
ND	Northern Dimension
OECD	Organisation for Economic Co-operation and Development
OMC	Open Method of Coordination
TEU	Treaty on European Union
TFEU	Treaty on the Functioning of the European Union
TSCG	Treaty on Stability, Coordination and Governance in the Economic and Monetary Union
US or USA	United States of America
WB	World Bank
WTO	World Trade Organization

List of Contributors

Hauke Brunkhorst is Professor for Sociology at the University of Flensburg (Germany). In 2009–2010 he was Theodor-Heuss-Professor at New School for Social Research New York/ NY.

Among his latest books are *Critical Theory of Legal Revolutions. An Evolutionary Perspective* (Continuum 2012) and *Solidarity. From Civic Friendship to a Global Legal Community* (MIT Press 2005). (Translation of *Solidarität. Von der Bürgerfreundschaft zur globalen Rechtsgenossenschaft*, Suhrkamp 2002).

Emilios Christodoulidis has been Professor of Legal Theory at the Glasgow University School of Law since 2006. Prior to this, he taught at the University of Edinburgh. He holds degrees from the Universities of Athens (LLB) and Edinburgh (LLM, PhD). His interests lie mainly in the area of the philosophy and sociology of law and in constitutional theory.

Michelle Everson has researched widely in the field of European Law and has particular interests in the areas of European regulatory law, European administrative and constitutional law and European citizenship. Professor Everson has recently published widely on financial and economic crisis in Europe.

Massimo Fichera is a Post-Doctoral Fellow at the University of Helsinki, Faculty of Law. He has been a member of the Centre of Excellence in Foundations of European Law and Polity Research, Faculty of Law, University of Helsinki. His research interests lie in the intersection between EU and international law and constitutional theory. He has co-edited *Law and Security in Europe: Reconsidering the Security Constitution* (with Jens Kremer, Intersentia 2013).

Sakari Hänninen is currently working as research professor at the National Institute for Health and Welfare, Helsinki. He has previously collaborated with the Centre of Excellence in Foundations of European Law and Polity Research, Faculty of Law, University of Helsinki. He is interested in a wide range of topics in law and political and social theory and European affairs.

Ari Hirvonen, LLD, is University Lecturer in Jurisprudence, Faculty of Law, at the University of Helsinki, Finland. He has been a member of the Centre of Excellence in Foundations of European Law and Polity Research, funded by the Finnish Academy.

Hirvonen has written extensively on legal theory, law and art, the idea of justice in Ancient Greek philosophy and tragedy, the problem of evil, and the relationship between law, democracy and politics. His main research areas are moral and legal philosophy, phenomenology, deconstruction and psychoanalysis.

Pia Letto-Vanamo, LLD, is a legal historian specializing in European legal history, history of European integration and conceptual history. Currently Professor Letto-Vanamo is working as Director of the Institute of International Economic Law at the University of Helsinki. She has in the past been Vice-Dean of the Faculty of Law responsible for research and researcher training and Co-Director of the research team 'Europe as Market' of the Centre of Excellence in Foundations of European Law and Polity Research funded by the Academy of Finland.

Giandomenico Majone is Emeritus Professor of Public Policy at the European University Institute. His latest book is *Rethinking the Union of Europe Post Crisis – Has Integration Gone Too Far?* (Cambridge University Press 2014).

Tore Vincents Olsen is Associate Professor in Political Theory at the Department of Political Science and Government at Aarhus University, Denmark. He holds a PhD in Political Science from the University of Copenhagen. He has worked on issues concerning the legitimacy of the EU, the Europeanization of national political institutions, anti-discrimination legislation in Europe and the relationship between political culture and immigrant inclusion.

Eva Sørensen is Professor of Public Administration and Democracy at the Department of Society and Globalization at Roskilde University. She holds a PhD in Political Science from the University of Copenhagen. She has over the years published extensively on the impact of new forms of governance on democracy.

Patricia Springborg DPhil (Oxon), is currently with the Centre for British Studies, Humboldt University, Berlin. She was previously *professore ordinario* in the School of Economics of the Free University of Bolzano and prior to that held a personal chair in Political Theory in the Department of Government at the University of Sydney.

Kaarlo Tuori is Academy Professor at the University of Helsinki, Faculty of Law. He has published extensively in the area of legal and constitutional theory, including the monographs *Critical Legal Positivism* (Ashgate 2002) and *Ratio and Voluntas* (Ashgate 2010). He has also co-edited *The Many Constitutions of Europe* (with Suvi Sankari, Ashgate 2010) and co-authored *The Eurozone Crisis: A Constitutional Analysis* (with Klaus Tuori, Cambridge University Press 2014). He has directed the Centre of Excellence in Foundations of European Law and Polity Research (University of Helsinki) and is a member and former Vice-President of the Venice Commission.

RBJ Walker is Professor of Political Science and Contemporary Cultural, Social, and Political Thought at the University of Victoria in Canada and Professor of International Relations at PUC-Rio de Janeiro in Brazil. He has published widely in the field of international political theory, most recently *After the Globe, Before the World* (Routledge, 2010), is the long-term editor of the journal *Alternatives: Global, Local, Political*, and was the founding co-editor, with Didier Bigo, of the journal *International Political Sociology.*

Editors' Preface

European integration is an open-ended, ongoing process which has been deeply challenged by integral world capitalism. This has become especially evident when economic integration in Europe has been supplemented by efforts to advance political unity, constitutional coherence and social cohesion. In the present circumstances of Eurozone crisis this challenge has embodied not only an economic but also a political, constitutional, social and even existential threat to continuity. This is an epochal turning point where the formative character of the EU is at stake and under critical discussion.

The main issue addressed by this book concerns the question of the future of the EU as a polity to come following the recent economic and financial crisis. Can the interaction between law, market and community in the transnational setting be ultimately associated with a sustainable model of European democracy? There is no single answer to this multifaceted question, which is here approached from an inter- or, if you like, post-disciplinary perspective.

The constitutional and political dimensions of the crisis are intertwined and prompt us to reconsider whether and in what sense the EU could be, or could not be, understood as a democratic polity. By opening up perspectives on the EU from inside and outside the driving forces, obstacles and political possibilities of the EU are addressed in reference to nationally determined criteria for politico-legal action such as those embedded in the Nordic democratic and welfarist heritage and are examined in the context of post-nationally or supra-nationally evolved patterns of cross-border transactions, be they economic, political or juridical.

The chapters in this book are the result of a Conference on 'Democracy and Law in Europe', organized in September 2012 by the Centre of Excellence in Foundations of European Law and Polity (Faculty of Law, University of Helsinki), funded by the Academy of Finland. The Conference represents an attempt to promote a dialogue between diverse scholarly approaches to European law and to address the legal theoretical implications of European integration and Europeanization.

We wish to thank Ashgate for publishing this book. Our special thanks go to Alison Kirk, Aarne Granlund and Christopher Goddard for their assistance.

Massimo Fichera, Sakari Hänninen and Kaarlo Tuori
Helsinki, 22 April 2014

PART I
Constitutional Challenges of the Eurozone Crisis

Chapter 1

The Eurozone Crisis as a Constitutional Crisis[1]

Kaarlo Tuori

Relationality of the European Constitution

The Specificity of the European Constitution

The present crisis in the euro area is both an economic and a constitutional crisis. In turn, the constitutional implications are not only confined to the economic dimension but reach out to the political and social constitutions as well. The crisis also affects democracy and transparency, as well as social values and rights. To catch the various constitutional aspects of the crisis presupposes a constitutional approach which the group of researchers making up the Helsinki Centre of Excellence in the Foundations of European Law and Polity Research has termed 'relational analytic'. The necessity for this approach is related to specific features of the European constitution which distinguish it from its nation state counterparts.

The first of these is the evolutionary nature of the European constitution; instead of a constitution as a fixed, standstill normative entity it is more appropriate to speak of a continuous process of a constitutionalisation. In the European context, the tripartite conceptual whole of constituent power (*pouvoir constituant*), demos and constitutional moment does not find application: in European constitutional history, no clearly definable constitutional moment exists where the European demos would have exercised its constituent power and given birth to a European constitution. The European process of constitutionalisation does include such manifest, high-profile constitutional speech acts as the Founding Treaties and their amendments; say, the treaties of Rome, Maastricht and Lisbon. But the discourse giving rise to continuous mutations to European constitutional law also comprises speech acts by many constitutional actors other than the European constitutional legislator: the ECJ as the constitutional court, other EU institutions, Member State constitutional courts, constitutional scholars and so on. Indeed, an important task for European

---

1 This chapter summarises the approach and some of the central conclusions of a longer study I have prepared together with Klaus Tuori. Kaarlo Tuori and Klaus Tuori, *The Eurozone Crisis: A Constitutional Analysis* (Cambridge University Press 2013).

constitutional scholars is to identify these constitutional actors and to assess the mutual weight of their contributions. The Eurozone crisis exemplifies the particular process-nature of the European constitution: the EU constitutional legislator or constitutional court has played but a peripheral role in the constitutional mutation the crisis has occasioned.

Distinct from the European constitution, too, is the differentiated nature of the process of constitutionalisation. In the nation state setting, we are used to treating the constitution not only as a result of an identifiable decision at an identifiable (constitutional) moment, but also as a unitary normative entity. In the European context, it is necessary to distinguish between various dimensions of constitution(alisation) or – if you like – between various European constitutions; instead of *the* constitution of Europe, we should actually talk about the many constitutions of Europe. I have suggested[2] that we distinguish between the following constitutional dimensions: the economic constitution; the juridical constitution; the political constitution; the security constitution; and the social constitution. This distinction between different dimensions of the European constitution – or, you could say, different European constitutions – is backed up by the first aspect of the approach termed relational analytic: the interrelation between constitutional law and its societal object of regulation.

The various European constitutions have not emerged simultaneously but, rather, successively, following a certain order. A third peculiarity of the European constitution is the multi-temporality of the process of constitutionalisation: the European constitution consists of a differentiated multi-temporal process of constitutionalisation. This entails a further research task for European constitutional scholars: to track the diverse temporalities of European constitutionalisation and to detect the internal logic inherent in its course provided, naturally, that such logic exists!

In previous contributions,[3] I have also defended the claim that distinct periods can be discerned in European constitutionalisation; these receive their particular colouring from a particular constitution. Reflecting the temporal and functional primacy of economic integration, the first wave proceeded under the auspices of the economic constitution. The landmark decisions of the ECJ defining the basic principles characterising Community law as an independent legal system manifested the significance of the juridical constitution. The Maastricht Treaty epitomised at least the temporary dominance of the political constitution. The Amsterdam Treaty (1998), with its new provisions on the Area of Freedom, Security and Justice, inaugurated the prominence of the security constitution, which was further reinforced by 9/11. Finally, the Eurozone crisis has again

---

2   Kaarlo Tuori, 'The Many Constitutions of Europe' in Kaarlo Tuori and Suvi Sankari (eds), *The Many Constitutions of Europe* (Ashgate 2010) 3; Kaarlo Tuori, 'The Relationality of European Constitution(s)' in Ulla Neergaard and Ruth Nielsen (eds), *European Legal Method: Towards a New European Legal Realism?* (DJØF Publishing 2013).

3   Tuori (n 2).

catapulted the economic constitution back to the pacemaker role.[4] However, if the emphasis in the Rome Treaty and the subsequent case law of the ECJ lay on what can be called the microeconomic constitution, the crisis has highlighted the role of the second, macroeconomic layer of the European economic constitution. The pacemaker role of the macroeconomic constitution entails that ongoing constitutional mutation is not restricted to the economic aspect and that, accordingly, the present constitutional crisis should not merely be conceived of in economic terms. It extends to the political and social dimensions; it also affects democracy and transparency, as well as social values and rights.

The Relational Nature of the European Constitution I: Constitutional Law and its Object of Regulation

The proposal for distinguishing between different dimensions of the European constitution – an economic, juridical, political, social, and security constitution – is based on a differentiation of constitutional objects, i.e., the regulatory objects of constitutional law. 'Constitution' is understood as a relational concept, referring to the interrelation between constitutional law and its societal object of regulation.[5] Such a reading of 'constitution' has affinities with two theoretical positions which at least at first glance seem widely diverse: Niklas Luhmann's application of autopoietic systems theory and the institutional theory of law already instigated by Carl Friedrich von Savigny and in recent decades expounded by, first of all, Neil MacCormick and Ota Weinberger.[6] What unites these seemingly disparate approaches to constitutions or law in general is a relational emphasis. The institutional theory of law has taught us that the law generates legal-institutional facts where the social or psychological factual side and the legal normative side are intertwined, and that this, arguably, is the very point of law. In turn, Luhmann points to the structural coupling that a constitution establishes between two differentiated sub-systems of modern society: the legal and political systems.[7]

---

4   Such a temporal succession should not be interpreted in the sense of an emerging constitutional aspect replacing or supplanting a previous one; rather, the constitutional dimensions complement each other. Thus, the history of the economic constitution did not end with the first period of constitutionalisation. Emphasis on the juridical constitution should not be taken as signifying a standstill or an eclipse of the economic constitution; the latent and manifest development of the economic constitution has continued, and the economic constitution has always retained its functional primacy.

5   A juridical constitution is a reflexive constitution where the object of constitutional law is law itself. It should be emphasized that not only the juridical constitution but all other constitutional dimensions, too, are legal phenomena in the sense of including constitutional law as the 'formal' element of the constitutional relation. What distinguishes the juridical constitution from the other dimensions is the legal character of both poles of the constitutional relation.

6   Neil MacCormick and Ota Weinberger, *An Institutional Theory of Law* (Kluwer 1986).

7   Niklas Luhmann, *Law as a Social System* (Oxford University Press 2004) 404ff.

I embrace the idea of the relational character of constitution but detach it from its Luhmannian context and give it a more general twist. Luhmann examines merely a sub-species, albeit a paradigmatic one, of constitution: the political constitution, with the political system as the constitutional object. Moreover, his systems-theory framework allows for only one particular type of relationship between constitutional law and its object of regulation, namely, structural coupling.

The relational concept of a constitution has important consequences for an examination of the Eurozone crisis. Economic analysis is needed, not as an external introduction to, but as an integral element of the constitutional discussion: mutation of the economic constitution should be understood as resulting from an interaction between economic and legal developments. Here constitutional lawyers and economists should engage in a genuine interdisciplinary enterprise which includes mutual learning processes. As a source of inspiration, the German ordoliberal school, where lawyers and economists sought to lay a common conceptual and theoretical ground, is much more relevant than recent law and economics where lawyers are confined to the receiving end and where the offering of economics for them consists merely of rather simplistic economic assessments of alternative readings of law. For ordoliberals, the need for a dialogue between lawyers and economists arose from the perceived necessity for an *ordo* – a legal and institutional framework – for the functioning of the economic system. A central means for facilitating dialogue consisted of common concepts which had their place in both law and economics; Luhmann would probably have discerned structural couplings here between law and economics. One of these key concepts – if not the very key concept – was 'economic constitution'. Indeed, as regards the economic constitution, ordoliberals must be regarded as precursors to the relational analytic proposed here.

In one important respect, I would like to emphasise the distance of our relational analytic from ordoliberal tenets. For ordoliberals the economic constitution signified a fundamental decision in favour of a market economy, based on free competition. Yet, the concept can be detached from its link to a specific economic model of the economy and defined simply through the interrelation between constitutional law and economy. Furthermore, use of the concept in discussing the Eurozone crisis requires an important specification. As I have argued together with Klaus Tuori,[8] in the European economic constitution one should distinguish between two layers: the microeconomic constitution, centred around free movement and competition law and introduced by the Treaty of Rome (1958), and the macroeconomic constitution, centred around aggregate economic objectives and economic policies, and introduced by the Treaty of Maastricht (1993). In its constitutional aspect, the Eurozone crisis is primarily a crisis of the Maastricht macroeconomic constitution.

However, one should bear in mind the interdependence of the two layers of the European economic constitution. The microeconomic constitution of the

---

8   Tuori and Tuori (n 1).

Treaty of Rome relied on macroeconomic presumptions, such as price stability, which was to be achieved at the Member State level. The Rome Treaty also exhorted Member States to heed the externalities of their economic policies: Member States were to consider their economic policies as a matter of common concern. In turn, the Maastricht economic constitution testifies to the continuing significance of the objectives of the microeconomic constitution for the macroeconomic layer. In Treaty provisions, the main principles of the microeconomic constitution were made obligatory for monetary and economic policy, too. Furthermore, in preparations for the Maastricht Treaty the step from micro- to macroeconomic constitution was seen as a consequent sequence of economic (and legal) development. On the other hand, the success of the Maastricht macroeconomic constitution, especially common monetary policy, was seen to depend on full realisation of the microeconomic constitution: completion of the single market.

Still, significant differences exist between the micro- and macroeconomic constitution, especially with regard to the significance of law and the courts. The microeconomic constitution of free movement and competition law deals with the behaviour of individual economic actors, which has enabled the central role of the law and the courts. The field of the macroeconomic constitution, with its focus on objectives, aggregate economic values and policies, is much less susceptible to juridification. Contrary to developments within the microeconomic constitution, the courts, both the ECJ and national courts, have hardly played any role in implementing or further elaborating the European macroeconomic constitution. Before the *Pringle* case,[9] the only ruling of the Court explicitly pertaining to the macroeconomic constitution was *Commission v. Council* in 2004, which dealt with the sanctions regime of the excessive deficit procedure.[10] In *Pringle* the Court discussed some of the main doctrinal constitutional issues raised by European management of the crisis, such as interpretation of the Treaty prohibition on bailouts and availability of the intergovernmental option in crisis resolution. Yet, *Pringle* mainly confirms the constitutional mutation which had already occurred, while landmark rulings in the field of the microeconomic constitution, such as *Dassonville* or *Cassis de Dijon*,[11] really created new constitutional law. *Pringle* is essentially reactive and, in this sense, backward looking, while the latter rulings focused on the future.

The Relational Nature of the European Constitution II:
Surface-Level Constitutional Law and its Underpinnings

Constitutional law as the legal pole of the constitutional relation should not be conceived of solely in terms of surface-level normative material, such as

---

9   Case C-370/12 *Thomas Pringle v Government of Ireland*, judgment of 27 November 2012 (not yet reported).

10   Case C27/04 *Commission v Council* [2004] ECR I6649.

11   Case 8/74 *Procureur du Roi v Benoît and Gustave Dassonville* [1974] ECR 837; Case 120/78 *Rewe-Central AG v Bundesmonopolverwaltung für Branntwein* [1979] ECR 649.

explicit constitutional provisions and precedents. A constitution also comprises a legal cultural level through which individual constitutional provisions or constitutionally relevant precedents are read and interpreted, and which lends surface-level normative material a certain coherence. The legal cultural level includes – so I claim – a particular view of the constitutional object; a hidden social theory, as if it were, which is an important manifestation of the interrelation between constitutional law and its object of regulation. Without legal cultural underpinnings, scattered individual provisions of the formal constitution (the Founding Treaties) or fragmentary constitutional case law would hardly give rise to a distinct constitutional dimension. At the European level, too, constitutional law should be examined, not only in its relation to the constitutional object, but also as an interplay between surface-level normative material – such explicit speech acts as Treaties and constitutional precedents issued by the ECJ – and its legal cultural underpinnings – such as varieties of the European social model informing attempts to construe a social constitution or the notion of security underlying the Treaty provisions in the areas of freedom, security and justice and justifying talk of a distinct security constitution.[12]

An insight into the multi-layered nature of the constitution and its 'hidden social theory' is highly relevant in a constitutional discussion of the Eurozone crisis. Constitutional scrutiny should penetrate beneath the surface level of explicit Treaty provisions and ECJ case law, and into the underlying principles and economic assumptions on which these are based. The constitutional crisis is not manifest only in, say, debatable readings of single Treaty provisions but also – and, indeed, most importantly – the teetering of the central Maastricht principles of the macroeconomic constitution. When trying to grasp the crisis of the macroeconomic constitution at this deeper level, the first task is to reconstruct the central Maastricht principles. Here a brief summary, with a primary focus on the Eurozone, must suffice.

In monetary policy, the Maastricht constitution established the Union's exclusive competence in the euro area and defined price stability as the primary objective. The institutional position of the ECB was characterised by an enhanced independence and a strict definition of its mandate. The Treaty-based mandate did not comprise prudential supervision of financial institutions and stability of the financial system, which remained the primary responsibility of Member States. In contrast to monetary policy, Member States retained sovereignty in fiscal and economic policy with the Union having the task of facilitating coordination of national policies. Yet, Member States were obliged to consider their economic policy as a common concern. In the relationship between monetary and fiscal policy, price stability pursued by Europeanised monetary policy set limits to Member States' leeway in national fiscal policy objectives. Various instruments

---

12   I have presented my view of the multi-layered nature of modern law in *Critical Legal Positivism* (Ashgate 2002) and *Ratio and Voluntas* (Ashgate 2011). I have also discerned diverse relations connecting the layers of law and channelled through legal practices; relations such as sedimentation, constitution, justification, criticism and limitation.

were adopted to ensure sound public finances and fiscal discipline in Member States. These included Member State fiscal liability and prohibition of shared liability for government debt, laid down by the no-bailout clause (present Art. 125(1) TFEU).

The Maastricht principles relied on particular economic assumptions which make up the 'hidden social theory' of the macroeconomic constitution. As regards monetary policy and the institutional position of the ECB, the assumptions concern, for example, the role of inflation and the major task of central banks in combating it. Indeed, the post-Keynesian consensus which emerged in the 1980s was an important factor facilitating the establishment of EMU after a long run-up phase. The Maastricht principles gave expression to an optimistic view of the EU approaching an optimal currency area, where completion of the single market would produce the factor mobility necessary for absorbing asymmetric economic shocks and pursuing common monetary policy. The no-bailout clause manifested a confidence in the disciplining effects of financial markets on Member State finances. Yet, an awareness of the limitations of market discipline also existed, which explains the emphasis put on the monitoring procedures established in Maastricht and further specified by the 1997 Stability and Growth Pact, in particular, the excessive deficit procedure. A sovereign debt crisis was not seen as a possibility or, if it was, the assumption was that the prohibition on bailouts would be taken seriously and the Member State concerned would be allowed to default. Consequently, no crisis resolution mechanism was included in the Maastricht constitution. In turn, prevention (and resolution) of financial crises was deemed to be primarily a national responsibility, and no Union-level resolution mechanisms were designed to meet them, either.

Economic developments which culminated in the Eurozone crisis have quashed central elements of the 'hidden social theory' which the Maastricht principles implied. Completion of the single market has proved to be a much more time-consuming procedure than the Maastricht optimists expected. The fiscal constraints imposed by the Maastricht Treaty and the Stability and Growth Pact were not able to prevent a sovereign debt crisis in several Member States, while the financial integration of the euro area, as well as links between banks and sovereigns, made default by a Member State unacceptable. Invalidation of essential economic assumptions led to the shaking of central Maastricht principles. The financial stability of the euro area as a whole has been elevated to become a primary overriding objective of European economic measures, including monetary measures. The ECB has been deeply involved in resolving the financial and fiscal crises, which has had repercussions for its independence and led it to interpret its constitutionally defined mandate rather liberally. Yet, perhaps most dramatic are the consequences for Member States' fiscal liability and sovereignty.

The rescue packages and mechanisms, starting with the Greek loan facility in May 2010 and concluding with the launch of the European Stability Mechanism (ESM) in October 2012, signified retreat from observation of the no-bailout provision and the underlying principle of exclusive Member State fiscal liability.

In *Pringle*, the ECJ not only constitutionally sanctioned the rescue packages and mechanisms produced by the experimentalism of the preceding two and a half years; it also confirmed that the macroeconomic constitution had been complemented with and modified by three new elements. First, with regard to Member State fiscal policy, the macroeconomic constitution provides not only for crisis prevention but for crisis management as well. The bailout prohibition is valid only for preventive purposes; in a situation of threatening insolvency of a Member State, bailout measures may be permissible. Secondly, preventive fiscal policy constraints and crisis resolution share the same higher objective of financial stability of the euro area as a whole; this higher objective also justifies divergence from strict compliance with the bailout prohibition. And, thirdly, crisis resolution by means of financial assistance for the purpose of financial stability of the euro area as a whole is only permitted if accompanied by strict conditionality imposed on the recipient state.

Pringle is complemented by an amendment to Art. 136 TFEU confirming Member States' competence to establish a stability mechanism which can be activated for the purpose of safeguarding the stability of the euro area as a whole, provided that assistance is accompanied by strict conditionality.[13] *Pringle* and the amendment are important not only as speech acts introducing changes to the surface-level constitutional level; they also give expression to a constitutional mutation at the level of underpinning principles. They manifest the new overriding objective of financial stability of the euro area as a whole; restriction of scope of application of Member States' exclusive fiscal liability; and reduction of Member States' sovereignty in fiscal (and economic) policy. Curtailment of autonomous political decision making is of course most conspicuous in Member States receiving financial assistance, where it derives from the strict conditionality defined in the Memoranda of Understanding drafted and monitored by the troika of the Commission, the ECB and the IMF. Yet nor has the fiscal sovereignty of the assisting Member States been spared from restrictions. The liabilities related to various rescue operations and mechanisms are huge and, if realised, would considerably curb assisting states' budgetary autonomy, perhaps even affecting their ability to meet their constitutional fiscal obligations.

The leeway of Member States' fiscal and economic policies has been further reduced by the tightening of general European economic governance; here the catchwords are the six-pack and two-pack, as well as the Fiscal Compact. The six-pack and two-pack consist of EU secondary regulation, with a specific focus on the Eurozone, while the Fiscal Compact is Title III of the Treaty on Stability, Coordination

---

13   'Member States whose currency is the euro may establish a stability mechanism to be activated if indispensable to safeguard the stability of the euro area as a whole. The granting of any required financial assistance under the mechanism will be made subject to strict conditionality'. European Council Decision of 25 March 2011 amending Art. 136 TFEU with regard to a stability mechanism for Member States whose currency is the euro (2011/199/EU) [2011] OJ L91/1.

and Governance, an international agreement concluded by 25 Member States but mainly pertaining to the euro area. In the monitoring procedures established by Arts 121 and 126 TFEU and further specified by the Stability and Growth Pact, decisive steps have been taken from soft-law instruments to formal sanctions. Introduction of voting based on reversed majorities has strengthened the Commission's position; this, together with formal sanctions, has stripped governance of much of its peer review character. With introduction of the new excessive imbalances procedure, the scope of surveillance has been enlarged from fiscal to general macroeconomic policy. In fiscal policy, monitoring has been extended from Member States' multi-annual planning to both substantive and procedural aspects of annual budgetary processes. The two-pack established for euro-area states includes the obligation to submit their draft annual budgets for a check-up by the Commission. It is true, though, that Member States retain the final formal decision over their budgets. Still, European constraints have been considerably widened and deepened beyond those adopted in Maastricht.

The Relational Nature of the European Constitution III:
Relations Between Constitutional Dimensions

European integration has been primarily an economic project, and in spite of the expansion of EU activities into ever-new policy domains, economic integration has, arguably, always retained its functionally dominant position. This has left its imprint on the third relational aspect which an examination of the European constitution as a differentiated and multi-temporal process of constitutionalisation should address: relations between the various constitutions or constitutional dimensions. The non-economic constitutional dimensions largely owe their original impetus to demands raised or consequences set off by the economic dimension. Here we can talk of relations of implication. These relations may be specified as relations of support: for instance, development of the juridical constitution has supported realisation of the economic constitution.

Relations between constitutional dimensions can also be of a conflictual nature. Though the emergence of non-economic constitutional dimensions may have started out as a reaction to impulses from the economic constitution, in their further development they have acquired a dynamic of their own. Such a development may also lead to normative results which contradict the functional demands of the economic constitution. Thus, the normative implications of the economic constitution may clash with those of, say, the political or social constitution. Before the ECJ, such conflicts often assume the guise of contests between different types of rights: between, on the one hand, rights related to market freedoms and, on the other hand, civil and political or social rights. Generally speaking, in its conflicts with the economic constitution the social constitution has usually been the loser: the economic constitution has defined the space for social constitutionalism. This warrants talk of a relation of limitation between these two constitutional dimensions.

The idea of specific periods in the European process of constitutionalisation characterised by the dominance of a pacemaker constitution points to relations of implication detectable between constitutional dimensions. Since the eruption of the Eurozone crisis, the economic constitution – or more precisely, its macroeconomic layer – has clearly taken the lead in change. In the second part of the chapter, I will turn to the implications that developments in the field of the economic constitution have had for the political dimension. Equally important to paying attention to political developments is to be aware of the implications that changes in the macroeconomic constitution entail within the fledgling European social constitution. These implications, however, must be analysed in another context.

The Relational Nature of the European Constitution IV: The European Constitution and Member-State Constitutions

The fourth crucial relational aspect concerns the vertical interaction between the transnational European constitution and Member-State constitutions: the transnational constitution cannot be examined without paying due attention to its relations with the national constitutions of the Member States. An analytical conceptual apparatus, at least partly analogous to the conceptual apparatus tailored with a view to the interplay between the various dimensions of the transnational constitution, is also needed for dissecting relationships between the transnational and national constitutional levels. Thus, relationships of support, conflict and limitation may be discernible here, too.[14] In crucial respects, the European (micro) economic constitution relies on support from Member-State constitutions. National constitutions, for instance, guarantee the fundamental rights indispensable for the functioning of the market economy, such as the right to property, freedom of contract and freedom of trade. On the other hand, the European economic constitution, e.g., the subjection of healthcare and social security to free market and competition law, has considerably reduced Member States' leeway in designing their welfare regimes.

During the last 20 years, scholarly discussion on the European constitution has largely been dominated by the issue of constitutional pluralism. The Maastricht decision of the German Constitutional Court[15] was the crucial catalyst which brought the issue into the focus of academic constitutional discourse, too. The debate on constitutional pluralism explicitly thematises the co-existence of a European constitution with national constitutions. Yet the debate shows some deficiencies, the overcoming of which requires a fresh approach to the important issues the debate has addressed. The question of the exact nature of the relationships between the transnational, European constitution and the national, Member-State constitutions should be posed separately in the diverse constitutional dimensions. Relationships prevailing within the juridical constitution – the primary focus of

---

14   For a succinct exposition of the relational analytic see Tuori, 'Relationality' (n 2).
15   BVerfGE 89, 155, 2 October 1993.

the debate on constitutional pluralism – are not necessarily identical or analogical to those prevailing within, say, the economic or social constitutions. Moreover, one should be attentive to what could be termed diagonal relations: developments within a particular dimension of the European constitution may have implications in another dimension at the national level. For instance, the social repercussions of mutation of the macroeconomic constitution are mostly felt at the national level. Finally, the one-sided emphasis on conflictual relations, typical of discussion on constitutional pluralism, should be broadened and other types of relationship, such as those of implication and support, brought into the discussion, too.

In the debate on constitutional pluralism, two camps have stood out: radical pluralists emphasising the intractability of fundamental conflicts of authority between EU law and municipal law and dialogists pointing to interfaces and spaces for mutual dialogue and cooperative search for normative harmony.[16] These debates seem to have reached a deadlock. New insights and openings in the discussion on constitutional pluralism can only be attained through bringing in the other senses of the relationality of the European constitution.

The Eurozone crisis accentuates the necessity for European constitutional analysis attending to the dialectic of transnational and national as well. The crisis has constitutional implications at both the European and national levels, and these two-level implications are closely interrelated. For instance, Member States' national fiscal sovereignty is a principle of both European and national constitutional law and encroachments on this sovereignty hint at a crisis of both European and national constitutions; a crisis which extends to the field of the political constitution as disturbances of the two-level mechanism of democratic legitimation. In turn, the social consequences of austerity programmes should be assessed by both European and national constitutional yardsticks.

Repercussions of the crisis in Member States vary, depending, first, on the division into assisting and receiving states, and, secondly, national constitutional particularities. As regards assisting states, the repercussions for national constitutions have in particular been highlighted in Member States where the constitution enjoys high prestige in the political and legal culture, and where *ex ante* constitutional review is possible with regard to international agreements and European draft secondary legislation. These Member States include, for instance, Germany and Finland. The role of, in particular, the German Constitutional Court also manifests the fact that national constitutional courts participate in European

---

16 In his path-breaking articles, Neil MacCormick gave birth to the radical pluralist view. See Neil MacCormick, *Questioning Sovereignty* (Oxford University Press 1999). As examples of the dialogist position see N Walker, 'The Idea of Constitutional Pluralism' (2002) 65 *Modern Law Review* 317; Miguel Poiares Maduro, 'Contrapunctual Law: Europe's Constitutional Pluralism in Action', in N Walker (ed.) *Sovereignty in Transition* (Hart 2003); Mattias Kumm, 'The Jurisprudence of Constitutional Conflict: Constitutional Supremacy in Europe Before and After the Constitutional Treaty' (2005) 11 *European Law Journal* 262.

constitutional discourse, too. Even some opinions of the Constitutional Law Committee, which is responsible for *ex ante* constitutional review in Finland, may have impacted European developments.

The Eurozone Crisis and Democracy

Division of Competences as a Democratic Issue

As argued above, the Eurozone crisis has lifted the macroeconomic constitution into a pacemaker position among the many constitutions of Europe. Thus, the economic constitution is clearly defining the agenda for the political dimension. The obvious danger is that the economic constitution also dictates the terms of development, so that insufficient attention is paid to specifically political constitutional values such as democracy, transparency, legitimacy and accountability. This danger is enhanced by the sneaking, piecemeal mode in which the political constitution is being remoulded under the impact of the economic one. As the German Constitutional Court has repeatedly argued, in assessing the requirements of democracy and realising the principle of democracy, both the European and the Member State level must be involved.[17]

The division of competences between the national, Member State and transnational, European level is an issue not only of expediency but of democracy, too. Often enough, the default assumption is that transfer of competences from the national to transnational level signifies a defeat for democracy. Coverage of national democratic procedures is reduced in a manner which cannot be compensated for at the European level, due to the still largely lacking sociological and cultural prerequisites for transnational democracy. The standard position may grant an exception to 'non-political' policy fields such as monetary or competition policy, or 'non-political' public functions such as adjudication, which are considered more suitable for Europeanisation. These fields and functions are exempted from the requirement of democratic input legitimacy; if the legitimacy issue is considered at all relevant, it is conceived of in terms of output legitimacy, guaranteed by specific economic or juridical expertise.

Yet, things are not that simple. The standard view which brackets off expert fields and functions and claims the democracy argument for the side of national decision making is open to contestation. The basic idea of democracy is to give those concerned, that is, those affected by a decision, a possibility to have a say in its making. National sovereignty and democracy go together where the effects of decisions are confined within national boundaries. But the wider and deeper the cross-border effects that decisions have, the more national sovereignty loses its privileged linkage to democracy. At a certain point, retaining decision making

---

17   Of principal significance are the Lisbon and Maastricht rulings. BVerfGE 89, 155, 2 October 1993; BVerfG, 2 BvE 2/08, 30 June 2009.

under national sovereignty produces a democratic deficit by excluding from participation those affected by the externalities.

The cross-boundary consequences of national policies are a major reason and justification for the European project as a whole and for transnational developments in general.[18] Democratic arguments exist not only for defending national sovereignty but also for reducing its scope: transfer of competences from national to transnational level may be construable as a remedy for the democratic deficit which derives from the externalities of national policies. Still, another solution exists to at least alleviate, if not resolve, the problem of externalities; namely, their inclusion in national decision making, i.e., the internalisation of the interests and viewpoints of other nation states and their peoples. By and large, this has been the preferred way of the European economic constitution ever since the Treaty of Rome.[19] It may be recalled that one of the principles underpinning the macroeconomic constitution introduced in Maastricht is Member States' obligation to treat their economic policies as a common concern (Art 121(1) TFEU). The reasoning underlying the Treaty provisions on economic policy appears to be that when Member States live up to this obligation, the Union may confine itself to facilitating coordination of national policies.

One of the lessons from the Eurozone crisis is that transcending a narrow nationalistic perspective in economic policymaking and internalising the perspective of others has proved to be harder to achieve than expected. This lesson has been a major background factor to efforts to tighten European economic governance and develop it beyond the primarily soft methods of coordination set out in the Maastricht constitution. The original approach left it mainly to national discretion to ensure that national fiscal policy would not burden the common monetary policy and fiscal policies of other Member States. This discretion did not yield the expected results, but in many cases failed to heed even national medium-term considerations, let alone negative externalities.

Moreover, privileging the intergovernmental way in rescue measures and mechanisms appears to have further enhanced the nationalistic perspective in Member States. Emphasis in national discussions often enough seems to be on short-term national optimisation. Be that as it may, our discussion has demonstrated that the assumption inherent in the standard view that the democratic argument always weighs in support of national decision making is far too straightforward.

Of course, the democratic deficit at the Member-State level, related to the externalities of national policies, does not suffice in providing transnational decision-making with democratic justification. Meeting the externalities criterion

---

18   In his doctoral thesis, Maduro already invoked the externalities of national measures as a major justification for the ECJ's role as a constitutional court in the field of the microeconomic constitution. Miguel Poiares Maduro, *A New Governance for the European Union and the Euro: Democracy and Justice* (European University Institute, 2012).

19   Art. 103(1) obliged the Member States to regard their conjunctural policies as a matter of common concern.

can be deemed a necessary but insufficient condition for such a justification. The problem remains how to ensure the necessary democratic input legitimation for Union policies and actions.

Narrowing the Reach of National Democratic Legitimation

Democratic arguments played a part in determining the division of competences between the national and transnational level in the Maastricht macroeconomic constitution. A major reason for leaving the economic union incomplete was the perceived need for democratic input legitimation for fiscal and other economic policies; that need, in turn, could only be satisfied at the Member State level. This remains the principal line of reasoning of the German Constitutional Court, too, although it has consented to significant curtailing of national budget autonomy.[20]

The reduction of Member States' sovereignty in fiscal and economic policy as a central part of the recent mutation of the macroeconomic constitution has affected the democratic input legitimacy not only of national but even of European policies and actions. The German Constitutional Court has repeatedly pointed out that democratic national budgetary decision making is a requirement not only of the Basic Law but of the Treaties as EU constitutional law, too; national democratic procedures are necessary for the democratic legitimation of Union action, as well. This normative argumentation has its sociological counterpart in Fritz Scharpf's observations on the two-level legitimation structure of the EU. The effects of European policies on European citizens have been mediated through Member States, and citizens have confronted EU institutions, policies or the impacts of these policies in their daily lives not directly, but indirectly, via Member State action.[21] Consequently, Member States have borne the burden of providing input legitimacy for the EU as well. This they have largely been able to accomplish, due to national democratic procedures and the controlling power of national parliaments, electorates and civil societies.

The discontent in both recipient and assisting states that finds expression in, for instance, the electoral success of populist parties riding on nationalistic and anti-European themes, testifies to increasing legitimation problems. This poses a grave

---

20   See rulings on Greek loans and the EFSF, and the ESM. BVerfG, 2 BvR 987/10, 7 September 2011; BVerfG, 2 BvR 1390/12, 12 September 2012.

21   '... (t)he higher level of the European polity is generally beyond the horizon of citizens' expectations and political demands; it is not the target of public debates and party competition, and most importantly, it is not vulnerable to electoral sanctions ... . Citizens will not usually know the origin of the rules with which they are asked to comply, but they know that the only government which they might hold politically accountable is their own. In effect, therefore, national governments must generally bear the full burden of political accountability for unwelcome exercises of governing authority, regardless of how much European law may have contributed to these'. Fritz W Scharpf, *Legitimacy Intermediation in the Multilevel European Polity and its Collapse in the Euro Crisis* (Max Planck Institute for the Study of Societies 2012) 19.

danger for the future of European integration. European citizenry experiences the consequences of European policies without the dampening and legitimating mediation of national democratic procedures: 'In the present euro crisis ... the shield of legitimacy intermediation has been pushed aside as citizens are directly confronted with the massive impact of European policies – and with their manifest lack of democratic legitimacy'.[22] In crisis states, governments and parliaments implement the austerity programmes agreed on by the troika of the Commission, the ECB and the IMF, giving effect to the strict conditionality of assistance. National democratic institutions are widely conceived of as mere executors of policies imposed from the outside. In these circumstances, parliamentary and electoral mechanisms are hardly able to procure input legitimation even for national decision making, not to speak of channelling that legitimation to the European level. In assisting Member States, too, the European level is increasingly held responsible for policies affecting citizens, and the national parliament is not seen to possess much leeway in their implementation.

Two alternative responses exist to the legitimacy dilemma of fiscal and economic policy which has resulted from the gradual erosion of national sovereignty and the consequent shrinking of the legitimating power of national democratic procedures. The first of these is to redefine fiscal and economic policy and negate their need for democratic input legitimation. This strategy implies de-politicising fiscal and economic policy, labelling them fields of non-political expertise where decisions should be grounded in objectively given economic parameters. Thus, the model already applied to monetary policy would be extended to non-monetary economic policy as well. The door to re-definition was already left ajar by the Maastricht macroeconomic constitution through its constraints on national fiscal policy, relying on quasi-objective, quantitative reference values. However, the reference values still left the content and size of the public sector at national discretion, as long as it was considered to be prudently financed. The expansion and deepening of European economic governance and the increasing substantive and procedural requirements imposed on national budgetary frameworks have widened the crack and enhanced the non-political features of fiscal policy. The new excessive imbalances procedure, with its scoreboard of macroeconomic parameters monitored by the Commission, has extended the tendency of de-politicisation to general macroeconomic policy. This tendency has taken institutional forms as well. Proposals for creating independent budget offices or councils at both the Member-State and European level have abounded. With adoption of the two-pack, they have reaped their first practical results. Eurozone states are obliged to establish independent bodies monitoring compliance with fiscal rules. These must be structurally independent or 'endowed with functional autonomy *vis-à-vis* the fiscal authorities of the Member State in charge of monitoring the implementation of national fiscal rule'.[23]

---

22   Scharpf (n 21).

23   European Parliament and Council Regulation (EU) No 473/2013 of 21 May 2013 on common provisions for monitoring and assessing draft budgetary plans and ensuring

The strategy of de-politicisation has obvious limits. The need for legitimation arises from the impacts that policies have on citizens' lives. Democratic input legitimation has responded to the re-distributive effects of fiscal and economic policy. European citizens have experienced these effects very profoundly during the Eurozone crisis. The need for legitimation has not disappeared; on the contrary, it has intensified. Re-definition of fiscal and economic policy signifies an effort to shift the emphasis from democratic input legitimation towards output legitimation, guaranteed by non-political, independent experts. But even if concrete results, testifying to the benefits of increasing the weight of non-political expertise, were to be seen, legitimacy expectations cannot be manipulated at will from above. Moreover, national budgetary processes are not only about the budget; they are about politics in general. In many nation-state democracies, the budgetary process lies at the very centre of political discourse and opinion formation, as the German Constitutional Court has repeatedly pointed out.

The obvious alternative to de-politicisation would be to try to remedy the notorious democracy deficit at the European level and to introduce or reinforce democratic federalist structures. In this respect, developments during the Eurozone crisis have not been very encouraging. The European Parliament and the national parliaments have been accorded but a peripheral position in both financial stability mechanisms and European economic governance. In rescue measures and mechanisms, intergovernmentalism has been the privileged option; moreover, the amendment to Art. 136(3) TFEU and the establishment of the European Stability Mechanism have confirmed it as permanent, constitutionally anchored policy. Sidestepping the EU legislative and institutional framework has not conceded the European Parliament any role at all in either the design or administration and monitoring phase. In turn, the leeway and influence of national democratic procedures have depended, apart from pressures from the European level, on national constitutional arrangements.

Even in European economic governance, the European Parliament has, from the very installation of multilateral surveillance and excessive deficit procedures, played but a minor role, restricted mainly to the right to receive information. The rather modest efforts by the six- and two-pack to engage the European Parliament and national parliaments in European economic governance, as well as to increase its transparency, are hardly able to affect the general picture. However, because of a potential institutional or – we could also say – democratic asymmetry, a more far-reaching involvement of the European Parliament is not unproblematic, either. Both stability mechanisms and deepening European economic governance focus in particular on the euro area. The increasing impact of the European Parliament, representing the citizenry of the EU as a whole, raises democratic worries about the congruence of influence on, and effects of, decision making. Democracy requires that all those concerned be given a chance to participate.

---

the correction of excessive deficit of the Member States in the euro area, OJ L140/11, Arts 2(1) and 5.

But, arguably, it also requires that those not concerned and not contributing be left without a voice.

The weak formal position of the European Parliament in both financial stability mechanisms and European economic governance is not the only and, arguably, not even the main obstacle to democracy at the European level. The major problems now as before concern sociological and cultural presuppositions: the still embryonic European civil society and public sphere, as well as the weak self-identity and frail mutual solidarity of European citizenry. If the self-identity of European citizens is measured by electoral turnout, the development is rather discouraging: as the formal powers of the European Parliament have increased, electoral turnout has decreased. Consequently, the institution which is supposed to channel direct democratic legitimacy into the EU's institutional structure is suffering from a crisis of democratic legitimacy. However, no election for the European Parliament has been held since the eruption of the crisis, so its impact on electoral activity is still untested.

If the Eurozone crisis has in general had positive consequences for democracy, one of these could be awakening a sense of European interconnectedness both in the media and among the general public. For the first time in many Member States, European issues have occupied the forefront of national electoral campaigns. A sense of interconnectedness is an indispensable prerequisite for a functioning European democracy. Unfortunately, this in itself positive development has been tainted by a nationalistic distortion: more often than not, events in other Member States and in Europe at large have been observed through the lenses of narrowly conceived national interests. On balance, the crisis has probably done more to destroy than to promote sociological and cultural presuppositions for the emergence of a European demos, the subject of European democracy. One of the crucial issues for the future of European integration is how to end the inopportune marriage between rising European awareness and rising nationalism.

New Intergovernmentalism

Instead of enhancing control by the European Parliament and its Member-State counterparts or civil society, developments in the field of the political constitution are labelled by, on the one hand, the rise of new intergovernmentalism and, on the other hand, the strengthening of the position of expert bodies, primarily the ECB and the Commission. Reliance on intergovernmental legal and institutional structures is especially conspicuous in the creation and administration of financial stability mechanisms.[24] The first Greek rescue package in May 2010 was based

---

24   The rise of new intergovernmentalism is a central theme in Chiti and Teixeira's discussion of the constitutional implications of European responses to the financial and public debate crisis. Edoardo Chiti and Pedro Gustavo Teixeira, 'The Constitutional Implications of the European Responses to the Financial and Public Debt Crisis' (2013) 50 *Common Market Law Review* 683.

on a Loan Facility Agreement between Greece and the other euro-area states, settling the availability of credits in the form of pooled bilateral loans for Greece; an Intercreditor Agreement was drawn up among the creditor states; the European Financial Stability Facility (EFSF) was established as a limited liability company under Luxembourg law, and, subsequently, the euro-area states and the EFSF concluded a Framework Agreement, laying down the institutional structure of the EFSF, as well as the forms and conditionality of available assistance, and the procedure for granting it; and the European Stability Mechanism (ESM), replacing the EFSF, was founded through an Intergovernmental Agreement among the Member States. Furthermore, decision making in both the EFSF and the ESM is entrusted to intergovernmental bodies outside the institutional structure of the EU. Only the rather insignificant EFSM (European Financial Stability Mechanism) has been established using the Union method, i.e. through secondary legislation (Regulation) and is administered by EU institutions.

Obvious reasons exist for opting for the intergovernmental way in financial assistance, the most important of these being lack of EU fiscal capacity. But the intergovernmental option was also adopted in strengthening European economic governance where this justification does not apply. Efforts to amend the Founding Treaty in order to oblige Member States to introduce the debt brake and the balanced budget requirement ran into a veto by the UK and the Czech Republic. The way out was seen in the Treaty on Stability, Coordination and Governance, concluded without these two Member States. The intergovernmental way may be justified as an emergency policy, in particular in the field of financial assistance. Still, it also raises grave constitutional concerns. Here I confine myself to discussing the implications for democracy.

The Eurozone crisis has spawned an abundance of new official, semi-official and unofficial intergovernmental bodies, some of them with formal decision-making powers, others without formal competence but still exercising considerable influence. Not only has the European Parliament been largely kept on a side-track but even the Commission and the Council have found rivals in novel organisational forms. Rescue measures and mechanisms, in addition to tightening fiscal discipline, have been planned and negotiated not only within the institutions acknowledged by the Treaties but also in, for instance, the Working Group of the President of the European Council, the Working Group of the Eurogroup, the Euro Summit, 'Merkozy' meetings and so on. The European Council, with its President, and the Euro Summit, both epitomising executive, intergovernmental federalism *par excellence*, clearly took the lead in determining measures to be taken to overcome the crisis.

The federalist structures which the crisis has gradually engendered are largely based on intergovernmentalism, supported by expertise-based institutions such as the Commission and the ECB. The sneaking federalism we see emerging has rightly been termed 'executive federalism'.[25] Given the two-level structure

---

25   Jürgen Habermas, *Zur Verfassung Europas: Ein Essay* (Suhrkamp 2011) 43.

of legitimation in the EU and the formidable obstacles to an emergent European demos, intergovernmentalism might be seen as the institutional solution that democratic considerations call for. However, the two-level process of democratic legitimation can only function and contribute to the overall legitimacy of European policies on two conditions. First, executive participation in European policy making should be subjected to constant supervision by national parliaments and civil societies. And secondly, bearing in mind the complementary nature of Europe-wide and national democratic procedures, intergovernmentalism and the related intermediated legitimation should contribute to rather than destroy the socio-cultural prerequisites for European democracy. Arguably, the new intergovernmentalism meets neither of these preconditions.

Stability mechanisms, such as the EFSF and the ESM, operate as separate financial institutions outside the Treaty framework, with their own intergovernmental decision-making bodies. They remain outside the scope of application of Treaty provisions on the principle of transparency and complementary secondary legislation, as well as the EU Charter of Fundamental rights.[26] Disregarding the promises of openness and the general right to access to documents expressed by Art. 15 TFEU and Art. 42 of the Charter, stability mechanisms work behind the shield of far-going confidentiality and immunity. This has raised constitutional concerns in, for instance, Germany and Finland. Both the German Constitutional Court and the Finnish Constitutional Law Committee have underlined the necessity for parliamentary control, not only over establishment of the ESM, but its functioning, too, in particular decision-making affecting national liabilities. This control requires that adequate information be provided to Parliament.[27]

Perhaps even more detrimental to the possibility of democratic control is the institutional fragmentation which has accompanied the new intergovernmentalism. Fragmentation has been further accentuated by differentiation of the Eurozone from the rest of the Union. Bodies such as the Euro Summit and Eurogroup, as well as the President and Working Group of the Eurogroup, have gained in importance and within the field of the macroeconomic constitution have at least partially surpassed corresponding bodies where all Member States are represented.[28] Hurdles to democratic supervision posed by institutional disintegration are further elevated by the mounting complexity of legislative instruments which determine the substance and procedures of European policies. The six- and two-pack, as well as intergovernmental agreements and complementary guidelines regulating

---

26   In addition to the provisions on democratic principles in Title II TEU-Lisbon, Art. 15 TFEU lays down in more detail the obligations of EU institutions and EU citizens' access to documents. The most important piece of secondary legislation is European Parliament and Council Regulation (EU) No. 1049/2001 of 30 May 2001 regarding public access to European Parliament, Council and Commission documents, OJ L 145/43.

27   BVerfG, 2 BvR 1390/12, 12 September 2012; PeVL 13/2012.

28   Such institutional parallelism may, though, be democratically justified by reference to the need to restore symmetry of influence and effects in Union decision making.

the rescue mechanisms, have created an extremely complicated rule-work; a dense and opaque jungle of rules where but few specialists are able to orient themselves. In these circumstances, control by national parliaments and civil societies, implicit in the idea of two-level democratic legitimation, remains largely a fiction.

At the same time, the intergovernmental way of managing the sovereign debt crisis has taken the EU towards a 'transfer union' effected through financial transfers between Member States. By the same token, it has induced in Member States a very nationalistically determined view on European policies. It has put national democracies on a collision course, re-enlivened old and spawned new prejudices among European states and peoples. For European democracy, this is perhaps the most worrisome consequence of the crisis. Unfortunately, the crisis appears not to have brought European citizenry closer to the kind of solidaristic civic community which could act as the subject of European democracy, but has further distanced it from it.

It is evident that a European stability fund is needed in the future as well. But what is not evident is the need to opt for an intergovernmental way which is apt to set Member States against each other and enhance nationalist sentiments among both the general public and decision makers. The alternative to intergovernmentalism would obviously require considerably strengthening the fiscal capacity of the EU (or the euro area), financed through, not increased payments from Member-State budgets, but EU taxation, as has been proposed by, among others, Miguel Poiares Maduro and Mattias Kumm.[29]

In economic governance, the Council is the epitome of intergovernmentalism. However, two-level legitimation can only function with regard to common European rules applicable to all (Eurozone) Member States. In two-level legitimation, each Government represented in the Council channels the consent of the national parliament and electorate to European policies and norms which concern the respective state, in the same way as other Member States. But, as Scharpf has observed, emphasis in economic governance has shifted away from common policies and rules to country-specific guidance and sanctions: 'What needs to be legitimated, therefore, are European controls over national policy choices and national resources, rather than choices about common European policies and the allocation of European resources'. Especially if country-specific measures cannot be based on clear rules, the two-level legitimation mechanism of intergovernmentalism runs short of its objective:

> Concededly, the governments represented in the Council may be constitutionally and democratically legitimated to agree to common rules binding, and obligations burdening, their own polities. But there is no way in which German

---

29 Maduro (n 18); European Parliament, Mattias Kumm, 'Democratic Challenges Arising from the Eurocrisis: What kind of a Constitutional Crisis is Europe in and what should be Done about it?'(Challenges of Multi-Tier Governance in the EU Workshop, 4 October 2012) <www.eui.eu/Events/download.jsp?FILE_ID=3543> accessed 20 September 2013.

or Finnish voters and parliaments, or the voters and parliaments of most member states, could authorise their governments to impose special sacrifices on the citizens of Greece or Portugal or of any other member state. In other words, intergovernmental input legitimacy may sustain general rules applying to all member states, but it cannot legitimate discretionary interventions in individual member states.[30]

The Role of Expert Bodies

Expert bodies have played a central role in implementing and further elaborating the European economic constitution. Realisation and development of the microeconomic constitution has, to a great extent, relied on the Commission as the European Anti-Trust Authority and the ECJ as a constitutional court *vis-à-vis* both EC/EU institutions and – in the context of free movement, even primarily – Member-State legislatures. In the field of the macroeconomic constitution, the ECJ's contribution has been rather peripheral. In contrast, the Commission has been assigned important functions in European economic governance – in monitoring and coordinating procedures under Arts 121, 126 and 136 TFEU – as well as in recent rescue measures and mechanisms. Yet, the ECB is undoubtedly the most important expert body in the field of the macroeconomic constitution.

Independent expert bodies are exempted from the coverage of democratic input legitimation. This calls for both specific justification and a compensatory guarantee of legitimacy. The justification is based on a belief that specific expert functions exist in society which require application of specific scientific or quasi-scientific knowledge and tools. Experts are expected to perform their tasks independently of external, particularly political, influences. The input information processed by experts is solely defined by the 'scientific' needs of their functions. As scientific rationalisation leaves only one available option, there is no longer any room or need for political decision making. Courts of law are the classic epitome of an independent expert function, competition (anti-trust) authorities, in turn, a later example. The independent expert role of central banks is an even more recent phenomenon; its underpinning intellectual foundation was only laid in the 1970s.

In terms of the distinction between input and output legitimacy, the emphasis with regard to expert bodies is on the latter. Independent courts are expected to guarantee individual rights and the rule of law in general; independent competition authorities are expected to guarantee economic freedoms and a liberal market economy; and independent central banks are expected to guarantee monetary stability and consequent economic prosperity. Furthermore, they are supposed to produce their expected outcome in virtue of their expertise: their knowledge of the juridical or scientific laws which govern their field of action and which they apply to individual cases. Here lies the justification for their independence: expert bodies

---

30   Scharpf (n 21).

must be shielded from all influence which would derail them from a rigorous and disinterested employment of their expertise.

In Maastricht the ECB was constitutionally protected as an independent expert institution with a clear and restricted mandate. Instead of supervision and guidance by European or national political authorities, it was expected to maintain accountability through the transparency and trustworthiness of its actions. However, the picture has become blurred in the course of the financial and fiscal crisis, as the ECB has been involved in actions concerning the banking sector and Member State fiscal positions. The decisions the ECB has taken in the new fields of action hardly live up to the technocratic model based on rational application of scientific information and exclusion of value judgments. The major issue, of course, is how sound the underlying premises justifying the position of independent expert bodies, such as the ECB, really are: how objective are the objectives and means of the policy field involved. The more the premise of objectivity and the concomitant claim of the absence of alternatives are contested and the more value choices are perceived to play a role, the more expert legitimacy loses its power. Accusations of transgressing legitimate boundaries and of imposing value choices under the robe of neutral expertise are familiar from criticism of the judiciary, both national and transnational; the ECJ, the main institutional actor in implementing and elaborating the first layer of the European economic constitution, has not been spared from such accusations, either. It is inevitable that similar reproaches are directed at the ECB, too. It may be debated whether even the aim and policies of price stability live up to objectivist premises. But especially if the ECB ventures outside the framework of a monetary policy aiming at price stability, criticism for overstepping its mandate and including value judgments in its decision making is inevitable. For the moment, however, the status of the ECB seems to be buttressed by a relatively highly valued output legitimacy. The ECB has managed to position itself as the saviour of the Eurozone and questions about its mandate and the relation of its measures to basic constitutional principles are relegated to the background.[31]

In addition to the ECB, the Commission, too, emerges from the Eurozone crisis more powerful than ever. The Commission has been a central actor in country-specific rescue measures, and even the European Stability Mechanism relies not only on its own institutional structure but on the Commission, too. Along with the IMF and the ECB, the Commission is the third limb of the famous troika, which drafts and monitors financial assistance programmes. Tightening, remodelling and expanding European economic governance, especially in the Eurozone, has increased the competences of the Commission and left the Council, the epitome of intergovernmentalism, in the shadows. At the same time, the focus

---

31 A central topic in Christopher Lord's discussion on the legitimacy of the monetary union consists of the consequences of the ECB's alleged move from rule-based to discretionary decision making. Christopher Lord, *On the Legitimacy of Monetary Union* (Swedish Institute for European Policy Studies 2012).

of competences has shifted towards country-specific monitoring. In particular, the crisis has enhanced the position of the Commissioner for Economic and Monetary Affairs and the Directorate-General for Economic and Financial Affairs of which he is in charge.

The institutional position of the Commission has always been marked by a fundamental ambivalence. From Rome to Lisbon, the Commission has been treated mainly as an expert body. Yet, the fact that the Member States have possessed the right to nominate the Commissioners has added a distinct intergovernmental flavour to it. But as the Commissioners are not, despite the procedure for nomination, supposed to act as representatives of the Member States, the characteristic of an expert body has prevailed. This is also how the present Founding Treaties portray the Commission. Art. 17(3) TEU lays down that 'in carrying out its responsibilities, the Commission shall be completely independent' and that 'the members of the Commission shall neither seek nor take instructions from any Government or other institution, body, office or entity'. Furthermore, in Art. 245(1) TFEU, Member States pledge to respect the independence of the members of the Commission and not to seek to influence them in the performance of their tasks. A third, parliamentary feature has been introduced by the provisions on the election of the President of the Commission by the European Parliament: the vote of consent in the Parliament preceding the appointment of the Commission; the collective responsibility of the Commission before the Parliament; and the availability of a motion of censure of the Commission. Instead of an expert body, intergovernmental and parliamentary traits point to the role model of a politician. The peculiar constitutional combination of features of an expert, intergovernmental and parliamentary institution entails that in terms of legitimacy expectations, too, the Commission is a hybrid body. The role of independent expert evokes the expectation of outcome legitimacy, guaranteed by unbiased application of expertise, while the role of politician implies the need for democratic input legitimacy. The picture is further complicated by the multiplicity of functions of the Commission; different functions may imply different roles and legitimacy expectations. In competition policy, the role of independent expert has been particularly accentuated.

Great uncertainty seems to reign over how the Commission's increased tasks and powers in economic governance and fiscal crisis resolution should be defined. The six-and two-pack have accentuated the expert role of the Commission in fiscal and economic surveillance procedures as a counterweight to the intergovernmental Council, fulfilling a politician role. On the other hand, open contestation of the economic theory underlying the conditionality of financial assistance and country-specific economic governance has undermined belief in objective, scientifically proved foundations of austerity programmes and supply-side reforms.[32] It is

---

32 The contributions of such academic observers as Paul de Grauwe have been complemented by the self-criticism of the IMF for the Troika measures in Greece. See Paul de Grauwe, 'Who cares about the survival of the Eurozone?' (2011) CEPS Commentary

increasingly difficult to present the goals and means of fiscal and economic policy as objectively given, admitting of no alternatives and involving no value choices. Critics discern a politician making value judgments under the Commission's robe of an independent expert.

The proposals for developing the Commission reflect this vacillation between expert and politician roles. On the one hand, proposals exist to assign the fiscal policy function of the Commission to an independent European Budget Office, complementing and crowning the structure of independent national offices or councils. These proposals are countered by plans to develop the Directorate-General for Economic and Financial Affairs into a European Ministry of Finance, and to enhance the parliamentary accountability of the Commission and especially the Commissioner of Economy and Finance.

Is There a Way Out?

The Eurozone crisis has been, first of all, an economic crisis and, accordingly, its direct constitutional repercussions have been felt in the field of the (macro) economic constitution. Hence, it is no surprise that reform proposals, too, focus on the economic dimension. Still, all the major initiatives, such as the scheme produced by a Working Group consisting of the Presidents of the European Council, the Commission, the Eurogroup and the ECB[33] or the Commission's 'blueprint for a deep and genuine economic and monetary union'[34] at least pay lip service to the central values of the political constitution: democracy, legitimacy and accountability.

From the very beginning, the implications of an economic and monetary union for political integration have figured prominently on the agenda. Yet, the political decision makers have always retreated from following up the implications to the very end. Of the initiatives now under debate in the EU, the Commission's blueprint is most explicit in pondering the repercussions that completion of EMU would have in the political dimension. The Commission argues that a full fiscal and economic union would 'involve a political union with adequate pooling

---

<www.ceps.eu> accessed 20 September 2013; Paul de Grauwe, 'Design Failures in the Eurozone: Can they be Fixed?' (2013) LSE LEQS Paper No. 57 <www.lse.ac.uk/europeanInstitute/LEQS/LEQSPaper57.pdf> accessed 20 September 2013; Paul de Grauwe and Yuemei Ji, 'More Evidence that Financial Markets Imposed Excessive Austerity in the Eurozone' (2013) *CEPS Commentary* www.ceps.eu accessed 20 September 2013; IMF, 'Greece: Ex Post Evaluation of Exceptional Access under the 2010 Stand-By Arrangement', Country Report No 13/156, June 2013 <www.imf.org/external/pubs/ft/scr/2013/cr13156.pdf> accessed 20 September 2013.

33　European Council, 'Towards a Genuine Economic and Monetary Union', Brussels, 25.06.2012 EUCO 120/12.

34　Communication from the European Commission, 'A Blueprint for a Deep and Genuine Economic and Monetary Union – Launching a European Debate, Communication from the Commission', Brussels, 30.11.2012 COM (2012) final.

of sovereignty with a central budget as its own fiscal capacity and a means of imposing budgetary and economic decisions on its members, under specific and well-defined circumstances'. The Commission is also much more detailed than the Van Rompuy Working Group in its ideas for ensuring democratic legitimacy and accountability in the stage-by-stage development of a banking, fiscal and economic union.

The Commission sets out two basic principles for enhancing EMU's democratic legitimacy. First, accountability should be ensured at the level where decisions are taken; due attention, though, should be paid to the (other) level where decisions have an impact. This principle entails a crucial position for the European Parliament in ensuring democratic accountability for decisions taken at the Union level, particularly by the Commission. Accordingly, many of the Commission's more detailed initiatives imply a deepened involvement of the Parliament. Yet the Commission points out that 'the role of national parliaments will always remain crucial in ensuring legitimacy of Member States' action in the European Council and the Council but especially of the conduct of national budgetary and economic policies even if more closely coordinated by the EU'. The Commission's second basic principle relates the need for democratic legitimacy at the European level to the degree of transfer of sovereignty from Member States to the Union. This leads the Commission to distinguish between implications of short-term action, realisable through secondary legislation, and further stages which involve Treaty amendments. As regards short-term reforms, the Commission is rather complacent towards the mechanisms of democratic legitimacy under the Lisbon Treaty and seems to downplay the quite significant changes in the macroeconomic constitution initiated by European responses to the Eurozone crisis. These changes have not involved Treaty amendments, except for the new Art. 136(3) TFEU, which has been declared to have been of a merely clarifying character. The Commission does, though, draw attention to issues raised by intergovernmental action, both with regard to compatibility with EU primary law and organisation of parliamentary accountability. The Commission underlines that in future reinforcement of governance structures in EMU, the Union's institutional framework and the Community method should be preferred. Yet, considering the profundity of the legitimacy crisis in the Union, in particular in the Eurozone, the Commission's short-term proposals appear fairly unpretentious. The Commission goes somewhat further in suggestions which address the mid-term situation where EMU is strengthened through Treaty amendments, but where a full fiscal and economic union is not yet established. The Commission proposes using co-decision to legitimise Union power to require revision of a national budget and advocates integrating the European Stability Mechanism into the EU framework. In an institutional respect, the euro committee of the Parliament could even be granted decision-making powers, and a specific relationship of confidence and scrutiny could be created between this committee and the Commission Vice President for Economic and Monetary Affairs. This would be part of a development towards 'political direction and enhanced democratic accountability of a structure akin to an EMU Treasury within the Commission'. The parliamentary supervision the Commission envisages for the ECB is confined to allowing normal budgetary control by the Parliament over the ECB's activity as a banking supervisor and falls short of any political responsibility. Finally, the Commission discusses the implications for democracy and accountability of mutualising sovereign debt underpinned by a joint and several guarantee by all Eurozone states in a 'full' fiscal and economic union where Member States would not be jointly and severally liable for each other's sovereign debt. Such a union would itself dispose of a substantial central budget, the resources for which would be derived from an autonomous power of taxation, complemented, if necessary, by the EU's own sovereign debt. This would be concomitant with a large-scale pooling of sovereignty over the conduct of economic policy at EU level. The European Parliament would then have reinforced powers to co-legislate on Union taxation and provide the necessary democratic scrutiny for all decisions taken by the EU executive.

A perusal of the initiatives which European institutions and bodies have produced for strengthening democratic legitimacy and accountability, particularly in the Eurozone, leaves one somewhat perplexed. They do not really appear to grasp adequately either the roots or the gravity of the legitimacy crisis or the multifaceted nature of the democracy issues spawned by the Eurozone crisis. The Van Rompuy Working Group's report and the Commission's blueprint bypass most of the critical developments which relate to grave disturbances in the two-level legitimation mechanism and narrowing of the reach of legitimacy coverage that Member States' democratic procedures can offer; the rise of nationalist sentiments due to the intergovernmental way of coping with the Eurozone crisis; and expert bodies, such as the ECB and the Commission, assuming stakeholder or politician roles. And if the diagnosis is deficient, the remedies cannot be appropriate, either.

The initiatives discuss transfer of competences to the European level but not as a democracy issue. By contrast, Miguel Poiares Maduro, who has produced a report on 'a New Governance for the European Union and the Euro' for the European Parliament,[35] has grasped this perspective and, indeed, considers it the fundamental democracy issue in Europe. He is also more sensitive to the detrimental consequences for the legitimacy of the European project of the intergovernmental way of dealing with the Eurozone crisis. It is true, though, that official initiatives, too, call for incorporating intergovernmental agreements, including the Treaty on Stability, Coordination and Governance, and intergovernmental mechanisms, such as the European Stability Mechanism, into the Union framework. But Maduro makes clear the contribution of intergovernmentalism to the rise of narrow nationalism in both assisting and recipient states. For him, this is a central reason for strengthening Union (EMU) fiscal capacity and financing it through Union taxation, instead of transfers from national budgets. Moreover, Maduro is conscious of the social and cultural prerequisites of a functioning European

---

35 Maduro (n 18).

democracy and does not confine his perspective merely to the interplay of European institutions among themselves or with their national counterparts. Yet, in the end, his recipe for fostering European civil society and European belongingness among the citizenry is rather mild: it boils down to the suggestion that in order to raise interest and participation among the electorate, political parties should nominate their candidates for the Commission Presidency.

If progress is not made towards a civic European demos and if the damage caused by the unfortunate intergovernmental crisis-resolution mechanisms is not undone, institutional solutions for patching up the democracy deficit cannot result in very much. This conclusion is shared by many observers. Now, the real task is to show how such progress could be possible.

Not an entirely new conclusion either, I am afraid.

Bibliography

Adamski D, 'National Power Games and Structural Failure in the European Macroeconomic Governance', (2012) 49 *Common Market Law Review* 1319

Amtenbrink F and de Haan J, 'Economic Governance in the European Union – Fiscal Policy Discipline Versus Flexibility' (2003) 40 *Common Market Law Review* 1057

Antoniadis A, 'Debt Crisis as a Global Emergency: The European Economic Constitution and Other Greek Fables' in A Antoniadis, R Schütze and E Spaventa (eds), *The European Union and Global Emergencies: A Law and Policy Analysis* (Hart Publishing 2011)

Balzacq T, Bigo D, Carrera S and Guild E, *Security and the Two-Level Game: The Treaty of Prüm, the EU and the Management of Threats* (Centre for European Policy Studies 2006)

Baquero Cruz J, *Between Competition and Free Movement: The Economic Constitutional Law of the European Community* (Hart Publishing 2002)

Barro RJ, 'Rational Expectations and the Role of Monetary Policy' (1976) 2 *Journal of Monetary Economy* 1

Bean C, *The Great Moderation, the Great Panic and the Great Contraction* (European University Institute 2010)

Belke A, *Driven by the Markets? ECB Sovereign Bond Purchases and the Securities Markets Programme* (Ruhr Economic Papers 2010)

Benati L and Surico P, *VAR Analysis and the Great Moderation* (European Central Bank 2008)

Bernanke BS, 'Remarks by Governor Ben S. Bernanke: Great Moderation' Meetings of the Eastern Economic Association, 20 February 2004

Bernoth K, von Hagen J and Schuknecht L, *Sovereign Risk Premia in the European Government Bond Market* (European Central Bank 2004)

Blundell-Wignall A and Slovik P, 'The EU Stress Test and Sovereign Debt Exposures' *OECD Working Papers on Finance, Insurance and Private Pensions* 4 (OECD Financial Affairs Division 2010)

Böhm F, 'Das Problem der Privaten Macht' (1928) 3 *Die Justiz* 324
—— *Wettbewerb und Monopolkampf. Eine Untersuchung zur Frage des Wirtschaftlichen Kampfrechts und zur Frage der Rechtlichen Struktur der Geltenden Wirtschaftsordnung* (Carl Heymanns Verlag 1933)
—— 'Privatrechtsgesellschaft und Marktwirtschaft' (1966) 17 *ORDO* 75
Borger V, 'The ESM and the European Court's Predicament in *Pringle*' (2013) 14 *German Law Review* 113–40
Busch K, Hermann C, Hinrichs K and Schulten T, *Euro Crisis, Austerity Policy and the European Social Model: How Crisis Policies in Southern Europe Threaten the EU's Social Dimension* (Friedrich Ebert Stiftung 2013)
Calliess C, 'Perspektiven des Euro Zwischen Solidarität und Recht – Eine Rechtliche Analyse der Griechenlandhilfe und des Rettungsschirms' (2011) 14 *Zeitschrift für Europäische Studien* 213
Calmfors L, Flam H, Gottfries N, Matlary JH, Jerneck M, Lindahl R, Nordh Berntsson C, Rabinowics E and Vredin A, *Calmforsraportten* (SOU 1996); also published in English as *EMU – A Swedish Perspective* (Kluwer Academic Publishers 1997)
Cappelletti M, Seccombe M and Weiler J (eds), *Integration through Law, European and the American Federal Experience* (Walter de Gruyter 1985)
Cecchetti SG, Mohanty M and Zampolli F, *The Real Effects of Debt* (Bank for International Settlements 2011)
Chen R, Milesi-Ferretti G-M and Tressel T, 'External Imbalances in the Euro Area' (IMF Working Papers 2012)
Chiti E and Teixeira P, 'The Constitutional Implications of the European Responses to the Financial and Public Debt Crisis' (2013) 50 *Common Market Law Review* 683
Chiti E, Menéndez A and Teixeira P, 'The European Rescue of the European Union' in E Chiti, A Menéndez and P Teixeira (eds), *The European Rescue of the European Union* (ARENA Centre for European Studies 2012) 391
Codogno L, Favero C and Missale A, 'Yield Spreads on EMU Government Bonds' (2003) 18 *Economic Policy* 37 503–32
Craig P, 'The Stability, Coordination and Governance Treaty: Principle, Politics and Pragmatism' (2012) 37 *European Law Review* 231
Crouch C, 'What Will Follow the Demise of Privatised Keynesianism?' (2009) 80 *The Political Quarterly* Issue Supplement s1 302
Davis EP, *Debt, Financial Fragility, and Systemic Risk* (Clarendon Press 1992)
de Grauwe P, 'Design Failures in the Eurozone: Can they be Fixed?' (2013) LSE LEQS Paper No. 57 <http://www.lse.ac.uk/europeanInstitute/LEQS/LEQSPaper57.pdf> accessed 20 September 2013
—— 'Who cares about the survival of the Eurozone?' (2011) *CEPS Commentary* <http://www.ceps.eu> accessed 20 September 2013
—— and Ji Y, 'More Evidence that Financial Markets Imposed Excessive Austerity in the Eurozone' (2013) *CEPS Commentary* <http://www.ceps.eu> accessed 20 September 2013

de Gregorio Merino A, 'Legal Developments in the Monetary and Economic Union During the Debt Crisis: The Mechanisms of Financial Assistance' (2012) 49 *Common Market Law Review* 5 1613–46

de Laroisière J, *The High-Level Group on Financial Supervision in the EU Report*, 25 February 2009 <http://ec.europa.eu/internal_market/finances/docs/de_larosiere_report_en.pdf > accessed 15 May 2014

de Witte B, 'Old-fashioned Flexibility: International Agreements between Member States of the European Union' in G de Búrca and J Scott (eds), *Constitutional Change in the EU – From Uniformity to Flexibility* (Hart Publishing 2001)

—— 'The European Treaty Amendment for the Creation of a Financial Stability Mechanism' (2011) 6 *European Policy Analysis* 1

Dworkin R, *Taking Rights Seriously* (Ducksworth 1978)

Eucken W, *Grundsätze der Wirtschaftspolitik* (JCB Mohr 1952)

Fabbrini F, '*The Fiscal Compact, the "Golden Rule", and the Paradox of European Federalism'* (2013) 36 *Boston College International and Comparative Law Review* 1

Fassbender K, 'Der Europäische "Stabilisierungsmechganismus" im Lichte von Unionsrecht und Deutschem Verfassungsrecht' (2010) 13 *Neue Zeitschrift für Verwaltungsrecht* 799

Faust J, Rogers J and Wright J, 'News and Noise in G-7 GDP Announcements' (2005) 37 *Journal of Money, Credit and Banking* 403

Fossum JE and Menéndez A, *The Constitution's Gift: A Constitutional Theory for a Democratic European Union* (Rowman & Littlefield 2011)

Friedman M, 'The Quantity Theory of Money: A Restatement' in *Studies in the Quantity Theory of Money* (1956), reprinted in *The Optimum Quantity of Money* (Aldine Transaction 2005)

Fuller LL, *The Morality of Law* (New Haven: Yale University Press 1969)

Gaitanides C, 'Intervention des IWF in der Eurozone – Mandatswidrig?' (2011) 14 *Neue Zeitschrift für Verwaltungsrecht* 848

Garriga C, Gavin W and Schlagenhauf D, 'Recent Trends in Homeownership' (2006) 88 *Federal Reserve Bank of St. Louis Review* 5 397

Gerber D, 'Constitutionalizing the Economy: German Neo-liberalism, Competition Law and the "New Europe"' (1994) 42 *American Journal of Comparative Law* 25

Giannone D, Lenza M and Reichlin L, *Explaining the Great Moderation: It is not the Shock* (European Central Bank 2008)

Gilbert M, *European Integration: A Concise History* (Rowman & Littlefield Publishers 2012)

González Cabanillas L and Ruscher E, *The Great Moderation in the Euro Area: What Role have Macroeconomic Policies Played?* (European Commission 2008)

Habermas J, *Toward a Rational Society: Student Protest, Science, and Politics* (Heinemann 1971)

—— *Zur Verfassung Europas: Ein Essay* (Suhrkamp 2011)

Hacker B and van Treeck T, *What Influence for European Governance? The Reformed Stability and Growth Pact* (Friedrich Ebert Stiftung 2010)

Häde U, 'Haushaltsdisziplin und Solidarität im Zeichen der Finanzkrise' (2009) 12 *Europäische Zeitschrift für Wirtschaftsrecht* 399

Hänninen S, 'Social Constitution in Historical Perspective: Hugo Sinzheimer in the Weimar Context' in K Tuori and S Sankari (eds), *The Many Constitutions of Europe* (Ashgate 2010) 219

Heipertz M and Verdun A, *Ruling Europe: The Politics of the Stability and Growth Pact* (Cambridge University Press 2010)

Höpner M and Rödl F, 'Illegitim und rechtswidrig: Das neue makroökonomische Regime im Euroraum' (2012) 92 *Wirtschaftsdienst* 219

Hufeld U, 'Zwischen Notrettung und Rütlischwur: der Umbau der Wirtschafts- und Währungsunion in der Krise' (2011) 34 *Integration* 117

Issing O, *The Birth of the Euro* (Cambridge University Press 2008)

—— 'Communication, Transparency, Accountability: Monetary Policy in the Twenty-First Century' (2005) 87 *Federal Reserve Bank of St. Louis Review* 2 (Part 1) 65

——, Gaspar V, Angeloni I and Tristani O, *Monetary Policy in the Euro Area Strategy and Decision Making at the European Central Bank* (Cambridge University Press 2001)

James H, *Making the European Monetary Union* (The Belknap Press 2012)

Knopp L, 'Griechenland – Nothilfe auf dem Verfassungsrechtlichen Prüfstand' (2010) 63 *Neue Juristische Wochenschrift* 1777

Koukiadaki A and Kretsos L, 'Opening Pandora's Box: The Sovereign Debt Crisis and Labour Market Regulation in Greece' (2012) 41 *Industrial Law Journal* 276

Kumm M, 'The Jurisprudence of Constitutional Conflict: Constitutional Supremacy in Europe Before and After the Constitutional Treaty' (2005) 11 *European Law Journal* 262

Lord C, *On the Legitimacy of Monetary Union* (Swedish Institute for European Policy Studies 2012)

Losada Fraga F, 'Exacerbated Economic Governance in the European Union – Or when did we Forget about Democratic Legitimacy?' Helsinki Legal Studies Research Paper No. 24 (2013)

Louis J-V, 'Guest Editorial: The No-bailout Clause and Rescue Packages' (2010) 47 *Common Market Law Review* 4 971–86

Luczak JM, *Die Europäische Wirtschaftsverfassung als Legitimationselement europäischer Integration: Ein Beitrag zur wirtschaftsverfassungsrechtlic hen Analyse des Unionsrechts durch den Vertrag von Lissabon* (Duncker & Humblot 2009)

Luhmann N, *Law as a Social System* (Oxford University Press 2004)

MacCormick N, *Questioning Sovereignty* (Oxford University Press 1999)

—— *Institutions of Law: an Essay in Legal Theory* (Oxford University Press 2007)

—— and Weinberger O, *An Institutional Theory of Law* (Kluwer 1986)

Maduro MP, *We the Court: The European Court of Justice and the European Economic Constitution* (Hart Publishing, 1998).

—— 'Contrapunctual Law: Europe's Constitutional Pluralism in Action' in N Walker (ed.) *Sovereignty in Transition* (Hart 2003)

—— *A New Governance for the European Union and the Euro: Democracy and Justice* (European University Institute 2012)

Majone G, 'Patterns of Post-National Europe: The Future Integration after the Crisis of the Monetary Union' in M Fichera, S Hänninen and K Tuori (eds), *Polity and Crisis* (Ashgate 2014) forthcoming

—— 'The General Crisis of the European Union: A Genetic Approach' Presented at the conference 'Europe in Crisis: Implications for the EU and Norway' 14–15 March 2013, Oslo

—— 'The Parable of EMU: Maastricht as the Decisive Constitutional Moment in EU History' Presented at the conference on 'Constitutional Implications of the European Union Economic Crisis' 28–29 March 2012, Helsinki

Mankiw GN, 'The Inexorable and Mysterious Tradeoff between Inflation and Unemployment' (2001) 111 *The Economic Journal* 45

Marsh D, *The Euro: The Battle for the New Global Currency* (Yale University Press 2011)

Mayer T, *Europe's Unfinished Currency* (Anthem Press 2012)

Mestmäcker EJ, *Wirtschaft und Verfassung in der Europäischen Union: Beiträge zur Rechtstheorie und Politik der europäischen Integration* (Nomos 2003)

Mosley L, 'Government-Financial Market Relations after EMU' (2004) 5 *European Union Politics* 181

Mundel RA, 'A Theory of Optimum Currency Areas' (1961), reprinted in M Blejer, D Cheney, J Frenkel, L Leiderman and A Razin (eds), *Optimum Currency Areas: New Analytical and Policy Developments* (International Monetary Fund 1997)

Pattison B, Diacon D and Vine J, *Tenure Trends in the UK Housing System* (Building and Social Housing Foundation 2010)

Pech L, '"A Union Founded on the Rule of Law": Meaning and Reality of the Rule of Law as a Constitutional Principle of EU Law' (2010) 6 *European Constitutional Law Review* 359

Pernice I, 'Der Beitrag Walter Hallsteins zur Zukunft Europas: Begründung und Konsolidierung der Europäischen Gemeinschaft als Rechtsgemeinschaft' (2001) Walter Hallstein Institute Paper 9/01

Piris J-C, *The Future of Europe: Towards a Two-Speed EU* (Cambridge University Press 2012)

Pisani-Ferry J, Sapir A and Wolff G, 'EU-IMF Assistance to Euro Area Countries: An Early Assessment' (2013) 16 *Bruegel Blueprint* <www.bruegel.org/download/parent/779-eu-imf-assistance-to-euro-area-countries-an-early-assessment/file/1661-eu-imf-assistance-to-euro-area-countries-an-early-assessment/ > accessed 9 October 2013

Raz J, *The Authority of Law: Essays in Law and Morality* (Oxford University Press 1979)

Reinhart CM and Rogoff KS, 'Growth in a Time of Debt' (2010) 100 *American Economic Review* 573

Ruffert M, 'The European Debt Crisis and European Union Law' (2011) 48 *Common Market Law Review* 1777

Sauter W, 'The Economic Constitution of the European Union' (1998) 4 *Columbia Journal of European Law* 1 27

Scharpf FW, *Legitimacy Intermediation in the Multilevel European Polity and its Collapse in the Euro Crisis* (Max Planck Institute for the Study of Societies 2012)

—— 'The Asymmetry of European Integration, or why the EU Cannot be a "Social Market Economy"' (2010) 8 *Socio-Economic Review* 211

—— *Reflections on Multilevel Legitimacy* (Max Planck Institute for the Study of Societies 2007)

Schneider K, 'Yes, But … One More Thing: Karlsruhe's Ruling on the European Stability Mechanism' (2013) 14 *German Law Journal* 53

Schorkopf F, 'Gestaltung mit Recht – Prägekraft und Selbststand des Rechts in einer Rechtsgemeinschaft' (2011) 136 *Archiv des Öffentlichen Rechts* 323

Schuknecht L, Moutot P, Rother P and Stark J, *The Stability and Growth Pact – Crisis and Reform* (European Central Bank 2011)

Schütze R, *European Constitutional Law* (Cambridge University Press 2012)

—— 'Supremacy without Pre-emption? The Very Slowly Emergent Doctrine of Community Pre-emption' 43 (2006) 4 *Common Market Law Review* 1023

Smits R, 'The European Constitution and the EMU: An Appraisal' (2005) 42 *Common Market Law Review* 425

Thym D, 'Euro-Rettungsschirm: Zwischenstaatliche Rechtskonstruktion und Verfassungsgerichtliche Kontrolle' (2011) 5 *Europäische Zeitschrift für Wirtschaftsrecht* 167

Tomkin J, 'Contradiction, Circumvention and Conceptual Gymnastics: The Impact of the Adoption of the ESM Treaty on the State of European Democracy' (2013) 14 *German Law Journal* 169 <www.germanlawjournal.com/index. php?pageID=11&artID=1500> accessed 9 October 2013

Tommaso Padoa-Schioppa Group, 'Completing the Euro: A Road Map towards Fiscal Union in Europe' June 2012 <www.eng.notre-europe.eu/011–3317-Completing-the-EuroA-road-map-towards-fiscal-union-in-Europe.html> accessed 9 October 2013

Tridimas T, *The General Principles of EU Law* (3rd edn Oxford University Press 2013)

Tuori K, *Critical Legal Positivism* (Ashgate 2002)

—— 'The Many Constitutions of Europe' in K Tuori and S Sankari (eds), *The Many Constitutions of Europe* (Ashgate 2010) 3

—— *Ratio and Voluntas: The Tension between Reason and Will in Law* (Ashgate 2011)

—— 'The Relationality of European Constitution(s)' in U Neergaard and R Nielsen (eds), *European Legal Method: Towards a New European Legal Realism?* (DJØF Publishing forthcoming)

Tuori K and Tuori K, *The Eurozone Crisis: A Constitutional Analysis* (Cambridge University Press 2013)

van Riet A, *Euro Area Fiscal Policies and the Crisis* (ECB Occasional Paper Series No 109 2010) <http://www.ecb.europa.eu/pub/pdf/scpops/ecbocp109. pdf> accessed 15 May 2014

Vits C and Kennedy S, 'Weber to Leave Bundesbank in April, Throwing Race of ECB Chief Wide Open', 11 February 2011, ≤www.bloomberg.com/ news/2011–02–11/weber-to-leave-bundesbank-in-april-throwing-race-for-ecb-chief-wide-open.html> accessed 9 October 2013

Walker N, 'The Idea of Constitutional Pluralism' (2002) 65 *Modern Law Review* 317

Wegmann M, *Früher Neoliberalismus und Europäische Integration; Interdependenz der Nationalen, Supranationalen und Internationalen Ordnung von Wirtschaft und Gesellschaft (1932 – 1965)* (Nomos 2002)

Weiler J, *The Constitution of Europe* (Cambridge University Press 1999)

Zilioli C and Selmayr M, 'The Constitutional Status of the European Central Bank' (2007) 44 *Common Market Law Review* 355

Ziller J, *Le Traité de Prüm: Une Vraie-Fausse Coopération Renforcée dans l'Espace de Sécurité de Liberté et de Justice* (European University Institute 2006)

Official Documents

BIS, *Annual Report 2009* (Bank for International Settlements 2009) <http://www. bis.org/publ/arpdf/ar2009e.pdf> accessed 9 October 2013

CEBS, 'Press Release on the Results of the EU-wide Stress Testing Exercise' 1 October 2009 <http://eba.europa.eu/documents/10180/15977/CEBS-2009–180-Annex-2-%28Press-release-from-CEBS%29.pdf> accessed 9 October 2013

Committee for the Study of Economic and Monetary Union (Delors Committee), 'Report on an Economic and Monetary Union in the European Community' 17 April 1989 <http://aei.pitt.edu/1007/1/monetary_delors.pdf> accessed 9 October 2013

Committee on the Elimination of Discrimination against Women, 'Seventh Periodic Report Greece' 14 March 2011 <http://www.un.org/ga/search/view_ doc.asp?symbol=CEDAW/C/GRC/7> accessed 9 October 2013

Council of the European Union, 'Economic and Financial Affairs – Extraordinary Council Meeting Press Release' 9–10 May 2010, 9596/10 <http://europa.eu/ rapid/press-release_PRES-10–108_en.htm> accessed 9 October 2013

—— 'Extraordinary Council Meeting: Economic and Financial Affairs' 9–10 May 2010, Press Release 9596/10 <http://www.consilium.europa.eu/uedocs/cms_ data/docs/pressdata/en/ecofin/114324.pdf> accessed 9 October 2013

ECB, 'Transcript of Press Briefing' 2 August 2007 <http://www.ecb.int/press/pressconf/2007/html/is070802.en.html> accessed 9 October 2013

—— 'Introductory Statement with Q&A with J.-C. Trichet' 2 October 2008 <http://www.ecb.int/press/pressconf/2008/html/is081002.en.html> accessed 9 October 2013

—— 'Introductory Statement with Q&A with J.-C. Trichet' 7 May 2009 <http://www.ecb.int/press/pressconf/2009/html/is090507.en.html> accessed 9 October 2013

—— 'Press Release' 4 June 2009 <http://www.ecb.int/press/pr/date/2009/html/pr090604_1.en.html> accessed 9 October 2013

—— 'Introductory Statement with Q&A with J.-C. Trichet' 4 February 2010 <http://www.ecb.int/press/pressconf/2010/html/is100204.en.html> accessed 9 October 2013

—— 'Statement by the ECB's Governing Council on the Additional Measures of the Greek Government' 3 March 2010 <http://www.ecb.int/press/pr/date/2010/html/pr100303.en.html> accessed 9 October 2013

—— 'Introductory Statement with Q&A with J.-C. Trichet' 4 March 2010 <http://www.ecb.int/press/pressconf/2010/html/is100304.en.html> accessed 9 October 2013

—— 'Introductory Statement with Q&A with J.-C. Trichet' 6 May 2010 <http://www.ecb.int/press/pressconf/2010/html/is100506.en.html> accessed 9 October 2013

—— 'Press Release' 31 March 2011 <http://www.ecb.europa.eu/press/pr/date/2011/html/pr110331_2.en.html> accessed 9 October 2013

—— 'Press Release' 7 July 2011 <http://www.ecb.europa.eu/press/pr/date/2011/html/pr110707_1.en.html> accessed 9 October 2013

—— 'Press Release' 6 September 2012 <http://www.ecb.int/press/pr/date/2012/html/pr120906_1.en.html> accessed 9 October 2013

— 'Press Release', 21 February 2013 <http://www.ecb.int/press/pr/date/2013/html/pr130221_1.en.html> accessed 9 October 2013

—— 'Intra-Euro Area Trade Linkages and External Adjustment' *Monthly Bulletin* 1 (2013) <http://www.ecb.int/pub/pdf/other/art2_mb201301en_pp59–74en.pdf> accessed 9 October 2013.

—— 'The Definition of Price Stability', *Monetary Policy – Strategy* <http://www.ecb.europa.eu/mopo/strategy/pricestab/html/index.en.html> accessed 9 October 2013

EFSF Framework Agreement consolidated version <http://www.efsf.europa.eu/attachments/20111019_efsf_framework_agreement_en.pdf> accessed 9 October 2013

Euro Area Loan Facility Bill 2010, Schedule 1 <http://www.oireachtas.ie/documents/bills28/bills/2010/2210/b2210d.pdf> accessed 9 October 2013

Euro Area, 'Conclusions of the Heads of State or Government of the Euro Area' 11 March 2011 <http://www.european-council.europa.eu/council-meetings/conclusions?lang=en> accessed 9 October 2013

—— 'Summit Statement' 29 June 2012 <http://www.consilium.europa.eu/uedocs/cms_data/docs/pressdata/en/ec/131359.pdf> accessed 9 October 2013

Eurogroup, 'Draft Statement' 2 May 2010 <http://www.consilium.europa.eu/media/6977/100502-%20eurogroup_statement%20greece.pdf> accessed 9 October 2013

—— 'Statement' 16 March 2013 <http://eurozone.europa.eu/media/402209/Eurogroup%20statement%20CY_final__16%203%202013%20_2_.pdf> accessed 9 October 2013

—— 'Statement' 25 March 2013 <http://eurozone.europa.eu/media/404933/E.G.%20EG%20Statement%20on%20CY%2025%2003%202013.pdf> accessed 9 October 2013

European Commission, 'External and Intra-European Union Trade' *Statistical Yearbook* (2004 and 2011) <http://epp.eurostat.ec.europa.eu/cache/ITY_OFFPUB/KS-CV-04–001/EN/KS-CV-04–001-EN.PDF> and <http://epp.eurostat.ec.europa.eu/cache/ITY_OFFPUB/KS-GI-11–001/EN/KS-GI-11–001-EN.PDF> accessed 9 October 2013

—— 'Making it Happen – the European Semester' <http://ec.europa.eu/europe2020/making-it-happen/index_en.htm> accessed 15 May 2014

—— *The Economic Adjustment Programme for Greece: Third Review – Winter 2011* (Directorate-General for Economic and Financial Affairs 2011)

—— *The Economic Adjustment Programme for Greece: Fifth Review – October 2011* (Directorate-General for Economic and Financial Affairs 2011)

—— *The Economic Adjustment Programme for Ireland: Spring 2011 Review* (Directorate-General for Economic and Financial Affairs 2011)

—— *The Economic Adjustment Programme for Portugal: Fifth Review – Summer 2012* (Directorate-General for Economic and Financial Affairs 2012)

——, Spain, 'Memorandum of Understanding on Financial-Sector Policy Conditionality' 20 July 2012 <http://ec.europa.eu/economy_finance/eu_borrower/mou/2012–07–20-spain-mou_en.pdf> accessed 23 June 2014

—— 'A Blueprint for a Deep and Genuine Economic and Monetary Union – Launching a European Debate – Communication from the Commission' 30 November 2012, COM(2012) 777 final/2 <http://ec.europa.eu/commission_2010–2014/president/news/archives/2012/11/pdf/blueprint_en.pdf> accessed 9 October 2013

—— 'Towards a Deep and Genuine Economic and Monetary Union: The Introduction of a Convergence and Competitiveness Instrument – Communication from the Commission' 20 March 2013, COM(2013) 165 final <http://ec.europa.eu/economy_finance/articles/governance/pdf/2039_165_final_en.pdf> accessed 9 October 2013

—— 'MIP Scoreboard' updated 20 March 2013 <http://ec.europa.eu/economy_finance/economic_governance/macroeconomic_imbalance_procedure/mip_scoreboard/index_en.htm> accessed 9 October 2013

European Committee of Social Rights, 'Decision on the Merits General Federation of employees of the national electric power corporation and Confederation of

Greek Civil Servants' Trade Unions' Complaint No. 66/2011, 23 May 2012 <www.coe.int/T/DGHL/Monitoring/SocialCharter/Complaints/CC66Merits_en.pdf> accessed 9 October 2013

European Council, 'Statement by Heads of State and Government of the Euro Area' 25–26 March 2010 <http://ec.europa.eu/economy_finance/focuson/crisis/2010–03_en.htm> accessed 9 October 2013

—— 'Conclusions' 28–29 October 2010 <www.consilium.europa.eu/uedocs/cms_data/docs/pressdata/en/ec/137634.pdf> accessed 9 October 2013

—— 'Conclusions' 16–17 December 2010 <www.consilium.europa.eu/uedocs/cms_data/docs/pressdata/en/ec/118578.pdf> accessed 9 October 2013

—— 'Conclusions' 24–25 March 2011 <www.consilium.europa.eu/uedocs/cms_data/docs/pressdata/en/ec/120296.pdf> accessed 9 October 2013

—— 'Conclusions' 1–2 March 2012 <www.consilium.europa.eu/uedocs/cms_data/docs/pressdata/en/ec/128520.pdf> accessed 9 October 2013

—— (President H van Rompuy), 'Towards a Genuine Economic and Monetary Union Report' 26 June 2012, 120/12 <http://ec.europa.eu/economy_finance/focuson/crisis/documents/131201_en.pdf> accessed 9 October 2013

—— 'Towards a Genuine Economic and Monetary Union' 5 December 2012, <www.consilium.europa.eu/uedocs/cms_data/docs/pressdata/en/ec/134069.pdf> accessed 9 October 2013

European Monetary Institute, *Convergence Report: Report Required by Article 109j of the Treaty establishing the European Community* (European Monetary Institute 1998)

European Parliament (Matthias Kumm), 'Democratic Challenges Arising from the Eurocrisis: What kind of a Constitutional Crisis is Europe in and what Should be Done about it?'(Challenges of Multi-Tier Governance in the EU Workshop, 4 October 2012) <www.eui.eu/Events/download.jsp?FILE_ID–3543> accessed 20 September 2013

Corriere della Sera 'Trichet e Draghi: Un'Azione Pressante per Ristabilire la Fiducia degli Investitori, 6 August 2010 <www.corriere.it/economia/11_settembre_29/trichet_draghi_inglese_304a5f1e-ea59–11e0-ae06–4da866778017.shtml> accessed 9 October 2013

Finfacts Team, 'Government's Emergency Legislation to Provide €400 Billion Guarantee for Irish Banking System to be Passed by Oireachtas Today' *Finfacts Ireland* 1 October 2008 <www.finfacts.i.e./irishfinancenews/article_1014861.shtml> accessed 9 October 2013

German Council of Economic Experts, 'European Redemption Pact' <www.sachverstaendigenrat-wirtschaft.de/fileadmin/dateiablage/download/publikationen/working_paper_02_2012.pdf> accessed 9 October 2013

German Federal Court, 'ESM/Fiskalpakt – Anträge auf Erlass Einer Einstweiligen Anordnung' Press Release 2 July 2012 <www.bundesverfassungsgericht.de/pressemitteilungen/bvg12–047.html> accessed 9 October 2013

Greek Financial Assistance Facility Agreement <www.efsf.europa.eu/attachments/efsf_greece_fafa.pdf> accessed 9 October 2013

IMF, 'Greece: Ex Post Evaluation of Exceptional Access under the 2010 Stand-By Arrangement' Country Report No 13/156 June 2013 <www.imf.org/external/pubs/ft/scr/2013/cr13156.pdf> accessed 20 September 2013

IMF, 'Changing Patterns of Global Trade' prepared by the Strategy, Policy, and Review Department and approved by Tamim Bayoumi (2011) <http://www.imf.org/external/np/pp/eng/2011/061511.pdf> accessed 15 May 2014

IMF, 'Cyprus: Letter of Intent, Memorandum of Economic and Financial Policies, and Technical Memorandum of Understanding' 29 April 2013 <http://www.imf.org/External/NP/LOI/2013/CYP/042913.pdf> accessed 15 May 2014

IMF, 'Greece: Ex Post Evaluation of Exceptional Access under the 2010 Stand-By Arrangement' Country Report No 13/156 June 2013 <www.imf.org/external/pubs/ft/scr/2013/cr13156.pdf> accessed 20 September 2013

International Labour Office, 'Report on the High Level Mission to Greece' 19–23 September 2011 <www.ilo.org/global/standards/WCMS_170433/lang--en/index.htm> accessed 9 October 2013

Limburg Principles on the Implementation of the International Covenant on Economic, Social and Cultural Rights, UN Doc. E/CN.4/1987/17 (1987) 9 *Human Rights Quarterly* 122–35

Master Financial Assistance Agreement between European Financial Stability Facility, Kingdom of Spain as Beneficiary Member State, Fondo de Reestructuración Ordenada Bancaria as Guarantor and the Bank of Spain <www.efsf.europa.eu/attachments/efsf_spain_ffa.pdf> accessed 9 October 2013

Merkel A, 'Regierungserklärung von Bundeskanzlerin Merkel zu den Euro-Stabilisierungsmaßnahmen', speech before the *Bundestag* 19 May 2010 <www.bundesregierung.de/Content/DE/Regierungserklaerung/2010/2010-05-19-merkel-erklaerung-eu-stabilisierungsmassnahmen.html> accessed 9 October 2013

OECD, 'Debt and Macroeconomic Stability' *OECD Economics Department Policy Notes* 16 (2013)

OECD, 'Strengthening Euro Area Banks' *Economic Outlook, Analysis and Forecasts* <www.oecd.org/eco/outlook/strengtheningeuroareabanks.htm> accessed 9 October 2013

TESM, 'Declaration on the European Stability Mechanism' 27 September 2012 <www.consilium.europa.eu/uedocs/cms_data/docs/pressdata/en/ecofin/132615.pdf> accessed 9 October 2013

UN Committee on Economic, Social and Cultural Rights, 'Concluding Observations: Greece' 7 June 2004 <www.refworld.org/publisher,CESCR,CO NCOBSERVATIONS,GRC,42d26c904,0.html> accessed 9 October 2013

Werner Committee, 'Report to the Council and the Commission on the Realization by Stages of Economic and Monetary Union in the Community (Werner Report)' 8 October 1970 <http://ec.europa.eu/economy_finance/emu_history/documentation/chapter5/19701008en72realisationbystage.pdf> accessed 9 October 2013

Newspaper Articles

Elliot L, 'EU Should Control Member States' Budgets, Says Bank Boss' *Guardian* 2 June 2011 <http://www.guardian.co.uk/business/2011/jun/02/trichet-wants-eu-central-finance-ministry> accessed 15 May 2014

Müller P, Pauly C and Reiermann C, 'ECB Chief Economist Quits: Jürgen Stark's Resignation is Setback for Merkel' *Spiegel Online* 12 September 2011 <http://www.spiegel.de/international/europe/ecb-chief-economist-quits-juergen-stark-s-resignation-is-setback-for-merkel-a-785668.html> accessed 15 May 2014

Spiegel P, 'EU's Olli Rehn Lashes out at IMF Criticism of Greek Bailout' *Financial Times* 7 June 2013 <www.ft.com/cms/s/0/ed72d2ac-cf4e-11e2-be7b-00144feab7de.html#axzz2Y3GjWyda> accessed 9 October 2013

'Former Central Bank Head Karl Otto Pöhl: Bailout Plan is all about "Rescuing Banks and Rich Greeks"' *Spiegel Online* 18 May 2010 <www.spiegel.de/international/germany/former-central-bank-head-karl-otto-poehl-bailout-plan-is-all-about-rescuing-banks-and-rich-greeks-a-695245.html> accessed 9 October 2013

'Merkel ECB Candidate: German Central Bank Head Axel Weber Resigns' *Spiegel Online* 11 February 2011 <www.spiegel.de/international/germany/merkel-ecb-candidate-german-central-bank-head-axel-weber-resigns-a-745083.html> accessed 9 October 2013

Chapter 2

The European Crisis – Paradoxes of Constitutionalizing Democratic Capitalism

Hauke Brunkhorst

In the beginning, European Unification was not the affirmation of *peace* – the protection of which led to the European Union receiving the Nobel Prize in 2012 (despite the fact that the Union, or some of its Member States, was at war in several parts of the world).

In the beginning was not peace but the *negation of fascism*: that is the emancipation of Europe from the dictatorship of the Third Reich.

In the beginning was not the *managerial mindset* of possessive individualism and 'peaceful competitive struggle'.[1]

In the beginning was political autonomy.

In the beginning was not rational choice and strategic action enabled by rule of law – but the emancipation from any law that is not the law to which we have given our agreement.[2]

Martti Koskenniemi calls the latter, in contrast to the managerial mindset, the *Kantian mindset*.[3] For Kant in his time the scandal of so-called absolutism was not a lack of *Rechtsstaat* or rule of law. Kant had no doubt that the contemporary monarchy was a *Rechtsstaat*. For Kant the scandal of that monarchy was its lack of political 'autonomy' and 'self-legislation', and the absence of 'structures of political representation'.[4] Historically the Kantian constitutional mindset is the mindset of the French Revolution as it once was expressed strikingly by the young Karl Marx in one short sentence: 'Die gesetzgebende Gewalt hat die

---

1   Karl Marx, *Der 18. Brumaire des Louis Bonaparte* (Die Revolution, New York 1852) 97, English quoted from: <www.marxists.org/archive/marx/works/1852/18th-brumaire/ch01.htm> accessed 19 March 2012.

2   Alexander Somek, 'Europe: From emancipation to empowerment', *LSE 'Europe in Question'Discussion Paper Series LEQS Paper No 60/2013* 8.

3   Martti Koskenniemi, 'Constitutionalism as Mindset: Reflections on Kantian Themes About International Law and Globalization' (2006) 8 *Theoretical Inquiries in Law* 9; for a similar argument see also Martti Koskenniemi, 'Formalismus, Fragmentierung, Freiheit – Kantische Themen im heutigen Völkerrecht' in R Kreide and A Niederberger (eds), *Transnationale Verrechtlichung. Nationale Demokratien im Zeitalter globaler Politik* (Campus 2008).

4   Koskenniemi, Cosmopolitanism as Mindset (n 3) 26.

Französische Revolution gemacht'. – The legislative power has made the French Revolution.[5]

1   The Hour of the Legislator

Today the memory that it was the same constituent legislative power of the peoples of Europe that instigated the beginning of European unification between autumn 1944 (the last year of World War II in Europe) and 1957, has been repressed and displaced by the managerial mindset that had already become hegemonial in the 1950s. However, European unification did not begin with the Treaty of Paris in 1951 and the Treaty of Rome in 1957 but with the new constitutions that all founding members (France, Belgium, Italy, Luxemburg, Netherlands and West Germany) had established for themselves between 1944 and 1948. Moreover, the foundation of the first Communities of 1951 and 1957 was in effect a global revolutionary transformation of national and international law that was as deep as that of the French Revolution.[6] All constitutions of the founding members were made by new representatives of their respective peoples.

1. All founding members had changed their political leaders and had replaced large parts of the former ruling classes with former resistance fighters or emigrants who had defected. They gained a power that had not existed before or during the time of the Nazi occupation. Rebels, guerrillas and exiled politicians became heads and members of government. They had risked their lives, not solely as patriots, but as democrats or socialists who had struggled for certain rights and universal constitutional principles.[7]

2. All constitutions of the founding members were new or in important aspects revised and more democratic than ever before. Only now *all* of them stipulated universal adult suffrage.

---

5   Karl Marx, *Kritik des Hegelschen Staatsrechts* (§§ 261–313) in MEW 1 (Dietz 1972) 203, 260. Because of the *indeterminacy* of law-application also the application and concretization of legal norms is not simply a politically neutralized business of managerial experts but, as Kelsen, Merkel and Heller rightly have argued already in the 1920s, *any* 'determining the content of the legal norm [is] a political question'. Koskenniemi (n 4) 29.

6   See Hauke Brunkhorst, *Legitimationskrisen – Verfassungsprobleme der Weltgesellschaft* (Nomos 2012).

7   Jürgen Osterhammel and Niels P Petersson, *Geschichte der Globalisierung* (Beck 2007) 85; Eric Hobsbawm, *Das Zeitalter der Extreme. Weltgeschichte des 20. Jahrhunderts* (Hanser 1994) 185–187. This does not mean that there did not remain strong continuities in all countries; in Germany in particular the Nazi continuities of the elites were still strong but silenced and displaced, strikingly described by Hermann Lübbe as 'kommunikatives Beschweigen brauner Biographieanteile', see speech by H Lübbe, 'Fünfzig Jahre Danach – Der Nationalsozialismus im politischen Bewußtsein der Gegenwart' (15 January 1983, Reichstag, Berlin).

3. All had eliminated the remains (or after 1918 newly invented structures) of corporative political representation of society. For the first time the system of political democracy was completely autonomous and could cover and control the whole society through parliamentary or popular legislation alone (as was the case with Kelsen's Austrian constitution of 1918 that was a lone exception then).[8] The German *Grundgesetz* even constituted a completely new state.[9]

4. All constitutions of the founding members expressed a strong emphasis on human rights and had opened themselves (more or less) to international law. The founding members of the European Communities designed their newly constituted states as open states – open for the incorporation of international law and international cooperation (an important example of this is, in German Basic Law (*Grundgesetz*), the obligatory *Völkerrechtsfreundlichkeit* (openness to international law) established in Art. 24(1)).[10]

5. Finally, and crucial for the foundation of Europe, the new constitutions declared the strong commitment of their respective peoples to the project of European unification, which was to be realized in the near future (for example: Preamble in combination with Art 24(1) of Basic Law). All founding members of the European Communities bound themselves by the constituent power of the people to the project of European unification, which then, from 1951 onwards, became constitutive for all European constitutional (or quasi-constitutional) treaties.[11] The only instance of a constitution of a founding member that made no declaration on Europe, the Constitution of Luxemburg, is of itself a revealing case. In this case the Luxemburg *Conseil d'Etat* decided in 1952 that the Constitution implicitly committed the representatives of the people to join the European Coal and Steel Community, and to strive for further European unification.[12]

---

8 See Dietrich Jesch, *Gesetz und Verwaltung. Eine Problemstudie zum Wandel des Gesetzmäßigkeitsprinzips* (Mohr 1961).

9 See Hans Kelsen, 'The legal status of Germany according to the Declaration of Berlin' (1945) 39 *American Journal of International Law* 518.

10 See Rainer Wahl, *Verfassungsstaat, Europäisierung, Internationalisierung* (Suhrkamp 2003); Udo Di Fabio, *Das Recht offener Staaten. Grundlinien einer Staats- und Rechtstheorie* (Mohr 1998).

11 John Erik Fossum, Agustin José Menéndez, *The Constitution's Gift. A Constitutional Theory for a democratic European Union* (Rowman 2011) 175.

12 It is argued that, even if the constitution of Luxemburg did not contain anything vaguely resembling a proto-European clause, the Conseil d'Etat constructed its fundamental law along very similar lines. When reviewing the constitutionality of the Treaty establishing the Coal and Steel Community, the Conseil affirmed that Luxembourg not only could, but should, renounce certain sovereign powers if the public good so required. See the Report on the 1952 judgment of the Conseil d'Etat; Fossum and Menéndez (n 11).

For the latter reason the Founding Treaties of Paris and Rome were directly legitimated by the constituent power of the peoples.[13] In consequence, it can be concluded that, from the outset, the European Union was not founded as an international association of states. On the contrary, it was founded as a community of peoples who legitimated the project of European unification directly and democratically through their combined, but still national, constitutional powers (represented later in the Council of the European Union and the European Council). At the same time and with the same founding act, these peoples, acting plurally, constituted a single European citizenship, embodying new rights for the European citizen, which were different from the rights of the citizens of the respective Member States (represented later by the European Parliament). These remained implicit for the first decades, but the ECJ made them explicit in *van Gend en Loos* and *Costa* in 1963 and 1964. The community of European citizens as a whole thus now constitutes a second and independent 'subject of legitimization'.[14] From the beginning, the Treaties were not just intergovernmental, but legal documents with a constitutional quality.

2   Full-fledged Democracy – But Nobody Knows It

However, as one also can observe in other cases of national or transnational constitutionalization, the constitutional moment was followed by unspectacular evolutionary incrementalism and a silent but gradual and steady process of ever denser integration. The managerial mindset took over soon after the first big changes. However, it has not only replaced and repressed the Kantian mindset of revolutionary foundation but also stabilized and realized it step by step legally.[15]

---

13   Fossum and Menéndez (n 11).

14   On the double legitimization of the EU by the community of peoples of the member states and the people of the European Union see Jürgen Habermas, 'Die Krise der Europäische Union im Licht einer Konstitutionalisierung des Völkerrechts' (manuscript of a lecture given at the Humboldt University, Berlin, 16 June 2011) 201. For a striking comparison with the development of the United States founded by a similar kind of 'double sovereignty' (which is still a technical term of constitutional law in the US), see C Schönberger, *Föderale Angehörigkeit* (Habilitationsschrift 2005). See also Murray Forsythe, *Unions of States. The Theory and Practice of Confederations* (Holmes 1981). Agustín Menéndez has made an important contribution to that thesis, comparing in a case study the implementation of federal taxes in the US and the EU, demonstrating the striking parallels: See AJ Menéndez, 'Taxing Europe – Two cases for a European power to tax' 3 *Cidel Working Papers* (2003).

15   An illuminating case study is by Mikael Rask Madsen, *The Protracted Institutionalization of the Strasbourg Court: From Legal Diplomacy to Integrationist jurisprudence* in Jonas Christoffersen and Mikael Rask Madsen (eds), *The European Court of Human Rights between Law and Politics* (Oxford University Press 2011) 55. On the general need of the 'Kantian' mindset of normative social integration for systemic and

In European law today the Kantian mindset is expressed in the references of the preambles of the European Treaties to 'solidarity', 'democracy', 'social progress' 'human rights' and 'rule of law'. It is implemented in many single articles and legal norms of primary and secondary European law, such as the famous Art. 6 of the Treaty of Maastricht, or Articles 9–12 of the Lisbon Treaty. Moreover, the Kantian mindset also determines legal precedents such as the famous cases of *Costa* and *van Gent en Loos* from the early 1960s which refer to the subjective rights that we have as European citizens ('direct effect' plus 'European law supremacy'). Finally, the Kantian mindset found its way into numerous juristic comments and treatises: this was the emergence of a European *Rechtsdogmatik* (legal doctrine)[16], and became part of the European common law.[17]

At the end of the day, and after the symbolic re-establishment of state sovereignty through the constitutional court of the European hegemon in Karlsruhe – the counter-hegemonial Czech constitutional court in its judgment on the Lisbon Treaty stated that the European Union today forms a complete and gapless system of democratic legitimization, and rightly so.[18] Legally Europe no longer has a crucial democratic deficit. It is already a full fledged democracy on both levels: the national *and* the transnational.

The problem is that nobody knows it.

'managerial' stabilization see Jürgen Habermas, *Theorie des kommunikativen Handelns II* (Suhrkamp 1981) 228; A Nassehi, *Der soziologische Diskurs der Moderne* (Suhrkamp Verlag 2006) 126–7.

16   A good explication of the Kantian democratic and even cosmopolitan mindset of the Lisbon Treaty is Armin von Bogdandy, 'The European Lesson for International Democracy: The Significance of Articles 9–12 EU Treaty for International Organizations' (2012) 23 *The European Journal of International Law* 315; See (with respect to the Maastricht-Amsterdam Treaty and in particular the Constitutional Treaty that failed in 2005 but to a large extent is identical with the Lisbon Treaty) Christian Callies, 'Das Demokratieprinzip im Europäischen Staaten- und Verfassungsverbund' in J Bröhmer, RB Callies, C Langenfeld, S Weber and J Wolf, (eds) *Internationale Gemeinschaft und Menschenrechte* (Heymanns 2005) 399, 402–4.

17   What German lawyers observe as the emergence of an *autonomous legal doctrine* is reflected by a Scottish observer as the emergence of *European common law* that transcends the *pacta sunt servanda* validity of international law. European 'institutions and organs', Neil MacCormick argues, 'have had a continuous existence over several decades and through many changes of personnel. They have become central institutional facts in the thinking of Europeans. Citizens and officials throughout Europe have interpreted the norms of and under the treaties as having direct effect on private persons and corporations as well as on states. Over more than four decades this has proceeded with impressive continuity': Neil MacCormick, *Questioning Sovereignty. Law, State and Nation in the European Commonwealth* (Oxford University Press 1999) 139.

18   Isabelle Ley, 'Brünn betreibt die Parlamentarisierung des Primärrechts. Anmerkungen zum zweiten Urteil des tschechischen Verfassungsgerichtshofs zum Vertrag von Lissabon vom 3.11.2009' (2010) 65 *Juristen-Zeitung* 170.

The problem is not just the managerial mindset but the hegemony of the managerial mindset, and the reduction of politics to technocracy that today allows the political and economic elites to bypass and manipulate public opinion and democratically legitimated public law on both levels: the European *as well as* the respective national level. At the same time as it is growing legally, the public power of the people and its representative organs is more and more deprived of real power and replaced by grey networks of informal government,[19] called 'good governance',[20] instead of democratic government, called 'administrative accountability',[21] instead of parliamentary responsibility, called 'deliberative democracy', instead of egalitarian decision making.[22] In a world where good governance has replaced democratic government, where administrative accountability has replaced parliamentary responsibility, where deliberative democracy of educated middle-classes has replaced egalitarian procedures of decision making, in a world where the semantics of pluralized civil societies has replaced the unity of capitalist society, where competition has replaced cooperation, where the managerial mindset of individual empowerment has replaced the Kantian mindset of emancipation – public contestation over real issues, public debate and public struggle over substantial alternatives are just 'not helpful' (*nicht hilfreich*), to say it in the matchless managerial language of Angela Merkel. In Angela Merkel's world deliberative democracy begins when the doors are closed.

Hence, and this is my overarching thesis, the Kantian mindset of revolutionary foundation has been concretized and stabilized throughout the gradual evolutionary process of constitutionalization. This evolutionary process was performed under the lead of the managerial mindset of Europe's political elites and professional experts. However, the hegemony of the managerial mindset had the paradoxical result that the Kantian mindset at the same time was preserved and repressed

---

19   Christophe *Möllers*, 'Transnationale Behördenkooperation. Verfassungs- und völkerrechtliche Probleme transnationaler administrativer Standardsetzung' (2005) 65 *Zeitschrift für ausländisches öffentliches Recht und Völkerrecht* 351; Christophe Möllers, *Gewaltengliederung* (Habilitationsschrift 2003). For accumulation of informal power in flexible, widely dispersed and rapidly changing networks, see also Michael Hardt and Antonio Negri, *Empire. Die neue Weltordnung* (Campus 2002); Thore Prien, *Fragmentierte Volkssouveränität* (Nomos 2010); Andreas Fischer-Lescano and Gunther Teubner, *Regime-Kollisionen* (Suhrkamp 2006); on white, grey and black networks see W Matiaske, 'Gullivers Fesseln: Corporate Social Responsibility als Normbildung?' (Lecture at Flensburg University, 5 June 2012).

20   Michael Zürn, *Regieren jenseits des Nationalstaates* (Suhrkamp 2004).

21   Ruth W Grant, Robert O Keohane, 'Accountability and Abuses of Power in World Politics' (2005) 99 *American Political Science Review* 2943.

22   For a sound criticism of these tendencies see SP Rieckmann, 'Constitutionalism and Representation: European Parliamentarism in the Treaty of Lisbon' in P Dobner, M Loughlin (eds), *The Twilight of Constitutionalism?* (Oxford University Press 2010) 120.

(or displaced), constitutionalized and de-constitutionalized – again and again on every stage of the twisted paths of European constitutionalization.[23]

3   Combining Functionalism (Tuori) and Critical Theory (Koskenniemi)

Before I come back to the gradual evolution of European constitutional law over several stages I have to make a short conceptual remark. I borrow from Koskenniemi the distinction between the two constitutional mindsets, the *Kantian* and the *managerial*. But I do not think that they are just mindsets which work as closed language games, and are the only way to get from the one to the other, that to get from the Kantian self-legislator Dr Jekyll to the neoliberal rule of law manager Mr Hyde is a gestalt switch such as in Robert L Stevenson's 1886 novel and John Carl Buechler's 1912 silent movie.

On the contrary, I will try to show that both mindsets are related internally and inferentially to one another in a dialectical way. To do that, I will use Kaarlo Tuori's (managerial) schema of the gradual and incremental evolution of the many constitutions of Europe. What I want to demonstrate is that managerial constitutionalization has always presupposed some Kantian qua constitutional law (and this is true already of the modern form of law that cannot be reduced totally to the managerial mindset). My thesis is that both contradicting mindsets are internal driving forces of the constitutional evolution, and Europe in this respect is only one of many cases.[24]

4   Hegemony of Economic Constitution

As Tuori has shown, Europe now has not only many national (and sub-national) constitutions but also many transnational constitutions that evolved gradually and in stages. The first evolutionary step was taken in 1957 with the establishment of a functional economic constitution that consisted in the structural coupling of the legal and the economic system (stage I of the constitutional evolution of the European Union).

Originally the idea of an economic constitution was an invention of the German socialist left at the end of World War I, in particular Hugo Sinzheimer and his student Franz Neumann. Sinzheimer and Neumann strictly followed the Kantian presupposition that the political constitution and the parliamentary legislator

---

23   On the stages see Kaarlo Tuori, 'Multi-Dimensionality of European Constitutionalism: The Many Constitutions of Europe' in K Tuori and S Sankari (eds), *The Many Constitutions of Europe* (Ashgate 2010) 3.

24   I cannot go into details and further examples here but have tried to develop some major points of such a theory in my new book: Hauke Brunkhorst, *Critical Theory of Legal Revolutions – Evolutionary Perspectives* (Bloomsbury 2014) 294–316.

should maintain absolute supremacy over the economic constitution. The economic constitution should have a mere service function: It should improve the possibilities of the democratic legislator, to get the markets, and in particular the private sphere of domination within the capitalist firm under democratic control.[25]

At the end of the Weimar Republic ordoliberals 'rather hi-jacked' the idea of an economic constitution from Sinzheimer and Neumann, watered it down and reversed it severely.[26] During the 1950s they turned the idea upside down, trans-nationalized the economic constitution, decoupled it from the national political constitution and subsumed the latter under the former. Now the whole society should be 'subsumed' under the 'principle of market-compliance', as the (at that time pious) former Nazi Alfred Müller-Armack wrote in 1960.[27] In the 1957 treaty negotiations the German ordoliberals under the lead of Müller-Armack, and strongly supported by the American government, finally won the battle against the recalcitrant French government that, at the time, defended a constitutional project that was much closer to the original ideas of Sinzheimer and Neumann.[28] Therefore *Wettbewerbsrecht* (competition law) became the 'axis of the economic order'.[29]

My thesis is that with the establishment of the economic constitution in 1957 a Schmittian constitutional *Grundentscheidung* (basic decision) was made. It consisted in the radical 'negation of a political constitution of Europe'.[30] Instead of subsuming the economic under the political constitution, the political constitution was subsumed under the economic constitution. In case of doubt the 'concrete order' of *law and economics* trumps the formal constitution of *law and democracy*.[31]

---

25   Cf. Franz Neumann, *Wirtschaft, Staat und Demokratie* (Suhrkamp 1978) 70, 72, 74, 87–90, 95–6.

26   See Tuori, 'Multidimensionality' in Tuori and Sankari (n 23) 16. The hi-jacking was organized by Franz Böhm, *Wettbewerb und Monopolrecht* (Nomos 2010) 1933.

27   Alfred Müller-Armack, *Studien zur Sozialen Marktwirtschaft* (Institut für Wirtschaftspolitik 1960) 11–12, 15 (my translation). For a brief and powerful criticism of the imperial tendencies of Ordoliberalism see Gunther Teubner, *Constitutional Fragments. Societal Constitutionalism and Globalization* (Oxford University Press 2012) 30–34.

28   Milène Wegmann, 'European Competition Law: Catalyst of Integration and Convergence' in Tuori and Sankari (n 23) 91, 93.

29   Wegmann (n 28).

30   Tuori, 'Multidimensionality' in Tuori and Sankari (n 23) 15.

31   'Diese Asymmetrie ist bereits in den Gründungsverträgen angelegt, was sich daran zeigt, dass im Gegensatz zu den meisten Rechtsordnungen der Mitgliedstaaten die Wettbewerbspolitik der Union verfassungsrechtlich abgesichert ist, während die Bewältigung der sozialen Folgen den Mitgliedstaaten überlassen bleibt. Auf diese Weise fallen Deregulierung und Regulierung institutionell auseinander. *Legitimationstheoretisch lässt sich das nicht begründen.* Die Aufspaltung in eine bloß formelle Legitimation des gemeinsamen Marktes und eine materielle, über die Mitgliedstaaten vermittelte Legitimation der Marktkorrektur macht angesichts der vielfältigen wechselseitigen Abhängigkeiten heute keinen rechten Sinn mehr. Will man Freiheiten über Grenzen hinweg

Whereas formal constitutional law still adhered to the Kantian priority of democratic legislation, the concrete order of *law and economics* became Europe's informal prerogative constitution – Europe's 'hidden curriculum'.[32] The legal link between visible constitutional law and the invisible prerogative constitution was Art. 2 TEEC.[33] One of the most crucial effects was that the negation of any transnationalization of the political constitution and the hegemony of the hidden curriculum of the transnational economic constitution stimulated and reinforced the Europeanization of big enterprises and employers' federations, but at the same time strictly limited union activities and employee organizations to the sphere of the national state.[34]

Ordoliberals today are proud of the fine differences that distinguish them from Neoliberalism. But it was indeed ordoliberalism that disclosed the historical path to the latest great transformation of globalization that has lasted since the 1980s. If we resume the three basic ideas of ordoliberalism, it becomes evident that only one idea is different. Therefore, the relation between ordo- and Neoliberalism resembles more a cooperative historical division of business than a fierce opposition:

---

ausdehnen, müssen auf Ebene der Union politisch hinreichend verantwortete Kompetenzen für eine Umverteilung geschaffen werden'. (Claudio Franzius, Ulrich K Preuß, *Europäische Demokratie* (Ms 2011) 70.

32   On the 'hidden curriculum' see Claus Offe, 'The European Model of "Social Capitalism": Can it Survive European Integration?' (2003) 11 *The Journal of Political Philosophy* 437, 463. On the distinction between the two constitutional orders, see Ernst Fraenkel, 'Der Doppelstaat' (1999) 2 *Gesammelte Schriften* 33 (published 1974, originally finished 1938); see Christian Joerges, 'Europas Wirtschaftsverfassung in der Krise' (2012) 51 *Der Staat* 357, 360–61, 366–7, 377–81.

33   Wegmann (n 28) 94. Art. 2 ECC: 'It shall be the aim of the Community, by establishing a Common Market and progressively approximating the economic policies of Member States, to promote throughout the Community a harmonious development of economic activities, a continuous and balanced expansion, an increased stability, an accelerated rising of the standard of living and closer relations between its Member States'. Today it is replaced by Art. 2 EC: 'The Community shall have as its task, by establishing a common market and an economic and monetary union and by implementing common policies or activities referred to in Articles 3 and 4, to promote throughout the Community a harmonious, balanced and sustainable development of economic activities, a high level of employment and of social protection, equality between men and women, sustainable and non-inflationary growth, a high degree of competitiveness and convergence of economic performance, a high level of protection and improvement of the quality of the environment, the raising of the standard of living and quality of life, and economic and social cohesion and solidarity among Member States'. On the term 'invisible constitution', but with a slightly different meaning, see A Wiener, *The Invisible Constitution of Politics* (Cambridge University Press 2008).

34   See S Buckel, 'Welcome to Europe' – Juridische Auseinandersetzungen um das Staatsprojekt Europa, (unpublished Habilitationsschrift, Goethe-Universität 2012) 20.

- The *first* basic idea of ordoliberalism is to rid markets of state control. The spectre of 'socialism' and 'communism' must be banned as long as it still haunts Europe under the mask of macroeconomic state interventionism. Here ordo- and Neoliberalism agree from the beginning. Today's representatives of the power elite, such as the President of the German Bundesbank, Jens Weidmann, or the former judge of the Verfassungsgericht, Udo DiFabio, accuse even the President of the ECB, Mario Draghi, of creeping socialization (*schleichende Sozialisierung*) and planned central states economy (*planwirtschaftliche Zentralität*) – Draghi, the creeping socialist who learned his job at the communist cadre training centre Goldman & Sachs.[35]
- However, ordoliberalism not only distrusts the (bureaucratic) state but also large-scale (that is bureaucratic) capitalism and its tendency towards concentration and centralization of capital that has led to monopoly capitalism since the beginning of the twentieth century.[36] Therefore the *second* basic idea of ordoliberalism is to get rid of monopoly capitalism. Competition law should maintain equal economic opportunities for all market participants at any time. This idea is called market justice, but it is a very poor idea of justice.[37] From the beginning it was mere ideology. In fact (as Kelsen demonstrated in his scathing criticism of Hayek in 1955) it worked in favour of the 'haves' who maintained control over the means of production, and at best regulated *their* competition.[38] However, in this respect ordoliberalism is clearly different from Neoliberalism. Neoliberalism bluntly has abolished competition law and reduced so-called market justice to shareholder value that then has been identified with the common good by Milton Friedman and others.[39] That's why we can no longer side step the bright lights of the latest stock market news everywhere we go.
- The *third* (and in terms of constitutional law most crucial) basic idea of ordoliberalism is to get rid of democratic legislative control. Here again ordo- and Neoliberals meet in applying the categorical imperatives:

---

35   See Jens Weidmann, 'Die Stabilitätsunion sichern' 27 *Frankfurter Allgemeine Zeitung* (Frankfurt, 8 July 2012) 33; J Weidmann, 'Der Euro verlangt eine Stabilitätsunion' 146 *Frankfurter Allgemeine Zeitung* (Frankfurt 27 June 2012) 28 (quoting the following article of Udo Di Fabio); Udo Di Fabio, 'Das europäische Schuldendilemma als Mentalitätskrise' 143 *Frankfurter Allgemeine Zeitung* (Frankfurt, 22 June 2012) 9.

36   See Karl Marx, *Das Kapital I* (1867) 650–57.

37   See Milton Friedman, *Capitalism and Freedom* (Chicago University Press 1982) 15–26, especially at 20–21.

38   See Hans Kelsen, 'Demokratie und Sozialismus' (1954) in N Leser (ed) *Demokratie und Sozialismus. Ausgewählte Aufsätze* (Verlag der Wiener Volksbuchhandlung 1967) 170; Ernst Tugendhat, 'Liberalism, Liberty and the Issue of Economic Human Rights' in E Tugendhat (ed) *Philosophische Aufsätze* (Suhrkamp 1992) 352; Wolfgang Streeck, 'Zum Verhältnis von sozialer Gerechtigkeit und Marktgerechtigkeit' (unpublished e-manuscript of a lecture, Verona 20 September 2012).

39   Colin Crouch, *The Strange Non-Death of Neoliberalism* (Polity 2011).

Give the judges what you have taken from the democratic legislator and the parliamentary bound government! Promote the judges to guardians of functional *Ordnungsrecht* (regulatory law)! In the words of Ernst Joachim Mestmäcker: 'Die wichtigsten Aufgaben obliegen nicht der Legislative oder der Regierung, sondern der Rechtsprechung'. ('The most important decisions have to be taken not by the legislator or the government but by the judges').[40] The beheading of the legislator is the true end of the French Revolution and the Kantian political era.[41] If it really comes true, it will be the final triumph of the counter-revolution that in this case is the counter-revolution against 1789: Never again shall a legislator be able to make a revolution. That was Margaret Thatcher's actual message. In 2002 Alec Stone Sweet could only state that in 'today's multi-tiered European polity, the sovereignty of the legislator, and the primacy of national executives, are dead. In concert or in rivalry, European legislators govern with judges'.[42] One has to add that in combination transnational and national constitutional jurisdiction have reinforced one another, and in a way the European *Verfassungsgerichtsverbund* (Udo DiFabio) has reserved for itself the most basic functions of all three classical state powers – at least in normal times of incremental and managerial evolutionary constitutionalization.[43]

For these reasons, the implementation of the Euro without political government was not just a mistake, or the worst possible compromise – as seen at least from the perspective of the negotiating parties[44] – but actually nothing else than, as

---

40 Ernst Joachim Mestmäcker, 'Einführung' in Franz Böhm (ed), *Wettbewerb und Monopolkampf* (Berlin 1933) 5, 9; the same argument seems to fit the present crisis, see EJ Mestmäcker, 'Ordnungspolitische Grundlagen einer politischen Union' *Frankfurter Allgemeine Zeitung* (Frankfurt 11 September 2012) 12. In the same way Milton Friedman and the Chicago School argues that the main threat to political and economic freedom 'arises out of democratic politics' and must be 'defeated by political action' (Gabriel A Almond, 'Capitalism and Democracy' 24 *Political Science and Politics* 467).

41 For the theory that transnational law already has realized a mutation to a law that is no longer related to the legislative power see Marc Amstutz and Vaios Karavas, 'Rechtsmutationen' (2006) *Rechtsgeschichte* 14, 20; for a sceptical view: Karl-Heinz Ladeur, 'Die Evolution des Rechts und die Möglichkeit eines "globalen Rechts" jenseits des Staates – zugleich eine Kritik der "Selbstkonstitutionalisierungsthese"' (2012) *Ancilla Juris* 220; Mathias Albert and Rudolf Stichweh, *Weltstaat und Weltstaatlichkeit* (VS 2007).

42 Alec Stone Sweet, *Governing with Judges: Constitutional Politics in Europe* (Oxford University Press 2000) 193, quoted from Buckel (n 34) 26.

43 See Andreas Voßkuhle, 'Multilevel Cooperation of the European Constitutional Courts. Der Europäische Verfassungsgerichtsverbund' (2010) 6 *European Constitutional Law Review* 175.

44 See Henrik Enderlein, *Grenzen der europäischen Integration? Herausforderungen an Recht und Politik*, DFG-Rundgespräch in Zusammenarbeit mit der Friedrich-Ebert-Stiftung Berlin (Ms 2011).

Wolfgang Streeck says, a 'frivolous experiment' to realize a 'market economy emancipated' from all political bonds and to establish 'a political economy without parliament and government'.[45] The implementation of the Euro finalized the prerogative constitution and perfected the hidden curriculum of European governmentality by 'immunizing the markets against democratic corrections'.[46] This immediately resulted in an increase of the social differences between the rich North and the poor South. When finally the crisis came, European *Ordnungsrecht* derogated national as well as transnational constitutional law.[47] As a result, the social gap separating the North from the South grew dramatically in favour of the northern hegemon that is Germany.[48]

Hence, by beheading the legislator ordoliberalism opened the evolutionary path for the neoliberal globalization of capital beyond state control. Whether it did so intentionally or not, doesn't matter. Once Neoliberalism had taken over, the great transformation of the last 30 years could begin: the transformation of state-embedded and state-controlled markets into market-embedded and market-controlled states.[49] The new world order of market-embedded states makes it extremely hard for any political actor to get rid of the pressure of market compliance, to gain independence from the nervousness of a highly sensitive class of investors, and to get back to macroeconomic steering, be it national or transnational.

5 Juridical Constitution

For all that, economic constitutionalization is not the only evolutionary formation of European constitutional law, and even if it remains the hegemonial constitution to date, it was and is not the last stage of Europe's constitutional evolution. The latter is, as we have seen, conducted by the managerial mindset of law and

---

45   Streeck (n 38) 8.

46   Streeck (n 38) 6 (my translation); on the unity of ordo- and neoliberalism see also Fritz Scharpf, 'Integration versus Legitimation: Der Euro. Thesen', (e-manuscript presented at DFG-Rundgespräch Grenzen der europäischen Integration? Berlin 25 November 2011).

47   See Florian Rödl, 'EU im Notstandsmodus' (2012) 5 *Blätter f. deutsche u. int. Pol.* 5; Joerges (n 32); EW Böckenförde, 'Kennt Europas Not kein Gebot?' in Ernst-Wolfgang Böckenförde and Dieter Gosewinkel, *Wissenschaft, Politik, Verfassungsgericht* (Suhrkamp 2011) 299; Gerd Grözinger, *Alternative Solutions to the Euro-Crisis* (Ms 2012). Grözinger calls the 'financial markets' strikingly a 'second constituency'.

48   Paul Krugman rightly states: 'Fifteen years ago Greece was no paradise, but it wasn't in crisis either. Unemployment was high but not catastrophic, and the nation more or less paid its way on world markets, earning enough from exports, tourism, shipping and other sources to more or less pay for its imports'. (Paul Krugman, 'Greece as Victim' *New York Times* (New York, 17 June 2012, <www.nytimes.com/2012/06/18/opinion/krugman-greece-as-victim.html> accessed 3 November 2012).

49   Wolfgang Streeck, 'Sectoral Specialization: Politics and the Nation State in a Global Economy' (37th World Congress of the International Institute of Sociology, Stockholm 2005).

economics. However, once the Kantian mindset has been constitutionalized and integrated into the public authority of European law, it counteracts the managerial mindset of blind evolutionary adaption as a *normative constraint*. However weak it may be, it operates no longer as a Kantian (allegedly) 'empty ought' but as a Hegelian existing concept (as a moment of objective spirit).[50]

In European constitutional history, the Kantian mindset of autonomy had already come back in the early 1960s, together with the rapidly increasing volume of European regulations. It came back in the reduced and, for professional lawyers, manageable form of individual lawsuits over issues of private autonomy. In two landmark decisions of the European Court from 1963 (*van Gent & Loos*) and 1964 (*Costa*) the emancipatory side of the legal form flashed up. As public authority with binding legal force the Kantian mindset remained, it is true, privatized. However, to establish only private autonomy, the judges (in a bold teleological interpretation of the Treaties) had to create an autonomous European citizenship and European citizens' rights as the rights of an autonomous legal community.[51] The two decisions from 1963 and 1964, therefore, were described emphatically (by European law jurists) as 'the declaration of independence of Community law'.[52]

However, the Kantian flash of the two landmark decisions would have disappeared immediately from the trajectory of constitutional evolution, if the two decisions had not been followed by thousands of cases appealing to European law in national courts of all Member States (and the backing of the national courts by the ECJ submission procedure under Art. 267 TFEU).[53] In this case the old

---

50 On the 'existing concept' see Georg Wilhelm Friedrich Hegel, *Wissenschaft der Logik II*, (Suhrkamp 1969) 481. On the (very one-sided) critique of the empty, or as Hegel says 'abstract' see Hegel, *Vorlesungen über die Geschichte der Philosophie III* (Suhrkamp 1971) 369–72. Kant is not that far away from modern historical and evolutionary thinking as his critics since Hegel regularly assume, see Karl Vorländer, *Kants Leben* (Meiner 1921) 100. Such a concept then can work in both directions dialectically: as a mechanism of stabilizing the so-called *Sittlichkeit* (ethical life) of the *social systems* of bourgeois society, capitalist or bureaucratic class-rule and authoritarian economic government, or – in dialectical retaliation – 'can strike back' (Friedrich *Müller, Wer ist das Volk? Eine Grundfrage der Demokratie, Elemente einer Verfassungstheorie VI* (Duncker & Humblot 1997) 56. It can strike back because law, and in particular *constitutional law* can be used by the have-nots, by peripheral states and lower classes as a legal principle, a legal claim, or even as a legal remedy to contradict its own interpretation and implementation that is in the service of the respective ruling classes.

51 See Damian Chalmers, Christos Hadjiemmanuil, Giorgio Monti, Adam Tomkins, *European Union Law* (Cambridge University Press 2006); Paul Craig, Gráinne De Búrca, *EU Law. Text, Cases and Materials* (4th edn, Oxford University Press 2007).

52 Tuori, 'Multi-Dimensionality' in Tuori and Sankari (n 23) 3, 17.

53 See Karen J Alter, 'The European Court's Political Power' (1996) 19 *West European Politics* (1996) 458; Karen J Alter, 'Who are the "Masters of the Treaty"'? (1998) 52 *International Organization* 121; Tanja Hitzel-Cassagnes, *Entgrenzung des Verfassungsbegriffs. Eine institutionentheoretische Rekonstruktion* (Nomos 2012).

evolutionary insight became true that it is not the elites but the masses that drive evolution, and here I mean the masses of negative legal communications that filled the variety pool of the legal evolution, and finally engendered a new constitutional formation: the European *Rechtsstaatsverfassung*, the juridical constitution of Europe (stage II of the constitutional evolution of the European Union). The European *Rechtsstaatsverfassung* consists in the (reflexive) structural coupling of law and law – or maybe better: the structural coupling of law and subjective rights.[54] The European *Rechtsstaat* finally transformed Europe into one single, internally differentiated legal order, negatively described as fragmented, positively as pluralized[55] – and it is an order that is not toothless, as Hungary recently experienced.[56]

However, all these legal advances remained limited to legal experts and individual plaintiffs. On the rule-of-law-stage-II of the constitutional evolution of Europe the Kantian mindset was constitutionalized under private law (in a kind of Teubnerian *Zivilverfassung*[57]). However, at the same time it was repressed and displaced again in public.[58] On the second stage of constitutional evolution we become aware of a paradox: *Constitutionalization at once advances and is de-constitutionalized by its own advances.*

This paradoxical structure is due to the emergence and continuation of formal constitutional law together with its opposite, that is, informal prerogative law. Both constitutional formations constitute a European double-state.[59] Whereas, for example, the Kantian mindset of the formal constitution is reflected by the

---

54   Tuori, 'Multi-Dimensionality' in Tuori and Sankari (n 23) 3, 18.

55   On the ambivalence of the fragmentation diagnosis (which is true also for all larger national states) see Christoph Möllers, 'Fragmentierung als Demokratieproblem' in Claudio Franzius, Franz C Meyer and Jürgen Neyer (eds), *Strukturfragen der Europäischen Union* (Nomos 2010) 150.

56   Case C-286/12 *Commission v Hungary* [2012] ECR I-0000.

57   Gunther Teubner, 'Globale Zivilverfassungen: Alternativen zur Staatszentrierten Verfassungstheorie' (2003) 63 *Zeitschrift für ausländisches öffentliches Recht und Völkerrecht* 1.

58   Joseph Weiler, 'To be a European citizen – Eros and civilisation' (1997) 4 *Journal of European Public Policy* 495. Weiler writes: '[Y]ou could create rights and afford judicial remedies to slaves. The ability to go to court to enjoy a right bestowed on you by the pleasure of others does not emancipate you, does not make you a citizen. Long before women and Jews were made citizens they enjoyed direct effect'. (503). In cases such as *Walrave, Bosman, Viking* and *Laval* for the European Court the basic freedoms prevail over basic rights. In an antidemocratic way basic rights are now constrained by the four basic freedoms, and in particular by the freedoms of big money, capital etc., and not – as it should be at least in an egalitarian democratic society – the other way round, see S Buckel and L Oberndorfer, 'Die lange Inkubationszeit des Wettbewerbs der Rechtsordnungen – Eine Genealogie der Rechtsfälle Viking/Laval/Rüffert/Luxemburg aus der Perspektive einer materialistischen Europarechtstheorie' in A Fischer-Lescano, F Rödl and C Schmid (eds), *Europäische Gesellschaftsverfassung. Zur Konstitutionalisierung sozialer Demokratie in Europa* (Nomos 2009) 277, 285.

59   Fraenkel (n 32).

court's interpretation of the basic freedoms of EU Law as anti-discrimination norms that are constraining the basic freedoms through the basic rights of all European citizens, the managerial mindset of the informal constitution is reflected by the court's interpretation of the basic freedoms (in particular of big money and big capital) as constraints of basic rights (*Walrave, Bosman, Viking* and *Laval*).[60] It is this contradiction between the formal and the informal constitution of Europe that causes a latent crisis of legitimization. The contradiction between the two constitutional mindsets is productive as long as it becomes a driving force for further constitutionalization.

6   Political Constitution

Since the middle of the 1970s the long latent conflict between the ever-closer united executive powers of Europe and the parliamentary legislative bodies has become more and more manifest. At the same time the European Court of Human Rights has turned into an active court. Now backed by the ECJ's doctrines of European law supremacy and uniform application, it has radicalized its human rights jurisdiction.[61] This was important for the process of democratization because – different from civil and economic law – human rights have an internal relation to democracy and cannot be dissociated from public autonomy and public self-determination.[62] The pressure to reduce the growing democratic deficit of Europe finally urged the political and professional power elites to take into account the Kantian mindset's longing for public autonomy. Again it became evident that the Kantian mindset of emancipation can be repressed, 'can be halted or inhibited. But it cannot be eliminated', once it is constitutionalized.[63]

After the first direct elections to the European Parliament in 1979 the power of the Parliament increased persistently. The managerial mindset and stubborn incrementalism of everyday parliamentary work over a quarter-century made the weak and restricted European Parliament into a controlling and law-shaping parliament that is now one of the strongest institutions of the EU.[64] The final step in the parliamentary legislative procedure, taken in the Treaty of Lisbon, largely

---

60   Buckel and Oberndorfer (n 58) 285.

61   Madsen (n 15) 55.

62   Ingeborg Maus, *Zur Aufklärung der Demokratietheorie* (Suhrkamp 1992); Jürgen Habermas, *Faktizität und Geltung* (Suhrkamp 1997); Hauke Brunkhorst, *Solidarity* (MIT Press 2005); for the present legal-philosophical discussion see Samantha Besson, 'Das Menschenrecht auf Demokratie – Eine moralische Verteidigung mit einer rechtlichen Nuance' in G Haller, K Günther and U Neumann (eds), *Menschenrechte und Volkssouveränität in Europa – Gerichte als Vormund der Demokratie?* (Campus 2011) 73–7.

63   With reference to the historical concept of *emancipation* see Somek (n 2) 8.

64   See Philipp Dann 'Looking through the federal lens: the Semi-parliamentary Democracy of the EU' (2002) *Jean Monnet Working Paper* 5; John Erik Fossum and Agustin José Menéndez, 'The Constitution's Gift' (2005) 11 *European Law Journal* 123.

completed the political constitution of Europe (stage III of the constitutional evolution of the European Union).[65] The third stage of structural coupling of law and politics had been reached.

However, even this time the managerial mindset came back and kept control. The polling stations and the market places remained empty. To the same extent as the shaping power of the parliament increased, its public legitimacy decreased dramatically from election to election.[66] The most crucial act of the Kantian mindset, the political implementation of representative government based on fierce public debate ('Freiheit der Feder'), had the paradoxical effect of democratic public legislation without democratic public life. The increase of constitutionalization of public legislation again was gained at the cost of a de-constitutionalization of public discourse.

Again the managerial mindset – the ever-closer united executive bodies in concert with the politico-economic power elites, supported by the chief-economists of the big banks, present everywhere, by the willing legal and political experts, and by partisan journalists (who are much better paid than ever before and trained in the same economic vocabulary, at the expense of freelance journalists who are paid much less than ever before) – seems to prevail over the Kantian power of the people.[67] Public debate is not oppressed or limited but – more effectively – bypassed by political and economic power; or as the German foreign minister, Westerwelle, once put it during the Euro-crisis, public remarks are 'not helpful'. Again *Ordnungsrecht* derogates constitutional law and stabilizes the new collective Bonapartism of Europe.[68]

7   Social Welfare Constitution

However, these days, the repressed returns. The economic crisis, and in particular the banking crisis can no longer be displaced by the budget crisis. As a consequence, the long latent crisis of political legitimization suddenly becomes manifest. The Kantian mindset gangs up in the streets, in Athens as well as in Madrid and elsewhere. The disregarded constitutional text books are striking

---

65   Jürgen Bast 'Europäische Gesetzgebung – Fünf Stationen in der Verfassungsentwicklung der EU' in Franzius, Meyer and Neyer (n 55) 173.

66   See 'An Ever-Deeper Democratic Deficit' *The Economist* (New York, 26 May 2012) www.economist.com/node/21555927 accessed 18 November 2012.

67   On the strangely sustainable triumph of ordo- and neoliberal economy in global media see Wolfgang Streeck, 'Public Sociology as a Return to Political Economy' in *Transformations of the Public Sphere* (SSRC) <http://publicsphere.ssrc.org/streeck-public-sociology-as-a-return-to-political-economy/> accessed 19 November 2012; Stephan Schulmeister, 'Statt Sparen – New Deal für Europa' 1 *Le Monde Diplomatique* (Paris, 9 November 2012) 12, 12.

68   Hauke Brunkhorst, 'Bologna oder der sanfte Bonapartismus der transnational vereinigten Exekutivgewalten' (2006) 1 *Zeitschrift für Philosophie und Sozialwissenschaft* 1.

back: 'Stop law and economics! Support law and democracy!' they say. They have opened up the quarrel over the social welfare constitution of Europe (stage IV of the constitutional evolution of the European Union).

As it stands, the structural coupling of law with the systems of social welfare and security can no longer be performed silently behind closed doors and at low cost. The crisis makes it evident that there is no modern mass-democracy without the rough equality of stakeholders, at the very least.[69]

The national state looked like the big winner after the outbreak of the global economic crisis in autumn 2008 (and many political theorists and analysts triumphed: *Totgesagte leben länger* – 'The condemned live longer'). But in fact the state was already weak, and therefore became one of the greatest losers of the crisis. Wolfgang Streeck rightly headed an essay two years later with: *Noch so ein Sieg und wir sind verloren* ('Another victory like that and we are lost'). The great crisis of 2008 has proven that the national state was already deprived of its most basic alternatives in economic and social politics.[70]

The national state's capacity to act and shape the future always relied on the existence of two major instruments to get modern capitalism under control, and to enforce the legislative will of democratic majorities: either the stick of the law, or the carrot of money.[71]

However, it seems that from the beginning of the present crisis, the national states as well as the European Union (and other continental regimes such as the US, China, Brazil or India) were no longer able to perform macroeconomic steering through an effective mix of stick and carrot, of legislation and investment. The political actors had already lost most of the legislative power that is needed to regulate and control a capitalist economy. Up to now they have not regained it at the global level. On the contrary, during the last 30 years of neoliberal global hegemony, the fragile balance of power between democracy and capitalism has dramatically shifted in favour of capitalism.

---

69   Colin Crouch, *Post-Democracy* (Polity Press 2004); see also the quintessence of the last books of the economists Paul Krugman and Joseph Stiglitz: Jacob S Hacker and Paul Pierson, 'What Krugman & Stiglitz Can Tell Us' (2012) 14 *New York Review of Books* 55; with instructive statistics and observations: Tony Judt, *Ill Fares the Land* (Penguin 2010). On rough equality of stakeholders see Thomas Christiano, 'Democratic Legitimacy and International Institutions' in S Besson and J Tasaioulas (eds), *The Philosophy of International Law* (Oxford University Press 2010) 119, 130–32; on 'rough equality' as a necessary condition of modern mass-democracy see Colin Crouch, *Post-Democracy* (Polity Press 2004) Chapter 1.

70   Wolfgang Streeck, 'Noch so ein Sieg, und wir sind verloren. Der Nationalstaat nach der Finanzkrise' (2010) 38 *Leviathan* 159; Wolfgang Streeck, 'The Crisis of Democratic Capitalism' (2011) 71 *New Left Review* 1.

71   See Renate Mayntz 'Die Handlungsfähigkeit des Nationalstaats in der Regulierung der Finanzmärkte' (2010) 38 *Leviathan* 175.

As long as a modern, functionally differentiated economy (with capitalist markets) is embedded in democratically controlled state power, the parties of the have-nots, either the exploited social classes, or the nations who are the losers of the global economic competition between states and regions, have two means to enforce rough compensatory justice.[72] They can perform macroeconomic steering in times of crisis: (a) *nationally* by legal regulation and investment, in particular increasing taxes for high incomes and assets, and/or (b) *internationally* by devaluating their national currency.[73]

Franklin D. Roosevelt's New Deal administration in the 1930s, supported and pushed by a fighting working class and young and strong Unions who had nothing to lose, finally regulated and controlled Wall Street, increased taxes for the rich, split up banks and industrial corporations, created jobs administratively, and printed money. This way New Dealers and other social democrats and socialists in advanced societies were able to square the circle: to socialize the means of production within the capitalist mode of production.

However, this no longer seems possible. Since 2008, nowhere have taxes increased in measures comparable to those of the US and other western countries in the 1950s and 1960s. Not one of the banks too big to fail was nationalized or split up. Apart from Lehmann, all were bailed out again and again. Moreover, in Europe the common currency excluded all possibilities of currency devaluation. Deprived of its legislative power to regulate the economy, the state no longer had an alternative, except to spend the rest of its money.[74]

Therefore the state has become susceptible to blackmail, and Margaret Thatcher's lie, that there is no alternative, became true as a self-fulfilling prophecy.[75] Former democratic governments are now in the hands of bankers and their staff of technocrats – directly or indirectly. In states where the bankers have not yet taken the lead, their advice resembles the advice of the old Roman Senate, the *senatus consultum*. That was advice without any legally binding force: soft law. But whoever did not follow it, was already a dead man, even if he left the room alive.

Once the money comes to an end, the state loses the power to enforce the legislative will of democratic majorities. The *taxing state* that is in control of

---

72   On states as global economic actors see Tobias ten Brink, *Geopolitik: Geschichte und Gegenwart kapitalistischer Staatenkonkurrenz* (Westfälisches Dampfboot 2008).

73   Claus Offe, Unpublished Interview, e-manuscript, 3; Streeck (n 38).

74   See Mayntz (n 71) 175; Streeck, 'Noch so ein Sieg' (n 70) 159; see also the long term case study by Wolfgang Streeck and Daniel Mertens, 'Fiscal Austerity and Public Investment. Is the Possible the Enemy of the Necessary?' 11/12 *MPIfG Discussion Paper* <www.mpifg.de/pu/mpifg_dp/dp11–12.pdf> accessed 19 November 2012.

75   See Jens Beckert and Wolfgang Streeck, 'Die Fiskalkrise und die Einheit Europas' (2012) 4 *Aus Politik und Zeitgeschichte* 7.

capitalism becomes a *borrowing state* that is controlled by capitalism.[76] The problem is that the borrowing state can no longer (a) increase taxes – or (b) devaluate the currency, and make use of the other means of macroeconomic steering. Therefore it must (c) execute the neoliberal programme with microeconomic means and 'devalue labor and the public sector', 'put pressure on wages, pensions, labor market regulations, public services'[77] – and then sell the whole thing as 'reform', 'modernization', 'new public management' and 'individual empowerment', best served by Third Way labour parties, reformed social democrats and red-green coalitions of the 'new bourgeoisie' (*neue Bürgerlichkeit*).[78]

Unfortunately neither Keynesians nor Marxists have ever tried to develop transnational continental and global alternatives to national state power. They have socialized the means of production not only within the capitalist mode of production but also within one country. They have not even drawn up a plan to establish a transnational political power that can measure up with global big money and the unleashed communicative forces of the world market. The ordo- and Neoliberals (and that is the historical truth of Neoliberalism) had such a plan, as we have seen, and it worked, even if finally with catastrophic results. Only that explains the strange non-death of Neoliberalism – after a crisis that, following the pure Chicago doctrine, should only happen once every 50,000 years.

Now national state power is over, at least as the power of the so-called sovereign state. To borrow a metaphor from Eyal Benvenisti (an Israelian international lawyer): In the process of globalization the state politically, legally, economically and culturally has been completely transplanted from a detached villa into a condo in the middle of a house of 200 condos with many different and overlapping forms

---

76   Offe (n 73) 6. On the genealogy see Streeck, 'The Crisis of Democratic Capitalism' (n 70). What is crucial for the neoliberal triumph and sharply recognized by Reagan and Thatcher and their economic advisers: that the Unions first are losing their formerly strong political influence, and then their organizational power, either by direct oppression such as in the UK, the US and in the low intense democracies of the formerly so-called Third World, or by internal reform that makes them sometimes a powerful, quasi council-democratic participant in globally operating industrial enterprises such as *Volkswagen*, but at the price of the general interest of the working class. On the latter see the case study: Gary Herrigel, 'Roles and Rules: Ambiguity, Experimentation and New Forms of Stakeholderism in Germany' (2008) 15 *Industrielle Beziehungen* 111.

77   Offe (n 73) 3; see Fritz W Scharpf, 'Rettet Europa vor dem Euro!' *Berliner Republik* (Berlin 2012) <www.b-republik.de/aktuelle-ausgabe/rettet-europa-vor-dem-euro> accessed 8 May 2012.

78   See Somek (n 2). See Hauke Brunkhorst, 'Raus aus der Neuen Mitte! Umrisse einer künftigen Linken' 13 *Die Zeit* (25 March 1999) 28; Hauke Brunkhorst, 'Schluss mit der Kritik! Die Generation Berlin und der Affekt gegen den Egalitarismus' 45 *Die Zeit* (4 November 1999) 54; Hauke Brunkhorst, 'Bürgerlichkeit als Philosophie der Postdemokratie. Ein Beitrag zur Debatte um Jens Hackes Philosophie der Bürgerlichkeit' (2007) 5 *Deutsche Zeitschrift für Philosophie* 22.

of real estate ownership.[79] However, the network of transnational public (and arguably also constitutional) law and politics, and the already emerging formation of transnational statehood[80] is by far too weak to bring the global markets under control again. The coordinated state powers together with international organizations can at best *make* the global market (negative integration) but nowhere are they able to *constrain* it *normatively*: that is in the general interest of all of us (positive integration).[81] In 30 years of globalization (for good *and* for bad) by far the most powerful states in history – the Western democracies – have been turned, as Wolfgang Streeck writes, 'into debt-collecting agencies on behalf of a global oligarchy of investors, compared to which C. Wright Mills's "power elite" appears a shining example of liberal pluralism'.[82]

If this is the right diagnosis, Angela Merkel's warning was right: The fall of the Euro will lead immediately to the fall of Europe, and to a decay of what still remains of its democratic welfare state systems (including Germany's). The likelihood that this will happen is very high, simply because it will be easy to break the big egg of the already legally, politically, economically and even culturally highly integrated EU-organism, but it will be hard to rebuild broken shells and diffluent yolk and egg white into a lot of different (and fruitful) national eggs again, or at least to rebuild the pre-Euro state of Maastricht.[83] Therefore, there is only one way out: that way is towards a more or less fully fledged economic and financial government of the Eurozone. Hence, this way has been taken, reluctantly at first, now with more and more boldness and determination. This has already resulted in an authoritarian European economic government that is on the road to finalizing the replacement of law and democracy by law and economics, that is, the collective Bonapartism of Europe's ever closer united executive bodies under the lead of the German hegemon.[84]

To overcome hegemony, collective Bonapartism and authoritarian economic government there seems only one way open, and that is the complete legal

---

79   Quoted from Armin von Bogdandy, 'Grundprinzipien von Staat, supranationalen und internationalen Organisationen' in Handbuch des Staatsrechts XI: Internationale Bezüge (Müller 2012).

80   Albert and Stichweh (n 41).

81   See Offe (n 32); on the concept of solidarity as the general or universal interest of all of us, see Brunkhorst (n 62); on normative constraints see Hauke Brunkhorst, 'Critical Theory of Legal Revolutions; on the distinction between 'positive' and 'negative integration' in Fritz Scharpf (ed), *Regieren in Europa. Effektiv und demokratisch?* (Campus 1999).

82   Streeck (n 76). As a consequence popular sovereignty has been fragmented and marginalized, beyond and within the national state, see Prien (n 19).

83   Enderlein (n 44).

84   Rödl (n 47); Brunkhorst (n 6) 341–67; Jürgen Habermas, Peter Bofinger and Julian Nida-Rümelin, 'Für einen Kurswechsel in der Europapolitik', *Frankfurter Allgemeine Zeitung* (Frankfurt, 3 August 2012) <www.faz.net/aktuell/feuilleton/debatten/europas-zukunft/kurswechsel-fuer-europa-einspruch-gegen-die-fassadendemokratie-11842820.html> accessed 3 December 2012.

formalization, procedural integration and subsumption of the ESM, the IMF, the troika, the European Council, the Commission, the Council of Ministers and the Central Bank under the parliamentary legislative procedure of the Treaty of Lisbon. Moreover, the not yet concretized and implemented democratic potential of Articles 9–12 of the Lisbon Treaty should be expanded by legislative concretization and public action (Referendum-initiatives etc.).[85] Such a massive constitutional change must not necessarily be enacted by a new constitutional treaty but could also be managed by 'unconventional' (constitutional) legislation, such as the great turns of American history during and after the Civil War, or during the New Deal.[86] What is needed is massive democratic change (including Parliament's right to initiative) – but it would be less massive than the already massive change from democratic capitalism over capitalist democracy to authoritarian economic government. This needs massive public support, and not less but more public struggles between nations and classes over the future of Europe than we already have. Class struggle is the very medium of normative learning processes, and conflict unites, according to old sociological insights going back to Marx, Spencer and Durkheim. The crisis has opened the window. For the first time a European public is emerging that has already made Europe a topic around every table and in every family. The last elections to the European Parliament (which were performed long after finishing this essay in May 2012) for the first time were performed as real campaigns. Whether taking this trajectory will finally be more successful than breaking the egg is an open question. Even if it works, this does not mean that capitalist democracy (that is no longer really democratic) can be turned into a new form of democratic capitalism (not to mention democratic socialism). But only a democratically legitimated European government could have an interest in and mobilize the generalizable collective interests of the democratic majorities that are needed to make global capitalism subject to democratic correction again.

Bibliography

Ackerman B, *We the People, Volume 2: Transformations* (Harvard University Press 1998)

Albert M and Stichweh R, *Weltstaat und Weltstaatlichkeit* (VS 2007)

Alter KJ, 'Who are the "Masters of the Treaty"'? (1998) 52 *International Organization* 121

—— 'The European Court's Political Power' (1996) 19 *West European Politics* (1996) 458

Almond GA, 'Capitalism and Democracy' 24 *Political Science and Politics* 467

Amstutz M and Karavas V, 'Rechtsmutationen' (2006) *Rechtsgeschichte* 14

---

85   See von Bogdandy (n 16).

86   See Bruce Ackerman, *We the People, Volume 2: Transformations* (Harvard University Press 1998).

Bast J, 'Europäische Gesetzgebung – Fünf Stationen in der Verfassungsentwicklung der EU' in C Franzius, FC Meyer and J Neyer (eds) *Strukturfragen der Europäischen Union* (Nomos 2010) 173

Beckert J and Streeck W, 'Die Fiskalkrise und die Einheit Europas' (2012) 4 *Aus Politik und Zeitgeschichte* 7

Besson S, 'Das Menschenrecht auf Demokratie – Eine moralische Verteidigung mit einer rechtlichen Nuance' in G Haller, K Günthger and U Neumann (eds), *Menschenrechte und Volkssouveränität in Europa – Gerichte als Vormund der Demokratie?* (Campus 2011)

Böckenförde EW, 'Kennt Europas Not kein Gebot?' in EW Böckenförde and D Gosewinkel, *Wissenschaft, Politik, Verfassungsgericht* (Suhrkamp 2011) 299

Böhm F, *Wettbewerb und Monopolrecht* (Nomos 2010)

Brink T ten, *Geopolitik: Geschichte und Gegenwart kapitalistischer Staatenkonkurrenz* (Westfälisches Dampfboot 2008)

Brunkhorst H, *Critical Theory of Legal Revolutions – Evolutionary Perspectives* (unpublished)

—— 'Critical Theory of Legal Revolutions; on the distinction between 'positive' and 'negative integration' in F. Scharpf (ed), *Regieren in Europa. Effektiv und demokratisch?* (Campus 1999)

—— *Solidarity* (MIT Press 2005)

—— 'Bologna oder der sanfte Bonapartismus der transnational vereinigten Exekutivgewalten' (2006) 1 *Zeitschrift für Philosophie und Sozialwissenschaft* 1

—— 'Bürgerlichkeit als Philosophie der Postdemokratie. Ein Beitrag zur Debatte um Jens Hackes Philosophie der Bürgerlichkeit' (2007) 5 *Deutsche Zeitschrift für Philosophie* 22

—— *Legitimationskrisen – Verfassungsprobleme der Weltgesellschaft* (Nomos 2012)

Buckel S, 'Welcome to Europe' Juridische Auseinandersetzungen um das Staatsprojekt Europa (unpublished Habilitationsschrift, Goethe-Universität 2012)

—— and Oberndorfer L, 'Die lange Inkubationszeit des Wettbewerbs der Rechtsordnungen – Eine Genealogie der Rechtsfälle Viking/Laval/Rüffert/Luxemburg aus der Perspektive einer materialistischen Europarechtstheorie' in A Fischer-Lescano, F Rödl and C Schmid (eds), *Europäische Gesellschaftsverfassung. Zur Konstitutionalisierung sozialer Demokratie in Europa* (Nomos 2009) 277

Callies C, 'Das Demokratieprinzip im Europäischen Staaten- und Verfassungsverbund' in J Bröhmer, RB Callies, C Langenfeld, S Weber and J Wolf, (eds) *Internationale Gemeinschaft und Menschenrechte* (Heymanns 2005) 399

Chalmers D, Hadjiemmanuil C, Monti G and Tomkins A, *European Union Law* (Cambridge University Press 2006)

Christiano T, 'Democratic Legitimacy and International Institutions' in S Besson and J Tasaioulas (eds), *The Philosophy of International Law* (Oxford University Press 2010) 119

Craig P and de Búrca G, *EU Law. Text, Cases and Materials* (4th edn, Oxford University Press 2007)

Crouch C, *Post-Democracy* (Polity Press 2004)

—— *The Strange Non-Death of Neoliberalism* (Polity Press 2011)

Dann P, 'Looking through the federal lens: the Semi-parliamentary Democracy of the EU' (2002) *Jean Monnet Working Paper* 5

di Fabio U, *Das Recht offener Staaten. Grundlinien einer Staats- und Rechtstheorie* (Mohr 1998)

—— 'Das europäische Schuldendilemma als Mentalitätskrise' 143 *Frankfurter Allgemeine Zeitung* (Frankfurt, 22 June 2012) 9

Enderlein H, *Grenzen der europäischen Integration? Herausforderungen an Recht und Politik*, DFG-Rundgespräch in Zusammenarbeit mit der Friedrich-Ebert-Stiftung Berlin (Ms 2011)

Fischer-Lescano A and Teubner G, *Regime-Kollisionen* (Suhrkamp 2006)

Forsythe M, *Unions of States. The Theory and Practice of Confederations* (Holmes 1981)

Fossum JE and Menéndez AJ, 'The Constitution's Gift' (2005) 11 *European Law Journal* 123

—— *The Constitution's Gift. A Constitutional Theory for a democratic European Union* (Rowman 2011)

Fraenkel E, 'Der Doppelstaat' (1999) 2 *Gesammelte Schriften* 33 (published 1974, originally finished 1938)

Franzius C and Preuß UK, *Europäische Demokratie* (Ms 2011)

Friedman M, *Capitalism and Freedom* (Chicago University Press 1982)

Grant RW and Keohane RO, 'Accountability and Abuses of Power in World Politics' (2005) 99 *American Political Science Review* 2943

Grözinger G, *Alternative Solutions to the Euro-Crisis* (Ms 2012)

Habermas J, *Theorie des kommunikativen Handelns II* (Suhrkamp 1981)

—— *Faktizität und Geltung* (Suhrkamp 1997)

—— 'Die Krise der Europäische Union im Licht einer Konstitutionalisierung des Völkerrechts' (manuscript of a lecture given at the Humboldt University, Berlin, 16 June 2011)

Hacker JS and Pierson P, 'What Krugman & Stiglitz Can Tell Us' (2012) 14 *New York Review of Books* 55

Hardt M and Negri A, *Empire. Die neue Weltordnung* (Campus 2002)

Hegel GWF, *Wissenschaft der Logik II*, (Suhrkamp 1969)

—— *Vorlesungen über die Geschichte der Philosophie III* (Suhrkamp 1971)

Herrigel G, 'Roles and Rules: Ambiguity, Experimentation and New Forms of Stakeholderism in Germany' (2008) 15 *Industrielle Beziehungen* 111

Hitzel-Cassagnes T, *Entgrenzung des Verfassungsbegriffs. Eine institutionentheoretische Rekonstruktion* (Nomos 2012)

Hobsbawm E, *Das Zeitalter der Extreme. Weltgeschichte des 20. Jahrhunderts* (Hanser 1994)

Jesch D, *Gesetz und Verwaltung. Eine Problemstudie zum Wandel des Gesetzmäßigkeitsprinzips* (Mohr 1961)

Joerges C, 'Europas Wirtschaftsverfassung in der Krise' (2012) 51 *Der Staat* 357

Judt T, *Ill Fares the Land* (Penguin 2010)

Kelsen H, 'The legal status of Germany according to the Declaration of Berlin' (1945) 39 *American Journal of International Law* 518

—— 'Demokratie und Sozialismus' (1954) in N Leser (ed) *Demokratie und Sozialismus. Ausgewählte Aufsätze* (Verlag der Wiener Volksbuchhandlung 1967) 170

Koskenniemi M, 'Constitutionalism as Mindset: Reflections on Kantian Themes About International Law and Globalization' (2006) 8 *Theoretical Inquiries in Law* 9

—— 'Formalismus, Fragmentierung, Freiheit – Kantische Themen im heutigen Völkerrecht' in R Kreide and A Niederberger (eds) *Transnationale Verrechtlichung. Nationale Demokratien im Zeitalter globaler Politik* (Campus 2008)

Krugman P, 'Greece as Victim' *New York Times* (New York, 17 June 2012, <www.nytimes.com/2012/06/18/opinion/krugman-greece-as-victim.html> accessed 3 November 2012

Ladeur KH, 'Die Evolution des Rechts und die Möglichkeit eines "globalen Rechts" jenseits des Staates – zugleich eine Kritik der "Selbstkonstitutionalisierungsthese"' (2012) *Ancilla Juris* 220

Ley I, 'Brünn betreibt die Parlamentarisierung des Primärrechts. Anmerkungen zum zweiten Urteil des tschechischen Verfassungsgerichtshofs zum Vertrag von Lissabon vom 3.11.2009' (2010) 65 *Juristen-Zeitung* 170

Lübbe H, 'Fünfzig Jahre Danach – Der Nationalsozialismus im politischen Bewußtsein der Gegenwart' (15 January 1983, Reichstag, Berlin)

MacCormick N, *Questioning Sovereignty. Law, State and Nation in the European Commonwealth* (Oxford University Press 1999)

Madsen MR, *The Protracted Institutionalization of the Strasbourg Court: From Legal Diplomacy to Integrationist jurisprudence* in J Christoffersen and MR Madsen (eds), *The European Court of Human Rights between Law and Politics* (Oxford University Press 2011) 55

Marx K, *Der 18. Brumaire des Louis Bonaparte* (Die Revolution, New York 1852)

—— *Das Kapital I* (1867)

—— *Kritik des Hegelschen Staatsrechts* (§§ 261–313) in MEW 1 (Dietz 1972) 203

Matiaske W, 'Gullivers Fesseln: Corporate Social Responsibility als Normbildung?' (Lecture at Flensburg University, 5 June 2012)

Maus I, *Zur Aufklärung der Demokratietheorie* (Suhrkamp 1992)

Mayntz R, 'Die Handlungsfähigkeit des Nationalstaats in der Regulierung der Finanzmärkte' (2010) 38 *Leviathan* 175

Menéndez AJ, 'Taxing Europe – Two cases for a European power to tax' 3 *Cidel Working Papers* (2003)

Mestmäcker EJ, 'Einführung' in F Böhm (ed), *Wettbewerb und Monopolkampf* (Berlin 1933) 5

—— 'Ordnungspolitische Grundlagen einer politischen Union' *Frankfurter Allgemeine Zeitung* (Frankfurt 11 September 2012) 12

Möllers C, *Gewaltengliederung* (Habilitationsschrift 2003)

—— 'Transnationale Behördenkooperation. Verfassungs- und völkerrechtliche Probleme transnationaler administrativer Standardsetzung' (2005) 65 *Zeitschrift für ausländisches öffentliches Recht und Völkerrecht* 351

—— 'Fragmentierung als Demokratieproblem' in C Franzius, FC Meyer and J Neyer (eds) *Strukturfragen der Europäischen Union* (Nomos 2010) 150

Müller F, *Wer ist das Volk? Eine Grundfrage der Demokratie, Elemente einer Verfassungstheorie VI* (Duncker & Humblot 1997)

Müller-Armack A, *Studien zur Sozialen Marktwirtschaft*, (Institut für Wirtschaftspolitik 1960)

Nassehi A, *Der soziologische Diskurs der Moderne* (Suhrkamp Verlag 2006)

Neumann F, *Wirtschaft, Staat und Demokratie* (Suhrkamp 1978)

Offe C, 'The European Model of "Social Capitalism": Can it Survive European Integration? (2003) 11 *The Journal of Political Philosophy* 437

—— Unpublished Interview, e-manuscript, 3

Osterhammel J and Petersson NP, *Geschichte der Globalisierung* (Beck 2007)

Prien T, *Fragmentierte Volkssouveränität* (Nomos 2010)

Rieckmann SP, 'Constitutionalism and Representation: European Parliamentarism in the Treaty of Lisbon' in P Dobner and M Loughlin (eds), *The Twilight of Constitutionalism?* (Oxford University Press 2010) 120

Rödl F, 'EU im Notstandsmodus', (2012) 5 *Blätter f. deutsche u. int. Pol.* 5

Scharpf FW, 'Integration versus Legitimation: Der Euro. Thesen', (e-manuscript presented at DFG-Rundgespräch Grenzen der europäischen Integration? Berlin 25 November 2011)

—— 'Rettet Europa vor dem Euro!' *Berliner Republik* (Berlin 2012) <www.b-republik.de/aktuelle-ausgabe/rettet-europa-vor-dem-euro> accessed 15 May 2014

Schönberger C, *Föderale Angehörigkeit* (Habilitationsschrift 2005)

Somek A, 'Europe: From emancipation to empowerment', *LSE 'Europe in Question' Discussion Paper Series LEQS Paper No 60/2013* 8

Stone Sweet A, *Governing with Judges: Constitutional Politics in Europe* (Oxford University Press 2000)

Streeck W, 'Sectoral Specialization: Politics and the Nation State in a Global Economy' (37th World Congress of the International Institute of Sociology, Stockholm 2005)

—— 'Noch so ein Sieg, und wir sind verloren. Der Nationalstaat nach der Finanzkrise' (2010) 38 *Leviathan* 159

—— 'The Crises of Democratic Capitalism' (2011) 71 *New Left Review* 1

—— 'Zum Verhältnis von sozialer Gerechtigkeit und Marktgerechtigkeit' (unpublished e-manuscript of a lecture, Verona 20 September 2012)

—— 'Public Sociology as a Return to Political Economy' in *Transformations of the Public Sphere* (SSRC) <http://publicsphere.ssrc.org/streeck-public-sociology-as-a-return-to-political-economy/> accessed 8 June 2014

—— and Mertens D, 'Fiscal Austerity and Public Investment. Is the Possible the Enemy of the Necessary?' 11/12 *MPIfG Discussion Paper* <www.mpifg.de/pu/mpifg_dp/dp11-12.pdf> accessed 8 June 2014

Teubner G, 'Globale Zivilverfassungen: Alternativen zur Staatszentrierten Verfassungstheorie' (2003) 63 *Zeitschrift für ausländisches öffentliches Recht und Völkerrecht* 1

—— *Constitutional Fragments. Societal Constitutionalism and Globalization* (Oxford University Press 2012)

Tugendhat E, 'Liberalism, Liberty and the Issue of Economic Human Rights' in E Tugendhat (ed) *Philosophische Aufsätze* (Suhrkamp 1992) 352

Tuori K, 'Multi-Dimensionality of European Constitutionalism: The Many Constitutions of Europe' in K Tuori and S Sankari (eds), *The Many Constitutions of Europe* (Ashgate 2010) 3

von Bogdandy A, 'The European Lesson for International Democracy: The Significance of Articles 9–12 EU Treaty for International Organizations' (2012) 23 *The European Journal of International Law* 315

—— 'Grundprinzipien von Staat, supranationalen und internationalen Organisationen' in Handbuch des Staatsrechts XI: Internationale Bezüge (forthcoming e-manuscript 2012)

Voßkuhle A, 'Multilevel Cooperation of the European Constitutional Courts. Der Europäische Verfassungsgerichtsverbund' (2010) 6 *European Constitutional Law Review* 175

Vorländer K, *Kants Leben* (Meiner 1921)

Wahl R, *Verfassungsstaat, Europäisierung, Internationalisierung* (Suhrkamp 2003)

Wegmann M, 'European Competition Law: Catalyst of Integration and Convergence' in K Tuori and S Sankari (eds), *The Many Constitutions of Europe* (Ashgate 2010) 91

Weidmann J, 'Der Euro verlangt eine Stabilitätsunion' 146 *Frankfurter Allgemeine Zeitung* (Frankfurt 27 June 2012) 28

—— 'Die Stabilitätsunion sichern' 27 *Frankfurter Allgemeine Zeitung* (Frankfurt, 8 July 2012) 33

Weiler J, 'To be a European citizen – Eros and civilisation' (1997) 4 *Journal of European Public Policy* 495

Wiener A, *The Invisible Constitution of Politics* (Cambridge University Press 2008)

Zürn M, *Regieren jenseits des Nationalstaates* (Suhrkamp 2004)

Cases

Case C-286/12 *Commission v Hungary* [2012] ECR I-0000

Newspaper Articles

Brunkhorst H, 'Raus aus der Neuen Mitte! Umrisse einer künftigen Linken' 13
Die Zeit (25 March 1999) 28
—— 'Schluss mit der Kritik! Die Generation Berlin und der Affekt gegen den
Egalitarismus' 45 *Die Zeit* (4 November 1999) 54
Habermas J, Bofinger P and Nida-Rümelin J, 'Für einen Kurswechsel in der
Europapolitik', *Frankfurter Allgemeine Zeitung* (Frankfurt, 3 August 2012)
'An Ever-Deeper Democratic Deficit' *The Economist* (New York, 26 May 2012)
www.economist.com/node/21555927
Schulmeister S, 'Statt Sparen – New Deal für Europa' 1 *Le Monde Diplomatique*
(Paris, 9 November 2012) 12

Chapter 3

The Economics of Constitutional Renewal

Emilios Christodoulidis

The Semantics of Crisis

Thinking about crisis in Europe is rife. Political discourse has been largely re-aligned to its co-ordinates. Such has been the semantic inflation that we find ourselves at a point where recourse to the language of 'limit' is becoming normalised. Running alongside this normalisation, even banalisation of the concept of crisis, is the rhetoric of renewal; while Europe's directorate continues to unleash its austerity programmes with unrelenting barbarity on the States of the South, the 'Europe 2020 Strategy' put forward by the European Commission as a successor to the 2000 Lisbon Strategy promises to deliver Europe from crisis 'setting out a vision of Europe's social market economy for the 21st century' and aspiring to 'show how the EU can come out stronger from the economic crisis and how it can be turned into a smart, sustainable and inclusive economy delivering high levels of employment, productivity and social cohesion'.

Certainly not everyone shares this optimism. Even those involved in systemic thinking, and who take the autonomy of the economy as a non-negotiable starting point – functional differentiation, said Luhmann, like modernity's original sin, cannot be undone – are now calling for a significant change of direction at this 'tipping point'. They are calling to rein in the kind of excess that led the spiralling downwards of capitalist economies to 'hit the bottom'.[1] Gunther Teubner's important paper 'Constitutionalising Polycontexturality'[2] for example, culminates in an argument and a warning about preventing '*catastrophe*'. His concern is that 'freed up energies' may 'spin out of control', to have corrupting or even destructive social effects when a 'tipping point' is reached, at which we may even have a 'collision' between the reproduction of function systems and a 'comprehensive rationality of world society'. 'This requires massive interventions', he says, most effective when 'they are translated into self-limiting impulses and transformed into a regime constitution'.[3]

---

1   Gunther Teubner, 'A Constitutional Moment? The logics of 'Hitting the Bottom', in P Kjaer, G Teubner and A Febbrajo (eds), *The Financial Crisis in Constitutional Perspective* (Hart 2011).

2   Gunther Teubner, 'Constitutionalising Polycontexturality' (2011) 19 *Social and Legal Studies*.

3   Teubner (n 2) 225.

I want to take the warning about catastrophe seriously and to attempt to understand why it is that amidst so much devastation we are still to such an extent in thrall to the structures and logic of a destructive system of financial economics and confronted, in Colin Crouch's memorable title, by the 'strange non-death of neo-liberalism'.[4] And perhaps the best way to address this is to take a step back and ask a preliminary, diagnostic, question: How would we *know* that tipping points have been reached, that destructive energies can no longer be tolerated? What societal register would carry that message? Not just from Marx but from Polanyi too, we know that the market system has in the past had a series of massive collisions with society, and what in Marx's analysis of capitalism's early clearing exercise of 'primitive accumulation' is a history of pillage, exaction and devastation, Polanyi describes as the radical disembedding of the market system from the society that harboured it, a violent extraction that marks social devastation.[5] Worlds have been lost in these collisions and where the incidence of a 'tipping point' in Marx is postponed to the future proletarian revolution, in Polanyi it takes the form of the 'double movement', with social forces storming the market to restore something of an original *embeddedness* of the economy in its society, though both scenarios remain highly unlikely under current conditions of radical differentiation. That is all to say that functional sub-systems not only outlive catastrophic events but feed off them, making them productive. In which case, 'tipping point' incidents are re-integrated into business-as-usual, giving those responsible for the crisis yet another financial instrument to play with, recycling catastrophe into the vortex of profit as another toxic commodity to be sold, and importing financial interests into the state and governmental structures to the point of making a nonsense of democratic sovereignty. We witness a functionalisation in the direction of new systemic operations and a renewed impetus for accumulation. It is also an argument that resonates all too disturbingly with how capitalist economies 'think'. Capitalism has proven to be extraordinarily resilient before and it is showing this again. We may project that the only thing that might usher in radical change will do so *not* because it *is* read (and reacted to) by the paradigm that it challenges but precisely because it *cannot* be. But that is a different argument. For now let us just say this. As is always the case in the deployment of collective categories, the notion of a *collective* 'hitting the bottom' is both over- and under-inclusive. The crisis is a catastrophe for the lives and livelihoods only of *some*. There are indeed many who are angry; references abound in the literature to Durkheim's '*colère publique*'. But there are also those who remain largely untouched by the 'catastrophe' and there are those who are profiting from the crisis. And then, of course, there are those who are well past the 'tipping point', for whom it is already too late, and for whom our talk of 'renewal' is an insult.

---

4   Colin Crouch explains in some depth why the inherent instabilities of the financial model in place will not change the economic system that drives the world.

5   Karl Polanyi, *The Great Transformation: The Political and Economic Origins of Our* Time (Beacon Hill Press 1944).

In this context we might ask whether the diagnosis that we have 'hit the bottom' is not perhaps, ironically but strikingly, premature. As devastating austerity programmes are mobilised to meet the costs of propping up the collapsing system, the depressing spectrum of a new appropriation looms: a neo-liberal onslaught to exact surplus-value from the very devastation it created: 'disaster capitalism' as Naomi Klein popularly defined it.[6] As we now look back on a looted landscape that the system leaves behind as an effect of it having spiralled downwards out of control, let us pause to take stock and assess this risk: that we do not stand again powerless before this conjuncture, confronted with a system that *renews itself through crisis*, both through its ordinary and, now, even its exceptional manifestations.

In what follows I will take issue with two versions of what we might identify as an 'internal critique' of the autonomy of 'the economic'. In both cases critical voices have been raised over excess, though in neither case are they prepared to see this as anything other than a need for recalibration of an economic system that has spiralled out of control to the point where it can no longer secure its own reproduction. Both strands of internal critique – both systems theory and the theory of 'capabilities' – share a founding premise: that the autonomy of the economy conceived in its market form cannot and should not be compromised. Against this, but only briefly, I will contrast the outlines of an alternative that sees the inability of capitalism to reproduce itself as the limit of the logic of a catastrophic system, and where the current crisis is the expression of the profound contradictions that beset its functioning.

Crisis as a Pathology of Functional Differentiation

Zygmunt Bauman is perhaps an unlikely reference point in this context, but he offers a useful insight in respect of functional differentiation and (sub-) system autonomy. He says:

> However free the subsystems of that order may be singly or severally, the way in which they are intertwined is rigid, fatal and sealed off from any freedom of choice. *The overall order of things is not open to options*. It is far from clear what such options could be, and even less clear how an ostensibly viable option can be made real in the unlikely case of social life being able to conceive it and gestate. Between the overall order and every one of its agencies, vehicles and stratagems of purposeful action there is a cleavage – a perpetually widening gap with no bridge in sight.[7]

For Bauman, it is the inability to establish and act upon the continuity of the macro- and the micro-levels of society that undercuts political action and radically hedges in the opportunity to challenge the sources of disempowerment.

---

6   Naomi Klein, *The Shock Doctrine. The Rise of Disaster Capitalism* (Picador 2008).
7   Zygmunt Bauman, *Liquid Modernity* (Polity 2000) 4–5, my italics.

The complexity of modern society spells paralysis to the extent that any attempt to act politically to challenge the order of the market is virtually precluded as inadequate, futile or even dangerous because it undermines differentiation and the integrity of systems. *What differentiation entrenches is a distance between the right to self-assertion and the control of the social settings which would make it feasible.* It is in this process that the exercise of 'constituent power', which sustains the 'constitutional perspective', arguably disappears into the gap.

Amongst the most insightful of the internal critiques is Teubner's, *internal* to functional differentiation but *critical* of the state in which autopoietic systems find themselves in the absence of an overall functional balance. Teubner invites us to think about the recent crisis as the opportunity for an alternative thinking about society. The theory of social constitutionalism which he has been developing for the last few years[8] involves confronting constitutionalism with the new task of delivering a recalibration of systemic equilibria. Or, more simply, of providing an adequate answer to the question: how can a sufficiently large degree of external pressure be exerted on the sub-systems to push them into self-limitations of their options? It focuses on the possibility of reflexive readjustment on the part of each system's 'internal constitution', the emphasis on self-limitation, expressed in terms of 'self-discipline', aimed at countering the systems' imperialist tendency to grow. The focus has thus shifted from the constitutive to the limitative. It refers no longer to the question: what are the institutional preconditions of the autonomy of functional sub-systems? It refers rather to the question: where are the limits of their expansion? Also much of the concern now has, understandably, shifted away from 'juridification' and 'politicisation' towards the economy. One has to begin of course from the 'constitutive' dimension, of self-foundation, of systems, in order to understand what the options available in the first place are to rein in self-expansion. For Teubner, the constitution of the economy, science, the media, etc., all perform the same constitutive function by securing for each sphere the autonomy of their specific medium, today on a global scale. Each partial constitution makes use of 'constitutive rules' to regulate the abstraction of a homogeneous communicative medium – power, money, law, knowledge – as an autonomous social construct within a globally constituted function system. At the same time the constitutions make sure that the society-wide impact of their communicative media is guaranteed under different historical conditions. They develop organisational rules, procedures, competences, and subjective rights for both these orientations, codifying the separation between the social spheres and, in this way, shore up the functional differentiation of society.

As in older writings on 'reflexive law',[9] the emphasis is yet again on self-steering, and the challenge is to combine 'external pressures with internal processes of

---

8   See in particular Gunther Teubner, *Constitutional Fragments. Societal Constitutionalism and Globalization* (OUP 2012).

9   Gunther Teubner, 'Substantive and Reflexive Elements in Modern Law' (1978) 17/2 *Law & Society Review* 239ff.

discovery' to enable such steering. The state we are told often, Teubner here quotes Ladeur, is not to superimpose its rationality, to attempt to achieve results – 'it must direct its intervention at their [functional systems'] self-transformation'.[10] While 'high cognitive demands' will be made of 'national and international interventions by the world of states', especially in a situation of economic crisis it is assumed, the temptation must be resisted to substitute their – the states' – reason for that of the focal system, here the economy. Instead their intervention should consist in the 'selective' generation of 'constitutional irritants' that will translate into self-steering, that will liberate systems from pathologies in the form of 'self-blockades' as Ladeur puts it, but not superimpose state rationality. State-run command economies is the (not so) implicit message that failed for attempting precisely such a substitution and buttressing it, when it inevitably failed, with state terror – hence Teubner's warning that 'following the experiences of political totalitarianism in the last century, a permanent subordination of the subsystems to the state is no longer a valid option'.[11] Hence there is 'no alternative but to experiment with constitutionalisation' in the hope that 'with a bit of luck' 'the external and internal programmes' – of irritating and irritated systems – 'will play out together along the desired course'.[12]

Teubner is certainly not alone in putting the emphasis on the policing of proper boundaries of systemic autonomy, the handling of crisis, as we saw, having to do with the recalibration of the overall logic of systemic balance. In a similar vein, and under the eloquent title 'Eroding boundaries', another systems theorist, Marc Amstutz, identifies crises as 'boundary disorders',[13] where the 'closure mechanism' of a system generates a 'deleterious' interdependence between systems, which is no longer premised on their mutual closure (and thus their healthy cognitive openness to each other) but on the undermining of that very condition that sustains functional differentiation. And to bring it closer to the financial crisis, Amstutz puts the question in this way: 'If financial crises are, in fact, an instance of systemic boundary dissolution, what are the conclusions to be drawn in terms of market regulation or, more specifically, in terms of financial law?'[14] A very interesting typology of forms of regulatory crisis follows from this. In the first place we have crises induced by the fact that the coding of a system is incapable of aligning complex information to its logic and is instead thrown off kilter by information it is unable to process through its own coding; they are in other words *crises of disproportionate reaction* to the environment. In the second category of crises fall those that result from insufficiently differentiated systems, typically those that have not evolved towards differentiation but have been artificially created through

---

10   Teubner (n 1) 14.

11   Teubner (n 1) 13.

12   Teubner (n 1) 15.

13   Marc Amstutz, 'Eroding Boundaries', in P Kjaer, G Teubner and A Febbrajo (eds), *The Financial Crisis in Constitutional Perspective: The Dark Side of Functional Differentiation* (Hart 2011).

14   Amstutz (n 13) 224.

programming interventions. Finally, and these I would suggest in the current context are by far the most interesting, are crises that have to do with *parasitic functioning*, or the creation of a 'parasitic chain'. In its striving to maximise profits the economic system exploits the code of the political system, which seeks in turn to enhance its legitimacy by exploiting the code of the legal system, which, for its part, allows itself to be exploited as a means of asserting an authority (regulatory powers) which it does not, in reality, possess.[15]

What does all this mean in practice? Take the example of corporations deemed 'too big to fail'. These were corporations whose insolvency, it was deemed, would carry intolerable costs for the economy. By having the 'issue framed in its own terms' and in this particular semantics, the economic system translates the economic costs into political costs; the second, now insidious move involves translating the political response back into economic benefits for the 'so-called systemically relevant' financial institutions. The new semantics thus provides the economy with a new reservoir for siphoning off further profits. The insinuation of private economic interests into the code of the political system (in the public interest/not in the public interest) allows economic decisions to be made on the basis of political criteria, closing the cycle of parasitic behaviour of the economic on the political system which, at the same time, allows it (the economy) to redeem itself in the guise of the pursuit of the common good. No 'self-limitation' is conceivable to stem this course. The parasite has intercepted the reproductive cycle of the political system feeding off its energies: capitalism capitalises on the crisis and renews itself through precipitating and then 'managing' catastrophic trajectories.

The Ordoliberal Legacy and the 'Capacitas' Argument

If the improbable solution to the crisis that the first 'critical' theoretical direction suggests has to do with the restoration of disturbed equilibria between functional sub-systems, another critical orientation providing a platform for a second set of responses to the crisis draws on the ordoliberal legacy and its insistence on 'economic constitutionalism'. We can again identify this orientation as 'internal', although here the 'internality' is somewhat more stretched than in the case just discussed, of functional differentiation.

For all the much vaunted difference between ordo- and neo-liberalism, usually associated with Hayek's 'turn' (Hayek was a marginal figure amongst the ordoliberals but, following his term in Chicago, became a luminary of neo-liberalism and the New Right in the mid-70s) the seeds of neo-liberalism are already clear in the ordoliberal phobia of the State and the need to establish the economic constitution on a plane cleansed of State control.[16] Michel Foucault's

---

15   Amstutz (n 13) 256.

16   For an analysis of economic constitutionalism in its original (Weimar) Left-wing conceptualization see Ruth Dukes, 'Constitutionalising Employment relations: Sinzheimer,

1982 lectures at the College de France capture something of the novelty and radical import of the conceptual shift.[17] It consists of the revolutionary move to conceive of the economic first and foremost in market terms and to set it up as conceptually cleansed of political categories. With this, inevitably, comes a radical divestment of economic activity (and the organisation of production) from democratic control. As Kaarlo Tuori puts it, it involves the 'negation of a political constitution of Europe'.[18] And Hauke Brunkhorst explains:

> With the establishment of the economic constitution in 1957 a Schmittian constitutional *Grundentscheidung* (basic decision) was made. Instead of subsuming the economic under the political constitution the political constitution was subsumed under the economic constitution. In case of doubt the 'concrete order' of *law and economics* trumps the formal constitution of *law and democracy*. Whereas formal constitutional law still adhered to the Kantian priority of democratic legislation, the concrete order of *law and economics* became Europe's informal prerogative constitution – Europe's 'hidden curriculum'.[19]

The eclipse of political constitutionalism is sealed by a further substitution: that of legislative for judicial organs. Brunkhorst quotes Ernst Joachim Mestmäcker here: 'The most important decisions have to be taken not by the legislator or the government but by the judges'.[20] In 2002 Alec Stone Sweet enthused that 'today's multi-tiered European polity, the sovereignty of the legislator, and the primacy of national executives, are dead. In concert or in rivalry, European legislators govern with judges'.[21]

If the economic constitution reconfigured along ordoliberal lines involves its evacuation from democratic categories, it is also buttressed by the new emphasis

---

Kahn-Freund and the role of Labour Law' (2008) 25 *Journal of Law and Society* 341; Brunkhorst describes to co-option of the 'economic constitution' by the ordoliberals in 'The Beheading of the Legislator' in *University of Brasilia LJ* (forthcoming), also supra. For other incisive interventions in the debate see Kaarlo Tuori, 'The Many Constitutions of Europe' in K Tuori and S Sankari (eds), *The Many Constitutions of Europe* (Ashgate 2010). For an excellent account of the legacy of ordoliberalism and its roots in German political and economic thinking, see Keith Tribe's *Strategies of Economic Order; German Economic Discourse 1750–1950* (Cambridge 1995).

17   Michel Foucault, *The Birth of Biopolitics* (Palgrave Macmillan 2004).

18   Tuori, *The Many Constitutions of Europe* (n 16) 15.

19   Hauke Brunkhorst, 'The Return of Crisis' in P Kjaer, G Teubner and A Febbrajo (eds), *The Financial Crisis in Constitutional Perspective: The Dark Side of Functional Differentiation* (Hart 2011). On the 'hidden curriculum' see Claus Offe, 'The European Model of "Social" Capitalism: Can it Survive European Integration?' (2003) 11/4 *The Journal of Political Philosophy* 437–69, at 463.

20   Brunkhorst (n 19).

21   Alec Stone Sweet, *Governing with Judges: Constitutional Politics in Europe* (Oxford 2002) 193.

on rights as guarantees against the abuse of political power. After all the ordoliberal position is one profoundly antithetical to the State and its constitutive orientation (at least for those amongst them who developed their thinking in the shadow of and in reaction to the National-socialist State) is a rights-based individual protection from State power.

But there is more to the economic constitution becoming Europe's 'prerogative constitution' and 'hidden curriculum' than the displacement of democratic legislation. Economic constitutionalism – remember, as autonomous from the political – also finds expression in the rise of market thinking associated with the 'capabilities' argument. The turn to 'capabilities' associated with the theories of Amartya Sen is an argument about market inclusion, that is familiar at least since Offe's *Contradictions of the Welfare State*, except no longer developed on the terrain of contradiction but instead on that of aspiration. The critical insight that it carries into the response to crisis, is its attempt to introduce something of a corrective to 'total market' thinking; potentially a sense of economic rationality that resists the collapse of the economic, and the agency proper to it, to the 'total' market.

In the last few decades Sen's work has been at the centre of a more general attempt to invest in the capabilities of the poor to engage in economic activity in order to address the problem that there are actors who do not possess the practical capability to pursue their interest – or to take action – within the market system as it stands. The *Idea of Justice* published in 2009 proclaims to be a 'realisation focused' approach directed to the actual possibility of implementing – of putting into practice – the conclusions of the more abstract theorisation of justice and away from, as Sen puts it, 'transcendental arguments about institutions'.[22]

But for a crucial qualification along the temporal dimension (more on this later) it is the market that is held up by the 'capabilities' theorists as the mechanism that best distributes social resources amongst possible uses. As David Campbell describes it well, 'in the neoclassical conception of the operation of the market, economic actors reveal their preferences through the choices they make and, if the market conforms to the conditions of general competition, a Pareto optimal equilibrium representing a perfectly efficient allocation of goods will be established'.[23] Once it is acknowledged, of course, (as Campbell, too, concedes) that the conditions of general competition will never obtain empirically, the efficiency of actual markets becomes questionable. What remains unquestioned and unquestionable however both for the theorists of the free market and for Sen in his overhauling of the defence of the market, is its clear superiority against planning. The capabilities approach is an attempt to consolidate, not substitute, the range of *information* that is available through the price mechanism. And the enhancement has to do with addressing – at the level of structure – the opportunities that economic actors

---

22   Amartya Sen, *The Idea of Justice* (Harvard University Press 2009) 7–8.

23   David Campbell, 'The Law of Contract and the Limits of the Welfare State' in Maksymilian del Mar and Claudio Michelon (eds), *The Anxiety of the Jurist* (Ashgate 2013) 199.

actually have of revealing their preferences through their choices. Opportunity-structure is what the capabilities theory is about: equality, as equal basic capability, measures itself against the promise of equal participation.

For Sen and the capabilities theorists, then, a market order must *complement* its distribution of formal bargaining positions (that secure equal formal participatory positions in the market economy) with the just distribution of 'conversion factors' that allow economic actors to pursue their advantage within the framework of the exchange, to furnish them, in other words, with the *capabilities* necessary to undertake autonomous action in the context of market exchange. As Simon Deakin puts it, in an important manifesto-like publication *Capacitas* that he has co-edited,[24] what is new are 'the elements of a new concept of *capacitas,* one that goes beyond purely formal guarantees of market access, to encompass the conditions needed for effective participation in the complex economic orders which characterise our time'.[25] 'Capacitas', he says, 'should be thought of as the juridical concept through which the legal system defines the conditions of access to the market by human persons ... In a narrow conception, capacity is defined as the ability to engage in rational economic action ... In a wider conception it is the sum total of the preconditions of effective participation in market relations'.[26] Against paradigms where 'resources, endowments and preferences are taken as given' and so 'exogenous to the operation of the market mechanism'[27] the *capacitas* argument asks whether the economic actor is self-sufficiently capable of revealing his preferences through his/her choices – and re-orients our attention to 'the process by which preferences and endowments are formed'[28] and thus to the conditions needed for effective participation in the economic order.

The argument, as developed over the last 30 years, is complex and, in any case, well beyond the reach of this chapter. Very briefly, for Sen, an economic actor's 'capability set' is what is essential as measure of her agency and autonomy. Since, as he insists, 'commodity command is *a means* to the end of well-being' rather than the end itself, the emphasis shifts on to the set of 'functionings' defined as 'what the person succeeds in *doing with* the commodities at his or her command'. What a person actually achieves ('advantage') is called the 'functioning vector', and a person's capability set is the set of functioning vectors within her reach.[29] 'Conversion factors' are crucially relevant to that capacity for Sen because they frame the conversion of 'endowment' to 'advantage' and undergird the actor's capacity to conduct market exchange.

---

24   Simon Deakin and Alain Supiot (eds), *Capacitas* (Hart 2009).

25   Simon Deakin "'Capacitas': Contract Law and the Institutional of a Market Economy' in Deakin and Supiot (n 24) 1

26   Deakin (n 25) 28.

27   Deakin (n 25) 28

28   Deakin (n 25) 19

29   Amartya Sen, 'Well-being, Agency and Freedom' (1985) 82 *Journal of Philosophy* 169, 200.

For a position that balances so finely between market-enhancing and market-correcting logics, its privileging of market over political allocations (in the final instance) leaves it tainted for the Left, while the fact that its prescriptions *must* involve some welfarist leverage (in order to materialise opportunity-structure for the powerless) and therefore cannot avoid regulatory 'coercive transfers' leaves it vulnerable to critiques from the Right. For the latter, take David Campbell's objection that 'the social welfare function can be identified only by government action. However we define it, we must use governmental computation processes to identify social welfare and if we are to put our welfare conclusions into practice, we must use government power to alter the outcomes of voluntarily agreed exchanges'.[30] To this critique we must surely add that for those who criticise capabilities from the Right, Sen has merely moved coercion one stage back: from government action directly imposing coercive transfers (against those voluntarily assumed by market players) to engineering 'social conversion factors'. And all engineering, however far *back* one takes it from what is *actually* implemented through planning, involves a compromise of what is 'voluntarily assumed' through market choice, which also, to find its legitimacy, must work all the way back, to fundamental choices and commitments that free market thinkers assume constitutive of social agency.

That is why, from the political perspective from which Campbell levels his critique, he is surely right when he says that the capabilities approach must compromise its procedural premise – its commitment to the neutrality of market allocations – at some point in the process of its own actualisation in favour of specifically prescribed outcomes. 'It is not possible', he says, 'to have a concrete policy towards specific choices that is amorphous' in the sense of an abstention from imposing patterns, because to promote opportunity one must in the end 'have a policy that pursues a particular goal of advantage to the economic actor in respect of a particular pattern of consumption'.[31]

For us it is of less concern how the capabilities approach might square its commitment to market neutrality on the one hand and on the other the 'discriminatory' enhancement of 'functioning vectors' and opportunity structures. More important is the question whether the capabilities approach can mediate the requirements of market entry and alleviate the brutality of market participation in the form of social dumping. At a time when the question for Europeans appears to be less that of qualifying, but rather of surviving, the processes of 'actually existing Europeanisation' (to borrow a formulation from Richard Hyman), the agency-enhancing market participation that the capabilities approach promises appears crucially vulnerable to participation *simpliciter* in the race to the bottom. Which means typically, short term profitability, relentless re-organisation (which as Samuel Jubé rightly says is *disorganisation*')[32] under the pressure of maximising

---

30   Campbell (n 23) 204.

31   Campbell (n 23) 207.

32   Samuel Jubé, 'La normativité comptable : un angle mort du droit social' (2009) 4 *Revue de Droit de Travail* 211.

returns for capital. Because what would *entice* the owners of productive capital in the EU to play the 'long game' and forgo the immediate maximisation of return on their capital in favour of the promise of a market-enhancing capabilities regime that cuts against market allocations?

This first quandary about the capabilities theory turns on the absence of any discernible political will in Europe to resist functionalist efficiency in favour of *political* allocation. But there is a second, philosophical, objection to capabilities that does not turn on the empirically verifiable absence of any democratic resistance to mainstream economics. The objection, which I cannot but put in a cursory form here, is that if capacity is a corrective to how agency is 'priced' in the total market (now) then the real difficulty is to conceive of how we will know when agency might *optimise* a projected capability and a projected value (in the future.) This is ultimately a question about information. If agency is still, in the medium and long term, to be mobilised in an activity where the value of capacity is harnessed to profitability, how would we assess or know what the significant future *thresholds* are (in terms of 'conversion factors'), at what point, that is, the investment in capabilities is to be cashed in? The price mechanism is after all that which cannot be second-guessed, and that, for Hayek, was its abstract beauty.

Nevertheless, the *capacitas* argument now occupies a central position in the discourse on Europe, claiming its leverage from art. 3 (3) TEU the (highly competitive) 'social market economy' – a formula that was formally introduced into Europe's constitutional parlance to 'correct' the neo-liberal tilt in the constitutional project, even if the possibility of a social Europe, or a 're-socialised' one, remains painfully unattained and increasingly unattainable. Let us see how the corrective to this neo-liberal 'tilt' is understood as an argument about symmetry and implemented in the thinking of 'proportionality'.

Symmetry and Proportionality

A certain confluence between the rise of rights-constitutionalism and the enhancement of 'capabilities' channelled – inevitably perhaps given the loss of faith in the capacity of steering – to an appeal to *social rights*, marks and underpins the emergence of a new understanding of constitutionality couched in the language of *symmetrical* protection and implemented as *proportionality*. I will say something more, in this section, about the confluence and the emergence and with it the comprehensive turn towards a Court-centred paradigm of constitutionalism that seals the eclipse of the democratic imaginary in Europe.

For the workers of the Nordic States who, in the wake of the *Laval/Viking* jurisprudence have felt the effect of 'governing with judges' on their backs, so to speak, little more needs to be said about how injurious the removal of key question of the organisation of labour and social protection from democratic fora has proven.[33] But the jurisprudence of EU Law remains strangely inattentive to this catastrophe, and under the loud proclamations of the 'new' members, a paralysing dissensus appears to be emerging over what precisely is at stake. Proportionality is the compensatory move that seals over such dissensus. How remarkable, in this context, that the dominant position in legal thinking has fallen behind this abdication from democracy and the transferral of key political decisions to the Courts.

If the transferral of political decision-making to the Courts is to fulfil its legitimating function it must perform the compensatory move: it must establish itself as the agent of symmetry, arbiter of proper balancing and guarantor of proportionate distributions of burdens. That is why the Court in its jurisprudence is at pains to justify its intervention as heeding both sets of demands, economic and social. This is what the CJEU says in *Viking*:

> Since the [Union] has thus not only an economic but also a social purpose, the rights under the provisions of the Treaty on the free movement of goods, persons, services and capital *must be balanced against* the objectives pursued by social policy, which include, as is clear from the first paragraph of Article [151 TFEU], inter alia, improved living and working conditions, so as to make possible their harmonisation while improvement is being maintained, proper social protection and dialogue between management and labour.[34]

Now arguably its decisions in these cases skewed the balance, and the CJEU, in subsequent decisions, has acknowledged that it perhaps went too far with the decisions in *Laval* and *Viking* in protecting economic freedoms at the expense of social rights. Nonetheless, in its agonising over how to re-think and re-operationalise *proportionality*, over how to restore it as a reconciliatory device between competing demands, freedoms and rights, over how to re-introduce it as central to its self-understanding, and finally over how to harness it to the creation of a highly competitive 'social market economy' (as art. 3(3) TEU demands) the Court is becoming something of an enigma to itself.

Let us look at one such subsequent effort. In her opinion in *Commission v Germany (occupational pensions)*,[35] Advocate General Trstenjak *is* at pains to be seen to temper the one-sided commitment to economic over social goals. Her clear intention is to restore *symmetry* between the two, her emphasis is on proper *balancing,* and *proportionality* is the means and measure of the undertaking. She criticises the decision in *Viking* for adopting a 'hierarchical relationship

---

33　*Laval & Viking* decisions of the CJEU: Case C341/05, *Laval un Partneri Ltd*, ECR 2007, I11767 and Case C438/05, *International Transport Workers' Federation and Finnish Seamen's Union v Viking Line ABP and OÜ Viking Line Eesti*, ECR 2007, I10779.

34　*Viking ITWF v Viking Line* (C-438/05) [2007] E.C.R. I-10779; [2008] C.M.L.R. 51 at [79].

35　*European Commission v Federal Republic of Germany* (Case C-271/08) [2010]

between fundamental freedoms and fundamental rights in which fundamental rights are subordinated to fundamental freedoms and, consequently, may restrict fundamental freedoms only with the assistance of a written or unwritten ground of justification'.[36] And she says:

> [I]t must be presumed that the realisation of a fundamental freedom constitutes a legitimate objective which may limit a fundamental right. Conversely, however, the realisation of a fundamental right must be recognised also as a legitimate objective which may restrict a fundamental freedom. (188) ... For the purposes of drawing an exact boundary between fundamental freedoms and fundamental rights, the principle of proportionality is of particular importance. (189) ... A fair balance between fundamental rights and fundamental freedoms is ensured in the case of a conflict only when the restriction by a fundamental right on a fundamental freedom is not permitted to go beyond what is appropriate, necessary and reasonable to realise that fundamental right. Conversely, however, nor may the restriction on a fundamental right by a fundamental freedom go beyond what is appropriate, necessary and reasonable to realise the fundamental freedom.[37]

This final 'realisation' has no longer anything to do with any *Albany*-type incompatibility. As in *Laval* and *Viking*, the Court will again find that the fundamental right to bargain collectively is important but not absolute. Like the previous cases the emphasis is again on 'reconciliation': the exercise of the fundamental right to bargain collectively must be reconciled with the requirements stemming from the freedoms protected by the FEU Treaty (para 44). The solution this delivers is not by kind, but by weight, like in *Laval* and *Viking*, except now weighted also in the direction of justifying restrictions on fundamental freedoms imposed by fundamental rights, or at least cognisant that 'the proportionality enquiry cuts both ways'.[38] It may be worth commenting that for all the rhetoric of symmetry and reconciliation and the Advocate General's 'scathing' attack on the 'one-sidedness' of *Laval* and *Viking*, the balancing arrived at in *Commission v Germany* is barely distinguishable from that of the 'one-sided approach'. While some commentators find 'staggering' the failure to apply the 'genuinely symmetrical approach',[39] one might suggest that the failure is hardly surprising. But I will not go further in that direction. Instead I will stay with the conceptualisation (rather than the operationalisation) of the two organising ideas of symmetry and proportionality.

The first challenge for the symmetrical approach is to establish the poles from which equi-distance is to be established. And to face up to the difficulty that those

---

36   All quotes in Catherine Barnard, 'A Proportionate Response to Proportionality in the Field of Collective Action' (2012) 37/2 European Law Review 117–35

37   Barnard (n 37) 125

38   P Syrpis, 'Reconciling Economic Freedoms and Social Rights – The Potential of *Commission v Germany* (2011) 40 I.L.J. 222, at 225

39   Syrpis (n 38) 227.

who are to gain 'market access' from the decisions are the first to attack the structuring work that the difference between the social and the economic is performing. They will suggest instead a reconfiguration along the same axis, arguing that the (social) right to work of the Estonian or Latvian workers 'sacrifices' the (social) right of the privileged Nordic workers to increased protection; their economic freedom to gain market access clashes with the Nordic workers' freedom to remain in that market. The clash is no longer between rights and freedoms, the social and the economic, but between those who are prepared to work for half the wage and those who are not prepared to recognise that as a legitimate comparative advantage.

It is interesting that Catherine Barnard who remains critical of the *Laval/Viking* jurisprudence quotes approvingly an author who makes precisely this point. It is interesting in that it reflects a general ambivalence that now characterises much labour law writing post-*Laval*.

> Like Wittgenstein's duck-rabbit picture, what appears as economic is social and what as social, is economic, depending on the angle from which we see the dilemma. The debate could just as well be framed in terms of social rights of [Estonian] workers against the [Finnish] interpretation of the freedom of movement provisions which ignores their realisation.[40]

In the above quote, Kukovec 'puts succinctly' a necessary 'caveat' for Barnard.

> The precedence of the economic over the social is not necessarily a bad thing for developing a social dimension of the European Union in the general sense, since opening up the markets will benefit the Estonian workers, improving their prosperity and thus giving effect to the aspiration originally expressed in art. 117 EEC.

But Barnard will qualify this endorsement:

> While this argument has much merit, it distracts from the general thesis of this article, namely that in terms of preserving the integrity of national social systems, the *Viking* judgment is severely damaging to rules developed by the states in the social field – the very area over which the initial Treaty of Rome settlement deliberately gave autonomy to the states – because fundamental (EU) economic rights take precedence in principle over fundamental (national) social rights.[41]

And yet, after all the qualifications, there remains something profoundly disturbing about 'the merit' of an argument that suggests a mutual substitution

---

40   Damjan Kukovek, 'Whose Social Europe?', talk delivered to Harvard Law School (April 16, 2010), SSRN <*http://papers.ssrn.com/sol3/papers.cfm?abstract_id=1800922*> accessed February 16, 2012. In Barnard (n 36) 123.

41   Barnard (n 36) 123.

('duck-rabbit') that *pivots* on market access understood in its functionality of sustaining a downward spiral of lowering wages (social dumping) and to assume market access in this modality as *sole* guarantor of *both* social rights *and* economic freedoms for Baltic workers. In this formulation market access comes to undergird the social market in giving leverage to social rights. Can the integrity of the market not resist the logic of this downgrading?

Against the aspirations of the *capabilities* argument to give some integrity to the market, market access, and with it social dumping, becomes the entry condition and arbiter of both economic participation and social capacities-building. Systems theorists' prescriptions for (internal) reflexive adjustments, given the overall institutional preconditions of the autonomy of functional sub-systems, are only meaningful *given* those conditions of autonomy of systems, and the problem is that there is nothing given about the autonomy of the 'social constitution' or of 'political decision-making' in the dilemmas at hand. This is revealed in the difficulties of even sustaining a concept of symmetry in the face of the market's overdetermination of what is social, and what might be a social right.

At this point the architecture of symmetry yields to the fluid balancings of proportionality. Barnard notes that A.G. Trstenjak's 'symmetrical' approach *may well have been inspired by German law principles and is in any case* 'reminiscent of the German Constitutional Court's approach to balancing rights of equal weight, namely 'practical concordance' (*praktische Konkordanz*).[42] The meaning of 'practical concordance' according to Konrad Hesse who coined it, requires the 'optimisation' of conflicting values. Where values conflict, both 'need to be limited so that each can attain its optimal effect. In each concrete case, therefore, the limitations much satisfy the principle of proportionality; that is, they may not go any further than necessary to produce a concordance of both legal values'. The principle of practical concordance matches the three-pronged test of proportionality that requires any limitation exercised in either direction to be (1) appropriate (*geeignet*); (2) no more restrictive than necessary (*erforderlich*); and (3) proportionate (*zumutbar*).[43] The latter requirement is also known as proportionality *stricto sensu.*

In the article that largely inaugurated the discussion of balancing constitutional principles back in 1987,[44] Aleinikoff explained 'proportionality' as the method that aims at the 'judicial opinion that analyzes a constitutional question by identifying interests implicated by the case and reaches a decision or constructs a rule of constitutional law by explicitly or implicitly assigning values to the identified

---

42 A point made by Barnard (n 36).

43 Donald P Kommers, *The Constitutional Jurisprudence of the Federal Republic of Germany* (2nd edn University of Chicago Press 1996) 46, quoting Konrad Hesse, *Grundzüge des Verfassungsrechts der Bundesrepublik Deutschland,* new print of 20th edn (Müller 1999) para.72.

44 T Alexander Aleinikoff, 'Constitutional Law in the Age of Balancing' (1987) 96 *Yale Law Journal* 943.

interests'. What made this method uncontroversial for the author was its 'resonance with current conceptions of law and notions of rational decision-making'.[45] Since then 'proportionality' has become a key concept around which constitutional review is organised. It has become key to judicial thinking and key to doctrinal and theoretical attempts to combine the requirements of pragmatic solutions with adequate justifications, and has been discussed at the most abstract levels of legal-theoretical discussion as significant to what *rational* decision-making means and requires today. Here is an indicative extract:

> Impartially applied, proportionality permits disputes about the limits of legitimate lawmaking to be settled on the basis of reason and rational argument. It makes it possible to compare and evaluate interests and ideas, values and facts, that are radically different in a way that is both rational and fair. It allows judgments to be made about ways of thinking that are as incommensurable as reason and faith. It provides a metric around which things as dissimilar as length and weight can be compared.[46]

I take Robert Alexy's hugely influential work on proportionality as its most interesting expression. In order to guarantee proportionality as rational reflection, Alexy will attempt to insulate the legal-reflexive balancings of constitutional principle that proportionality involves from political decision-making; and this bracketing off is achieved by entrusting the balancings to Constitutional Courts rather than legislatures. There is no shortage of allies here, from Dworkin, Michelman and the civic republican tradition that flourished in the 1980s, to the more recent endeavours of Kumm, Hirsch, Beattie, etc., in the many varieties of 'cosmopolitan' and legal' constitutionalism. Constitutional scrutiny secures a privileged position above the 'rough and tumble' of political bargaining, or the circumventing of proper reflection though majoritarian decisions, making it the ideal forum for rational deliberation. That is why proportionality is claimed not as a compromise of but as the very realisation of practical rationality. For Alexy, the fact that it is undertaken by Courts not at all compromises it as an exercise of universal uncoerced communication aiming at consensus because Courts represent us in the modality of participation. For him, the exercise of the proportionality test by judges in fact enjoys some superiority to the balancing that occurs in legislatures because while both rely on argumentative and discursive processes, and subject them to the 'test of public reason', judicial argument relies exclusively on such processes to the exclusion of the decisional element, and all the arbitrariness of political or majoritarian preferences, that characterise legislation. The argument about 'optimisation' must be understood as self-contained, and thus distinct from such political/decisionist elements.

Such is the nature of the defence of proportionality that has gradually come to replace other constitutional *problématiques* over the last couple of decades.

---

45 Aleinikoff (n 44) 944–5, 960.
46 Aleinikoff (n 44) 965.

Perhaps one way to explain the measure of its success, and certainly the one most relevant to our current discussion, is that it allows constitutional thinking to circumvent difficult choices between priorities that are the stuff of politics, and to replace them instead with a judgment over proportionate weightings, that now no longer presupposes or demands that an architecture of rights be upheld, with its internal hierarchisations and incommensurabilities, but instead collapses them all in an all-inclusive pooling where the language of optimisation will do all the work.

The Political Economy as Democratic Category

I would like to take up Rob Walker's invitation in this book to think democracy in relation to the economy. And this involves what in the current conjuncture is a near-impossible re-introduction of democratic categories in the organisation of social labour and the processes of production. 'Governments', as Michelle Everson puts it well, 'are trapped in a perverse non-logic' expressed as a blind faith 'in the continuing capacity of autonomous market operation to internalize increasingly brutal social externalities through ever more elusive growth'.[47] My own focus in this chapter has been on the preceding step involving the conditions of the distinction between what is properly democratic and what is economic. In this final section I will focus on the framing work that is done by the disjuncture in the following sense. That if one begins with the disjuncture in the way that both ordoliberalism and the theory of functional differentiation conceptualise the logics of the fields as distinct, one is caught up *ab initio* in a largely compensatory venture, that must provide reasons for their approximation rather than reasons against their disarticulation.

In an important recent paper,[48] Hauke Brunkhorst identifies the internal connection between functional differentiation, crisis and the reproduction of Capitalism. Against the background of Marxism's forever renewed reminder that 'capitalism is an inherently catastrophic system', Brunkhorst suggests a concept of crisis that is structural. It is structural because it is the outcome of the functional differentiation of the economy, which 'if not regulated and institutionalized appropriately' leads to a 'new kind of class rule'.[49] Conflict-positions proliferate and Brunkhorst is keen to resist their reduction to 'only one central social conflict, the conflict of capital and labour'; instead he is quick to draw our attention to the 'new' conflict between included and excluded populations. Insightfully, in relation to the latter Brunkhorst deploys a critical reading of Luhmann to argue that:

> The social and political success of the national states depended on their ability
> to exclude inequalities ... On the other hand, the exclusion of inequalities

---

47   Michelle Everson, 'The Fault of (European) Law in (Political and Social) Economic Crisis' (2013) 24 *Law & Critique* 109.

48   Brunkhorst (n 19).

49   Brunkhorst (n 19) 146.

is a functional requirement of highly specialized social systems which are constituted by open access to the system because they are in need of a never ending stream of more and more variation and integration ... .[T]he social and systemic integrative potential of the now ubiquitously comparably modern world society does not suffice to guarantee equal access to everybody, or to pen the systemic couplings (in particular of law, the economy and politics) at least far enough ... for the autopoiesis of the respective systems.[50]

And later:

Whereas the national state loses its ability to exclude inequalities effectively, there is no coercive power, no sufficient administrational mechanism to implement and enforce the exclusion of the inequalities on a global, or at least a regional, level (including the insufficiently empowered EU, which cannot break the economically exploitative hegemony of the North over the South, or of Germany over the rest, as we have seen during the world economic and financial crisis since 2008.)[51]

Brunkhorst's is a powerful analysis of the forms and modalities of exclusion, deploying Habermas's vocabulary of collective learning processes, the symbolic reproduction of the lifeworld, and legitimation crisis. Much of the critique is directed here to that aspect of social reproduction that Luhmann's analysis misses, and that theorists like Marcelo Neves have insightfully developed around the concept of integration.[52] Integration of the population in the functional differentiation of systems is a key premise of that tradition of social analysis that is inaugurated in Durkheim's writing on organic solidarity, and via Parsons and others, finds its apogee in the radical, autopoietic, differentiation of functional systems in Luhmann. But the premise of such differentiation is the partial (differentiated) inclusion of *everyone* in those systems. The economic sub-system depends on everyone producing and consuming, the political system on generalised citizen participation, the legal system on everyone being able to sue one another, etc. The effects of the capitalist system, which became so blatantly evident during the crisis, involved the creation of a privileged 'over-included' class and a class of those whose life-chances diminished to the point where their participation in society was rendered vacuous. Despite Brunkhorst's occasional notes of optimism ('there are at least some hopeful constellations of class conflict that could lead to further learning processes')[53] the spectre of exclusion of vast swathes of the world's populations from meaningful participation in social life is the devastating insight of his contribution.

---

50   Brunkhorst (n 19) 159–60.
51   Brunkhorst (n 19) 168–9.
52   See indicatively Marcelo Neves, 'Zwischen Subintegration und Überintegration: Bürgerrechte nicht ernstgenommen' (1999) 4 *Kritische Justiz*.
53   Brunkhorst (n 19) 163.

Under conditions of crisis, social exclusion is radicalised. It is absurd to seek to correct the effects of such exclusion through the facilitation of labour mobility in a 'race to the bottom'. Everson puts this well. She says, 'only the most neo-liberal of economic commentators could hope … that labour mobility would compensate for the inequalities in national economic development'.[54] Market access, or labour mobility, under these conditions is no longer simply the economic motor for growth within the economic sphere of a functionally differentiated society. It becomes the route to – or modality of – inclusion itself, and thus the condition of meaningful participation in a functionally differentiated society. Since market access by definition involves a distribution of access and non-access, it also by definition deprives those excluded from participation in a functionally differentiated society (see Brunkhorst and Neves above) and thus undercuts its very condition. The effect is the creation of 'surplus' or 'redundant' populations.

In a devastating account of 'the crisis of democratic capitalism',[55] Wolfgang Streeck analyses the current crisis not as the disruption of normalcy, but as the very expression of the contradictory articulation of markets and democracy – in his words, the 'inherently conflictual transformation of the social formation we call 'democratic capitalism'.[56] In the years immediately after the Second World War, says Streeck, 'there was a widely shared assumption that for capitalism to be compatible with democracy, it would have to be subjected to extensive political control – for example, nationalisation of key firms and sectors, or workers' 'co-determination', as in Germany – in order to protect democracy itself from being restrained in the name of free markets'.[57] This 'conflictual transformation' organised the space of political contestation, and in social democracy, in the decades after the War, the contradiction found its temporary accommodation. If, as Streeck puts it, 'Hayek withdrew into temporary exile'[58] during this period, the advent of neo-liberalism signalled his triumphant return: if the market is no longer the guarantor of efficiency but also the neutral register of *democratic* 'choices' as expressed though our purchases (putting one's money where one's mouth is, as it were) the contradiction is undone and the accommodation installs itself no longer as precarious but rather as subtending both efficiency and democracy. The result of this undoing for Streeck involves the 'frivolous experiment' to realise a market economy emancipated from all political bonds.

> Mainstream economics have been obsessed with the 'irresponsibility' … of interfering with otherwise efficient markets, in pursuit of objectives – such as full employment and social justice – that truly free markets would in the

---

54   Everson (n 47) 107.

55   Wolfgang Streeck, 'The Crises of Democratic Capitalism' (2011) 71 *New Left Review* 5–29 and 'Markets and Peoples' (2012) 73 *New Left Review* 63–71

56   Streeck (n 55) 5.

57   Streeck (n 55) 6.

58   Streeck (n 55) 6

long run deliver anyway, but must fail to deliver when distorted by politics. Economic crises, according to standard theories of 'public choice', essentially stem from market-distorting political interventions for social objectives. In this view, the right kind of intervention sets markets free from political interference; the wrong, market-distorting kind derives from an excess of democracy.[59]

In concluding I will return to my title and the dystopia of an economics of constitutional renewal. The terms of constitutional renewal – 'constituent power', 'self-understanding', 'political community', 'self-determination' – remain constitutively oriented towards democracy. And yet the effective collapse of our political capacity as political community is mediated through the move that supplants political with economic thinking. And with this as European citizens we stand powerless before the loss of the language with which to confront and redress our current disposition. Our political and constitutional vocabularies ill-equip us to deal with crisis, where the categories at our disposal are either *constitutively complicit* with the crisis or at least *exhausted* to the point where they can no longer deliver us from it. More urgently than before, this alerts us to the danger that our ability to *act back* typically folds back into the very categories our action might have attempted to place in doubt.

Bibliography

Aleinikoff TA, 'Constitutional Law in the Age of Balancing' (1987) 96 *Yale Law Journal* 943

Amstutz M, 'Eroding Boundaries' in P Kjaer, G Teubner and A Febbrajo (eds), *The Financial Crisis in Constitutional Perspective: The Dark Side of Functional Differentiation* (Hart 2011)

Barnard C, 'A Proportionate Response to Proportionality in the Field of Collective Action' (2012) *European Law Review*

Bauman Z, *Liquid Modernity* (Polity 2000)

Brunkhorst H, 'The Return of Crisis' in P Kjaer, G Teubner and A Febbrajo (eds), *The Financial Crisis in Constitutional Perspective: The Dark Side of Functional Differentiation* (Hart 2011)

Brunkhorst H, 'The Beheading of the Legislator' in *University of Brasilia LJ* (forthcoming)

Campbell D, 'The Law of Contract and the Limits of the Welfare State' in M del Mar and C Michelon (eds), *The Anxiety of the Jurist* (Ashgate 2013)

Deakin S and Supiot A (eds), *Capacitas* (Hart 2009)

Dukes R, 'Constitutionalising Employment Relations: Sinzheimer, Kahn-Freund and the role of Labour Law' (2008) 25 *Journal of Law and Society* 341

---

59   Streeck (n 55) 7

Everson M, 'The Fault of (European) Law in (Political and Social) Economic Crisis' (2013) 24 *Law & Critique* 109

Foucault M, *The Birth of Biopolitics* (Palgrave Macmillan 2004).

Hesse K, *Grundzüge des Verfassungsrechts der Bundesrepublik Deutschland*, new print of 20th edn (Müller 1999)

Jubé S, 'La normativité comptable : un angle mort du droit social' (2009) 4 *Revue de Droit de Travail* 211

Klein N, *The Shock Doctrine. The Rise of Disaster Capitalism* (Picador 2008)

Kommers DP, *The Constitutional Jurisprudence of the Federal Republic of Germany* (2nd edn University of Chicago Press 1996)

Kukovek D, 'Whose Social Europe?', talk delivered to Harvard Law School (April 16, 2010), SSRN, *http://papers.ssrn.com/sol3/papers.cfm?abstract_id=1800922* [Accessed February 16, 2012]

Neves M, 'Zwischen Subintegration und Überintegration: Bürgerrechte nicht ernstgenommen' (1999) 4 *Kritische Justiz.*

Offe C, 'The European Model of "Social" Capitalism: Can it Survive European Integration?' (2003) 11/4 *The Journal of Political Philosophy* 437–69

Polanyi K, *The Great Transformation: The Political and Economic Origins of Our Time* (Beacon Hill Press 1944)

Sen A, 'Well-being, Agency and Freedom' (1985) 82 *Journal of Philosophy* 169, 200

Sen A, *The Idea of Justice* (Harvard University Press 2009)

Stone Sweet A, *Governing with Judges: Constitutional Politics in Europe* (OUP 2002)

Streeck W, 'Markets and Peoples' (2012) *New Left Review*

Streeck W, 'The Crises of Democratic Capitalism' (2011) *New Left Review*

Syrpis P, 'Reconciling Economic Freedoms and Social Rights – The Potential of *Commission v Germany* (2011) 40 I.L.J. 222, at 225

Teubner G, 'Substantive and Reflexive Elements in Modern Law' (1978) 17/2 *Law & Society Review* 239ff

Teubner G, 'A Constitutional Moment? The logics of "Hitting the Bottom"' in P Kjaer, G Teubner and A Febbrajo (eds), *The Financial Crisis in Constitutional Perspective: The Dark Side of Functional Differentiation* (Hart 2011)

Teubner G, 'Constitutionalising Polycontexturality' (2011) 19 *Social and Legal Studies*

Teubner G, *Constitutional Fragments. Societal Constitutionalism and Globalization* (OUP 2012)

Tribe K, *Strategies of Economic Order; German Economic Discourse 1750–1950* (Cambridge 1995)

Tuori K, 'The Many Constitutions of Europe' in K Tuori and S Sankari (eds), *The Many Constitutions of Europe* (Ashgate 2010)

Cases

Case C-271/08 [2010] *European Commission v Federal Republic of Germany*
Case C341/05, *Laval un Partneri Ltd*, ECR 2007, I11767
Case C438/05, *International Transport Workers' Federation and Finnish Seamen's Union v Viking Line ABP and OÜ Viking Line Eesti*, ECR 2007, I10779

Chapter 4

Finding our Way Back to Europe?

Michelle Everson

Introduction

If belatedly, the once rose-tinted lenses of EU scholarship are darkening. As combined sovereign-debt crisis and paradox-laden response to crisis have been recognised to constitute an emergency moment, pregnant with peril for traditional democratic process, the perennial complacency of European academic debate has given way to a new urgency, to a belated understanding that technocratic institutions of supranational governance do not always play host to miraculously conjured and mutually beneficial processes of deliberation but may, by contrast, be driven by a normatively voided functionalism, which is dedicated only to ever closer Union, without thought for the legitimate character of European *finalité*. At the forefront of movements to counter this growing 'technicity', we find Jürgen Habermas who has demanded corrective retort in a voluntaristic moment of constitutive European politics. Yet, just as crisis unmasks the long-standing absences within Habermasian theory, it similarly defies immediate constitutionalised solutions for Europe. Although also marked by specifically European trends, crisis is similarly located within a far longer (global) durée of totalising scientification; it is rooted within economic and legal technologies, which, in their quest for objective universalisms have denatured politics and denuded political capacity. A path back to Europe – *as organising political ideal* – is discernible. However, it is long and necessarily contingent, dependent upon the uncertain outcomes of grassroots-led socio-economic and political renewal. In the meantime, the EU must learn to manage its affairs with a – *for it* – revolutionary modesty, a post-functionalist preparedness to accept greater diversity and less, rather than more Europe.

'Ohne Recht gibt es keine Freiheit'

Paul Kirchhof, one-time President of the German Constitutional Court (FCC) has recently thrown his considerable weight behind voices urging the current FCC to take a strict adjudicative line on European crisis measures, including, at the time of writing (June 2013), the unlimited guarantee given by the ECB for the (secondary) state bonds of members of the Eurozone. Intimating that, '[D]em Bürger mehr Wohltaten zu gewähren, als ihm steuerlich zustehen, ist verfassungswidrig',[1] Kirchhof takes a strict line, requiring continued individualised assumption of non-collectivised risk within the EU, arguing that current functionalist longing for a centralised European competence, in order to ensure immediate financial and fiscal stability, undermines the constitutional jurisdiction, and does so, to the exact degree that functionally driven executive assumption of the moral hazard of debtor nations, private banks, as well as private citizens, pre-empts democratically accountable delineation of the established community of risk-bearing fate.

The argument is prescient, infinitely more complex than might at first be thought: Kirchhof is not by any means a Hayekian, negating all mutualisation of economic risks; instead, the constitutional jurist's declaration that 'without law there is no freedom', is also a reflection of an instinctive understanding of the Weberian paradox of law that haunts all constitutional jurisdictions (Everson and Joerges 2013). Constitutional courts are never legitimated simply by the formal norms of their jurisdictions. Rather, constitutional legitimacy is established by the constant and impossible process of '*Rechtsverfassungsrecht*',[2] whereby indeterminate constitutional norms are promulgated within the tension between legal certainty and dynamic social value formation, or in the interplay between the formal caution of constitutional justices and their responsiveness to cultural immanence, or ever-evolving material demands for social justice. To Paul Kirchhof, ensconced within the post-war constitutional settlement of the Federal Republic – and admittedly also marked by its ordo-liberal traditions (Joerges 2004) – proper social value formation, especially with regard to 'solidarity', or the establishment of communities of fate, is to be found in democratic process; in structured self-determination, or a socially embedded construction of 'freedom' as the joint utilisation of jointly pooled resources, and the mutual bearing of mutually demarcated risks. Hence the German Court's historical appreciation of democratic, cultural and legal indeterminacy in its judgment on the Maastricht Treaty;[3] its openness to the European political process and its sovereignty defying insistence that a European competence might evolve in step with the emergence of a European citizen (Everson 2010); hence also, however, Kirchhoff's current existential opposition to increasing accumulation of 'redistributive' emergency powers in the executive hands of the European Council and the managerialist Commission, both mere functionalist servants of the need to ensure European stability, and both blind to the cultural imperative to affirm mutualisation of economic burdens.

The accumulation of managerial competences by a European executive in the course of crisis is shocking both in its ubiquity and character. Crisis law departs

---

1   It is unconstitutional to promise the citizen greater benefits than are due to him by virtue of taxes paid (author's translation). See P Kirchoff, Verfassungsnot! *FAZ*, 12.07.2012

2   A term coined by the German legal theorist Rudolf Wiethölter.

3   Judgment of 12 October 1993, 2 BvR 2134/92 and 2 BvR 2159/92, 89 BVerfGE 155 (1993) [Brunner v European Union Treaty, CMLR 57 (1994) 1]

significantly from European law and governance as we once knew it. Crisis summits have become routine and the drafting of ever more ersatz-legislation – or international law substituting for European Union law[4] – memoranda and policy papers is breathtaking.[5] More comprehensive accounts are available (Ruffert 2011). Highlights nonetheless include: the 'Europe 2020 strategy'[6] and the 'European Semester'[7] of March and May 2010, designed by the Commission; the EFSF Framework Agreement of June 2010,[8] and the European Council's 'Euro Plus Pact' of March 2011.[9] Simultaneously, on the basis of the simplified revision procedures laid down in Article 48 Paragraph 6 TEU, the European Council also decided, on 25 March 2011, to add a new Paragraph 3 to Article 136 TFEU, permitting the establishment of a stability mechanism and the granting of financial assistance, effective as of 1 January 2013.[10] This was followed in November 2011 by a bundle of legislative measures aimed at reinforcing budgetary discipline on the part of Member States. The package, bequeathed to posterity under the catchy title 'Six Pack', entered into force on 13 December 2011.[11] The cornerstone of the whole new edifice, however, is the Treaty on Stability, Coordination and Governance (TSCG), drafted in December 2011, approved at an informal meeting of the European Council on 30 January 2012,[12] and signed on 2 March 2012 by 25 out of 27 Member States. A debt brake, designed according to the German model, will be introduced and will be subject to judicial review by the Court of Justice of the European Union (CJEU), as borrowing use is made of EU institutional arrangements, whereby one Member State may bring an action against another in cases of default. Support from the European Stability Mechanism (ESM),

---

4   That term, coined by a German lawyer, was taken up in the ESM judgment of the German Constitutional Court at paragraph 226 to denote the resort to international law for measures which European law does not foresee <http://www.bundesverfassungsgericht.de/entscheidungen/rs20120912_2bvr139012en.html> accessed August 2013

5   For continuously updated information see <http://www.consilium.europa.eu/press/press-releases/economic-and-financial-affairs?lang=en&BID=93> accessed August 2013

6   Communication from the Commission of 3 March 2010, COM(2010) 2020 final.

7   Communication from the Commission of 12 May 2010, COM(2010) 250 final.

8   Confirmed in the conclusions of the European Council, Brussels, 17 June 2010, EUCO 13/10, CO EUR 9, CONCL 2. The Framework Agreement was concluded by the ECOFIN Council and confirmed by the European Council, Brussels on 17 June 2010.

9   Conclusions of the European Council, Brussels, 24/25 March 2011, EUCO 10/11, CO EUR 6, CONCL 3 (Annex I).

10   Dec 2011/199/EU amending Art 136 TFEU with regard to a stability mechanism for Member States whose currency is the euro, OJ 2011, L 91/2011, 1.

11   The five regulations 1173–1177/2011/EU and directive 2011/85/EU of 8 November 2011, OJ L 91/2011, 1.

12   See the Communication of the euro area Member States as well as the Treaty on Stability, Coordination and Governance in the Economic and Monetary Union in the version of 20 January 2012 <http://european-council.europa.eu/media/639235/st00tscg26_en12.pdf> accessed August 2013

a permanent crisis fund, will be available only to countries in the Eurozone that have signed the pact. Finally, in March 2013 the 'Two Pack' submitted back in 2011 was adopted with parliamentary blessing.[13]

The emergency moment – or 'state of exception' *sensu* Carl Schmitt – within crisis law is readily apparent in academic responses which, even at their most optimistic, struggle to find an appellation for the form of European governance now emerging, but jointly settle for categorisations that stress the preponderance of the executive competence within the new regime. Characterisations by commentators oscillate between notions such as 'Executive Federalism' (Habermas 2012)', 'Distributive Regulatory State' (Chalmers 2012), 'Consolidating State' (Streeck 2013 and 'Authoritarian Managerialism' (Joerges and Weimar 2013). Academic struggle to characterise our new Europe, however, is partnered by grave concerns about the constitutionality – or, indeed, simple legality – of emerging governance at both European and national level. First, through the supervision and control of budgetary imbalances, it disregards the principle of enumerated powers (Article 13 TEU), and, by the same token, disrespects the democratic legitimacy of national institutions, in particular, the budgetary powers of parliaments. Second, in its departure from the one-size-fits-all philosophy orienting European integration in general and monetary policy in particular, it nonetheless fails to achieve a variation, which might be founded in democratically legitimated choices; quite the contrary, individualised scrutiny of national administrations is geared to the objective of budgetary balance and seeks to impose an accompanying discipline, whereby Member States are left with only one response to the conditions of monetary unity – austerity measures (Everson and Joerges 2013). Third, the machinery of the new regime is necessarily indeterminate, or regulatory in nature, establishing a 'political administration' outside the realm of democratic politics, which defies accountability under the rule of law, not least because the core concepts deployed by new economic governance – more particularly, in the hands of Commission experts – to assess macro-economic balance within Member States cannot be defined with any precision, either by economists or by lawyers (Adamski 2012).

Although, as argued below, divergent historical conditions defy claims of exact theoretical congruence, the new European economic governance established within Europe forcefully recalls Carl Schmitt's description of the process of the secession of powers to 'the Political' during the *Außnahmezustand* that plagued the declining years of the Weimar Republic. In particular, the European Council would now appear definitively to have taken on the guise of the *Reichspräsident*,

---

13   The 'Two-Pack' provides for 'enhanced monitoring and assessment of draft budgetary plans of euro area member states, with closer monitoring for those in an excessive deficit procedure, and furthermore enhanced surveillance of euro area member states that are experiencing or threatened with serious financial difficulties, or that request financial assistance'; for details see <http://www.europarl.europa.eu/pdfs/news/expert/infopress/201 303121PR06439/201303121PR06439_en.pdf> accessed August 2013

wielding competence beyond normal legality.[14] Yet, Schmitt's more detailed theorising of the state of exception may also be argued to provide this analysis with an additional perspective on European crisis, one which similarly reveals the futility of Paul Kirchhof's appeal for the maintenance of, or a return to, legality and the constitutional jurisdiction. Schmitt, after all, had a limited tolerance for the political personified by the *Reichspräsident*, whose 'constitutional guardianship' could only extend to immediate protection for the *Volk* he embodied (Schmitt 1931): Schmitt did not conceive of the state of exception as a permanent condition; his justification for 'commissarial dictatorship' similarly encapsulated the effort to overcome the problems that precipitated departure from the rule of law, and to regain normal constitutionality (Schmitt 1938). Within the EU at least, such a return currently appears impossible, stopped by the 'incompleteness' of the European constitutional jurisdiction.

The core problem here, however, is not the long-identified one of the immutable clash of sovereign legal orders within a European jurisdictional space (MacCormick 1998). Certainly tensions remain, say, between national constitutional courts and the CJEU. Nevertheless, the prediction made by Neil MacCormick, over a decade ago, that national and supranational orders would muddle through together, or create a new form of pluralist constitutional jurisdiction, would seem to have been realised, not least in the contemporaneously contentious and constructive 'European Judgments' of the FCC, which may – in their 'offers to treat' to an emerging legal order (Everson and Eisner 2007) – be viewed as a unilateral, but radical re-writing of the unfolding texts of contending sovereign laws (Everson 2010). Instead, the measure of current jurisprudential malaise is to be found in the matching cases of the *ESM Treaty and Fiscal Compact*[15] (FCC) and *Pringle*[16] (CJEU), which jointly and severally demonstrate the extraordinary degree to which a pluralist constitutional jurisdiction within Europe is held in thrall to a technical – rather than legal, or socially constructed – concept of 'conditionality'.

Decided on 12 September 2012, the FCC's Judgment on the compatibility of the ESM Treaty and the Fiscal Compact with the German Constitution is an extraordinary exercise in constitutional subtlety. At the same time, however, it is a deeply ambivalent Judgment, notable not only for the Court's continuing openness to Europe and equal determination to place democratic (German) limitations upon the European Political, but also for its similar inability to constitutionalise its current restraint of our emergency situation within a joint European space of unfettered democratic process. Thus, on the one hand, the Court's willingness to

---

14 Although, the emergency powers of the Reichspräsident were given a legal basis by Article 48 of the Weimar Constitution.

15 An incomplete English translation is available at: <http://www.bundesverfassungsgericht.de/entscheidungen/rs20120912_2bvr139012en.html> accessed August 2013

16 Case C-370/12 *Pringle* v *Ireland*, Judgment of 27 November 2012. Not yet reported.

support the outcome of European integration processes, most notably encapsulated within the novel constitutional concept of 'integration responsibility' evolved in its earlier Judgment on the Lisbon Treaty',[17] was once again never in doubt. 'The Court that barks but never bites' (Weiler 2009), readily approved Germany's participation within each of the proposed measures, albeit subject to the limitations demanded by Article 79(3) of the German Constitution guaranteeing the centrality of democratic process within the German state.[18] Translating this principle in this particular case, the justices accordingly concluded, first, that financial support for the peripheral members of the Eurozone might proceed apace, although similarly conditioned by the value of 'monetary stability', laid down in the Maastricht Treaty and given subsequent recognition by an amended German Constitution as a legal basis for transferral of the decisional competences of the German Parliament to the European Central Bank. Secondly, in vivid support for principles of democratic self-determination, the Court re-affirmed its earlier *Maastricht, Lisbon* and *Greek Rescue Package*[19] Judgments, underlining the eternal nature of the budgetary powers of the Bundestag within the German Constitution, and demanding that it be given sufficient powers to scrutinise the arrangements designed to effect stability and transfer packages,[20] especially as they relate to assessing conditionality.

With this, the Court preserved a democratic imperative within Germany but also continued to seek to open up the German Constitution to European integration, noting vitally – in unfolding legal text mode – that 'Article 79 (3)' does not preserve the law in aspic, but 'seeks to protect those structures and procedures which keep the democratic process open',[21] thus presumably allowing also for a

---

17   FCC, judgment of 30 June 2009, available at: <www.bundesverfassungsgericht. de>; English translation at: <http://www.bundesverfassungsgericht.de/entscheidungen/ es20090630_2bve000208en.html> accessed August 2013

18   Paragraph 220: 'Die haushaltspolitische Gesamtverantwortung des Deutschen Bundestags wird in Ansehung der Übertragung der Währungshoheit auf das Europäische System der Zentralbanken namentlich durch die Unterwerfung der Europäischen Zentralbank unter die strengen Kriterien des Vertrages über die Arbeitsweise der Europäischen Union und der Satzung des Europäischen Systems der Zentralbanken hinsichtlich der Unabhängigkeit der Zentralbank und die Priorität der Geldwertstabilität gesichert'.

19   FCC, Judgment of 7 September 2011, 2 BvR 987/10 – 2 BvR 1485/10 – 2 BvR 1099/10 – aid measures for Greece and against the euro rescue package; available at <http:// www.bverfg.de/entscheidungen/rs20110907_2bvr098710en.html> accessed August 2013

20   Paragraph 274; this section is not yet translated. The official translation is still incomplete. In view of the complexity and importance of this pronouncement, we add the German original: 'Da der Bundestag durch seine Zustimmung zu Stabilitätshilfen den verfassungsrechtlich gebotenen Einfluss ausüben und Höhe, Konditionalität und Dauer der Stabilitätshilfen zugunsten hilfesuchender Mitgliedstaaten mitbestimmen kann, legt er selbst die wichtigste Grundlage für später möglicherweise erfolgende Kapitalabrufe nach Art. 9 Abs. 2 ESMV'.

21   Paragraph 206 in the English extract, paragraph 222 in the German original.

future re-alignment of democratic process within a European political space. All is indeed still well in the 'open' German constitutional jurisdiction. And yet, on the other hand, the glue that holds all of this refined constitutional architecture together is, in a final analysis, a technical rather than a constitutional value, a scientific rather than cultural outlook, which paradoxically pre-conditions, just as it seeks to open up the space of European politics.

Currently, the FCC's prescriptions have given us a 'new Europe' within which the Bundestag receives and scrutinises the Irish budget before it is placed before the Irish Parliament, and Greece continues to writhe under the wholly counterproductive application to its affairs of economic conditionality. However, the true weakness in the FCC's cunning construction, one which has similarly externalised the ordo-liberal monetary caution of the Federal Republic within European economic governance structures (Everson and Joerges 2013), only becomes fully apparent when the Court's Judgment is juxtaposed with the CJEU's counterpart Judgment in *Pringle*. The CJEU's reasoning in *Pringle* shares very little of the FCC's constitutional sophistication; but that is, perhaps no surprise. In an emergency situation, Thomas Pringle's concerns about Europe's crisis management were legally well-founded and perhaps catastrophic for the entire machinery of European crisis management. What would have happened had the Court concluded that the EFSF and ESM support-mechanisms do indeed interfere with the exclusive European competence for monetary policy, or that the amendment of Article 136 TFEU was not at all possible under the simplified revision procedure enshrined in Article 48(6) TEU? What would have happened had the Court intoned that new policies adopted and pursued by the Member States jeopardised the primacy of price stability, that the bailout provision of Article 125 TFEU prohibited the granting of financial assistance to Eurozone members, that the functions assumed by the Commission and the ECB (as well as the IMF) were irreconcilable with the principles on the conferral of powers laid down in Article 13 TFEU, or that the mandate allocated to the CJEU in the ESM Treaty exceeded judicial powers? In two words: economic meltdown. To this degree then, the Court was obligated to dispense with its immediate commitment to legality and to identify grounds – however arbitrary – to support the new architecture. Nonetheless, in seizing in a wholly de-contextualised manner upon the saviour concept of 'conditionality', the CJEU has similarly blocked the path back from state of emergency to constitutionality within Europe.

Conditionality is ubiquitous throughout the Judgment, but appears only as simple technical orthodoxy:

1. Conditionality ensures respect for the exclusive European competence in monetary policy and thereby legality of the simplified amendment procedure:

   [T]he reason why the grant of financial assistance by the stability mechanism is subject to strict conditionality under paragraph 3 of Article 136 TFEU, the article affected by the revision of the FEU Treaty, is in order to ensure that that mechanism will operate in a way that will comply with European Union law, including the measures adopted by the Union in the context of the coordination of the Member States' economic policies.[22]

2. Conditionality is the glue that keeps transnational actors together:

[When granting assistance] the ESM Board of Governors shall entrust the European Commission – in liaison with the ECB and, wherever possible, together with the IMF – with the task of negotiating, with the ESM Member concerned, a memorandum of understanding ('MoU') detailing the conditionality attached to the financial assistance facility. The content of the MoU shall reflect the severity of the weaknesses to be addressed and the financial assistance instrument chosen. In parallel, the Managing Director of the ESM shall prepare a proposal for a financial assistance facility agreement, including the financial terms and conditions and the choice of instruments, to be adopted by the Board of Governors.[23]

3. Last, but by no means least, Article 125 TFEU retains its function thanks to conditionality:

[T]he purpose of the strict conditionality to which all stability support provided by the ESM is subject is to ensure that the ESM and the recipient Member States comply with measures adopted by the Union, in particular in the area of the coordination of Member States' economic policies, those measures being designed, inter alia, to ensure that the Member States pursue a sound budgetary policy.

Should the FCC really hope that if, with time, Article 79(3) of the German Constitution might be opened up to embrace democratic renewal within Europe, it should nonetheless note that the space for politics within Europe has been inexorably curtailed. It has been foreclosed, not least by a technical value of conditionality, which it itself has embraced to support its own transubstantiation beyond a German into a European jurisdiction. The European jurisdiction offers us very little hope of a return to normal constitutionality, being seized instead by a scientific outlook that currently pre-empts the constitutive moment of democratic self-determination, within which Paul Kirchof's community of European fate, with its joint utilisation of newly mutualised resources, might be established.

---

22 Paragraph 68.
23 Paragraph 18.

From the Political to Voided 'Technicity'

European Exceptionalism

Law within Europe has ceded its role as 'Hüter der Verfassung', offering us little no or no hope of a legally driven return to constitutional normality within Europe. This final failure of the 'integration through law' movement, however, should come as no surprise (Everson and Joerges 2012). Above all, normative abdication was surely long ago foretold in relation to an emergency moment, which – in terms of the establishment of *de facto* executive governance within the EU – both pre-dates economic crisis and, in one analysis (Majone 2005; Majone 2012; Majone 2014), resides in an original neo-functionalist sin of obsession with the totalising processes, rather than origins, or, more importantly, results of the whole process of European integration.

Citing influential US opinion (Majone 2012:9) Giandomenico Majone has correctly highlighted the dual failing in the construction of EMU, laid down by the Maastricht Treaty:

> Given the risks and uncertainties that pervade the process [of monetary integration] there would have to be a clear margin of benefits over costs for economic consideration, narrowly defined, to provide a justification for such a radical departure in policy. The absence of such a margin implies that the momentum for monetary union must therefore derive from other, primarily political factors (Eichengreen and Frieden 1995:274).

Certainly, EMU was a political project, a part of the neo-functionalist effort to perfect European Union through economic integration, but it was one which equally disguised its own elitist political origins, obfuscated the uncertainties inherent to its realisation, and refused to address the economic, social or political consequences of its possible failure. Application of the community method of total harmonisation to disparate economies was bound to produce default, first in the core of the Eurozone (Germany) and then in the periphery. The vaunted separation of economics and politics was wholly unsustainable with regard to a macro-economic policy mechanism with inevitable redistributive consequences (Majone 2012:12). No consideration was given to the vital need to win sustained support for a political project that would impose social costs (Majone 2012:6) and, most remarkably, no contingency plans were drawn up to address its failure.

For Majone, however, such neo-functionalist failings – accepted and sustained by the 'political culture of total optimism amongst European leaders' (Majone 2005; Majone 2012:6) – have similarly undermined the whole of the integration process since the 1980s, and have done so, above all, where no effort has been made to balance the redistributive burdens of harmonising strategies against the benefits of unitary outcomes, likewise leaving the European project prey always to disregarded social forces who bear the final costs of Union, and who cannot discern, let alone influence the motivations and outcomes of neo-functionalist sentiment.

This final observation, one which places our current emergency situation in a far longer durée of integration, accordingly also gains in significance for the analysis, or does so to the degree that it reminds us that the prime actor within contemporary economic crisis, the European Council, has emerged as an institutional player within the broad, and increasingly malleable EU Treaty framework not, in a constitutive moment, whereby the European Council has taken on the mantle of constitutional guardianship as representative of the European *Volk*, but, rather, in the context of the (failed) counter moment to neo-functionalism, the series of 'no' votes in popular referenda on the proposed European Constitutional Treaty. Established at institutional level, post the crisis-correcting Lisbon compromise, for the first time by Article 15 TEU – though given no formal powers – the European Council, with its President and permanent secretariat is itself simple pragmatic progeny of earlier *Außnahmezustand*, of the refusal of the people of Europe to ratify the European Constitution. The European Council now challenges the traditional balance of powers within the Union, especially as regards the right of supranational initiative afforded the European Commission, meeting in camera outside the normal course of Union political process, and making ready use of the simplified treaty revision process laid down in Article 48(6) TEU, as well as international law, to propel the accumulation of totalising competences by a European economic governance regime far beyond the wildest dreams of the most dedicated of neo-functionalists (Curtin 2013).

A Crisis of Democratic Capitalism?

This story of European exceptionalism, one which might thus be argued to have seen law within Europe cede constitutional guardianship to a 'normatively voided functionalism' – one more commonly associated with international regulatory regimens such as the IMF (Koskenniemi 2009) – of the EU regime of Commission and Council, must nonetheless similarly be augmented, and also challenged, by broader analyses of economic crisis, which, in their turn, cast further doubt on the potential for Europe to escape crisis through its own voluntaristic moment of refounding. In these several views, the financial crisis which precipitated monetary crisis within the Eurozone has far longer roots within the slow collapse of the whole edifice of democratic capitalism far beyond the workings of the EU (Crouch 2011; Scharpf 2011; Streeck 2012).

A common feature in this body of thought is the turning back of the clock: the stagflation of the 1970s sounded a death-knell for command interventionism and government-sponsored policies of full employment. From the 1980s onwards, a consensus established itself across the political spectrum. Direct government interventionism was ended and all political positions subsequently acquiesced in the new liberalising trend as monetary policy was entrusted to central bankers, and centralised steering capacities were divested in line with delegated economic efficiency principles. Vitally, however, the social unrest that negation of the post-war guarantee for public welfare might have engendered was simultaneously militated against by a silent process of 'privatised Keynesianism'. General support was won for liberalisation as the risks and, far more importantly, uncertainties – or non-calculable hazards – inherent to market operations that were once borne within the social state were transferred to private markets in line with a 'permissive consensus', in which private money (growth and/or debt) replaced state generated welfare (Crouch 2011).

Recent instances of counterfactual financial operation are thus readily explained as 'welfarist' commonplaces: provision of mortgages to the impecunious and subsequent resale of unsecured debt is not simply an egregious measure of the self-destructive logic of capital market operation. Instead, it is a destructive logic tolerated within the boundless optimism of a permissive consensus that has re-fashioned the state-financed 'social entitlements' of traditional welfare capitalism as privately constructed 'economic provisions', or contingent economic opportunities (Dahrendorf 2008; Everson and Joerges 2012). Economic opportunity has been 'universalised', or made available as cheap credit to all, within a liberalised financial market which has miraculously internalised all of the externalities and moral hazard inherent to its operations though ever more refined packaging of unsustainable private debt. At core a socio-political abdication of responsibility for public welfare, permissive consensus is similarly characterised by a depoliticisation paradox, or an inability to address enduring welfare concerns through anything other than market growth. It is this lack of political capacity that is most apparent at a time of European crisis. Although extreme positions decry the re-assumption of public responsibility for privatised welfare within governmental assumption of bank debt, collapse of financial markets was never a social option for western administrations of any political persuasion. Instead, governments are now trapped in a perverse non-logic, which combines (indirect) re-assumption of private debt and radical deficit reduction, with the preaching to publics of a 'counterfactual credo' (Streeck 2012) in the capacity of autonomous market operation to internalise increasingly brutal social externalities through ever more elusive growth.

It is similarly, at this exact point of paralysis that opinions upon future European governance diverge most starkly. As noted, for Jürgen Habermas, the 'technocratic moment' in crisis, or the normatively voided functionalism of the European regime within the emergency moment, is final justification for, as well as indicator of, the urgency of the voluntaristic European moment. So, per Habermas, escape from functionalist conditionality into a world of European solidarity will only be possible once the political moment is achieved at European level, wherein explicit solidaristic commitments might be established and pursued across the continent beyond the constraints of austerity (Habermas 2013). For Wolfgang Streeck by contrast, core incompatibilities between modern global capitalism and democratic imperatives can only be combated through – *grosso mondo* – 'retrenchment', or renewed recourse to comprehensive national citizenship, and the cultural and social ties of established risk-bearing communities (Streeck 2013).

   The debate is existential in nature and impacts far beyond the current European crisis, especially where it touches upon global relationships between capital and democracy. It is similarly hard for legal science to give any meaningful judgment on the core issue at dispute – one of if and how, at global level, markets might ever be brought under democratic control. Nevertheless, when viewed through the dual lenses of global democratic crisis and European exceptionalism, Habermas's faith in the ability of political process in Europe to re-establish meaningful political steering capacity must surely be doubted in the short-term. Permissive consensus might not have been the creation of the European Union, being instead a product of political and economic contingency at national level; however, as they have evolved from support of economic community to creation of Union, the supranational structures of European integration have also proven to be fertile ground for the development of rationalities – or a process of scientification – lying far beyond traditional democratic steering mentalities, which seem now likewise to act as a bulwark against the self-determination of political process.

   And herein lies one of the greatest paradoxes of European integration: certainly, founded within the constitutional traditions of the Member States of the Union, the EU aspires to far more than the normatively voided functionalism of Martii Koskenniemi's international regimes. Yet, at the same time, the European quest for universal value, or the Constitution of constitutions, leaves it particularly prey to the 'power' (bio-power) of rationalities in the Foucauldian sense. At structural, legal and judicial levels, the integration process has long been characterised by its devotion to objective rationalities, by its use of science, technology and expertise to unmask the national self-interest and protectionism, which has hindered the creation of a European marketplace. At the same time, however, the undoubted force and – more importantly – civilising, nature of objective rationality finds its more obscure flip-side, not in the growth of technocracy *per se*, but rather in the substitution of technocratic for substantive value. Recent slippages between procedural and substantive application of technocratic value are evident throughout and at all levels of the European regime. Firstly, within the free market jurisprudence of the CJEU, whereby the universalising concept of 'allocative efficiency' has come to govern the interface between (European) economic regulation, on the one hand, and (national) cultural and/or social regulation on the other (Everson 2013b), determining, most spectacularly, in the by now infamous *Viking* jurisprudence,[24] that national labour law within Europe, traditionally a guarantor for the assertion of social rights over markets, must cede to the ability of workers from less developed European economies to assert their competitive labour advantage, or to work for fewer wages and poorer conditions. Secondly, within regulatory regimes, and especially those focused upon the European flow of financial services within a banking union, where the important decision on the

──────────

   24   C-438/05, *International Transport Workers' Federation, Finnish Seamen's Union*
v *Viking Line*
   ABP, OÜ Viking Line Eesti [2007] ECR I-10779

degree of acceptable innovation within markets is no longer a political one, mediated by caution with regard to the unforeseeable hazards posed by such innovation, but is instead presented as a merely technical matter of the management of 'certain' risks which may be always be calculated (Everson 2012). And finally, and most notably, within monetary union itself, whereby conditionality, with its attendant austerity regime, is the sole technocratic value against which all political, expert or judicial action might be judged.

Habermas has long railed against technocracy; yet, in a realm of European exceptionalism, has perhaps fully to account for the extraordinary lure of its new, 'universalising character'. Firstly, not only with regard to the normative power of concepts such as allocative efficiency, which, where they overcome the stubborn closure of nationally and/or culturally negotiated social settlements, relocating welfare gain in the individual hands of economically empowered individuals, promise to overcome the economic and social exclusion of slower development, not simply in Europe, but far beyond.[25] But secondly, and perhaps far more importantly, in the light of a global scientification within society, as well as its governance, which has subsumed universal value within scientific method, replacing human value with 'material truth', as technical expertise promises, or is perhaps co-opted, in an incremental, yet totalising quest for universally applicable solutions. The effort is undoubtedly chimeric: as Hayek warns us, and Luhmann reminds us, economic processes are always uncertain, market values necessarily contingent, as market-led discovery processes make regulatory actions possibly only to the extent that they impose a partial order on an unknown and unknowable infinity of human relations. Yet, and herein perhaps lies the current absence in Habermasian theory, universalising impulses at both the level of a desire for justice and a belief in truth, when harnessed together with misunderstood, possibly misappropriated scientific method, can and do create a governing rationality of extraordinary power.

To this degree then, the absence of political will for the founding of Europe represents far more than fear – above all, the fear of national politicians, only heightened by the failure of the constitutional treaty process, that their populations will yet again reject a constitutional political founding that will contemporaneously create the steering freedoms but destabilising pressures of a European community of risk-bearing fate. Instead, as tentatively hinted at by Michel Foucault at the very outset of our post-modern period of liberalisation (2008),[26] a current lack of political capacity also derives from a new, materialising 'totalitarianism' within political liberalism; one which allows and encourages politicians and regulators alike to conflate the combatable risks with the unknowable uncertainties of market processes, such that the question of political responsibility for market failure need never arise; and one which prompts populations in general to conceive

---

25 Similarly assuaging the post-colonial 'guilts' of many European member states.

26 Foucault's later writings are tentative and to be treated with caution (Everson 2013b).

of themselves as economic rather than political actors, seeking individual and global welfare within a paradigm of scientific belief that posits final escape from overweening austerity within a permanent economic growth which is to be conjured by market forces.

Seen in this light, self-conscious moments of political founding are surely a matter for the future – postponed moments which will follow only upon a slow, intricate and necessarily messy re-evaluation of economic, political and social inter-relationships, which is equally sensitive to the gains as well as the losses of 30 years of post-modern liberalisation, above all with regard to the overcoming of the exclusionary nature of imagined settlements of national paradigms of economic organisation. To this degree then, the general admonition must be one of caution at all levels of political organisation – after all, the traditional nation state is equally beset by sites of technocratic organisation. Nevertheless, the particular characteristics of European exceptionalism are ones which have created their own form of voided 'technicity',[27] wherein European law – always in thrall to a scientific paradigm of self-legitimation (Joerges 2004) – has ceded constitutional guardianship only to the *de facto* functionalism of the European Council and its technocratic handmaiden, the European Commission. Seen in this light, both the total harmonisation and totalising political optimism that have been so characteristic of European integration may be posited to act as an immutable barrier to a return to normal constitutionality, or a form of new constitutionality, which will instead only be furnished by means of flexibility and realism at all levels of political, social and political organisation.

Muddling Through: Less Europe Now!

Refuting the analysis presented by Wolfgang Streeck, Jürgen Habermas argues that Streeck is overly pessimistic: new forms of global capitalism have not simply forced a conformity of human behaviour; instead, a feature of our new global marketplace has also been a greater degree of individualisation, with a large measure of economic creativity (Habermas 2013). Here, however, European experience indicates that Habermas is both wrong and right in his optimism. A notable feature of European integration is – as a side effect of total harmonisation strategies – the unravelling, not only of the variety of 'welfare capitalisms' that once characterised the continent (Esping-Andersen 1989), but also of the variety of capitalisms *per se* that varied European nations had crafted around their own particular cultural circumstances. European integration has not simply forced, for example, adoption of homogenised welfare entitlements such as the minimum wage throughout the continent (Everson 2013a). Instead, the assault on neo-corporatist structures underpinning national markets has extended far beyond limitations

---

27   The term 'technicity' is assigned to Schmitt's vision of normatively voided political organisation beyond the legitimating character of the Volk (McCormick 1999).

placed on social rights to undermine more general structural features of individual forms of capitalism; this movement is most apparent in the recent re-orientation of European competition policy away from the notion of 'fair' competition, and its ordo-liberal roots, to an abstract scheme of competitive advantage (Wigger 2008). With an eye to crisis, and in a loose analogy with evolutionary theory, the homogenisation of European capitalisms might thus be argued to present its own dangers, not simply as once quasi-public mechanisms of economic structuring – e.g. German *Landesbanken* – have, in their liberalised form, only contributed to economic collapse,[28] but also as, without access to the deep steering mechanisms that once structured national markets, Member State responses to crisis are also necessarily framed in the one dominant, competitive paradigm of economic organisation – one which leaves little room for experimental economic policy in the manner of an evolutionary advantage.

In crisis, it is apparent that homogenising European integration has undermined the game of the survival of the fittest economic structures, which might have provided the model for economic renewal. At the same time, however, it similarly should not be forgotten that 30 years of liberalisation have likewise witnessed the evolution of alternative markets, notable for their creativity (technology markets) and even for their ethical values (fair trade/directly sourced foods/organic goods etc.). In this regard then – though far beyond the scope of this limited 'legal' chapter – the long-term restructuring issue for the European economies which make up a European market must perforce, and far beyond current totalising austerity, be one of the experimental identification of various and varied means of re-establishing a variety of the deep economic structures, which can provide necessary support for and common steering capacity over liberated economic creativity, without however reproducing the negative exclusionary externalities of the traditional national market. All of this requires flexibility at national level and the evolution of cautiously restrained coordination capacity at European level. A direct reversal of the traditional community method, with its emphasis upon total harmonisation (Majone 2014), the notion of a partial retreat of the Union into a sensitively co-ordinating role of managing economic diversity may be currently challenging. Yet, political science has begun tentatively to provide us with models, whereby flexibility could be imbued with a measure of stability, should the Union simply admit of the always ever doubtful efficiency gains of total harmonisation and be prepared instead to work within a multi-speed paradigm building upon the real political will of national interests to effect those, and only those parts of an integration programme, which suit each Member State's very particular economic, social and political constellation (Majone 2014).

Such realism is nascent but refreshing; a small pragmatic voice acting as counterweight to counterproductively apocalyptic voices demanding the immediate federalisation of Europe. Europe can survive a period of 'muddling

---

28   See the part played by *WestLB* in the Irish crisis – the irony being that the bank had been forced into private capital markets by the European Commission.

through', giving itself and its peoples the necessary room and time to evolve their own steering capacity over newly liberated economic forces, and, perhaps, in time, to found a fully-fledged political Europe. In the meantime, however, law within Europe must learn to address its own very real failings. Here, however, 'muddling through' will not suffice. At both regulatory level and with regard to primary law (constitutional law), the pluralist European legal system must, as a matter of extreme urgency, rein in its own ambitions. Certainly, the integration through law movement played its own exceptional part in kick-starting a reluctant European integration process. Nevertheless, the recent totalising emergence of law within Europe as promulgator of objectively universal value not only causes consternation amongst a largely disenfranchised European populace,[29] it also threatens to undermine the rule of law within Europe. At regulatory or governance level, conflation of risk with uncertainty, is chimeric (Everson 2013b), simply implicating law in processes of scientification, ending all steering over matters of vital political choice. Similarly, putatively objective universalisms such as 'allocative efficiency' or 'conditionality' have no role to play in an ill-formed 'consitution-like' jurisdiction. Certainly, science and, not least economic science, can play their role within the courtroom. However, science, expertise and technocracy are not values of their own; merely yardsticks which might be used to uncover and test the sometimes ill-conceived motivations of political actors.

Bibliography

Adamski D, 'National Power Games and Structural Failures in the European Macroeconomic Governance' (2012) 49 *Common Market Law Review*, 1319 64

Chalmers D, 'The European Redistributive State and the Need for a European Law of Struggle' (2012) 18 *European Law Journal*, 667–93

Crouch C, *The Strange Non-Death of Neo-Liberalism* (Polity Press 2011)

Curtin D, 'Challenging Executive Dominance in Europe' (2013) 77/1 *Modern Law Review* 1–32

Dahrendorf R, 'Citizenship and Social Class' in R Dahrendorf, *The Modern Social conflict: the Politics of Liberty* (Transaction Publishers 2008)

Eichengreen B, and Frieden J, *The Political Economy of European Monetary Unification* (Westview Press 1995)

Esping-Andersen G, *The Three Worlds of Welfare Capitalism* (Polity Press 1989)

Everson M, 'Politics, Power, and a European Law of Suspicion' in J Neyer and A Wiener, *Political Theory of the European Union* (Oxford University Press 2010)
——— 'A Technology of Expertise: EU Financial Services Agencies' (2012) LSE 'Europe in Question' Discussion Paper Series' (LEQS Paper No. 49/2012)

---

29   See, for example responses to 'strike busting' developments in free movement law (Supiot 2010).

—— 'The Constitutional Structures of the National Political Economy: Barrier to or Precondition for European Integration?' (2013a) 13/1 *Journal of Industry, Competition and Trade* 119–28

'The Fault of (European) Law in (Political and Social) Economic Crisis' (2013b) 24 *Law & Critique* 107–29

—— and Eisner J, *The Making of the EU Constitution: Judges and Lawyers Beyond Constitutive Power* (Routledge-Cavendish 2007)

—— and Joerges Ch., 'Reconfiguring the Politics–Law Relationship in the Integration Project through Conflicts–Law Constitutionalism' (2012) 18/5 *European Law Journal* 644–6

—— and Joerges Ch., 'Who is the Guardian for Constitutionalism in Europe after the Financial Crisis?' (2013) LEQS working Paper No. 63 <www.lse.ac.uk/europeanInstitute/LEQS/LEQSPaper63.pdf> accessed August 2013

Foucault M, (2008) *Birth of Biopolitics: Lectures at the College de France, 1978–79* (Palgrave MacMillan)

Habermas J, 'A Pact for or against Europe?' in U Guérot and J Hénard (eds), *What does Germany Think about Europe?* (2012) (European Council on Foreign Relations) 83–9

—— 'Demokratie oder Kapitalismus' (2013) *Blätter für deustche und international Politik*, 5/2013

Joerges Ch., 'What is Left of the European Economic Constitution?' (2004) EUI Working Paper LAW No. 2004/13

—— and Weimar M, 'A Crisis of Executive Managerialism in the EU: No Alternative?' (2013) Maastricht Faculty of Law Working Paper 2012/7, Maastricht

Koskenniemi M, 'Miserable Comforters: International Relations as New Natural Law' (2009) 15 *European Journal of International Relations* 395

McCormick J, *Carl Schmitt's Critique of Liberalism: Against Politics as Technology* (Cambridge University Press 1999)

MacCormick N, 'Risking Constitutional Collision in Europe?' (1998) 18/3 *Oxford J Legal Studies* 517–32

Majone G, *Dilemmas of European Integration: The Ambiguities & Pitfalls of Integration by Stealth* (Oxford University Press 2005)

—— *Rethinking European Integration after the debt crisis*, (2012) UCL, The European Institute, Working Paper No 3/2012

—— *Rethinking the Union of Europe Post-Crisis: Has Integration Gone Too Far?* (Routledge 2014)

Ruffert M, 'The European Debt Crisis and European Union Law' (2011) 48 *Common Market Law Review*, 1777–806

Scharpf F, 'Monetary Union, Fiscal Crisis and the Pre-emption of Democracy' (2011) 9/2 *Zeitschrift für Staats- und Europawissenschaften* 163–98

Schmitt C, *Der Hüter der Verfassung* (Mohr/Siebeck 1931)

—— 'Vergleichender Überblick über die neueste Entwicklung des Problems der gesetzgeberischen Ermächtigungen (Legislative Delegationen)' (1938) 6 *Zeitschrift für ausländisches öffentliches Recht und Völkerrecht* 252–67

Streeck W, 'The Crisis of Democratic Capitalism' (2011) 71 *New Left Review* 5–29

—— 'Markets and Peoples: Democratic Capitalism and European Integration, (2012) 73 *New Left Review*, January–February

—— *Gekaufte Zeit. Die vertagte Krise des demokratischen Kapitalismus* (Suhrkamp 2013)

Supiot A, 'A Legal Perspective on the Economic Crisis of 2008' (2010) 149/2 *International Labour Review* 151–62

Weiler JHH, 'Does Europe Need a Constitution? Reflections on Demos, Telos and the German Maastricht Decision' (1995) 1 *European Law Journal*, 219–58

—— 'The "Lisbon Urteil" and the Fast Food Culture' (2009) 20 *European Journal of International Law*, 505–9

Wigger A, *Competition for Competitiveness: The Politics of the Transformation of the EU Competition Regime* (Rozenberg Publishers 2008)

PART II
Can European Democracy
Be Saved For Democracy?

Chapter 5

Thomas Hobbes Reading the EU as a Polity

Sakari Hänninen

The Challenge of Empire

In their book *Empire*, Michael Hardt and Antonio Negri emphasize that the Empire "establishes no territorial center of power and does not rely on fixed boundaries or barriers. It is a *decentered* and *deterritorializing* apparatus of rule that progressively incorporates the entire global realm within its open, expanding frontiers."[1] In this fashion the empire should be understood as an integral and global regime of rule and governance that cannot be directly connected or even less identified with any one territorially organized sovereign power, such as, for example, the US or China. They have articulated this standpoint with considerable precision.[2]

The lack of territorial and temporal boundaries characteristic of Empire is the basic argument of Hardt and Negri which, as such, could be seen as an "increasingly familiar cliché."[3] Even though Hardt and Negri offer us a cunning analysis of biopolitically constituted global capitalism understood as Empire, this basic premise must be questioned in spite of the fact that networking technologies

---

1 Michael Hardt and Antonio Negri, *Empire* (Harvard University Press 2000) xii.

2 "The concept of Empire is characterized fundamentally by a lack of boundaries: Empire's rule has no limits. First and foremost, then, the concept of Empire posits a regime that effectively encompasses the spatial totality, or really that rules over the entire 'civilized' world. No territorial boundaries limit this reign. Second, the concept of Empire presents itself not as a historical regime operating in conquest, but rather as an order that effectively suspends history and thereby fixes the existing state of affairs for eternity. From the perspective of Empire, this is the way things will always be and the way they were always meant to be. In other words, Empire presents its rule not as a transitory moment in the movement of history, but as a regime with no temporal boundaries and in this sense outside of history or at the end of history. Third, the rule of Empire operates on all registers of the social order extending down to the depths of the social world. Empire not only manages a territory and a population but also creates the very world it inhabits. It not only regulates human interactions but also seeks directly to rule over human nature. The object of its rule is social life in entirety, and thus Empire presents the paradigmatic form of biopower. Finally, although the practice of Empire is continually bathed in blood, the concept of Empire is always dedicated to peace – a perpetual and universal peace outside of history." See Hardt and Negri (n 1) xiv–xv.

3 RBJ Walker, *After the Globe, Before the World* (Routledge 2010) 57.

and rationalities of government play a crucial role in the functioning practices and institutions of empires. I broadly agree with Jean L Cohen who argues that the analysis of Hardt and Negri is inadequate especially in two respects: the imperial project has not yet globally triumphed and it likewise does have a center and a carrier.[4] In other words, there is good reason to talk about particular empires that have not yet sufficiently coalesced integrally or merged together so as to give reason to talk about the Empire. The best proof of this would be to consider the complex relation between the US empire and the Chinese empire. But this is not the topic of this chapter. I rather want to examine, in the classical light of Thomas Hobbes, what kind of polity is the EU when it is located at the complex inter-zone between the national and the transnational. This question can be asked even if the answer were that the EU cannot be treated as a proper polity.

It is often claimed or at least implied that there is a clear and distinct transition from the international system of states to empire, from international law to transnational law, from a politics of the international to a politics of the world. However, this transitionary path is anything but clear: it is ambiguously folded and tangled. It is practically impossible to draw straight lines or make one-line distinctions in this complex terrain. Therefore, one should pay careful attention to RBJ Walker's prudent advice:

> The journey that is proposed as a move from a politics of the international to a politics of the world may be easily understandable as a simple line drawn from one condition to another, but this line, especially with its capacity to mobilize claims about spatiotemporalities that must be at work in contemporary political life, ought to make us think much more carefully about how complex practices of drawing lines have come to be treated as such a simple matter.[5]

Walker emphasizes that one should pay "far greater attention to what goes on at the boundaries, borders and limits of a politics orchestrated *within* the international that simultaneously imagines the possibility and impossibility of a move *across* the boundaries, borders and limits distinguishing itself from some world beyond."[6] The global disappearance of all boundaries is not an option so long as the inter-zone of the international is the crucial site of *the political* as a problem of sovereignty, authority, judgment and action.[7] For this and similar reasons, the tricky problematic of setting boundaries, drawing lines and making distinctions should be studied punctually and transversally in this multifaceted context of the international whose cartographies are all too often imagined in too linear and continuous a fashion in international politics and political and legal theory.

---

4   Jean L Cohen, 'Whose Sovereignty? Empire Versus International Law' (2004) 18 *Ethics & International Affairs* 18.

5   Walker (n 3) 6.

6   Walker (n 3) 2–3.

7   Walker (n 3) 14, 175.

The inter-zone of the international is an active site for the often novel and paradoxical games of setting boundaries, drawing lines and making distinctions which simultaneously feed the re-imagining of political life and political possibilities. What is ultimately at stake here is the need for greater political imagination about our possible futures.[8] The need for greater political imagination is the political challenge of our times and it is the real challenge of Europe after 1989.

Invigorating the Political Imagination

With an eye to invigorating our political imagination and improving our political judgment to better meet today's and tomorrow's worldly challenges, what can we still learn from European classic political thinkers in terms of (un)timely meditations about the EU? This is the topical question of my chapter. The answer is unequivocal. Walker's book *After the Globe, Before the World* is a testimony of the power of an authentic political imagining of modern classics. This is evident from the way he reads Thomas Hobbes and Immanuel Kant as two master thinkers of political space-time. Walker offers an acute reading of Hobbes which carefully avoids picturing him as a protagonist of static, linear, taxonomic thinking – in spite of the known fact that Hobbes praised Euclidean geometry as the foundational example of proper reasoning.

Walker examines closely the relationship between sovereignties and boundary conditions. He unveils how both Hobbes and Kant, in their own peculiar mode, argue that drawing lines in terms of boundaries, distinctions, divisions, discriminations, exclusions and frames is necessary for the constitution of modern sovereign authority, but more than that, Walker points out how these authors are simultaneously quite aware of the difficulty, perhaps impossibility, of drawing those lines. This makes sovereignty a serious problem concerning the authorization of authority.[9] This paradox is connected to the fragility of modern forms of discrimination which becomes especially manifest when turning to the international context of pluralism.[10] Walker concludes that, in Hobbes, it is even possible to see that the international has a constitutive outside: an embryonic but highly abstract account of the spatiotemporal world within which international relations must occur.[11]

In his *De Corpore* Thomas Hobbes defines the small beginnings of motion within the body of Man as endeavor or *conatus*, understood as point motion through an indefinitely small space: "to be motion made in less space and time than can be given."[12] It is remarkable that the Hobbesian theory of motion, ultimately

---

8   Walker (n 3) 23–36, 45–6.
9   Walker (n 3) 63, 65, 95, 119, 123, 196–7.
10   Walker (n 3) 124.
11   Walker (n 3) 137, 141, 143.
12   Thomas Hobbes, *The English Works of Thomas Hobbes – Elements of Philosophy. The First Section CONCERNING BODY.* (Scientia Aalen 1962 [1655]) 206.

based on his notion of *conatus* as a motion through a point in an instant, can be seen to have also shaped his theory of sovereignty, and especially the molecular transformation of the multitude into sovereign subjects. This is the kind of drawing of infinitesimally thin lines that is recognized by Walker as characterizing the Hobbesian sovereignty:

> Modern political life does indeed affirm very sharp discriminations. Hobbes relied on an emerging intellectual culture that was much taken with the points, lines and planes of geometrical reason, and with an emerging world of secular authorities struggling with the legacy of authorities emanating from an apparently transcendent and infinite world beyond human knowing. Euclidean lines have zero width. Hobbesian sovereigns are constituted in a single instant.[13]

At stake politically in these debates and quarrels between the transcendental appeal to continuity and infinity and the more modest and sober acknowledgment of limits and boundaries was, and still is, the constitution of order and authorization of authority. This reminds one of how regimes in power are fond of presenting themselves as an order that effectively suspends history and thereby fixes the existing state of affairs for eternity, just like Hardt and Negri describe the Empire in action. Therefore, it is always and again important to challenge those foundational attempts in which a worldly, discrete and finite order is presented as if it were an actualization of the heavenly city on earth, for example, in terms of static economic equilibrium or other idols of stability.[14] Such a challenge must pay careful attention to how lines are drawn especially in those *fracture zones* where transformations take place. Walker makes the further observation that

> The fracture zones of modern life have become strangely mobile. Discriminations are increasingly a problem. Authorizations are increasingly a problem. Exceptionalisms are increasingly a problem. Boundaries, borders and limits are increasingly a problem. Consequently, sovereignties are increasingly a problem ... [And] [i]nternational relations ... [are also] ... becoming the site at which modern political judgments are coming to be most persistently problematic ... .[15]

At the Crossroads of the International

The European Union (EU) has been conceived as a *polity* but it remains controversial as to what kind of a polity it could be, if it can be one. Such

---

13   Walker (n 3) 142.

14   Stephen Toulmin, 'The Idol of Stability,' *The Tanner Lectures on Human Values* (University of California, February 9–11 1998) 326.

15   Walker (n 3) 147.

conceptions and designs are interpretative choices, drawings of lines, which can be always challenged or at least slightly removed. This puzzle is the central question of this article and it will be approached as a *problem of relative indeterminacy*.[16] Since the conceptual specificity of the EU as a polity can be approached from an "ascending" as well as "descending" perspective,[17] one easily arrives at a paradox of indeterminacy. The interpretation of the EU as a particular kind of polity is often doctrinally conditioned or framed and such doctrinal outcomes are controversial. Koskenniemi relates this situation to a politics of international law.[18] The site where the meaning of the EU as a polity must be constituted is the fracture zone or schizosphere of the international located between the national and the transnational.

Answers to the tricky question "What kind of a polity is the EU?" are relative to the selected perspective. There are basically three alternatives: past-bound, present-bound and future-bound. The past-bound perspective could be understood as the "ascending" perspective, while the future-bound perspective would be seen as the "descending" perspective. Koskenniemi connects, in the practice of international law, the "ascending" perspective to *apology* and the "descending" perspective to *utopia*. Koskenniemi concludes that international law is left to oscillate between these two poles.[19] Koskenniemi's distinction between the "ascending" and the "descending" patterns of justification – following Walter Ullman[20] – helps in figuring out how different attempts to define the EU as a polity have justified their claims. In Koskenniemi's analytical design the "descending" pattern is seen to privilege normativity over concreteness. The concrete starting point of the "ascending" pattern is linked with state behavior, will and interest.[21] It could thus be claimed that the EU seen as a particular kind of polity starting from the national state behavior, will, and interest would follow an "ascending" pattern of justification. Examples of such attempts are not only confined to descriptions of the EU as a superstate, but can be understood to cover all those attempts which take a State as an affirmative or critical point of origin for their reflections on the EU as a polity. The EU seen as a particular kind of polity starting from the transnational normative order could be claimed to follow a "descending" pattern of justification. Examples of such attempts include descriptions of the EU as an empire besides all other truly transnationally determined forms of organization. Finally, the present-bound perspective opens up to the discourse of constitutional pluralism.

---

16   Martti Koskenniemi, *From Apology to Utopia. The Structure of International Legal Argument* (Finnish Lawyers' Publishing Company 1989) 20–25.

17   Koskenniemi (n 16) 40–42.

18   Koskenniemi (n 16) 52–4.

19   Koskenniemi (n 16) 66.

20   Walter Ullmann, *Law and Politics in the Middle Ages. An introduction to the Sources of Medieval Political Ideas* (Cambridge University Press 1975) 30–31.

21   Koskenniemi (n 16) 41.

Martti Koskenniemi has pointed out how Thomas Hobbes argued in terms of this double movement by starting "from the non-existence of a constraining natural law to a[n ascending] justification of order by reference to individual ends, associated with a [descending] construction of these ends in terms of an overriding need for security."[22] Koskenniemi emphasizes that for Hobbes social order and legal standards cannot be legitimized by reference to any transcendentally normative ideas since such order is artificial and justifiable only when linked to the concrete passions, desires, wills and interests of individuals.[23] This claim does not, though, fully capture the paradoxical complexity of Hobbes's reasoning.

Martti Koskenniemi has analyzed the paradox of liberal theory of politics informing international law. The reasons for the lack of coherent justification for the international legal system can be found in the contradictory nature of the liberal doctrine of politics.[24] Thomas Hobbes was already aware of this paradox and actually tried to offer a foundational solution to it. Koskenniemi's reconstruction of Hobbes's argument could be understood along these lines. He claims that, in Hobbes, political legitimation loses its *political* character and becomes simply causal, and, therewith, practical reason is transformed into a study of the instrumentalities of power – a descriptive *techne*.[25] However, for this reason, Hobbes may have counted on the natural, autonomous power of artificial mechanisms to order men's living together in such an efficient fashion that there is no need for other than counterfactual political justification according to the concrete wills and interests of individuals. Hobbes seeks to offer a solution to the paradox of liberal political doctrine by displacing politics altogether so that, in the final analysis, politics is taken to express the vanity and vainglory of men driven solely by their passions and drives. Should Thomas Hobbes be then seen as the real founder of an apolitical doctrine or even anti political rationality of government? Would that not be a form of radical liberalism?

The Hobbesian Displacement of Politics

Leo Strauss argued that Thomas Hobbes was a radical liberal. He made the point that "Hobbes's absolutism is in the end nothing but militant liberalism *in statu nascendi*."[26] In these terms, absolutism expresses political indifference and profound skepticism about the problem-solving capacity of politics in motion. Strauss further claims that Hobbes provided a justification for liberalism "with a

---

22 Koskenniemi (n 16) 59.

23 Koskenniemi (n 16) 6, 59.

24 Koskenniemi (n 16) 44, 47.

25 Koskenniemi (n 16) 61–2.

26 Leo Strauss, *Hobbes's Critique of Religion and Related Writings* (The University of Chicago Press 2011) 122.

radicalness that has never again been achieved."[27] One cannot but be impressed by the force and acuity of Strauss's conclusion:

> It is to the opposition so understood (between vanity and fear) which is never again developed as purely, as deeply, and as frankly as it is by Hobbes, that one must go back if one wishes to understand the ideal of liberalism ... in its foundations. For each battle against the political in the name of the economic presupposes a preceding depreciation of the political. But this depreciation is carried out in such a way that the political, as the domain of vanity, prestige, the desire for importance, is opposed, either in a veiled or in an open manner, to the economic as the world of rational "matter of fact," modest work.[28]

Though I do not consider Hobbes to be any sort of a liberal[29] – rather a radical, authoritarian rationalist – I find Leo Strauss's arguments about the Hobbesian displacement of politics very perceptive. Hobbes's depreciation of the political can be understood to ultimately take place in the name of the economic.[30] The big picture of Hobbes's radically authoritarian and possessive reasoning can be figured out by first tracing carefully his inferential paths and then by looking at this complex geometrical configuration of lines, boundaries and distinctions at a distance. As already noted, it all starts with "[t]hese small beginnings of Motion, within the body of Man, before they appear in walking, speaking, striking, and other visible actions [that] are commonly called ENDEAVOUR."[31] This endeavor or *conatus* as point motion through an infinitely small space, or an "enhancement of vital motion," [32] is caused by passions called desire, appetite, aversion, hate, joy, grief, hate, love,[33] which also explains why there is a general inclination of

---

27   Strauss (n 26).

28   Strauss (n 26) 135.

29   Judith N Shklar is uncompromising on this point: "No theory that gives public authorities the unconditional right to impose beliefs and even a vocabulary as they may see fit upon the citizenry can be described as even remotely liberal. Of all the cases made against liberalism, the most bizarre is that liberals are really indifferent, if not openly hostile, to personal freedom. This may follow from the peculiar identification of *Leviathan* as the very archetype of liberal philosophy, but it is a truly gross misrepresentation which simply assures that any social contract theory, however authoritarian its intentions, and any anti-Catholic polemic add up to liberalism." See Judith. N Shklar, *Political Thought & Political Thinkers* (The University of Chicago Press 1998) 6.

30   Hobbes's understanding of the value of man makes this point clear: "The *Value* or WORTH of man, is as of all other things, his Price; that is to say, so much as would be given for the use of his Power; and therefore is not absolute; but a thing dependent on the need and judgement of another." See Thomas Hobbes, *Leviathan* (ed. CP Macpherson, Penguin Books 1976[1651]) 151–2.

31   Hobbes (n 30) 11.

32   Strauss (n 26) 128.

33   Hobbes (n 30) 119, 122.

all mankind, a perpetual and relentless desire for power after Power, a will to Power, "that ceaseth only in death."[34] Hobbes connects pure politics with this desire for power but understands it to take place all too often in such a disorderly and chaotic manner – reminding of his own times – that can only be explained by the passions of vainglorious men in action. He does not, though, deny that in their state of nature individuals are not only free but they have a natural right to strive for power, and get involved in politics, if that is seen as an attempt for the preservation of their life.

For Hobbes the absolute unrest and the entire dangerousness and endangeredness of man to man and of mankind in the world are the source of natural right.[35] The natural right refers to individual freedom. It signifies the liberty with which each individual uses his will and power for the preservation of his own life and nature, which is the "unqualifiedly justified claim by man."[36] Hobbes, then, makes a distinction between natural right and natural law. The preservation of life is the ground for natural right, but the fear of violent death due to an attack by other men, i.e. fear as a voice of reason,[37] is the ground for natural law. In the experience of fear of violent death the passions that incline men to peace are encouraged by reason. Therefore, for Hobbes, a law of nature (*Lex Naturalis*) is a general rule, discovered by reason, by which a man is forbidden to do that which is destructive to his life. Man is, thus, obliged to do something beneficial for himself. For this reason, Hobbes argues, law and right differ as much as obligation and liberty.[38]

This argumentation leads to the conclusion that to endeavor toward peace, security and order, men as the many (multitude) must transfer their natural right to the one that becomes *sovereign* due to this *contract* (*pact* or *covenant*) and by so doing they themselves become both obliged as subjects and, thereafter, bound together mainly by awe and fear as endeavoring humans in *society*. Therefore, it must be emphasized that just like the sovereign state can be understood as the outcome of the contract made by every one of the many with every other of the many,[39] so society can be understood as the outcome of the bond or bonds "that have their strength, not from their own Nature, but from Feare of some evil consequence upon the rupture."[40] In this way, the living together in society, intelligible as a market society, is a sign that the three principal causes of human quarrel (competition, diffidence, glory) are effectively governed. There is, though, another aspect to the bond between men, *the ban*, which draws a line or boundary between the many and those who are left out or cast out of society.[41]

---

34   Hobbes (n 30) 161.
35   Strauss (n 26) 141.
36   Hobbes (n 30) 189; Strauss (n 26) 133.
37   Strauss (n 26) 128–32.
38   Hobbes (n 30) 189.
39   Hobbes (n 30) 228.
40   Hobbes (n 30) 192.
41   Hobbes (n 30) 205.

The Hobbesian Baroque Reason

In the Hobbesian style of reasoning the "ascending" analysis and the "descending" analysis rotate rather than just follow each other. The "ascending" analysis starts with passions, liberty, state of nature, will to power, politics as vanity and natural right, and, in this trajectory, proceeds to the act of making a sovereign contract. In contrast to this, the "descending" analysis starts with the idol of stability (kingdom of God on earth), experience of fear of violent death, as a voice of reason and the ground for natural law, and thereby, proceeds to private acts materializing in those bonds – and bans – which actually make up the threads of society. The end result of this double movement is to safeguard order and security between men by obliging them doubly. In this way, society is finally sketched as a market society and the battle against the political (vanity) in the name of the economic reason has been conducted and concluded in unison with the constitution of sovereignty and state. This kind of double movement of the Hobbesian reasoning can be outlined in Figure 5.1 in such a manner that actually reveals even more of what is involved here than just the double lines drawn by the "ascending" and "descending" moves.

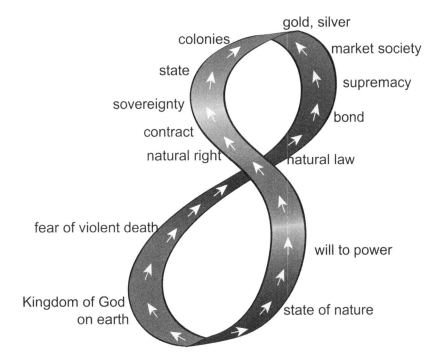

Figure 5.1   Hobbesian fold
Source: Puro S/THL.

This figure roughly illustrates how lines are drawn in the Hobbesian intellectual matrix not just as a double movement between "ascending" and "descending" lines but also as the generation of a baroque spiral or fold. The Hobbesian political imagination cannot be reduced to a sovereign obsession with absolute centers, countable numbers and unambiguous straight lines determinative of bounded strongholds, as Pickstock claims.[42] The baroque fold might be identified rather with the Möbius strip.[43] What actually is reflected here is the intertwining of *rule* and *governance*, the genealogy of which has been traced in detail by Giorgio Agamben in his book *The Kingdom and the Glory*.[44] He has demonstrated that two juxtaposed but functionally related paradigms derive from Christian theology: political theology and economic theology. He argues that "[p]olitical philosophy and the modern theory of sovereignty derive from the first paradigm; modern biopolitics up to the current triumph of economy and government over every other aspect of social life derive from the second paradigm."[45]

Leo Strauss claims that Hobbes does not borrow from the religious tradition and this is the key to his radical liberalism. This argument is actually challenged by Leo Strauss himself in his text *Hobbes's Critique of Religion and Related Writings*.[46] After making it clear that revelation is the true object of Hobbes's critique of religion, as it is opposed to reason, Strauss further argues that Hobbes introduced a thoroughly heterodox idea that man was created for immortality by God but in the meaning of *eternal life on earth*. In other words, Hobbes claimed or wanted to claim that God promised for humans an *earthly* reward for their obedience, i.e. a Kingdom of God on Earth.[47] Hobbes wanted to make sure that the fear and awe of death, the necessary precondition for the constitution of commonwealth, would not be jeopardized by the even stronger existential threat of eternal damnation. Hobbes reasoned that the Kingdom of God on Earth does not refer to any such automatically given natural order revealing God's invisible hand but to order and stability, which must be constitutionally constructed according to the rule of reason.

---

42   Catherine Pickstock, 'Numbers and Lines: Metaphysics and the Problem of International Order' *Oxford Journal of Law and Religion* (November 3 2012) 1 <http://ojlr. oxfordjournals.org/content/early/2012/11/03/ojlr.rws040.full> accessed 19 September 2013.

43   Didier Bigo and RBJ Walker, 'Political Sociology and the Problem of the International' (2007) 35 *Millenium: Journal of International Studies* 725.

44   Giorgio Agamben, *The Kingdom and the Glory. For a Theological Genealogy of Economy and Government* (translated from Italian by L Chiesa, Stanford University Press 2011).

45   Agamben (n 44). It is noteworthy that the "economic theology" which for centuries was concealed appeared again in the writings of Leibniz, who has been also recognized to be the true originator of the "spirit of capitalism." See Jon Elster, *Leibniz et la formation de l'esprit capitaliste* (Editions Aubier 1975).

46   Strauss (n 26).

47   Strauss (n 26) 40.

Leviathan can be read as an unfolding process depicted as a baroque spiral. It all starts with the state of nature. Though not a real state of war it can still be modally contrasted with the Kingdom of God on Earth, just as disorder can be contrasted with the potentiality of order; this idol of stability can, therefore, be seen as the utopian starting point for the descending analysis. Hobbes takes the next step by juxtaposing emotions as will to power with reason as fear of violent death, which is followed by the contrast between natural right as liberty with natural law as obligation,[48] and from there the analysis ascends to the foundational (p)act of contract or covenant.[49] Hobbes states doubly that by either transferring or renouncing one's natural rights by way of contract, a person is simultaneously said to become obliged or bound. Men are obliged by bonds which are sealed by contract and rationalized by natural law, and they are formatively linked to the governing practices of social life. Therefore, bonds do not have their strength from their own nature but from fear of some evil consequence.[50] It is possible to understand that there is another side to the governing practice of bonding, and that is the ban. If people are brought and kept together socially by bonds, some of them are simultaneously cast out of society by the ban. For this reason Giorgio Agamben has emphasized the contrast between contract and ban in Hobbes.[51]

The processes of contracting and bonding are displays of the transformation of the metamorphic subject of multitude. The multitude so united can be called COMMON-WEALTH.[52] Even though Hobbes identifies commonwealth with Leviathan, it must be understood to cover both state and society as an inclusive notion of *civitas*. This kind of double perspective is consistent with the double movement of ascending and descending analysis which further unveils how the constitution of Sovereignty could – in a Ciceronian fashion – be contrasted with Supremacy. In a commonwealth, supremacy cannot be understood, however, as a kind of ghostly authority which challenges sovereignty and the unity of the commonwealth as another master.[53] By calling it secular or temporal supremacy, I simply want to emphasize that sovereign rule and supreme governance must act in unison in an orderly commonwealth. The same request applies equally to the division between state and society, which is finally developed as a relation between absolutist state and market society.

The constitution of an absolutist sovereign state as the body of rule and the construction of a possessive market society as the body of governance together make up the two principal systems of commonwealth. Hobbes actually talks about public and private systems (*Systemes*) as twin parts of commonwealth and refers

---

48 Hobbes (n 30) 188–9, 264–8.

49 Hobbes (n 30) 189–96, 226–7.

50 Hobbes (n 30) 192.

51 Giorgio Agamben, *Homo Sacer: Sovereign Power and Bare Life* (Stanford University Press 1998).

52 Hobbes (n 30) 227.

53 Hobbes (n 30) 370–71.

to them as "any numbers of men joined in one Interest, or one Businesse."[54] The crucial thing to understand in Hobbes is that he develops the modern notion of the artificial absolutist sovereign state in close conjunction with the generation of a possessive market society in which individuals are totally free to pursue their own selfish private interests in order to achieve "commodious living" not violating the laws enacted by the sovereign ruler. According to his radical vision, the foundational task of the absolutist state is to constitutionally order and guarantee the free functioning of this market society by simultaneously recognizing that the self-interested action of commercially spirited individuals can be productive not only of money and riches but of security and stability in society since it displaces political passions with private vices. Hobbes, in fact, might be seen to antedate Mandeville in taking advantage of the rhetorical figure of paradiastole when he says that "(f)rom such reasoning as this, Successful wickedness hath obtained the name of Vertue."[55]

Stability, security and order are definitely the primary goals of Hobbesian radical authoritarian and possessive reasoning. He argues that an orderly commonwealth can be promoted and achieved only by the combined functioning of the rule-making sovereign state and the self-governing market society. In this systemic fashion the negative effects of political factions and strife can be minimized. However, it has been often claimed that Hobbes does not see any chance for such orderly conduct in the context of international relations, which are taken to manifest an anarchical and chaotic condition. This conclusion is understood to represent a realist vision of international politics. However, all those attempts that exploit the Hobbesian notion of the state of nature as a metaphor either for competitive economy, vainglorious politics or international anarchy miss the point; this image is only a starting point for a process of reasoning which, step by step, traces the generation of absolutist sovereign state and possessive market society, leading ultimately beyond these "*Systemes*," as can be recognized in his comments on colonies and money.

Hobbes clearly recognizes the limited possibility that between commonwealths there can be Leagues which "are not onely lawfull, but also profitable for the time they last."[56] He contrasts this occasion for international leagues with the leagues of subjects in a commonwealth, which he considers, for the most part, to be not only unnecessary but even unlawful as factions or conspiracies give good reason to keep politics under the tight control of the state. This comment should be read as a preamble to the section "Of the Nutrition, and Procreation of a Common-Wealth" where Hobbes addresses the questions of colonies and money. It is remarkable to notice that Hobbes assigns "Silver and Gold" not only the function of a common measure of commodities independent of the will of one or a few commonwealths, but also the privilege of making commonwealths move.[57]

---

54 Hobbes (n 30) 274.
55 Hobbes (n 30) 203.
56 Hobbes (n 30) 286.
57 Hobbes writes: "And because Silver and Gold, have their value from the matter itself; they have first this privilege, that the value of them cannot be altered by the power

In this way a commonwealth can stretch outwards, and this inter-generational procreation of a commonwealth can be called a Colony.[58]

The EU – Bound to Dissolve?

I have claimed that we could learn something about the EU by reading this European "polity in the making" through the looking glass of classics, such as Thomas Hobbes. I understand that such a reading represents highly speculative diagnostics that can pose questions and problems while not giving answers. The diagnostic strength of such speculation mainly derives from the quality of the said political imagination. For this reason, I have tried to outline carefully enough the Baroque rationalism of the Hobbesian imaginary which retraces the motions of body. Such an imagination is clearly, though quite unsuccessfully, at work in his mathematical writings, and less clearly but more successfully at work in his political writings. The first thing that must be underscored about Hobbesian imagination is that it is finite: "Whatsoever we imagine, it is Finite. Therefore there is no Idea, or conception of anything we call Infinite."[59] We could call this insight either rationalist or realist, but in doing so, we should again remember that it is as unsuccessful in mathematics as it is successful in politics and political theory.

The finite line of reasoning can be discerned in the way Hobbes visualizes commonwealth as a baroque fold, here, pictured anachronistically as a Möbius strip, or is it a double-helix? This is a particular sort of combinatorial structure which is, however, not a chiral object. In other words, the commonwealth pictured with the right and left edges moving in reverse direction have, thus, congruent counterparts in contrast to the Kantian treatment of the left hand and the right hand of the body as incongruent counterparts.[60] Such a congruence between rule and governance[61] can be understood as safeguarding the cohesion and security of the commonwealth, which is the primary objective of Hobbes's political theory. Hobbes actually claims that the commonwealth dissolves if its powers are divided: "For what is it to divide the Power of a Common-wealth but to dissolve it; for Powers divided mutually destroy each other."[62]

---

of one, nor of a few Common-wealths; as being a common measure of the commodities of all places. But base Mony, may easily be enhanced, or abased. Secondly, they have the privilege to make Common-wealths, move, and stretch out their armes, when need is, into forraign Countries; and supply, not only private Subjects that travel, but also whole Armies with Provision." (Hobbes (n 30) 300–301, also 372–3).

58   Hobbes (n 30) 201, 315, 368.

59   Hobbes (n 30) 99.

60   Immanuel Kant, 'Concerning the Ultimate Ground of the Differentiation of Directions of Space' in D Walford and R Meerbote (eds), *Immanuel Kant, Theoretical Philosophy 1755–1770* (Cambridge University Press 1992) 365.

61   See Shklar (n 29) 216.

62   Hobbes (n 30) 368.

Reading the EU from the Hobbesian perspective undoubtedly leads to the conclusion that as a "polity in the making" the EU has definitely divided its powers and faces the constant danger of fragmentation and dissolution. It might be particularly claimed that for a polity the EU is composed of incongruent counterparts in such a fashion that the right hand (ruling) does not know what the left hand (governing) is doing – indicating that the "Gothick Balance,"[63] or should we rather call it the "Baroque Balance," is in danger. This dilemma has been well captured by Fritz W. Scharpf in his analysis of the asymmetric institutional configuration of the EU. The EU is structured around multiple institutional asymmetries, but the principal one contrasts nationally anchored political ruling and legislative action with the apolitical governance and judicial action extending the Treaty-based rights of private individuals and firms and pushing transnationally forward with the internal market project. This contrast is illuminated in the "joint decision trap."[64]

In the order-thinking of Hobbes there is really no room for the separation of powers, which, it has been claimed, stems from Montesquieu who was also praised by Lord Keynes in his introduction to the French Edition of his *General Theory* as "the real French equivalent of Adam Smith, the greatest of your economists, head and shoulders above the physiocrats in penetration, clearheadedness and good sense."[65] The reason for reminding about Lord Keynes's praise for Montesquieu as the greatest of French economists is that it clearly expresses how Montesquieu, as the pioneer modern thinker believed that there are "laws of society." An example of this is what Albert O. Hirschmann has called the "Montesquieu-Steuart-position": good commerce (between nations) is the best guarantee of peace.[66] This thesis is actually quite analogous with the principle of the separation of powers, which also leans on the idea that antipodean or reciprocal forces or interests can balance each other. It is remarkable that, on this basis, Montesquieu also outlined a new theory of law, claiming that laws are the necessary relations arising from the nature of things.[67] This argument implies that there are laws pre-existing all human laws but that they are neither located definitely in the domain of natural law theology nor in the range of the Hobbesian contract: "That there were laws before laws makes it clear that there is no longer a contract, nor any of the political perils to which the very idea of a contract commits men and governments."[68] Montesquieu's modern

----

63   Shklar (n 29) 216.

64   Fritz W Scharpf, 'The Double Asymmetry of European Integration. Or: Why the EU Cannot Be a Social Market Economy' (2012) 9 *MPIfG Working Paper* 7, 13.

65   John Maynard Keynes, 'The General Theory of Employment, Interest and Money', *The Collected Writings of John Maynard Keynes: Vol II* (Macmillan 1973[1936]) xxxiv–xxxv.

66   Albert Hirschman, *The Passions and the Interests. Political Arguments for Capitalism before Its Triumph* (Princeton University Press 1977) 88.

67   Louis Althusser, *Politics and History. Montesquieu, Rousseau, Hegel and Marx* (Translated from French by B Brewster, NLB 1972) 31.

68   Althusser (n 67) 41.

understanding of law made it possible for him to give a new meaning also to the rule of law "as those institutional restraints that prevent governmental agents from oppressing the rest of society."[69]

These references to Montesquieu have been made to point out that the basic features of the EU as a political market project – peace and virtue through commerce, order and security by separation of powers, freedom and rights of individuals and firms through rule of law – are quite in line with the Montesquieuan heritage, but can be challenged by the Hobbesian radically authoritarian political reason. For Hobbes, just as for Aristotle,[70] the rule of law refers to the rule of reason, which can be trusted in constituting, ruling and governing a commonwealth in an orderly manner – otherwise, without a civil power, man must make custom and example the rule of his actions supplemented by an *Oath*.[71] The making and keeping of a covenant is for Hobbes a rule of reason,[72] which ultimately exploits the psychology of man for unveiling the causes of his actions in the will to power and fear of death.

Judith N. Shklar has aptly pointed out that "Montesquieu really has only one aim, to protect the ruled against the aggression of those who rule. While it embraces all people, it fulfills only one fundamental aim, freedom from fear, which, to be sure, was for Montesquieu supremely important."[73] Freedom from fear, guaranteed by the rule of law, is seen as a consequence of particular institutional restraints on rulers. Montesquieu is primarily worried about the possible despotism of the ruler (the Monarch) and to combat this threat can even be understood as proposing that a well-designed and automatically functioning system is worth striving at – just like functionalism has later found praiseworthy. However, for Hobbes the nature of things and their relations in a commonwealth appear in a totally different light, since without the decisive sovereign will or the genuine fear of sanctions, ultimately death, a commonwealth cannot be seen to be ruled and governed in an orderly fashion. From the Hobbesian perspective the EU has taken it all too much for granted that the internal market project can proceed smoothly as a functional system.

If a foreign ruler or envoy approached the EU from the Hobbesian perspective, his first question would be one of sovereignty and about the sovereign: who decides in this polity? The answer to this question would dictate his consequent behavior, and in a situation of ambiguity and perplexity, as is characteristic of the EU, he would simply have to turn elsewhere. Perhaps a more serious situation of ambiguity in the EU is connected with the immense amount of speech- and text-production, which really makes this "polity to come" look like a "shoot-off-your-mouth" community from the Hobbesian perspective. Hobbes insisted that the rule

---

69   Shklar (n 29) 22.
70   Shklar (n 29) 22–3.
71   Hobbes (n 30) 165, 200.
72   Hobbes (n 30) 189, 205.
73   Shklar (n 29) 24.

of reason entailed rule by words, but immediately added that to rule by words was charged with great risks. For this reason, "he only is properly said to Raigne that governs his Subjects by his Word, and by promise of Rewards to those that obey it, and by threatening them with Punishment that obey it not."[74] The nature of this ambiguity is that it easily entices men to avoid their obligations and even break their contract. Hobbes recognizes only two ways out of this ambiguous dilemma: "The force of Words, being too weak to hold men to the performance of their Convenants; there are in man's nature, but two imaginable helps to strengthen it. And those are either a Feare of the consequence of breaking their word; or a Glory or Pride in appearing not to need break it."[75]

Ever more rapid multiplication of words characterizes the EU as a speech-community that leaves its denizens often quite confused and puzzled. This state of affairs has been quite frankly acknowledged also officially by the EU institutions. In its *White Paper on European Governance*[76] the EU Commission states in the first page of its executive summary that "Many people are losing confidence in a poorly understood and complex system to deliver the policies they want. The Union is often seen as remote and at the same time too intrusive."[77] Understandably this confidence in the "System" has not increased following the severe financial, economic, political, social, and even existential crisis of the present EU.

The very first sentence of the *White Paper on European Governance* actually repeats the verdict of the Trilateral Commission's report *The Crisis of Democracy*[78] by referring to the paradox of democracy: on the one hand, citizens make more and more demands on democratic political institutions and want them to find solutions to the major problems confronting societies, but, on the other hand, people increasingly distrust these institutions and politics, or are simply not interested in them.[79] To solve this paradox the Trilateral Commission actually proposed that democracy should be better managed in order to shackle its excesses. In line with this proposition, new forms of governance have been introduced and many of their techniques have been borrowed from the managerial methods of private markets, as is evident in the New Public Management solutions.

It is not surprising that Mario Monti, the former European Chairman of the Trilateral Commission (until 2011) and a member of the EU Commission in charge of the Internal Market, Financial Services, Customs and Tax Policy (1995–1999) and later of Competition (1999–2004), explicitly requested in

---

74   Hobbes (n 30) 388–9.

75   Hobbes (n 30) 200.

76   Commission of the European Communities, *European Governance. A White Paper*, 25 July 2001. COM(2001) 428 final

77   Commission (n 76) 3.

78   Michel Crozier, Samuel Huntington and Joji Watanuki, *The Crisis of Democracy. Report on the Governability of Democracies to the Trilateral Commission* (New York University Press 1975).

79   Commission (n 76) 3; Crozier, Huntington and Watanuki (n 78).

2012, in circumstances of the EU financial crisis, that the Finns – obviously the power-holders – should keep better control of their parliamentary debates so as not to disturb the markets.[80] Even though Monti later qualified his statement, the Trilateral point remains: democracy must be managed in the market economy for reasons of order and stability. Even if similar points can be found in the White Paper, the overall tenor of this document is still rather different.

The requests that "democracy must be managed" or "politics must be domesticated" are familiar arguments to whoever reads carefully how Thomas Hobbes writes about the perils and pitfalls of vainglorious men, religious and political factions, and parties against the power of commonwealth.[81] Hobbes thinks that leagues of subjects that are in commonwealth are for the most part unnecessary,[82] especially since vainglorious desires for power and "perpetuell and restlesse desire of Power after Power" is seen by him to be characteristic of man.[83] And because genuine glory and pride of human character are so rare in practice, the only means to safeguard the order of commonwealth is by making men aware and fear that breaking their word has unavoidable consequences. Therefore "it is no wonder if there be somewhat else required (besides covenant) to make their Agreement constant and lasting; which is a Common Power to keep them in awe and to direct their actions to the Common Benefit."[84] This common power is sovereign authority.

From State to Empire

From the Hobbesian – radical, authoritarian, rationalistic – perspective, the EU lacks in sovereignty as common power. This lack of sovereignty can be best recognized in the inter-zone between the national and the transnational, which is still the principal space of EU action. In this space the EU, if seen as a polity, has been typically characterized, in various ways, as constitutionally pluralist. Constitutional pluralism is undoubtedly incompatible with the Hobbesian idea of sovereignty – or the sovereign – which is unitary to the core, as Ola Zetterquist has rightly emphasized.[85] However, he continues by claiming that "Nor can the EU, on a Hobbesian reading, have replaced the former constitutions (of member states)

---

80   Mario Monti, '"Eine Front zwischen Nord und Süd" Das Gespräch mit Mario Monti führten die Redakteure F. Ehlers und H. Hoyng' 32 *Spiegel* (August 6 2012) 44–6.

81   Hobbes (n 30) 125, 285–7.

82   Hobbes (n 30) 286.

83   Hobbes (n 30) 16.

84   Hobbes (n 30) 226–7.

85   Ola Zetterquist, 'Out with the New, in with the Old – Neo-Roman Constitutional Thought and the Enigma of Constitutional Pluralism in the EU' in M Avbelj and J Komárek (eds), *Constitutional Pluralism in the European Union and Beyond* (Hart Publishing 2012) 219.

since the EU is not a state."[86] In other words, Zetterquist claims that "sovereignty" and "state" go together or belong very closely together.[87]

Already in the first page of his introduction to *Leviathan* Thomas Hobbes equates commonwealth with the state: "For by Art is created that great LEVIATHAN called a COMMON-WEALTH or STATE (in latine CIVITAS) which is but an Artificial MAN ... ."[88] But it must be remembered, just as Judith N Shklar has emphasized, that "Hobbes did argue for sovereignty as a logical necessity and rejected historical arguments as uncertain and merely prudential."[89] In this rationalistic and counterfactual light it is quite possible to imagine a Hobbesian commonwealth which need not be confined to state boundaries, since "to draw a picture in little, or as great, or greater then the life, are different degrees of Art."[90] Therefore, to draw a picture of a commonwealth as an empire and not just as a state would express a different degree of the Hobbesian Art.

The latter-day neoconservatives, like Robert Kagan in the US, have found Thomas Hobbes viable for their advocacy and for the designation of the US global power as the "benevolent empire."[91] In this neoconservative discourse the US is pictured as a "Behemoth with a conscience,"[92] which is seen to champion not only the best interests of the US but also that of the world. Thomas Hobbes has been, thus, drawn on to extol the US as the hegemonic keeper of world order in this new era of unipolarity. Kagan argues that Europe lives now in a Kantian dream while America, as the unipolar global hegemon, acts in a Hobbesian reality.[93] This reality as practically seen is based on a reading of one passage in *Leviathan*, where Hobbes compares inter-state relations to the state and posture of gladiators.[94]

Different readings of Thomas Hobbes offer different political imaginaries for diagnosing the (history of the) present. Without mentioning the neocons, RBJ Walker clarifies how steps towards an empire can take place: "What counts for politics within one specific state is easily equated with what must count as politics in all other states, in the world as such. This is especially the prerogative

---

86   Zetterquist (n 85).

87   Zetterquist (n 85) 216.

88   Hobbes (n 30) 81.

89   Shklar (n 29) 217.

90   Hobbes (n 30) 138.

91   Robert Kagan, 'The Benevolent Empire' (1998) 111 *Foreign Policy* 24.

92   Robert Kagan, *Of Paradise and Power: America and Europe in the New World Order* (Knopf 2003).

93   Kagan (n 92); Jacobus Delwaide and Jorg Kustermans, 'Imperium en veiligheid: de zoektocht naar legitimiteit' (2008) 50 *Res Publica: politiek-wetenschappelijk tijdschrift van de Lage Landen* 5–30.

94   Hobbes (n 30) 187–8. There are, however, others like Anthony Pagden who have argued that the Europeans "by attempting to isolate the European Union as far as possible from all forms of external conflict that are considered to pose no immediate domestic threat – are the true Hobbesians" (Anthony Pagden, 'Imperialism, liberalism & the quest for perpetual peace' (2005) 134 *Daedalus* 56).

of the hegemonic: the hegemonic both in the sense of the great powers capable of imposing themselves upon all other states, thereby pushing at the limits of the distinction between a system of states that is the setting of modern politics and some other world for which we have tended to reserve the name (and the epithet) of empire."[95] But as Walker continues, there is a Hobbesian counter-reading to this imaginary and it emphasizes the role of hegemonic states and not that of a potential empire. What is ultimately at stake in these readings are such questions as "But which comes first? Who draws the line? Who, or what, decides?"[96]

However we draw a picture of the EU, it is quite impossible to make it meet the standards set by Hobbes for a secure and orderly commonwealth that can be seen as a state or superstate. For this it is an altogether too hybrid, composite, multipolar and heterarchical structure. No wonder then that many attempts have been recently made to characterize the EU as reminiscent of pre-modern empires. Jose Manuel Barroso has called it a non-imperial empire;[97] Ulrich Beck and Edgar Grande have talked about the cosmopolitan empire of Europe;[98] Magali Gravier has characterized the EU as the composite empire of all on all;[99] Kazuto Suzuki has defined the EU as a regulatory empire;[100] while Jan Zielonka, Ola Zetterquist, and Russell Foster have particularly seen the EU developing towards a kind of Neo-Roman empire.[101]

Jan Zielonka argues that the EU is no superstate but rather a new form of neo-medievalism in the making.[102] Ola Zetterquist considers that if there cannot be a sovereign EU, could there be a republican one? He thinks that the constitutional order of the EU echoes Cicero's definition of the republic as a community based on legal argument and community of interest.[103] Russell Foster explicitly connects the EU with Cicero's idea of *patrocinium* in contrast to *imperium*. He describes the EU as:

> This collective commonwealth of shared values, shared power and shared identity is "empire" in its classic Ciceronian context – not a vicious, expansionist

---

95   Walker (n 3) 76.

96   Walker (n 3) 76.

97   Jose Manuel Barroso, 'Non-Imperial Empire' *The Brussels Journal* (Brussels 11 July 2007) <www.brusselsjournal.com/node/2244> accessed 19 September 2013.

98   Ulrich Beck and Edgar Grande, *Das kosmopolitische Europa: Gesellschaft und Politik in der Zweiten Moderne* (Suhrkamp 2004).

99   Magali Gravier, 'The Next European Empire' (2009) 11 *European Societies* 627.

100   Kazuto Suzuki, 'EU as a "regulatory empire"' (2009) 2 *Shin-Sedai Houseisaku-Gaku Kenkyuu* (Sapporo) 141.

101   Jan Zielonka, *Europe as Empire. The Nature of the Enlarged European Union* (Oxford University Press 2006); Zetterquist (n 85); Russell Foster, '*Tege Imperium!*: a Defence of Empire' (Global Discourse 2010) <http://global-discourse.com/contents/tege-imperium-a-defence-of-empire-by-russell-foster> accessed 19 September 2013.

102   Zielonka (n 101).

103   Zetterquist (n 85) 227.

power bent on suppressing its neighbours but a benign empire. It differs from Cicero's model of *patrocinium* in that rather than a single paternalistic patron establishing its will upon its neighbours in order to establish peace beneficial to all, the modern European supra-state combines collective patronage and collective *imperium* to establish an ethnically heterogeneous empire and a universalistic normative order upon an otherwise perpetually-feuding continent of particularistic nation-states.[104]

These Neo-Roman and republican interpretations of the EU's future naturally exemplify a descending type of analysis which posit more or less a utopia. The utopian quality of such empire-projections for the EU is very conspicuous in the recent intervention by Giorgio Agamben, who suggested that the "Latin Empire" should strike back in this context of European transformation.[105] Taking Alexandre Kojève's famous 1945 memo *The Latin Empire: Outline of a doctrine for French Policy*[106] as a positive starting point, Giorgio Agamben suggested that there is now an urgent need for the "Latin Empire" as a counter-weight to the decisively dominant role of Germany in the European Union.[107] This is a most paradoxical proposal since it is motivated by the experienced danger of the disintegration of the Union. From the Hobbesian perspective, such a proposal, even though reasoned in terms of the balance of forces, would merely lead to further disintegration and dissolution of the Union seen as a polity. This kind of Hobbesian counterargument illustrates an ascending type of analysis that is anchored in the notion of state sovereignty.

But where are we now in the EU? Where and how should we draw the line between sovereignty of the state and supremacy of the empire? Talking in terms of constitutional pluralism does not help much in this cartographic exercise, since it only expresses some kind of indefinite "betweenness" and "indeterminacy." A more salient conceptual tool was already offered by Gottfried Wilhelm Leibniz, who applied in his early manuscripts on natural right and state the concept of *retrotraction* (*retrotractio*).[108] Retrotraction refers to "the process wherein a knowing subject realizes an event he is experiencing is part of a longer historical chain and hence attains genuine understanding of the event at hand for the first time."[109]

---

104   Foster (n 101).

105   Giorgio Agamben, 'L' "impero latino" contro l'egemonia tedesca' *Repubblica* (15 May 2013) <www.presseurop.eu/it/content/article/3593291-l-impero-latino-contro-l-egemonia-tedesca> accessed 19 September 2013.

106   Aleksandre Kojève, 'Outline of a Doctrine of French Policy' (2004[1945]) 126 *Policy Review* (translated by E de Vries) 3.

107   Agamben (n 105).

108   Gottfried Wilhelm Leibniz, *Frühe Schriften zum Naturrecht: lateinisch–deutsch.* Herausgegeben, mit einer Einleitung und Anmerkungen versehen sowie unter Mitwirkung von H Zimmermann (Translated by H Busche, Felix Meiner 2003[1669–1671] 160; William F Drischler, 'Retrotraction and the Young Leibniz's Critique of Hobbesian Sovereignty Notions' (2011) 5 *Kritike* 99,100.

109   Drischler (n 108) 99, 100.

If the event under consideration were the EU, then to understand its retrotraction dynamics would demand that it should be analyzed in the whole European cross-border history which is not circumscribed by national borders. The context of Leibniz's own anti-Hobbesian retrotractive analysis in his early 1669–1671 manuscript *Elements of Natural Right* (*Frühe Schriften zum Naturrecht*)[110] was primarily the Holy Roman Empire of Germany which certainly did not exhibit the unitary political order and indivisible sovereignty which Hobbes propagated. In sharp contrast to Hobbes, Leibniz did not argue that without such a unitary political structure and will, the federation in question was doomed to dissolve. On the contrary, Leibniz argued – taking the split sovereignty of the post-1648 *Reich* as his reference – that as long as the subjects do not "retrotract" unduly (connect local security problems historically with system-wide problems) "then it is not necessary that security be present factually (in the manner in which it has been claimed)."[111] Naturally the implied claim refers to the Hobbesian idea of a unitary security order characteristic of his modern sovereign state.

Instead of the unitary sovereign state imagined by Hobbes as the sole secure political order, Leibniz prefers to outline the dynamics of a qualitatively different polity, a "system of federated states" (*systema civitatum foederatarum*).[112] This system is a "pluralistic formation of entities which guarantee security for one another" (*civitas multitudo formam habens praestantium sibi securitatem*).[113] Such a "system of federated states," even though or even because it lacks unitary and indivisible sovereign structures, can be resilient, flexible and adaptive, as it does not easily dissolve even if security, due to crisis, for example, has been already partially broken up, but is not yet manifest to the public at large.

It is now quite easy to imagine that a similar kind of situation – retrotractive evental dynamics – characterizes the EU as "system of federated states to come." Whether this is the most probable future of the EU is an open question that has not been tackled directly in this chapter. But it can be, nevertheless, claimed that the Hobbesian alternative is not an option for the EU as long as its citizens' happiness is not subordinated to the stipulations of the sovereign or other unitary security order. The crucial difference between Hobbes and Leibniz is that for Leibniz the security of a polity is best guaranteed by the happiness of its citizens so that "security is the improbability of unhappiness" (*miseriae improbabilitas*).[114] If this is the *Leitmotiv* in the generation of the EU, then one is truly following Leibniz and Kant, rather than Hobbes.

---

110   Leibniz (n 108). Leibniz later continued in his magnum opus against Hobbes *Caesarini Fürstenerii* of 1677 (Gottfried Wilhelm Leibniz, *Caesarini Fürstenerii tractatus de jure suprematus ac legationis principum germaniae* (apud Joannem Danielem Tauberum 1696[1677]).
111   Leibniz (n 108) 158; Drischler (n 108) 99, 102.
112   Leibniz (n 108).
113   Leibniz (n 108).
114   Leibniz (n 108) 160; Drischler (n 108) 99, 103.

Bibliography

Agamben G, *Homo Sacer: Sovereign Power and Bare Life* (Stanford University Press 1998)

—— *The Kingdom and the Glory. For a Theological Genealogy of Economy and Government*, (Translated from Italian by L Chiesa, Stanford University Press 2011)

—— 'L'impero latino" contro l'egemonia tedesca' *La Repubblica* (15 May 2013) <http://www.presseurop.eu/it/content/article/3593291-l-impero-latino-control-egemonia-tedesca> accessed 19 September 2013

Althusser L, *Politics and History. Montesquieu, Rousseau, Hegel and Marx* (Translated from French by B Brewster, NLB 1972)

Antognazza MR, *Leibniz. An Intellectual Biography* (Cambridge University Press 2009)

Barroso JM, 'Non-Imperial Empire' *The Brussels Journal* (Brussels 11 July 2007) <http://www.brusselsjournal.com/node/2244> accessed 19 September 2013

Beck U, and Grande E, *Das kosmopolitische Europa: Gesellschaft und Politik in der Zweiten Moderne* (Suhrkamp 2004)

Bernstorff J von, 'Sisyphus was an international lawyer. On Martti Koskenniemi's "From Apology to Utopia" and the place of law in international politics' (2006) 7 *German Law Journal* 1015–35

Bigo D, and Walker RBJ, 'Political Sociology and the Problem of the International' (2007) *Millenium: Journal of International Studies* 725–40

Cohen JL, 'Whose Sovereignty? Empire Versus International Law' (2004) 18 *Ethics & International Affairs* 1

Commission of the European Communities, 25 July 2001, 'European Governance. A White Paper' COM(2001) 428 final

Crozier M, Huntington S, and Watanuki J, *The Crisis of Democracy. Report on the Governability of Democracies to the Trilateral Commission* (New York University Press 1975)

Delwaide J, and Kustermans J, 'Imperium en veiligheid: de zoektocht naar legitimiteit' (2008) 50 *Res Publica: politiek-wetenschappelijk tijdschrift van de Lage Landen* 5

Drischler WF, 'Retrotraction and the Young Leibniz's Critique of Hobbesian Sovereignty Notions' (2011) 5 *Kritike* 99

Elster J, *Leibniz et la formation de l'esprit capitaliste* (Editions Aubier 1975)

Foster R, '*Tege Imperium!*: a Defence of Empire' (Global Discourse 2010) <http://global-discourse.com/contents/tege-imperium-a-defence-of-empire-by-russell-foster> accessed 19 September 2013.

Gravier M, 'The Next European Empire' (2009) 11 *European Societies* 627

Hardt M, and Negri A, *Empire* (Harvard University Press 2000)

Hirschman A, *The Passions and the Interests. Political Arguments for Capitalism before Its Triumph* (Princeton University Press 1977)

Hobbes T, *Leviathan* (Edited with an introduction by CP Macpherson, Penguin books 1976[1651]
—— *The English Works of Thomas Hobbes – Elements of Philosophy. The First Section CONCERNING BODY.* (Scientia Aalen, 1962)
Kagan R, 'The Benevolent Empire' (1998) 111 *Foreign Policy* 24
—— *Of Paradise and Power: America and Europe in the New World Order* (Knopf 2003)
Kant I, 'Concerning the Ultimate Ground of the Differentiation of Directions of Space' in D Walford and R Meerbote (eds), *Immanuel Kant, Theoretical Philosophy 1755–1770* (Cambridge University Press 1992) 365
Keynes JM, 'The General Theory of Employment, Interest and Money' in *The Collected Writings of John Maynard Keynes: Vol II* (Macmillan 1973[1936])
Kojève A, 'Outline of a Doctrine of French Policy' (2004[1945]) 126 *Policy Review* (translated by E de Vries) 3
Koskenniemi M, *From Apology to Utopia. The Structure of International Legal Argument* (Finnish Lawyers' Publishing Company 1989)
Leibniz GW, *Frühe Schriften zum Naturrecht: lateinisch–deutsch.* Herausgegeben, mit einer Einleitung und Anmerkungen versehen sowie unter Mitwirkung von H Zimmermann (Translated by H Busche, Felix Meiner 2003[1669–1671]
—— *Caesarini Füstenerii tractatus de jure suprematus ac legationis principum germaniae* (Apud Joannem Danielem Tauberum 1696[1677])
Monti M, '"Eine Front zwischen Nord und Süd" Das Gespräch mit Mario Monti führten die Redakteure F Ehlers und H Hoyng' 32 *Spiegel* (August 6 2012) 44
Pagden A, 'Imperialism, liberalism & the quest for perpetual peace' (2005) 134(2) Daedalus 46–57
Pickstock C, 'Numbers and Lines: Metaphysics and the Problem of International Order' *Oxford Journal of Law and Religion* (November 3 2012) 1 <http://ojlr.oxfordjournals.org/content/early/2012/11/03/ojlr.rws040.full> accessed 19 September 2013
Scharpf FW, 'The Double Asymmetry of European Integration. Or: Why the EU Cannot Be a Social Market Economy' (2012) 9 *MPIfG Working Paper* 1
Shklar JN, *Political Thought & Political Thinkers* (The University of Chicago Press 1998)
Strauss L, *Hobbes's Critique of Religion and Related Writings* (The University of Chicago Press 2011)
Suzuki K, 'EU as a "regulatory empire"' (2009) 2 *Shin-Sedai Houseisaku-Gaku Kenkyuu* (Sapporo) 141
Toulmin S, 'The Idol of Stability' *The Tanner Lectures on Human Values* (University of California, February 9–11 1998) 326
Ullmann W, *Law and Politics in the Middle Ages. An introduction to the Sources of Medieval Political Ideas* (Cambridge University Press 1975)
Walker RBJ, *After the Globe, Before the World* (Routledge 2010)

Zetterquist O, 'Out with the New, in with the Old – Neo-Roman Constitutional Thought and the Enigma of Constitutional Pluralism in the EU' in M Avbelj and J Komárek (eds), *Constitutional Pluralism in the European Union and Beyond* (Hart Publishing 2012)

Zielonka J, *Europe as Empire. The Nature of the Enlarged European Union* (Oxford University Press 2006)

Chapter 6

Reinventing European Democracy
Democratization and the
Existential Crisis of the EU

Ari Hirvonen

'Soyez réalistes, demandez l'impossible'

May 1968 slogan

Introduction: 300 Years of European Union

The peace conference that produced the Treaty of Utrecht influenced one of its delegates, Charles-Irénée Castel, abbé de Saint-Pierre, to propose in 1713 a permanent and perpetual union of European sovereigns. For this reason, 'eighteen principal Christian sovereignties' ought to form 'l'Union européenne'.[1] The concept of the European Union was thereby launched.

Voltaire was not convinced of the proposal for the European Union. For him, this kind of peace union was nothing but a chimera which cannot exist 'among Princes any more than it does among elephants and rhinoceroses or between wolves and dogs'.[2]

As the European sovereign debt crisis, and also the broader European economic and financial crisis, has turned into a deep political and social crisis for the EU, one may wonder whether Voltaire had the last word. At the very least, in its profoundness the EU's multifaceted crisis is an existential one. To analyse and confront this crisis I will address two questions concerning the existential crisis and its relation to democracy at the European level.

Before David Marquand used the phrase 'the democratic deficit' in 1979 to describe the lack of democratic accountability and legitimacy of European Community institutions,[3] the phrase was mentioned in the manifesto of the Young European Federalists (JEF) dating back to 1977. The manifesto speaks of a sense of alienation and a lack of confidence in the ability of the European political and economic system to solve problems. For this reason, not only should institutions

---

1 Charles Irénée Castel De Saint-Pierre, *Projet pour rendre la paix perpétuelle en Europe* (Chez A Schouten 1713) vii–viii.

2 Voltaire, 'De la paix perpétuelle. Par le docteur Goodheart' (Oeuvres complètes. Tome I. Politiques et législation, Armand-Aubrée éditeur 1829) 25.

3 See David Marquand, *Parliament for Europe* (J Cape 1979).

capable of solving Europe-wide problems be created but also people ought to be given control over their own lives and the concept of democracy should be given meaning.[4]

Even if the phrase has become a commonplace, even a cliché, a lack of democracy in the EU plays a major part in the ongoing existential crisis.[5] Instead of the democratic deficit, I will speak of a lack of democracy, since deficit refers to an economic fact, a shortfall in revenue, which can be managed by means of rational and reasonable economic management. A shortfall in democracy is thus a gentrified version of a lack of democracy, which is a *political* issue and problem.

Therefore, the first question is, *has the process of democratization taken place in the EU?* To answer this, I will consider the democratization process not merely on the level of constitutional changes and as a process of parliamentarization but also as an enhancement of participation. Moreover, I will consider the fate of this process in the context of the EU crisis management.

Second question: Europe has always considered itself in the future tense. Europe, as something that is always yet to come, is on its way towards what it is not. It is a vision that looks at the horizon and beyond. Accordingly, is democracy on the horizon, that is, *what are the conditions for a democratic EU?* I will answer this by presenting four visions of Europe to come.

The Principle of Democracy

'A success story': so the Declaration for the Future of Europe adopted by the European Council in Laeken in 2001 praised the EU. The Laeken Declaration emphasized 'the democratic challenge facing Europe'. Even though democratic legitimacy is 'considerably strengthened', the declaration admitted that 'citizens are calling for a clear, open, effective, democratically controlled Community'. What is more, citizens 'want better democratic scrutiny'.[6]

The European Commission (the Commission) 2001 White Paper on European Governance says that the results of European integration – stability, peace and economic prosperity – have been achieved by democratic means. The EU has a double democratic mandate through the European Parliament representing EU

---

4   *JEF Manifesto*, First Chapter <http://www.federalunion.org.uk/the-first-use-of-the-term-democratic-deficit/> accessed 15 March 2013.

5   For critical perspectives on the democracy deficit see Giandomenico Majone, *Regulating Europe* (Routledge 1996); Giandomenico Majone, 'Europe's "Democratic Deficit": The Question of Standards' (1998) 4 *European Law Journal* 5; Andrew Moravcsik, 'In Defence of the "Democratic Deficit": Reassessing the Legitimacy of the European Union' (2002) 40 *Journal of Common Market Studies* 603.

6   European Council Presidency Conclusions, Laeken, Declaration of the Future on the European Union, 14–15 December 2001, <http://ec.europa.eu/governance/impact/background/docs/laeken_concl_en.pdf> accessed 2 October 2013.

citizens and the Council of the European Union (the Council) representing the elected governments of the Member States. In spite of this, many citizens are disenchanted and the gulf between the EU and the people has widened, the White Paper says. Thus, the White Paper proposes a reform of European governance so that its policy-making process would become more 'inclusive and accountable' and so that the EU would be more closely connected to its citizens.[7]

Even if a lack of democracy was admitted, the EU institutions maintained firm confidence in the European democratization process. The task was to transform weak democratic legitimacy into a true democratic foundation. 'Reform must be started now', the White Paper declared.[8] However, with – uncommon – modesty, the Commission acknowledged that this White Paper does not 'provide a magic cure' and that the Commission 'alone cannot improve European governance'.[9] The Europe to come would need concerted action by all the European institutions, Member States, regional and local authorities and even civil society.

At that time, a constitution for the EU seemed to be a relevant solution to the 'black hole at the heart of' the EU[10] in the shape of a lack of democracy. The Treaty establishing a Constitution for Europe (TCE) fell apart due to the joker in the pack, now in the shape of EU citizens who were much more disenchanted than the Commission had believed.

According to the President of the European Commission, José Manuel Barroso, this failure of the process of ratification created 'the shadow of division'. Therefore, he appealed to the Member States: 'please help us solve this', since the results of failure would lead to a very weak and divided Europe, a Europe of protectionism, egoisms and narrow national interests.[11] Plan B succeeded as the Treaty of Lisbon was ratified by the Member States. It seems to offer a promised democratic reform of the EU, which dissolves the shadow of insufficient democratic legitimacy.

In the Preamble and Article 2 of the Treaty on European Union (TEU) democracy is defined as one of the fundamental values of the EU. Democracy is defined as:

1. *Representative democracy*: a greater role for the European Parliament and greater involvement for national parliaments in EU legislation (Articles 10 and 12 TEU).

---

7   European Commission, European Governance – A White Paper, Brussels, 25 July 2001, COM(2001) 428 final 8.

8   European Commission (n 7) 3.

9   European Commission (n 7) 9.

10   David Martin, *European Union and the Democratic Deficit* (John Wheatley Centre 1990) 19.

11   José Manuel Barroso, 'The Political Priorities of New European Commission' European Commission (3 September 2009) <http://ec.europa.eu/commission_2010–2014/president/pdf/press_20090903_en.pdf> accessed 3 March 2013.

2. *Participatory democracy*: more rights for the citizens to participate in the democratic life of the EU, like the citizen's initiative, maintaining openness, transparency and regular dialogue with representative associations and civil society (Articles 10 and 11 TEU).

3. *Democratic equality*: the equality of its citizens and the obligation of the EU institutions to give equal attention to all citizens (Article 9 TEU).

The Treaty of Lisbon is a double answer to the democratic challenge. It is a constitutional reform that strengthens and deepens democracy in the EU. Moreover, as it reaffirms the principle of democracy – consisting of the aforementioned democratic principles of representation, participation and equality – it proclaims the essence of democracy as complementarity between representative and participatory democracy. Thus, it is both an institutional and ontological reform of democracy at the European level. As such, it continues the democratization process that had started with the Maastricht Treaty.

The Treaty of Lisbon is not so much a declarative statement about democracy at the European level but rather a normative statement asserting that the EU *ought* to be, or become, a democratic polity. In other words, Articles 2, 9, 10, 11 and 12 TEU assert that the EU *ought* to realize and implement the principle of democracy.[12] In these articles, we find the fundamental principles for the EU as an emerging democratic polity.

Then again, democracy is not established merely through legislative acts, statutory laws, court decisions and democratic policy programmes. Democratic principles and democratic rights must also, as Emilia Korkea-aho says, 'take root and gain practical importance in the EU'.[13] The democratic European polity must be constructed in a symbolic-normative democratization process that does not merely permeate the EU's institutional architecture, national parliaments and governments, procedures and practices, but also the European public sphere and civil society. Considering law as a multilayered phenomenon, here I follow Kaarlo Tuori, we can say that these principles and rights, which are at the moment explicitly and discursively formulated at the surface level of EU law, should be gradually sedimented into the deeper levels of EU law. During and through this process of sedimentation, they will become fundamental normative ideas of EU law.[14]

If this kind of democratization process, in which democratic principles, rights and values become an integral part of the European symbolic order (that is, political, cultural and juridical order) does not take place, then democracy in the

---

12   Cf. Martin Westlake, *A Modern Guide to the European Parliament* (Pinter 1994) 16.

13   Emilia Korkea-aho, *New Governance and the EU Courts. The Experimental Architecture of Judicial Decision-Making* (2010) LLD dissertation, Faculty of Law, University of Helsinki 35.

14   Kaarlo Tuori, *Critical Legal Positivism* (Ashgate 2002) 200–209.

EU will be nothing but a politico-juridical fantasy structure that masks a lack of democracy and democratic legitimacy.

Parliamentarization

Article 10 TEU notes that the EU is founded on representative democracy. EU citizens are directly represented in the European Parliament and indirectly through national parliaments. Therefore, democratization of the EU has unfolded along a model of representative democracy based on the parliamentary system.[15] The strengthening of the EU requires that it follows European democratic tradition, which in turn requires 'a movement toward a stronger parliamentary system'.[16] This has taken place through the gradual strengthening of the status and powers of the European Parliament, which has evolved from an unelected consultative European Assembly that was merely 'a multi-lingual talking shop' to an elected parliament, which has real 'legislative and executive oversight powers'.[17]

Granted, with the Treaty of Lisbon, the European Parliament obtained new legislative powers. New fields that came under the ordinary legislative procedure (former co-decision) under which it shares equal rights with the Council include, among others, agriculture, immigration, asylum, energy policy, public health and structural and cohesion funds. Together with the Council, the European Parliament now decides on the entire EU budget (Article 314 TFEU). Taking into account elections to the European Parliament, the European Council proposes to the European Parliament a candidate for the President of the Commission, who is elected by the European Parliament. The Commission is subject as a body to a vote of consent by the European Parliament, which may also vote on a motion of censure of the Commission (Article 17(7–8) TEU). In all its activities the European Parliament ought to be the guardian of fundamental rights. As an example, in the first consent vote on an international agreement in accordance with Article 218(6) TFEU, the European Parliament withheld consent to an agreement between the EU and the USA on the processing and transfer of financial messaging data, mainly on grounds of privacy, civil liberties and proportionality. It reiterated that a new agreement should comply with the new legal framework established by the

15   Berthold Rittberger, *Building Europe's Parliament* (Oxford University Press 2005). See also Julie Smith, *Europe's Elected Parliament* (Sheffield Academic Press 1999).

16   Svein S Andersen and Kjell A Eliassen, 'Introduction: Dilemma, Contradictions and the Future of European Democracy' in SS Andersen and KA Eliassen (eds), *The European Union: How Democratic Is It?* (Sage 1996) 43.

17   'Professor Farrell, The EP is now one of the most powerful legislatures in the world' European Parliament Press Releases (18 June 2007) <www.europarl.europa.eu/sides/getDoc.do?language=EN&type=IM-PRESS&reference=20070615IPR07837> accessed 13 March 2013. See also Simon Hix, Abdul G Noury and Gérard Roland, *Democratic Politics in the European Parliament* (Cambridge University Press 2007) 3.

Treaty of Lisbon, in particular with the Charter of Fundamental Rights.[18] A revised agreement was then approved by the European Parliament.[19]

The Treaty of Lisbon also enhanced the role of national parliaments by creating a direct political relationship between them and the EU institutions. According to the Protocol on the Application of the Principles of Subsidiarity and Proportionality, draft legislative acts must be forwarded to national parliaments (Article 4), which may send a reasoned opinion on whether a draft complies with the principle of subsidiarity (Article 6).[20] The European Parliament, the Council and the Commission must take account of these opinions (Article 7). According to the Protocol, national parliaments also have a possibility for ex post control. In the name of the national parliament (or one of its chambers) a Member State may bring a case before the CJEU if it considers that a legislative act does not comply with the principle of subsidiarity. The Committee of the Regions has the same right (Article 8). Moreover, Article 5(3) TEU refers explicitly to regional and local levels.

However, the democratization process as a gradual development of parliamentary democracy has various shortcomings.

First, the principle of representative democracy as parliamentary democracy, to which the EU subjected itself, was of course not created *ex nihilo* in the Treaty of Lisbon and previous constitutive acts, since it has been and remains a fundamental principle of European nation states. Together with human rights it even forms the cornerstone of European symbolic-normative power in the world where Europe has lost its former economic and military power. In this respect, the EU, which has been formed and structured in the context of European democratic rule-of-law states, imitates European democracies. Since in the process of mimesis, the imitator is affected by the object it imitates, it seems that the democratization of the EU is inevitable as the EU identifies itself with the principle of democracy that underpins national constitutions. Moreover, since the precondition of being integrated into the EU is to be integrated into democracy, applicants ought to imitate the democratic EU that imitates the principle of democracy of European democracies.

---

18   European Parliament legislative resolution of 11 February 2010 on the proposal for a Council decision on the conclusion of the Agreement between the European Union and the United States of America on the processing and transfer of Financial Messaging Data from the European Union to the United States for purposes of the Terrorist Finance Tracking Program (05305/1/2010/REV 1 – C7–0004/2010 – 2009/0190(NLE)). European Parliament Document 0029(2010).

19   European Parliament legislative resolution of 8 July 2010 on the draft Council decision on the conclusion of the Agreement between the European Union and the United States of America on the processing and transfer of Financial Messaging Data from the European Union to the United States for the purposes of the Terrorist Finance Tracking Program (11222/1/2010/REV 1 and COR 1 – C7–0158/2010 – 2010/0178(NLE)) OJ C 341 E/100. European Parliament Document 0279(2010).

20   See also Protocol on the Role of National Parliaments in the European Union, OJ C 115/203 Articles 2 and 3.

In spite of parliamentarization, the power and competence of the European Parliament remains too limited in comparison to the Commission, the Council and the European Council to call the EU a fully parliamentary democracy. Moreover, the enhancement of participatory democracy has challenged the ordinary legislative process, which paradoxically may have caused further depoliticization of the EU.

Second, 'Citizens are directly represented at Union level in the European Parliament' (Article 10(2) TEU) and its members are defined as 'representatives of the Union's citizens' (Article 14(2) TEU) instead of simply as 'representatives of the peoples of the States brought together in the Community' (Article 189(1) of the Treaty establishing the European Community).

In its decision concerning the constitutionality of the Treaty of Lisbon, the German Federal Constitutional Court took as a fundamental criterion the principle of democracy, which 'may not be balanced against other legal interests' and which is 'inviolable'.[21] Thus, democracy has a guarantee of eternity. The Court stated that measured against requirements of a constitutional state the EU lacks 'a political decision-making body created in equal elections by all citizens of the Union and with the ability to uniformly represent the will of the people'.[22] Moreover, 'the European Parliament is not a representative body of a sovereign European people'.[23] This is reflected in the fact that the European Parliament is 'designed as a representation of peoples in the respective national contingents of Members, not as a representation of Union citizens in unity without differentiation, according to the principle of electoral equality'.[24] Thus, the European Parliament is not the representative of the European people. In its decision the Court defended democracy as it stated that 'continuing sovereignty of the people ... is anchored in the Member States', which have to 'remain the masters of the Treaties'.[25] For the Court, the principle of democracy is first of all national representative and parliamentary democracy. However, as the Court interpreted the principle of democracy in a formal and statist way, it made a mistake in not problematizing the democratic shortcomings of the *Bundestag* and the *Bundesrat* at all.

Even if a national parliament is formally a representative body of the people, a gap exists between constitutional norms and the reality of the functioning of a national parliament as the representative of the people. This gap between norms and facts has taken place in spite of the EU. Representative institutions

---

21   BVerfG, 2 BvE 2/08, para. 216.

22   BVerfG, 2 BvE 2/08, para. 280. Already in 1974, in the Solange I case, the German Constitutional Court addressed the problematic of democratic legitimacy, stating that Community law could not take priority over the fundamental rights contained in the Basic Law for the Federal Republic of Germany. One of the arguments was that the European Parliament was not directly elected (BVerfGE 37, 2 BvL 52/71).

23   BVerfG, 2 BvE 2/08, para. 280.

24   BVerfG, 2 BvE 2/08, para. 280.

25   BVerfG, 2 BvE 2/08, para. 334.

do not represent what they are supposed to represent. Parliamentary democracy is undermined, according to Slavoj Žižek, because of the passivity of a large majority as well as growing executive privileges, which are 'implied by the spreading logic' of the state of emergency, which, I would add, is justified by various reasons: economic and environmental crises, the threat of terrorism and the protection of human rights.[26] If Jean-Jacques Rousseau strictly differentiated between the sovereign, which has the right to legislate, and government, which merely has executive power, this distinction has melted away insomuch that today there is 'an overwhelming domination of government and economy over popular sovereignty, which has been progressively run down in all senses'.[27]

Jacques Rancière speaks of post-democracy by which he refers to the following five phenomena. 1) Politics has been placed exclusively in the sphere of the state and has become merely a governmental practice, in which the managers of the state follow the advice of non-elected and non-accountable specialized elites and technical experts. In other words, power is exercised by, as Rancière says, 'the alliance of governmental and economic oligarchies and official experts'.[28] 2) Democracy is identified with consensual practice, which suppresses political disagreements, antagonisms and struggles, which are the necessary and essential elements of democracy. As a result, 'politics' becomes governance and management without alternatives. Consensus is 'the denial of the democratic ground of politics'.[29] 3) Post-democracy has given up posing as the power of the people. It is democracy after the *demos*, since it has eliminated the appearance of the people as a political subject. 4) Wrongs, instead of being issues of political struggles, have been subjected to the law as violations of subjective rights, especially fundamental freedoms and human rights, and resolved by juridical procedures. 5) Democratic politics is effaced under 'the exigencies of the limitlessness of global Capital'.[30] Sovereignty was stolen from the peoples of Europe 'by the "markets" a long time ago'.[31]

As a consequence, the democratic deficit is a problem not merely of the EU but also of European democracies, even if in the EU all these non-democratic traits are emphasized. The EU has become a model for post-democratic 'democracy'. The European representative democracies do offer normative criteria by which

---

26   Slavoj Žižek, 'From Democracy to Divine Violence' in G Agamben et al (eds), *Democracy in What State?* (Columbia University Press 2011) 101.

27   Giorgio Agamben, 'Note luminaire sur le concept de démocratie' in G Agamben et al (eds), *Démocratie, dans quel état?* (La Fabrique 2009) 11–12.

28   Jacques Lévy, Juliette Rennes and David Zerbib, 'Jacques Rancière: 'Les Territoires de la pensée partagée' EspaceTemps.net, Laboratoire, 8 January 2007 <www.espacestemps.net/document2142.html> accessed 1 October 2013.

29   Jacques Rancière, 'Dissenting Words. A Conversation with Jacques Rancière' (2000) 30 *Diacritics* 113, 125.

30   Jacques Rancière, *La haine de la démocratie* (La Fabrique 2005) 78.

31   Peter Bofinger, Jürgen Habermas and Julian Nida-Rümelin, 'Einspruch gegen Fassadendemokratie' *Frankfurter Allgemeine Zeitung* (4 August 2012).

to evaluate the democratic nature of the EU, only if we accept 'the status quo in Europe' and lower 'our democratic standards', but this would not be, says Anne Peters, 'a wise course to take'.[32]

Therefore, I cannot accept Andrew Moravcsik's defence of the EU against the allegation of its lack of democracy. He writes: 'constitutional checks and balances, indirect democratic control via national governments, and the increasing powers of the European Parliament are sufficient to ensure that EU policy-making is, in nearly all cases, clean, transparent, effective and politically responsive to the demands of European citizens'.[33]

Third, the extension of the powers of the European Parliament reflects the statist conception of representative democracy based on parliamentarism. Democratization has represented a will 'to re-establish a central power in the tradition of the nation state'.[34] But the parliamentary model adopted by modern constitutional nation states does not inevitably function at the supranational level. This model may even be 'irrelevant' to the EU.[35] One should take, as Neil MacCormick says, 'due account of the complexity of the democratic ideal applied to a commonwealth on this scale that brings together so many and such diverse parts, peoples and traditions'.[36]

At the EU supranational level, the challenge of democracy should not be answered by imitating European parliamentary democracies, since, on the one hand, contemporary European democracies suffer from a lack of democracy, and on the other hand, even though we would wish to hang on to the ideal model of parliamentary democracy, this would not as such be suitable at the level of a supranational polity.

Fourth, in addition to a lack of democracy and the problem of the suitability of the parliamentary model, one should ask a question usually ignored in discourse on democratization: whether the model of democracy is representative democracy, even if, as conventional democracy, it seems to be the only kind of political form and

---

32   Anne Peters, 'European Democracy after the 2003 Convention' (2004) 41 *Common Market Law Review* 37, 41.

33   Moravcsik (n 5) 605.

34   Karl-Heinz Ladeur, 'We, the European People ... Relâche' (2008) 14 *European Law Journal* 147, 160.

35   John Coultrap, 'From Parliamentarism to Pluralism: Models of Democracy and the European Union's "Democracy Deficit"' (1999) 11 *Journal of Theoretical Politics* 107, 109.

36   Neil MacCormick, 'Democracy, Subsidiarity and Citizenship in the "European Commonwealth"' (1997) 16 *Law and Philosophy* 332, 356. Arguments about democratic deficit are related to the standards of legitimacy which we use. Whether they derive from the theory and practice of parliamentary democracies or from the accomplishments of economic integration makes a big difference, as Giandomenico Majone has shown. See Majone, 'Europe's "Democratic Deficit"' (n 5) 15; Daniel Wincott, 'Does the European Union Pervert Democracy? Questions of Democracy in New Constitutionalist Thought on the Future of Europe' (1998) 4 *European Law Journal* 411.

regime deemed acceptable by emancipated humanity that has come of age.[37] The institutional architecture in representative democracy is top-down, hierarchical, formalized and centralized. The forms and procedures of relevant democratic practices are set by the constitution. Even if representative democracy is based on popular sovereignty the ultimate authority lies in the elected parliament, which uses its sovereign legislative power.

In aggregative democracy, the democratic participation of the people, means, first of all if not exclusively, voting representatives of the people. Popular sovereignty comes into being merely in and during regular general elections organized by established political parties. Otherwise, autonomous citizens are purely subjects of law who do not have proper knowledge of complicated political, legal and economic national and transnational issues. As Rousseau commented on the English parliamentary system, even though the people of England regard themselves as free, 'slavery overtakes it, and it is nothing' as soon as the members of parliaments are elected.[38]

If I may use Karl Marx's description of labour, I would say that citizens produce not only parliament as a commodity; they produce themselves and the constituency as commodities. The object, the parliament, which citizens produce – citizens' product – confronts and stands opposed to citizens as '*something alien*, as a *power independent* of the producer'.[39] The parliament is the constituency that is congealed in the parliament. The realization of the constituency in general elections is the objectification of the constituency as the loss of political reality for citizens and as the loss of the legislative body produced by it. Thus, the parliamentary system causes estrangement and alienation of citizens as they become dependent upon the parliament as an external agency that was their own product.

In the representative parliamentary model, democracy is reduced, on the one hand, to rule by voting, and on the other hand, to the authority of representative *and* external parliament to decide legislation and other matters by majority rule.

Thus, both the statist parliamentary model and representative democracy *as such* should not be taken as a pre-given vision, a figure or a model for Europe as a democratic polity.

The Enhancement of Participation

The democratization process requires that democracy in the EU is not reduced to general elections, the parliamentary system and a democratically controlled

---

37 See Jean-Luc Nancy, *Vérité de la démocratie* (Galilée 2008).

38 Jean-Jacques Rousseau, *The Social Contract and Later Political Writings* (Cambridge University Press 1997) 114.

39 Karl Marx, *Economic and Philosophic Manuscripts of 1844* (Foreign Language Publishing House 1959) 47.

government and administration. The EU should be committed to involving citizens in active participation in legislation and political choices. Hence, the principle of participatory democracy should become one of the fundamental principles of a democratic EU.

Already the White Paper on European Governance proposed a less top-down approach that would open up policy-making processes to involve more people and organizations in shaping and delivering EU policy. 'The aim should be to create a transnational "space" where citizens from different countries can discuss' the challenges for the EU.[40] Moreover, the EU and national policy makers should be receptive to what takes place in these transnational spaces. In that way, policy makers would be able to identify 'European projects which mobilise public support'.[41]

In order for the debate on the future of the EU to be broadly based and involve all European citizens, the European Convention, the task of which was to draft a constitutional treaty for Europe, not only deliberated in public and included representatives from the European and national parliaments, it also involved civil society in deliberating the proposition. For this purpose, a forum of civil society organizations – including non-governmental organizations, social partners, i.e. labour market players, academia and organizations representing other social and economic players – was established. Their contributions served as input in debates and deliberations.

Even if civil society organizations were involved, the chance to enhance participatory democracy at the European level misfired. The Treaty establishing a Constitution for Europe (TCE) signed in Rome on 29 October 2004 by the European political elite was drafted without any real involvement of European citizens.[42] The forum was not 'a transnational "space"' as demanded in the White Paper.[43] No Europe-wide public debates about the future of the EU in general and the TCE in particular had taken place since no European public space existed. One of the reasons for this was the text of the TCE itself, which was, as Perry Anderson says, 'bureaucratic elephantiasis without precedent' and 'a ponderous and rickety construction'.[44] The stylistic choices of the TCE were not accidental. According to Roberto M. Dainotto, the unreadability and boredom of the constitutional text was instrumental in making the EU 'a technocratic institution bureaucratically planned, decided, and managed by unelected representatives'.[45]

---

40   European Commission (n 7) 11–12.

41   European Commission (n 7) 12.

42   On 12 January 2005 the European Parliament voted a non-binding resolution in support of the TCE.

43   European Commission (n 7) 11–12.

44   Perry Anderson, *The New Old World* (Verso 2009) 57.

45   Roberto M Dainotto, 'Europe (in Practice): Which Culture for the Union?' (2011) 16 Lecture Paper, Nanovic Institute for European Studies 3.

After the French and Dutch public rejected the TCE in referendums, it was decided to have a reflection period. As the French President, Jacques Chirac said, 'I hope we can take a pause for reflection which will allow us to regain the confidence of the citizens'.[46] The TCE promised transparency and democracy but the process of its drafting and ratification did not become part of the democratization process. Instead of strengthening democratic legitimacy, the EU had lost the confidence of European citizens.

What the reflection period meant in reality was preclusion of the emergence of public debate, transnational spaces, European citizens and politics in general. The Action Committee for European Democracy (ACED), a group of high-level European politicians backed by the Commission, unofficially rewrote the TCE. They claimed that '[d]uring the reflection period European citizens and governments continued to express their support for a broader European reform project'. The members of the Committee were able to speak on behalf of EU citizens, because they defined themselves as 'engaged citizens'.[47]

All in all, a reform Treaty was discussed, prepared, drafted and accepted in non-transparent, exclusive and non-participatory processes. The principle of public participation was quietly dismissed. Finally, the Treaty of Lisbon, a decaffeinated version of the TCE, was marketed to European consumers. Having learned what kind of democratic scandals referendums may cause, it was reasonable that the ratification of the Treaty of Lisbon would be made by politically responsible, reasonable and rational parliamentarians and not by unpredictable, and even rogue, European citizens.[48]

There was merely one minor problem. In a seminal constitutional decision, *Crotty v. An Taoiseach*, the Supreme Court of Ireland found that the Single European Act could not be ratified unless the Irish Constitution was changed to permit ratification.[49] This case established that ratification of any significant amendments to the EU Treaties requires an amendment to the Irish Constitution. After having passed both Houses of the Oireachtas, every amendment must be 'submitted by a Referendum to the decision of the people' (Article 46(2) Constitution of Ireland). Therefore, Ireland had to hold a referendum.

In colonialist tones, the Irish people were warned about the consequences of rejecting the Treaty of Lisbon. The Treaty was 'the best preparation for Europe's

---

46   Patrick Wintour, 'EU scraps timetable for ratifying constitution' *The Guardian* (17 June 2005) <www.guardian.co.uk/politics/2005/jun/17/eu.politics> accessed 16 March 2013.

47   Action Committee for European Democracy. 'The Way Forward for the European Union', 8 July 2007 <http://web.archive.org/web/20070708035001/http://www.eui.eu/RSCAS/e-texts/ACED2007_DECLARATION_4JUNE07.pdf> accessed 15 March 2013.

48   Even parliamentarians may cause democratic scandals if they are responsive to the constituency. This is what happened on 19 March 2013 as the Cyprus Parliament overwhelmingly rejected the bailout levy on bank deposits.

49   *Crotty v. An Taoiseach* [1987] IESC 4; [1987] IR 713.l.

future', said the German Chancellor, Angela Merkel, in Dublin before the referendum, as she pressed the Irish to act like good Europeans.[50] Barroso warned that Europe, and also Ireland, would pay the price if the Treaty was voted down.[51] Daniel Cohn-Bendit claimed that the Irish people had an obligation to vote yes, since 'Europe had boosted' Ireland so much from 1970 on.[52] Instead of being good Europeans – like the members of the Action Committee had been – the Irish people used their popular sovereignty by rejecting the Treaty of Lisbon in the referendum. The result was 'a democratic catastrophe' by which I refer to democratic decisions that cannot be managed and governed by the democratic powers that be.[53] Actually, the catastrophically democratic Irish people were recidivists since they had also rejected the Treaty of Nice.

After the referendum, there were claims that a tiny European minority had taken hostage the silent majority of Europeans, whose silence the EU elite claimed to represent.[54] The Irish referendum was considered as a vote, not merely against the Treaty of Lisbon, but against democracy itself. This was the message of the frustrated President of the European Parliament, according to whom, 'It is of course a great disappointment for all those who wanted to achieve greater democracy ... that the majority of the Irish could not be convinced of the need for these reforms'.[55] There is some irony in this. A representative of the European representative democracy blames participatory democracy for watering down the European democratization process.

The Irish people learned their lesson and became good Europeans as they voted 'yes' in a follow-on referendum. When Ireland once again organized a referendum, which this time concerned the Treaty on Stability, Coordination and Governance in the Economic and Monetary Union (TSCG), the Irish people had to be reminded, once again, about the disastrous consequences of a 'no' vote, which would be 'a leap in the dark', as the Irish Finance Minister, Michael

---

50   Hans-Jürgen Schlamp, 'Fate of the European Union Lies with Ireland' *Der Spiegel* (10 June 2008) <www.spiegel.de/international/europe/lisbon-treaty-referendum-fate-of-the-european-union-lies-with-ireland-a-558893.html> accessed 13 March 2013.

51   Schlamp (n 49).

52   Constance Baudry, 'M. Cohn-Bendit: "Il y a une incertitude sur la présidence française de l'UE"' *Le Monde* (17 June 2008) <www.lemonde.fr/l-europe-a-l-heure-de-la-presidence-francaise/chat/2008/06/17/les-politiques-en-direct-invite-daniel-cohn-bendit_1059096_1058958.html> accessed 15 March 2013.

53   Cf. Jacques Rancière, 'Les démocracies contre la démocratie' in G Agamben et al, *Démocratie, dans quel état?* (La Fabrique 2009) 95.

54   Kristin Ross, *Democracy for Sale, in Democracy in What State?* (Columbia University Press 2011) 87.

55   Hans-Gert Pöttering, 'Pöttering hopeful reforms still achievable before 2009 Euro-elections' European Parliament Published Article (13 June 2008) 85 <www.europarl.europa.eu/sides/getDoc.do?pubRef=-//EP//TEXT+IM-PRESS+20080613STO31667+0+DOC+XML+V0//EN> accessed 13 March 2013.

Noonan described it.[56] Rejection of the TSCG would create a wave of panic on the international markets and force Ireland out of the euro. Therefore, 'there is only one vote, and it's a yes vote'.[57] The EU knows Bertolt Brecht's solution: if the people forfeit the confidence of the government, 'Would it not be easier / In that case for the government / To dissolve the people / And elect another?'[58]

When commenting on debates surrounding the French referendum on the TCE, Rancière says something general about political decision-making processes at European and national levels. According to him, there is 'huge distrust' of the popular vote in Europe, even though the popular vote is 'a part of the official definition of democracy'.[59] The European political elite have read their Walter Bagehot. In *The English Constitution*, Bagehot warns of the dangers of democracy: due to the suffrage of the lower classes, the supremacy of ignorance and numbers prevails over instruction and knowledge: *vox populi, vox diaboli*.[60]

The principle of participatory democracy does not include direct democracy in the form of binding or non-binding referendums and open public debate before referendums. Improving plebiscitary democracy has no role in the democratization process.

This suspicion concerning the referendums discloses the paradox of democracy in the EU and more generally in modern parliamentary democracies. On the one hand, individual subjects, who concentrate on their work, private aspirations and particular interests, whose desires circulate and are fixed on various objects (or who seek instant enjoyment), should become active citizens, who share the public space, *polis*, with other citizens. If an individual subject is constituted within the circulation of desire (or within addiction to enjoyment), a citizen subject, a *zoon politikon*, is constituted within the fabrication of the public and common world of collective existence. In a political community a citizen subject exercises worldly and public freedom as political action.[61]

On the other hand, an excess of democratic activity and vitality may disturb and interrupt the smooth operation of democratic government. Democracies should be prepared to diminish or subdue 'the feverish energy activated in public scenes' and also democratic scandals like the rejection of the TCE.[62] According to Rancière, democracies – by which he refers to democratic states and forms of

---

56   Colm Keena, 'No Vote "A leap in the Dark"' *Irish Times* (16 May 2012) <www.irishtimes.com/newspaper/breaking/2012/0516/breaking11.html> accessed 12 September 2012.

57   S O'Driscoll, chairman of Irish Glen Dimplex manufacturing group. See Henry McDonald, 'Irish referendum no to EU treaty will prompt euro exit, business leaders warn' *The Guardian* (15 May 2012) <www.guardian.co.uk/world/2012/may/15/irish-referendum-no-eu-euro> accessed 13 March 2013.

58   Bertolt Brecht, 'The Solution' *Poems 1913–1956* (edited by J Willett and R Manheim, Methuen 1976). See P Anderson, (n 44) 59.

59   Rancière (n 52) 96.

60   Walter Bagehot, *The English Constitution* (Oxford University Press 1928).

61   Hannah Arendt, *The Human Condition* (Chicago University Press 1958).

62   Rancière (n 30) 14.

government – consider democrats as the enemies of democracy. For constitutional democracies, the spontaneous, intensive and radical political activity of democrats is an anarchic threat.[63]

To manage this paradox, the EU seems to turn back to Aristotle's *politeia*, in which the best (*aristoi*), the educated elite possessing practical wisdom, rule with the consent of the many (*demos*). The EU blends an administrative, political, economic and juridical aristocracy (the Commission, the Council, the European Council, the European Central Bank (ECB), the CJEU – and also the European Parliament) with European citizens, whose democratic power is channelled, on the one hand, into elections, and on the other hand, into rational civil dialogue and public deliberation and activities in civil society organizations.

Participation as Deliberative Governance

If participatory democracy does not refer to referendums and democratic scandals caused by Europeans, how we should understand it? What did Barroso really mean as he outlined the political priorities of the Barroso Commission (2010–2014), one of them being 'reinforcing EU citizenship and participation' so that citizens would become empowered and involved in decisions affecting their lives?[64]

New governance is one answer that the EU has offered. Comitology, Social Dialogue and the Open Method of Co-ordination (OMC) can be mentioned as examples. Of these, the OMC best represents new governance as 'a soft policy co-ordination mechanism designed to offer a flexible way to address common issues',[65] 'a way of networking decentralized decision-making units by a common system of benchmarking'.[66] As such, the OMC combines decentralization with reintegration, local deliberating forums and their co-ordination.

Let me list the main distinctive features of new governance. First of all, it differs from the ordinary legislative process that produces binding legal norms; and more generally, from top-down regulations and policy-making. It emphasizes civil dialogue plus wider and better involvement of civil society. Participation in policy formulation and soft-law rule-making is expanded by various stakeholders – actors from civil society, target groups, partners and experts. The European Council defined this participation as the active involvement of 'the Union, the member states, the regional and local levels, as well as the social partners and civil society' that uses various forms of partnership.[67] This new governance mechanism

---

63   Rancière (n 53) 96.

64   Barroso (n 11) 16.

65   Korkea-aho (n 13) 51.

66   Burkard Eberlein and Dieter Kerwer, 'New Governance in the European Union: A Theoretical Perspective' (2004) 42 *Journal of Common Market Studies* 121, 130.

67   European Council Presidency Conclusions, Lisbon, 23–24 March 2000, point 38 <www.europarl.europa.eu/summits/lis1_en.htm> accessed 2 October 2013.

brings together actors from local, regional, national and European levels. Decision-making is decentralized and coordinated diversity is accepted. The mechanism and procedures of decision-making are flexible, experimental and based on soft-law guidelines. Knowledge is produced that reflects the views of civil society. Decisions are reached by deliberation among participants.[68]

The aforementioned White Paper, which lays down the principles of European governance, sets as the goal of European governance to 'integrate the people of Europe', since '[d]emocracy depends on people being able to take part in public debate'.[69] This kind of inclusion of civil society seems to enhance democracy in the EU. Moreover Articles 11(1) and (2) TEU require that the EU institutions should be responsive to citizens and civil society organizations. There ought to be both civil dialogue as a democratic and public opinion-forming process between civil society organizations and the EU institutions. This can be horizontal – dialogue between citizens and civil society organizations on EU development and policies – and vertical – structured and regular dialogue. Moreover, civil dialogue can be sectoral, that is, daily dialogue between civil society organizations and their contacts within the legislative and administrative authorities. In addition to civil dialogue, a part of EU participatory democracy is social dialogue, which is a mechanism that has quasi-legislative powers according to Articles 153 and 154 TFEU.

All in all, participatory democracy is understood, first of all, as an institutionalized form of participation, rational communication and deliberative decision-making – even though it may be in ad-hoc, non-hierarchical, flexible, fluid and bottom-up regulation mode. It is based on reciprocal commitment between civil society organizations and European institutional structures. But, as Emilia Korkea-aho points out, 'who is to decide the standards by which participants are included or kept outside and what are those standards like?'[70]

According to Beate Kohler-Koch, 'those who want to participate in policy-making have to prove that they are representative'.[71] This kind of restricted participation is also found in the European Economic and Social Committee. As a consultative body of the EU, it is an institutional forum for stable forms of structured civil dialogue with representatives of civil society organizations. It has constructed a home for organized civil society.[72] As such, it is a 'legitimate

---

68   Joanne Scott and David M Trubek, 'Mind the Gap: Law and New Approaches to Governance in the European Union' (2002) 8 *European Law Journal* 1, 5–6. About new governance in the EU see Korkea-aho (n 13) (esp. the democracy of new governance, 40–45; deliberative new governance, 50–59).

69   European Commission (n 7) 32.

70   Korkea-aho (n 13) 58.

71   Beate   Kohler-Koch,   'Civil   Society   and   EU   democracy: "Astroturf" Representation?' (2010) 17 *Journal of European Public Policy* 100, 101.

72   European Economic and Social Committee, 'A Roadmap for Participatory Democracy', CES/11/38 25 March 2011.

mouthpiece for *organized civil society*.[73] Thus, mechanisms of governance are exclusive if we consider them from the perspective of EU citizens. Participatory democracy has enabled construction of bridges between the EU and civil society, which is not synonymous with EU citizens. Therefore, decision-making in even more experimental forms of governance might not be less elitist or expert-oriented than in the deliberative supranational governance represented by comitology committees, the dynamic of which is top-down and in which reasoning experts seek consensus without links to the concerns of the citizens affected.[74] What is more, Kohler-Koch says, there is no proof that civil society organizations would be closer to citizens than democratically elected representatives, even though the Commission has required them to be accountable to those they represent – but only to those. In spite of this, representatives of civil society organizations in Brussels remain distant and highly autonomous.[75]

When it comes to the decision-making process, deliberation may transform political and ideological issues into depoliticized problems. Through rational argumentation and discussion the participants find reasonable, effective or technical solutions to various problems. EU citizens are not integrated in decision-making as political subjects to make political decisions but as stakeholders, partners, experts and representatives of civil society and non-governmental organizations. Moreover, these deliberative and decision-making processes are not necessarily transparent.

The primary aim of new governance seems to be more effective and efficient management, regulation and decision-making within the EU, not a more democratic EU. One could also speculate whether new governance is a means to enhance the legitimacy of the Commission and even transfer emphasis from the political European Parliament to non-political governance. In this case, strengthening participatory democracy would, paradoxically, result in de-democratization.

Another form of participatory democracy is the European Citizens' Initiative (ECI) (Article 11(4) TEU, Article 24(1) TFEU). This first transnational mechanism of direct democracy enables one million EU citizens to request the Commission to initiate a legislative proposal in an area of EU competence. In this respect, EU citizens share equal power with the European Parliament (Article 225 TFEU) and the Council (Article 241 TFEU), which may also request the Commission to submit proposals. According to Alex Warleigh, this provision of a citizens' initiative has 'potentially enormous significance'.[76] Even though the ECI is an

---

73   European Economic and Social Committee, 'Participatory Democracy in 5 Points' (2011) <http://www.eesc.europa.eu/?i=portal.en.publications.15525> accessed 20 June 2014.

74   Caroline De la Port and Patrizia Nanz 'The OMC – A Deliberative-democratic Mode of Governance? The Cases of Employment and Pensions' (2004) 11 *Journal of European Public Policy* 267, 270–71.

75   Kohler-Koch (n 71) 111.

76   Alex Warleigh, 'On the Path to Legitimacy? The EU Citizens' Initiative Right from a Critical Deliberativist Perspective' in V Della Sala and C Ruzza (eds), *Governance*

important step in the democratization process, it may turn out to be quasi-direct democracy, since the Commission, although obliged to consider an initiative, is not required to submit a proposal for new legislation. Due to the ultimate power of the Commission, the ECI is a manageable democratic mechanism, which does not cause democratic scandals.

To promote active citizenship and involvement of citizens and civil society organizations, the European Parliament and the Council has also adopted the Europe for Citizens Programme.[77] The European Year of Citizens (2013) aimed at encouraging European citizens to participate in civic forums on EU policies. Activities were organized at the grass-roots level, by citizens and civil society organizations themselves.[78] However, these kinds of programmes and theme years turn out to be democracy not *of* the people but *for* the people. In other words, democracy is inserted into EU citizens' socio-political practices, which are governed by the rituals of general elections, deliberative governance and civil society organizations. These democratic rituals are defined and steered by the EU apparatus, which is able to take the credit for opening transnational spaces for democrats.[79]

Crisis Management

In spite of what I have said above, the Treaty of Lisbon can be counted as a minor step in the democratization process. But its democratizing effects have remained at the surface level of law. The EU's symbolic-normative order has not been democratized. However, that is not all. Management of the sovereign debt crisis has meant a turn from the weak democratization process into a strong de-democratization process.

Democratic imperatives and aims rarely chime with economic ones, which require efficient technocratic management, utilitarian viewpoints, risk management, inside information and confidentiality in order to promote and realize EU objectives for European prosperity, the smooth operation of a single market, sustainable growth, global competitiveness, social cohesion and employment. There seems to be no articulation between popular sovereignty and capital,

---

and Civil Society in the European Union. Normative Perspectives (Volume 1, Manchester University Press 2007) 64.

77   EACEA, 'Europe for Citizens Programme 2007–2013' <http://eacea.ec.europa. eu/citizenship/> accessed 13 March 2013; see also Proposal for a Council Regulation establishing for the period 2014–2020 the programme 'Europe for Citizens' Brussels, 14.12.2011 COM(2011) 884 final.

78   European Commission, 'European Year of Citizens', <http://europa.eu/ citizens-2013/> accessed 13 March 2013.

79   Cf. Louis Althusser, *Lenin and Philosophy and Other Essays* (Monthly Review Press 1971) 153–9.

between democratization and economic integration in the shape of a preferential trading area, a free trade union, a customs union, a single market, an economic and monetary union and a harmonized fiscal policy.

If economic integration were subjected to democratic discussion and decision-making, this would not be a catastrophe (establishing transnational economic, monetary, fiscal and social policy may even undermine the dominance of markets and capital), but this is not the case. The EU institutions have intentionally ignored the views of citizens and their representative associations on temporary funding programmes, rescue packages and austerity measures that as a condition of bailout loans have had severe social effects (the growth of unemployment, increasing poverty and social exclusion) and which have saved financial institutions instead of people.

The processes that resulted in ratification of the amendment to Article 136 TFEU,[80] the Treaty establishing the European Stability Mechanism (ESM Treaty) and the TSCG, i.e. the fiscal pact, were undemocratic, since these were dictated to national parliaments and EU citizens. This is even more problematic, since the ESM and the fiscal pact diminish and restrict the power of national parliaments in economic, monetary and fiscal policies. These are excellent examples of 'politics' without alternatives.

The European Council agreed the amendment, which authorized the establishment of the ESM under EU law. The amendment was made by simplified treaty revision procedure instead of the ordinary one and it entered into force in 1 May 2013. Before this, an international treaty, the ESM Treaty, had entered into force on 27 September 2012. These undemocratic manoeuvres made it possible to establish the ESM without referendums, even if the ESM is 'an autonomous and permanent international institution with the objective of circumventing the prohibitions and restrictions laid down by the provisions of the FEU Treaty [TFEU] in relation to economic and monetary policy'.[81]

The TSCG, another international treaty, which entered in force on 1 January 2013, requires the Member States to enact legal norms which have 'binding force and permanent character, preferably constitutional, or otherwise guaranteed to be fully respected and adhered to throughout the national budgetary process' (Article 3(2) TSCG). These – preferably constitutional – norms require national budgets

---

80 Article 136(3) TFEU reads, 'The member states whose currency is the euro may establish a stability mechanism to be activated if indispensable to safeguard the stability of the euro area as a whole. The granting of any required financial assistance under the mechanism will be made subject to strict conditionality'.

81 This was one of the claims by which Thomas Pringle, a member of the Irish Parliament, challenged ratification of the ESM Treaty. The Irish Supreme Court referred this and two of Pringle's other claims to the CJEU , which dismissed those claims. Thus, the CJEU considered the ESM Treaty compatible with EU law. See Case C-370/12 *Thomas Pringle v Government of Ireland, Ireland and the Attorney General* 27 November 2012, not yet reported.

to be in balance or in surplus according to the Treaty's definition and a national automatic correction mechanism on the basis of the principles proposed by the Commission. The requirement for the Member States to ratify the TSCG, which essentially changes the nature of the EU, and transpose the required provisions into national law to be eligible to apply for bailout money from the ESM, is a derision of parliamentary and participatory democracy. This is a wonderful example of neo-liberal capitalist logic: everyone has an equal right to sell or not to sell their labour, but those who refuse to sell it have to bear the consequences, that is, to become impoverished.[82] All in all, the EU's economic constitution is drastically changed without European-wide democratic deliberations, discussions and referendums.

Instead of maintaining an open, transparent and regular dialogue with EU citizens during the existential crisis, the EU institutions have avoided all democratic dialogue. Additionally, national parliaments are disregarded as they have been forced to accept harsh economic austerity policies dictated by the Commission, the ECB and the International Monetary Fund (IMF). Moreover, the European Parliament has been merely a rubber stamp in economic, monetary and fiscal matters and integration. As a consequence, the EU institutions have violated one of the fundamental principles of EU law: the principle of democracy.

What is taking place is an undemocratic turning point in European democracy. Perhaps it is nothing but regression to the EU's constitutive moment, to the Treaty of Rome, when democratic commitment was not on the agenda and when Europe was to be united by bureaucratic management 'marked by technocracy and elitism', as Jean Monnet pointed out.[83] But the EU ought no longer to be a merely technocratic regulatory union, at least if we believe the President of the European Commission, Jacques Delors who, during the ratification process of the Treaty of Maastricht, said that even if Europe started as 'an elitist project', this 'phase of

---

82   In its judgment of 12 September 2012, the German Federal Constitutional Court dismissed for the most part applications for the issue of temporary injunctions to prevent ratification of the TSCG and the ESM Treaty. However, the Court imposed several democratic conditions for ratification: all future bailout deals that the ESM handles will have to be approved by the German Parliament, the liability of Germany is limited to 190 billion euros unless an increase is approved by the German Parliament, the confidentiality of information by the ESM does not prevent the German Parliament from getting information on the workings of the ESM. The fundamental criteria it used is familiar from its Lisbon ruling: the ability of a constitutional state to democratically shape itself. (BVerfG, 2 BvR 1390/12.) The same kind of argumentation is found in its ruling in the case concerning the Greek rescue package (BVerfG, 2 BvR 987/10). See also Kaarlo Tuori 'The European Financial Crisis – Constitutional Aspects and Implications' (EUI Working Papers 2012) 41–43.

83   Kevin Featherstone, 'Jean Monnet and the "Democracy Deficit" in the EU' (1994) 32 *Journal of Common Market Studies* 19, 150; see also Michael Burgess, *Federalism and European Union: Political Ideas, Influences, and Strategies in the European Community 1972–1986* (Routledge 1989) 59.

benign despotism is now over'.[84] However, still in 2011 Jürgen Habermas had to assert that the 'European project can no longer continue in elite modus'.[85]

In spite of the democratization process, management of the ongoing European crisis has intensified and cemented the position of the new European aristocracy and narrowed down the significance of EU citizens – and even their elected representatives. Benign despotism has surfaced to manage the EU. The *demos* of democracy has become an excess and residue for the EU institutions in their dealing with the Eurozone crisis and in their building a complete economic, monetary and fiscal union. Instead of democratization, de-democratization processes prevail in the EU as European democracy to come is trampled upon by a future of Europe dictated by the new aristocracy backed by private financial institutions and justified by the necessities of global financial capital. What is taking place in the EU is, Habermas writes together with Peter Bofinger and Julian Nida-Rümelin, the transformation of 'a citizen's democracy built on the idea of a social state into a sham democracy governed by market principles'.[86]

During the existential crisis, the representatives of EU citizens at the European and national level have given carte blanche to technical experts and bankers. This is the claim of a declaration signed by European intellectuals and artists, among them Alain Badiou, Étienne Balibar, Jean-Luc Nancy and Jacques Rancière. According to the declaration, what is taking place in Europe is a class war through finance, politics and law against society and democracy. The austerity measures have turned Greece into a laboratory of a neo-liberal model of society with curtailed fundamental democratic rights and without public services. Thus, the declaration says, defending the Greek people is 'a question of the future of democracy'.[87]

The Continuation of the European Project

Now, we can conclude that democracy is lacking in the EU. Therefore, the EU has insufficient democratic legitimacy. The main problems are: (1) the weakness of the only EU institution with a direct popular mandate: the European Parliament; (2) the Commission's central role in the EU; (3) the lack of democratic accountability not merely of the Commission, the CJEU and the ECB but also of the Council and the European Council; (4) the preponderance of economic, governmental

---

84   Vernon Bogdanor, 'Futility of a House with no windows' *The Independent* (26 July 1993)   <www.independent.co.uk/voices/futility-of-a-house-with-no-windows-1487252. html> accessed 12 September 2012.

85   Georg Diez, 'Habermas: The Last European. A Philosopher's mission to save the EU' *Spiegel on Line* (25 November 2011) <www.spiegel.de/international/europe/habermas-the-last-european-a-philosopher-s-mission-to-save-the-eu-a-799237.html> accessed 13 March 2013.

86   Bofinger, Habermas and Nida-Rümelin (n 31).

87   Vicky Skoumbi, 'Sauvons le peuple grec de ses sauveurs!' *Liberation* (22 February 2012).

and managerial rationality over political rationality and democratic legislative rationality; (5) decision-making and policy formulation and implementation processes that are inadequately transparent and politically responsive to public participation by European citizens; (6) the non-inclusive, non-transparent and secretive drafting of legislation; (7) the downplaying of political praxis and democratic input while emphasizing outcomes; (8) the reduction of participatory democracy to exclusive and depoliticized mechanisms of civil dialogue and governance; (9) the undemocratic process of treaty negotiations and ratification; and (10) the absence of a collective European identity and the absence of Europe-wide public sphere, political parties and European *demos*.

Based on the above, I propose four visions for the future of Europe: managerialism, anti-federalism, democratic federalism and democratic multiplicities.[88]

1. *Managerialism*: The oligarchic EU affirms that democracy has from the beginning been a secondary issue while economic integration and its principles have always had top priority. The EU's *Sonderweg*, its special way and identity, lies not in its being a post-national democratic commonwealth, but in its being a new kind of transnational regulatory system run by the Commission, nurtured by professionals and technical experts who possess economic, political, juridical and administrative capital, power and knowledge, and the CJEU, backed by the principles of direct effect and supremacy of EU law established by the CJEU itself (first articulated respectively in *Van Gend en Loos*[89] and *Costa v. ENEL*[90]).

Therefore, the democratic deficit is not an existential problem but an essential part of the EU from the beginning. Moreover, the EU does not actually require democratic legitimacy, since its existence is legitimated by its outputs: European peace, stability, prosperity and human security (personal, political, social, economic, environmental, health, food and community security). Democratic politics and legislation are ineffective forms of conducting policies, solving problems, preventing individual vulnerabilities and practising human security compared to managerial governing centred on and revolving around the Commission, the ECB and the IMF.

Thus, the EU should be developed towards a more efficiently and rationally managed and governed system which avoids the risk of (over-)politicization

---

88 Thomas Wallgren sees that the EU has three alternatives, which are (1) an authoritarian capitalism, (2) a democratic federal state and (3) the disintegration of the EU. According to him, crisis management may save the unity of the euro. However, the winners will be the economic and administrative elites. European democracy and the welfare state will be the losers. Thomas Wallgren, 'Suomen eurotiestä on päätettävä vaaleilla' *Helsingin Sanomat* (17 July 2012).

89 Case 26/62 *Van Gend en Loos v. Nederlandse Administratie der Belastingen* [1963] ECR 1.

90 Case 6/64 *Flaminio Costa v ENEL* [1964] ECR 585.

leading to democratic scandals. The demand 'more Europe' is not seen as synonymous with 'more democracy'.

2. *Anti-federalism*: The starting point of anti-federalism is the principle of national sovereignty. Anti-federalism calls for EU reform based on the sovereign integrity of the nation state coupled with democracy, accountability and openness. Transfer of legislative and budgetary powers from national parliaments to the EU ought to take place only to a necessary extent. Areas where EU policy supersedes national political choices and preferences should be kept minimal. National governments and parliaments are the ultimate decision-makers. Since the legitimacy of the intergovernmental institutions of the EU emanates from national sovereignty, they are preferred to supranational institutions.

Anti-federalist nationalism continues by claiming that if sovereignty is not given back to the Member States, the EU should be dissolved, or at least, one's own state should walk out. Europe should thus once again become a Europe of sovereign civic nation states, which offer the best guarantee against economic and social insecurities and the crisis of identities caused by globalization. And on the extreme right there are those who prefer a 'return' to ethnic nation states instead of civic ones.

3. *Democratic federalism*: Anti-federalist nationalism, based on the presupposition of the true democratic nature of European nation states, includes serious problems and risks. The end or freezing of the European project will not lead to a return to lost national democracy but instead to a Europe of more or less weak nation states, where global capitalism dictates national legislation and social, economic, monetary, fiscal and labour policies much more than today. Both the minimal EU and also the EU as it is are not realistic options. Either the EU should dissolve or become a political unity. Then again, we must keep in mind that that only a united Europe can become an effective counter-force to global capital and multinational finance institutions.[91]

However, even if the supporters of managerialism promise a more integrated and effective supranational union, this model is constitutionally unacceptable. It is contrary to the principle of democracy stated in the TEU and national constitutions. The Basic Law for the Federal Republic of Germany (Article 23(1)) even states explicitly that Germany will participate in the development of an EU that is 'committed to democratic, social and federal principles'. Even if the German Federal Constitutional Court defended national democracy, one could claim that inviolability of the principle of democracy is how the principle of democracy within the order of the TEU should be interpreted.[92] Actually, the CJEU ought to emphasize the enhancement, intensification and extension of the principle of democracy. Therefore, the non-democratic technocratic road will ruin the European project. Democratic reactions all around Europe against the management of the sovereign debt crisis give proof of this.

---

91   Daniel Cohn-Bendit and Guy Verhofstadt, *Für Europa. Ein Manifest* (Hanser 2012) 14.

92   BVerfG, 2 BvE 2/08, para. 216.

Habermas points out that as we are experiencing 'a dismantling of democracy' we have reached 'a crossroads'.[93] If the EU and European governments do not openly state what they are doing, they will 'continue to undermine the already weak democratic foundations' of the EU.[94] The sovereign debt crisis, which, as earlier noted, has developed into a political and social crisis, is the best thing that has happened to the EU. This ultimately existential crisis forces a reassessment of the EU and thus opens an opportunity to take a step towards democratic federalism, which would avoid the impasses of managerialism and anti-federalism. At the same time, it should be recognized that the democratization process has not merely suffered serious setbacks but has also failed to construct the EU as a democratic polity. The failure has been immanent in the process.

In other words, only a deeper unification and closer coordination of financial, economic and social policies can keep the European project going. However, this unification process ought to be at the same time a democratization process. Federalism without democracy is no option. As Daniel Cohn-Bendit and Guy Verhofstadt, who speak for a European federal Union with supranational European institutions, remind us: one ought to not replace one technocracy by another.[95]

Thus, the continuity of the democratization process is the only relevant possibility to continue the European political, juridical, economic and cultural project. The pressing task is to subject economic, monetary and fiscal policy and management, the ECB and the ESM, to proper democratic will-formation and/or control. Democracy in the EU should be effectively extended to the economic and social order.[96]

This requires, first of all, that the powers and competences of the European Parliament are increased.

This democratization-federalization of the EU may take place without new treaties, since the existing constitutional framework offers possibilities for strengthening democracy in the EU. If the European Parliament takes a more active role, if the CJEU and national constitutional and supreme courts give priority to the principle of democracy and democratic rights and if all other EU institutions take the principle of democracy seriously in their practices, then democratization is made possible. For democratic federalism, the central task

---

93   Diez (n 85).

94   Bofinger, Habermas and Nida-Rümelin (n 31). For the authors, 'The European federal state [*Bundesstaat*] is a wrong model'. The tone is different than in Habermas's text 'Why Europe Needs a Constitution' (2001) 11 *New Left Review*.

95   Cohn-Bendit and Verhofstadt (n 91) 11.

96   See Wolfgang Abendroth, *Zum Begriff des demokratischen und sozialen Rechtsstaates im Grundgesetz der Bundesrepublik Deutschland* (Gesammelte Schriften, Band 2, Offizin 2008) 346; Kolja Möller, 'After the Lisbon Ruling: Where Is Social Democracy?' in A Fischer-Lescano, C Joerges and A Wonka (eds), *The German Constitutional Court's Lisbon Ruling: Legal and Political Science Perspectives* (ZERP 2010) 86.

is not developing and strengthening participatory democracy, understood today mainly as deliberative governance, but strengthening representative democracy. In this process the European Parliament should become 'a representative body of a sovereign European people' about which the German Federal Constitutional Court spoke in its Lisbon ruling, even though it did not see this possibility in its fixation on the nation-state model of representative democracy.[97] Besides, the need exists for Europeanization of the European Parliament so that it would become European in its debates, elections, responsiveness and accountability.

This democratization-federalization process should take place in open and transparent processes. This is an unconditional normative requirement laid down by the democratic principle of the TEU and national constitutions. The democratization of the EU would pave the way for and give legitimacy to federalization of the EU. Even if the contemporary constitutional framework and institutional architecture enable the first steps towards a democratic federalism, in the last resort democratization-federalization is not possible without a constitutional reform.

For this purpose, a constitutional convention should be summoned. In open, transparent and inclusive deliberations, which would engage not merely representative civil society organizations and movements but also all European citizens, the convention would consider visions of European democratic political union. The convention would prepare a draft for a European constitution or constitutional treaty. Unlike the TCE (and also the TEU and TFEU), the draft constitution should be written in clear, readable and understandable language. This draft would be submitted to a Europe-wide referendum. Thus, EU citizens would ultimately decide, not merely about the draft, but also about the future of the EU. If the draft is accepted, the constitution would *constitute* a democratic and federalist EU. This constitution-making process would provoke transnationalization of the national public sphere and bring the European people into being, not as Europeans sharing a common identity or substance, but as European citizens sharing the principles of democracy, human dignity and human rights.[98] Thus, EU citizens would become a European *demos* in and through this constitutionalization process.[99]

A democratic and federalist constitution may seem unrealistic in an existential crisis when, on the one hand, the EU is dominated by managerialism, and, on the other hand, public debate is dominated by right- and left-wing anti-federalist nationalism. Even though I shun the idea of a multi-speed Europe, a realistic option would perhaps be that a European avant-garde would pave the way for democratic federalism in a constitutionalization process, which is the process of democratization and federalization.

---

97   BVerfG, 2 BvE 2/08, para. 280.

98   Jürgen Habermas, *Zur Verfassung Europas. Ein Essay.* (Suhrkamp 2011); Bofinger, Habermas and Nida-Rümelin (n 31).

99   On the constitutionalization see Kaarlo Tuori, 'The Many Constitutions of Europe' in K Tuori and S Sankari (eds), *The Many Constitutions of Europe* (Ashgate 2010).

This is not the only issue that has to be taken into consideration. Democratic federalism (re)politicizes European policy formation and decision-making and brings about democratic legitimacy. However, it may not bridge the gap between democracy as a constitutional form of government and democracy as the power of the people. Even democratic federalism may continue the tradition of representative democracy, where the parliamentary system has democratic hegemony over the *demos*.[100] A conflict exists between the principles of representative and participatory democracy. How to balance these two elements of the principle of democracy in a democratic European polity? How to bring to light the *demos*, which is the essential and necessary conceptual element of democracy?[101]

4. *Democratic multiplicities*: To answer these problems we have to rethink democracy. At the same time, we should rethink what European federalism is, since the model of a federal state is not suited to the EU. Is a transnational and non-statist federalism available that is based on democracy? Thus democracy and federalism needs to be reinvented. The fourth vision about the future of Europe outlines what democratic multiplicities could be without dictating the model, figure or foresight of a Europe to come.[102]

Democratic Multiplicities

Democracy is not, at root, a form of government or constitution, a certain type of political regime. It is not merely an identifiable legitimate authority, institutional architecture or procedures that proceed from constitutional authorization. From Plato to Lenin and beyond democracy has been wrongly considered as no more than a particular form of state, as a configuration of the formal exercise of sovereignty.[103]

The truth of democracy is the power of the people, the exercise of political *kratos*, power, by the *demos*. According to Rancière, the *demos* of democracy is not those who are the strongest, the richest or the best, who possess wisdom, practical reason or expertise, who represent the people, capital or civil society. Then again, the *demos* is not a constituency, a population, a community of those who share a common identity, a civil society or the majority of the people. This is the scandal of democracy: it is the power of those who have no special entitlement, capacity or status to exercise power. Democracy is the power of anyone at all. Hence, on the one hand, the *demos* names all the people in a political community, and on the other hand, it names those who have no part in institutionalized political decision making and governance (except as members of the constituency), but who declare themselves to be the *demos* in the name of wrong done them by

---

100   Cf. Alain Badiou, *Metapolitics* (Verso 2005) 122.
101   Cf. Nancy (n 37) 17.
102   Nancy (n 37) 27–9.
103   Rancière (n 30); cf. Alain Badiou, 'L'emblème démocratique' in G Agamben et al (eds), *Démocratie, dans quel état?* (La Fabrique 2009) 17.

the establishment. In this second sense, the *demos* refers to the division of the community.[104] Democracy begins when those who have no share in the political, legal, economic, regulatory and institutional order of things present themselves as political subjects in democratic events by seizing democratic equality that always already belongs to everyone. Democracy is 'the power of the people', that is, the power of anyone at all.[105]

European political subjects are not to be reduced to stakeholders, participants, actors of civil society and non-governmental organizations. A criterion for becoming a political subject is neither legal or institutional status nor representativeness or expertise. European political subjects are those who bring about a political dispute and challenge the existing European 'distribution of the sensible' (Rancière's term *le partage du sensible* refers to the implicit and explicit division and governance of the sensible order, to the distribution of competences and positions, to the forms and places of participation, to inclusion and exclusion, to the division between those whose voices are heard, whose bodies are seen, whose presence is recognized and those who are not counted in).[106]

As an example, European political subjects are those EU citizens – as well as legal immigrants and *sans-papiers* – who come together to oppose austerity measures and bailout agreements dictated by the Commission, the ECB and the IMF. Thus, a political subject is not something essential but a mode of being in a public event, which is a democratic event. In these democratic events, European political subjects make themselves heard and seen by creating democratic stages for their demands, arguments, discussions and actions. Thus, public and private spaces and social media are transformed into democratic stages. Political subjects bring forth wrongs and injustices, policy and legislative initiatives, rebellion and resistance. They present a critique of the European distribution of the sensible, interrupt it and make demands for its reconfiguration. European democracy is, *first of all*, a project, or more properly, a manifold movement where individuals are created as political subjects as they open political stages and participate in democratic events. Democracy is, *first of all*, participatory democracy that takes place in a multiplicity of democratic events, which can be considered as 'forms of decentralised participation'.[107] Democratic potentiality emanates from the direct participation. In and through these local, national, transnational and global events spontaneous, autonomous and non-hierarchical democratic spaces and stages are constituted. This is what the decentralized European public sphere is.

This is participatory democracy, which is what democracy, *first and foremost*, is. Organized civil society is secondary to these democratic events. European political

---

104 Jacques Rancière, *La Mésente. Politique et philosophie* (Galilée 1995) especially chapters 1 and 2.

105 Rancière (n 30) 56.

106 See Jacques Rancière, *Le Partage du sensible: Ésthetique et politique* (La Fabrique 2000).

107 BVerfG, 2 BvE 2/08, para. 272.

subjects constituted in and through these events are the true democratic partners of the EU. Thus, according to Article 11(2) TEU, the EU institutions 'shall maintain an open, transparent and regular dialogue with representative associations and civil society', which should not be interpreted exclusively as organized civil society but inclusively so that part of it is the multiplicity of democratic events.[108] This is in line with the principle of democratic equality (Article 9 TEU) according to which all EU citizens – including political subjects – should receive equal attention from the EU institutions, bodies, offices and agencies. This is what civil dialogue as 'a democratic and public opinion-forming process' is.[109] Thus, participatory democracy in the EU should not be reduced to more or less institutionalized forms of decentralized governance and deliberative decision-making mechanisms open to civil society actors, who are counted as representatives.

Rousseau, the advocate of direct democracy and the inalienable sovereignty of the people, wrote: 'If there were a nation of Gods, it would govern itself democratically. A government so perfect is not suited to men'.[110] What Rousseau did was to separate a sovereign people directly enacting laws in a general assembly and a subordinate executive authority, which has authority to apply laws to particular cases and a political and legislative initiative.[111] Europeans are not gods. Therefore, one could claim, democracy as democratic events does not suit the EU. It is a mere utopia compared to participating in deliberation in various governance mechanisms.

However, European direct participatory democracy is not a utopia but the premise of democratic politics and the presupposition of a democratic polity. EU democracy ought to consist of, *first of all*, of a multiplicity of democratic events. As a consequence, European democracy is not based on any *arkhe* or *principium*, not even on the democratic tradition of modern European nation states. The principle of democracy or a democratic constitutional government cannot as such guarantee democracy in the EU as we have seen. The foundation of democracy in the EU is the absence of any foundation. Because of this European democracy is

---

108   Article 11(1) TEU mentions explicitly 'citizens and representative associations' as it defines to whom the EU institutions shall '*give opportunity* to make known and publicly exchange their views' (italics mine). Article 11(2) TEU defines differently those with whom the EU institutions '*shall maintain* an open, transparent and regular dialogue' (italics mine). They are 'representative associations and civil society'. So it seems that for citizens it is enough to give opportunities but it is not demanded to maintain a dialogue with them. However, civil society is 'a collective term for all types of social action, by individuals or groups, that do not emanate from the state and are not run by it'. European Economic and Social Committee, (n 73).

109   European Economic and Social Committee (n 73).

110   Rousseau (n 38) 92.

111   Richard Fralin, *Rousseau and Representation* (Columbia University Press 1978); Simon Critchley, 'The Catechism of the Citizen: Politics, Law and Religion in, after, with and against Rousseau' in A Hirvonen and J Porttikivi (eds), *Law and Evil. Philosophy, Politics, Psychoanalysis* (Routledge 2010).

always yet to come. The democratization process is thus an ongoing process of democratic events in which the democracy of the EU is continually reinvented. The constituent power of the European people is not a transitory moment but immanent to incessant democratic events in which we should also count elections and referendums.

Then again, how to bring together democratic events, other forms of participatory democracy and representative democracy in the context of the EU? What role could democratic stages play in the EU's institutional architecture?

By emphasizing democratic events, I am not putting phantom masses against the EU institutions, national governments and deliberative governance mechanisms. Even if democratic events are constitutive events that constitute political subjects and stages, they are, as political processes, organized processes, as Alain Badiou would remark.[112] They are not organized by EU law and decisions. They often have no formal organization, representatives, rules and procedural guidelines. But they are organized at the moment when they come about.

As organized political processes, democratic events are, as I have already noted, partners in EU policy- and decision-making. Instead of considering them as democratic scandals, the EU should recognize the democratic potential that is immanent to these scandals. The White Paper points out that democracy 'depends on people being able to take part in public debates'.[113] The democratization of the EU requires that the EU institutions are responsive to these events.

As partners, the political subjects of democratic events may have multiple effects on and relationships with the EU institutions and the EU's multi-level decision-making mechanisms.

Democratic events could be seen as a form of 'directly deliberative polyarchy', about which Oliver Gerstenberg and Charles F. Sabel speak, in which stakeholders participate directly in political debate, problem solving and decision-making instead of delegating responsibility for their choices to representatives 'who command a language beyond them'.[114] This kind of direct participation of political subjects in decentralized political stages does not have to be merely local but may also be supranational events debating and deciding contested policy issues. In this connection, deliberation should be understood not merely as consensus-seeking rational argumentation but also as antagonistic debates and political struggles.

The mechanism of governance may integrate democratic events. The demands, claims, proposals – and also knowledge – produced by political subjects in these events would have a more or less direct effect on the EU's decentralized and coordinated deliberative and participatory policy- and rule-making processes.

---

112   Badiou (n 100) 121.

113   European Commission (n 7) 11.

114   Oliver Gerstenberg and Charles F Sabel, 'Directly-deliberative Polyarchy: An Institutional Ideal for Europe' in C Joerges and R Dehousse (eds), *Good Governance in Europe's Integrated Market* (Oxford University Press 2002) 340; see also De la Port and Nanz (n 74) 271.

Through the governance mechanism political subjects would have an indirect influence on the EU institutions. Including political subjects in European multi-level governance would democratize it.

Democratic events could be starting points for citizens' initiatives or have a direct impact on ordinary legislative procedures. Owing to democratic events, the Commission might start to submit proposals requested in these events. They also could have an effect on the decision-making process of the European Parliament and the Council. They might influence EU policies in various fields and compel the European Council to take an issue on its agenda as it defines the general political direction and priorities of the EU. The CJEU might become aware of injustices and fundamental rights violations as political subjects give them voice. In its judicial activity it could turn attention to the principle of democracy and establish it as an inviolable principle that could not be balanced against market freedoms or other legal, policy or economic interests. Democratic events might themselves refer to fundamental rights or other EU legislation as their arguments and thus politicize subjective rights and legal norms and turn European and national courts into 'arenas in a legal-political struggle for a social and democratic European law'.[115] Likewise, they could make the most of the judgments of the CJEU, the European Court of Human Rights and national constitutional or supreme courts.

Conclusion

These are just some possible ways for democratic events to partake in the exercise of European democratic politics and be in political dialogue with the EU institutions and the mechanism of governance (without identifying with them).[116] In these ways, democratic events would feed the views and concerns of political subjects into EU policy- and law-making processes and adjudication. As a consequence, a democratic EU would be based on the incessant democratization process.

All this is possible in the existing constitutional and institutional architecture of the EU. If the EU institutions would take the principle of democracy seriously, it would take into account not merely deliberative governance but also decentralized democratic events and also take political subjects as participants within decision-making.

However, rethinking and reinventing European democracy and federalism would require an 'organized' open, transparent and inclusive debate on the future of Europe followed by a constitutional convention. The convention should include in its discussions and decision-making new social movements and democratic events, among others. Finally, the new constitution, which would recognize

---

115   Andreas Fischer-Lescano, 'Judicial Sovereignty Unlimited? A Critique of the German Federal Constitutional Court's Ruling on the Lisbon Treaty' in Fischer-Lescano, Joerges and Wonka (eds) (n 96) 69.

116   See Rancière (n 104) Chapter 5.

europe/habermas-the-last-european-a-philosopher-s-mission-to-save-the-eu-a-799237.html> accessed 13 March 2013

Eberlein B and Kerwer D, 'New Governance in the European Union: A Theoretical Perspective' (2004) 42(1) *JCMS* 121

Farrell D, 'Professor Farrell, The EP is now one of the most powerful legislatures in the world' European Parliament Press Releases (18 June 2007) <http://www.europarl.europa.eu/sides/getDoc.do?language=EN&type=IM-PRESS&reference=20070615IPR07837> accessed 13 March 2013

Featherstone K, 'Jean Monnet and the "Democracy Deficit" in the EU' (1994) 32(2) *Journal of Common Market Studies* 19

Fischer-Lescano A, 'Judicial Sovereignty Unlimited? A Critique of the German Federal Constitutional Court's Ruling on the Lisbon Treaty' in A Fischer-Lescano, C Joerges and A Wonka (eds), *The German Constitutional Court's Lisbon Ruling: Legal and Political Science Perspectives* (ZERP 2010)

Fralin R, *Rousseau and Representation* (Columbia University Press 1978)

Gerstenberg O and Sabel CF, 'Directly-deliberative Polyarchy: An Institutional Ideal for Europe' in C Joerges and R Dehousse (eds), *Good Governance in Europe's Integrated Market* (Oxford University Press 2002)

'Greece holds key over EU bailout' *BBC News* (17 June 2012) <http://www.bbc.co.uk/news/world-europe-18472595> accessed 1 October 2013

Habermas J, 'Europe's post-democratic era' *The Guardian* (10 November 2011)

—— *Zur Verfassung Europas. Ein Essay.* (Suhrkamp 2011)

—— 'Why Europe Needs a Constitution' (2001) 11 *New Left Review*

Hix S, Noury AG and Roland G, *Democratic Politics in the European Parliament* (Cambridge University Press 2007)

Keena C, 'No Vote "A leap in the Dark"' *Irish Times* (16 May 2012) <http://www.irishtimes.com/newspaper/breaking/2012/0516/breaking11.html> accessed 12 September 2012

Kohler-Koch B, 'Civil Society and EU democracy: "Astroturf" Representation?' (2010) 17(1) *Journal of European Public Policy* 100

Korkea-aho E, *New Governance and the EU Courts. The Experimental Architecture of Judicial Decision-Making* (2010) LLD dissertation, Faculty of Law, University of Helsinki

Ladeur K-H, 'We, the European People … Relâche' (2008) 14(2) *European Law Journal* 147

Lévy J, Rennes J and Zerbib D, 'Jacques Rancière: "Les Territoires de la pensée partagée"' EspaceTemps.net, 2007 <http://www.espacestemps.net/document2142.html> accessed 1 October 2013

MacCormick N, 'Democracy, Subsidiary and Citizenship in the "European Commonwealth"' (1997) 16(4) *Law and Philosophy* 332

Majone G, *Regulating Europe* (Routledge 1996)

—— 'Europe's "Democratic Deficit": The Question of Standards' (1998) 4(1) *European Law Journal* 5

Marquand D, *Parliament for Europe* (J Cape 1979)

Martin D, *European Union and the Democratic Deficit* (John Wheatley Centre 1990)

Marx K, *Economic and Philosophic Manuscripts of 1844* (Foreign Language Publishing House 1959)

McDonald H, 'Irish referendum no to EU treaty will prompt euro exit, business leaders warn' *The Guardian* (15 May 2012) <http://www.guardian.co.uk/world/2012/may/15/irish-referendum-no-eu-euro> accessed 13 March 2013

Moravcsik A, 'In Defence of the "Democratic Deficit": Reassessing the Legitimacy of the European Union' (2002) 40(4) *Journal of Common Market Studies* 603

Möller K, 'After the Lisbon Ruling: Where Is Social Democracy?' in A Fischer-Lescano, C Joerges and A Wonka (eds), *The German Constitutional Court's Lisbon Ruling: Legal and Political Science Perspectives* (ZERP 2010)

Nancy J-L, *Vérité de la démocratie* (Galilée 2008)

Peters A, 'European Democracy after the 2003 Convention' (2004) 41 *Common Market Law Review* 37

Pöttering H-G, 'Pöttering hopeful reforms still achievable before 2009 Euro-elections' European Parliament Published Article (13 June 2008) <http://www.europarl.europa.eu/sides/getDoc.do?pubRef=-//EP//TEXT+IM-PRESS+2008 0613STO31667+0+DOC+XML+V0//EN> accessed 13 March 2013

Rancière J, 'Dissenting Words. A Conversation with Jacques Rancière' (2000) 30(2) *Diacritics* 113

—— *La haine de la démocratie* (La Fabrique 2005)

—— *La Mésente. Politique et philosophie* (Galilée 1995)

—— *Le Partage du sensible: Ésthetique et politique* (La Fabrique 2000)

——'Les démocracies contre la démocratie' in G Agamben et al (eds), *Démocratie, dans quel état?* (La Fabrique 2009)

Rittberger B, *Building Europe's Parliament* (Oxford University Press 2005)

Ross K, *Democracy for Sale, in Democracy in What State?* (Columbia University Press 2011)

Rousseau J-J, *The Social Contract and Later Political Writings* (Cambridge University Press 1997)

Schlamp H-J, 'Fate of the European Union Lies with Ireland' *Der Spiegel* (10 June 2008) <http://www.spiegel.de/international/europe/lisbon-treaty-referendum-fate-of-the-european-union-lies-with-ireland-a-558893.html> accessed 13 March 2013

Scott J and Trubek DM, 'Mind the Gap: Law and New Approaches to Governance in the European Union' (2002) 8(1) *European Law Journal* 1

Skoumbi V, 'Sauvons le peuple grec de ses sauveurs!' *Liberation* (22 February 2012)

Smith J, *Europe's Elected Parliament* (Sheffield Academic Press 1999)

Tuori K, *Critical Legal Positivism* (Ashgate 2002)

—— 'The Many Constitutions of Europe' in K Tuori and S Sankari (eds), *The Many Constitutions of Europe* (Ashgate 2010)

—— 'The European Financial Crisis – Constitutional Aspects and Implications' (EUI Working Papers 2012)

Ulrich B, 'Panik statt Politik' *Die Zeit* (19 August 2012)

Voltaire, 'De la paix perpétuelle. Par le docteur Goodheart' (Oeuvres complètes. Tome I. Politiques et législation, Armand-Aubrée éditeur 1829)

Wallgren T, 'Suomen eurotiestä on päätettävä vaaleilla' *Helsingin Sanomat* (17 July 2012)

Warleigh A, 'On the Path to Legitimacy? The EU Citizens' Initiative Right from a Critical Deliberativist Perspective' in V Della Sala and C Ruzza (eds), *Governance and Civil Society in the European Union. Normative Perspectives* (Volume 1, Manchester University Press 2007)

Westlake M, *A Modern Guide to the European Parliament* (Pinter 1994)

Wincott D, 'Does the European Union Pervert Democracy? Questions of Democracy in New Constitutionalist Thought on the Future of Europe' (1998) 4(4) *European Law Journal* 411

Wintour P, 'EU scraps timetable for ratifying constitution' *The Guardian* (17 June 2005) <http://www.guardian.co.uk/politics/2005/jun/17/eu.politics> accessed 16 March 2013

Žižek S, 'From Democracy to Divine Violence' in G Agamben et al (eds), *Democracy in What State?* (Columbia University Press 2011)

EU documents

Action Committee for European Democracy. The Way Forward for the European Union, 8 July 2007 <http://web.archive.org/web/20070708035001/http://www.eui.eu/RSCAS/e-texts/ACED2007_DECLARATION_4JUNE07.pdf> accessed 15 March 2013

EACEA, Europe for Citizens Programme 2007–2013. Programme Guide <http://eacea.ec.europa.eu/citizenship/programme/documents/2013/guide_2013_en_final%20.pdf> accessed 13 March 2013

European Commission. European Governance – A White Paper, COM (2001) 428 final, 25 July 2001

European Commission. European Year of Citizens <http://europa.eu/citizens-2013/> accessed 13 March 2013

European Commission. Proposal for Council Regulation establishing for the period 2014–2020 the programme 'Europe for Citizens', COM(2011) 884

European Council. Presidency Conclusions, 23–24 March 2000

European Council. Laeken Declaration of the Future on the European Union, 15 December 2001

European Parliament legislative resolution of 11 February 2010 on the proposal for a Council decision on the conclusion of the Agreement between the European Union and the United States of America on the processing and transfer of Financial Messaging Data from the European Union to the United States for purposes of the Terrorist Finance Tracking Program (05305/1/2010/

REV 1 – C7–0004/2010 – 2009/0190(NLE)). European Parliament Document 0029(2010)

European Parliament legislative resolution of 8 July 2010 on the draft Council decision on the conclusion of the Agreement between the European Union and the United States of America on the processing and transfer of Financial Messaging Data from the European Union to the United States for the purposes of the Terrorist Finance Tracking Program (11222/1/2010/REV 1 and COR 1 – C7–0158/2010 – 2010/0178(NLE)). European Parliament Document 0279(2010)

European Economic and Social Committee. A Roadmap for Participatory Democracy. Press Release, 25 March 2011European Economic and Social Committee. Participatory Democracy in 5 Points, 2011 <http://www.eesc. europa.eu/?i=portal.en.publications.15525> accessed 20 June 2014

President of European Commission, José Manuel Barroso. 'The Political Priorities of New European Commission'. European Commission, 3 September 2009 <http://ec.europa.eu/commission_2010–2014/president/pdf/press_20090903_ en.pdf> accessed 13 March 2013

Cases

Court of Justice of the European Union (CJEU)

Case 26/62 *Van Gend en Loos v. Nederlandse Administratie Belastingen* [1963] ECR 1

Case 6/64 *Flaminio Costa v. Ente Nazionale per L'Energia Elettrica (ENEL)* [1964] ECR 583

Case C-370/12 *Thomas Pringle v Government of Ireland Thomas Pringle v Government of Ireland, Ireland and the Attorney General* of 27 November 2012, not yet reported

Bundesverfassungsgericht
BVerfGE 37, 29.5.1974
BVerfG, 2 BvE 2/08, 30.6.2009
BVerfG, 2 BvR 987/10, 7.9.2011
BVerfG, 2 BvR 1390/12, 12.9.2012

Supreme Court of Ireland
Crotty v. An Taoiseach [1987] IESC 4; [1987] IR 713.1. (9 April 1987)

Chapter 7

Which Democracy for Which *Demos*?

RBJ Walker[1]

Few weeks pass without sharp reminders that democracy remains an open question everywhere; in some places more than others, perhaps, but in no place does a claim to democracy warrant complacency. Democracy names a question, indeed a large bundle of questions, some of them more difficult to engage than the concept of democracy itself.

Are we to understand democracy as a form of legitimate power/authority/ constitution/sovereignty/law or a practice/technique/art of government? Plato already had much to say about this. Are we destined to understand democracy as a form/practice that is always in danger of resolving into tyranny as its corrupt other? Plato, Aristotle and Rousseau remain essential reading here. Can we talk about democracy without engaging in some depth with concepts of civil society, republicanism, a rule of law, liberty, equality, freedom of thought and information, practices of representation, the structure of party systems, and many other things, or is some much narrower definition acceptable? Are we to understand democracy as a form or practice that is always conditional upon some prior delimitation of a *polis/demos*, some spatiotemporal/social condition of possibility and limit, which may be endlessly contested by the form/practice that is constituted or permanently fixed in some apparently natural place and time? Are we simply going to have to invent new variations on the familiar struggle between state sovereignty and popular sovereignty, assuming that we know what it means to talk about sovereignty, a state, or a people? Or must we hope/fear that we will have to re-imagine sovereignty in some other terms, or even envision some kind of politics that avoids principles of sovereignty altogether?

Many commentators seem to be exhausted not only by the conceptual breadth and density of the question, and its reach into the most basic assumptions about what we mean by politics, but also by a widespread sense that so many empirical tendencies suggest that many great hopes for democracy are being sharply constrained or even extinguished. Can't go on, but must go on, they seem to suggest. Jean-Luc Nancy's recent formulation speaks for many:

1   RBJ Walker is Professor of Political Science and of Cultural, Social and Political Thought at the University of Victoria, BC, Canada and Distinguished International Professor, Instituto de Relacionais Internacionais, Pontifica Universidade Catolica do Rio de Janeiro, Brazil. He is Editor of the journal *Alternatives: Global, Local, Political*, and founding co-editor of the journal *International Political Sociology.*

Is it at all meaningful to call oneself a 'democrat'? Manifestly, one may and should answer both 'no, it's quite meaningless, since it is no longer possible to call oneself anything else', and 'yes, of course, given that equality, justice and liberty are under threat from plutocracies, technocracies, and mafiocracies wherever we look'. *Democracy* has become an exemplary case of the loss of the power to signify: representing both supreme political virtue and the only means of achieving the common good, it grew so fraught that it was no longer capable of generating any problematic or serving any heuristic purpose. All that goes on now is marginal debate about the differences between various democratic systems and sensibilities. In short, *democracy* means everything – politics, ethics, law, civilization – and nothing.[2]

Democracy may or may not name a question that is now more difficult than ever before. Still, it is especially difficult to engage with it now not only because judgments about whether the name is appropriate in any particular place are so vigorously contested but because it is once again unclear what kind of political practice the concept of democracy could possibly name. To ask whether, say, Canada (my implicit starting point here), Turkey, Brazil, the USA (my intermediate stops) or Europe (my eventual destination) deserve to be called democratic is to juggle with indices of both yes and no; and to rely on precarious understandings of how we ought to interpret indices. To ask what we mean when we connect such places with such a concept is to risk seduction by many official stories that do not quite satisfy demands for either scholarly scruple or discriminating political judgment.

Despite many self-serving rhetorics, we clearly live among quasi-democracies at best. This is certainly not to denigrate many historical achievements. On the contrary, it is to insist that many historical achievements have been smothered and appropriated by many self-serving rhetorics. Few dare to shun the name; many doubt the connection between the name and its supposed referent. The gap between rhetoric and achievement breeds both bracing scepticism and corrupting cynicism. Many of the great achievements of even quasi-democracies have been hard won. It is also clear that many of these achievements have been seriously eroded in many places, my starting point included. Sometimes they have been eroded in the name of democracy itself, or at least in the name of concepts of democracy that are profoundly at odds with more established democratic norms. For there is, of course, no historical record of a single understanding of democracy, no matter how hard some of the most powerful forces of our time have tried to impose their preferred brand upon others, especially as a condition of appropriate policies of 'development' in more vulnerable societies. One of the necessary conditions for any kind of democratic politics, one might say, is the possibility of contesting what it means to engage in democratic politics, and it

---

2   Jean-Luc Nancy, 'Finite and Infinite Democracy' in G Agamben et al (eds) *Democracy in What State?* (Columbia University Press 2010) 58.

is the possibility of such contestation that might yet permit us to move on from the sense of exhaustion understandably expressed in so many contemporary commentaries.

Democracy is one of those 'essentially contested concepts' demanding their own application to any process that seeks to define them, so that, to stay with my example, the imposition of 'multiparty representation' as the appropriate definition of democracy for 'developing states' should always be met by an insistence on democratic discussion of what democracy should mean for those involved. In this respect democracy is closely related to the concept of sovereignty, a concept that, as Thomas Hobbes recognised with unmatched clarity, always demands sustained analysis of the practices of sovereign authorization constituting a sovereign capacity to authorize sovereign law. Many of the most worrisome trends of our time depend on a strong preference for essentially uncontested concepts in both cases. It is a preference that still counts as both scholarly authority and sustainable political judgment in far too many situations. It should not. Democracy is an open concept as well as an open question, and those who claim expertise in definitions of what democracy must be always risk authoritarian tendencies when they try to make their definitions stick.

To root a discussion of democracy in fairly remote – classical and other – historical sources would be to see that the name has referred to a great diversity of ambitions, many of them at odds with more recent conventions. Historical records may confirm a wide range of 'transitions to democracy', but they also confirm many struggles in the name of competing understandings of democracy. For my purposes here, just two traditions, both firmly in play in early twentieth-century Europe and still shaping contemporary events but already formulated with some clarity sometime between the eras symbolized by, say, Hobbes and Adam Smith, will be sufficient to begin with. Specifically, contemporary discussions about the status of democracy are still shaped by long-standing tensions about whether democracy is a political condition ultimately rooted in state law and enacted within the jurisdictions of sovereign nation states, within some kind of Hobbesian commonwealth, or in the laws of economic value generated by capitalist markets and the privatization of common wealth.

Many in 'the West' are now nostalgic for some kind of social democracy, for a political order predicated on something like a Keynesian accommodation between states and capital, or between states and markets in the current conventions. Others retain hopes for accommodations made in the name of a stronger flavour of nationalism: in the name of the kind of 'modernization from above' that has been familiar from the time of Otto von Bismark and Max Weber to the strategies of the so-called BRICS countries attempting to create a multipolar antidote to excessive expressions of American unipolarity or Western hegemony. For all their differences, both social democrats and statist nationalists have some sense of what they are talking about in relation to democracy because they can refer to some kind of state, and thus a familiar kind of *demos*, marked by a familiar kind of sovereign law, that can contain and sustain some form of democratic practice in which economic processes are more or less subservient to state law, with the difference between the more and the less being of critical consequence.

On the other hand, many of the dominant forces of our time care less about generalized categories of society or nation than about the promises of a market. This is the so-called neo-liberal move that has been reshaping not only the conventions of Keynesianism and liberal democracy but even the character of nation/state-led modernization from above. The general inspiration here comes less from Hobbes (and many others) than, again among many possible sources, from John Locke's account of private property and accounts of the transformation of private vices into public virtues celebrated those we now think of as 'economists'. Here the character and even the location of the *demos* is not quite so clear, although official stories still confirm its congruence with the *demos* of state law. The concept of private property may have much in common with the concept of the sovereign law of states, but once hitched to the mobile strategies of market processes and the universalizing tendencies of capitalist forms of production, distribution and exchange, the two primary sites of ultimate value in our supposedly post-theological modern political order – sovereign state law and an also sovereign economic law (money would be the shorthand version) – became more obviously in dramatic tension.

Attempts to resolve this tension have shaped and still shape many of the most important achievements of our most familiar forms of democracy, all of which struggle to reconcile claims to both liberty and equality in the context of the competing dynamics of states and markets. This is why so many accounts of democracy are still haunted by versions of the elite theories of democracy, once associated with the Italians Roberto Michels, Gaetano Mosca and Vilfredo Pareto, which valorized democracy as a practice of inequality that is fundamentally at odds with narratives about democracy as an equalitarian practice of representation or equal rights under a rule of law. Contemporary concerns are expressed in relation to the ever more extreme divergence between an extremely wealthy minority and the rest of us. From, say, some ugly experiments in Chile shaped by figures like Milton Friedman to the rush to the radical shifts associated with Margaret Thatcher, Ronald Reagan and their many heirs, and on to more recent attempts to justify bold policies of unequal redistribution as mere responses to a necessary austerity, claims about democracy have been caught ever more tightly between competing accounts of the *demos* to which democracy is supposed to refer. As with the achievements of social democracy, Keynesian political economy and the privileging of the 'high politics' of national-state power over the 'low politics' of economic power, much of the received wisdom about democratic possibilities has rested on the assumption that the *demos* constituted by state law and the *demos* constituted by capitalist markets can be made to converge, again more or less. Much of the substantive repertoire of modern democratic politics has hinged on the difference between the more and the less, on the appropriate forms of regulation, representation and redistribution necessary to sustain a political order ordained by these two gods of a modern secular political order. As divergence has become more and more apparent, not least as expressed in popular accounts of 'globalization' as well as in relation to the corruption and collapse of financial markets, democracy has become even less susceptible to assumptions that we know to which *demos* the term is supposed to refer.

So democracy is an open question, and an open concept, and it is especially open in relation to competing accounts of which *demos*, or which constellation of *demoi*, the concept is supposed to refer. The tension between 'political' and 'economic' versions has been with us for a long time, and now seems to lie behind much of the widespread scepticism or even cynicism about whether the name of democracy can be anything more than a rhetorical mask expressing an increasingly impossible ambition. The question of democracy becomes even more elusive as it becomes ever more obvious that it is indeed a bundle of questions, some of which are even more difficult to engage than the concept of democracy as we have come to know it: questions especially about what democracy might mean when the *demos* seems to be losing some of its moorings in any singular political community, or systemic order of singular political communities, rooted in state and international law. This is why some scholars are prepared to countenance other understandings of what it means to speak about a *demos*, whether larger (cosmopolitan, global) or smaller (local, urban) in scale. It is also why it is so difficult to speak about democracy in relation to Europe, whatever and wherever that may be; but not only in Europe.

II

Particular recent events have added further reminders that democracy is both an open question and an open concept. I only pick two sorts of event from many possibilities. These events are not explicitly European. They nevertheless speak to questions about democracy in the specific case of Europe in ways that I hope will become obvious as I move along. One sort of event, the eruption of popular dissent within highly centralized and rapidly modernizing states, occurred both in Turkey and in Brazil. Another sort of event, disclosure of still more information about the surveillance of entire populations through powerful networks of computerized agencies, some of them nominally public and some nominally private, occurred in the USA. Neither sort of event, however, is easily contained within these particular states, or separated from the dynamics shaping and limiting democratic practices in Europe.

In Turkey, very local protests against yet another imposition of 'development' sponsored by the familiar combination of large corporations and a modernizing state provoked an also familiar heavy-handed response from police and security forces. These local protests quickly triggered much broader expressions of discontent. These events in turn generated speculation about the possible retreat from an at least partly quasi-democratic government towards something more directly authoritarian as well as about the potential for new forms of democratic action by groups expressing new social forces thrown up by new forms of modernization.

Despite reminders of Ottoman rule, the underlying pattern here has been shaped by the standard narratives about the need for modernization from above, the narrative articulated with particular force in Weber's exemplary diagnosis of the need for some functional replacement for the middle class as the driver of modernization given the desire to 'catch up' with hegemonic states in an increasingly internationalized political order. This, it is worth noting, is precisely the narrative that has largely gone missing from most Anglo-American accounts of that internationalized order, which prefer to erase history in favour of more elegantly spatialized accounts of structural form while simultaneously pushing history into the narratives about 'development' that have so corrupted many literatures about comparative politics and their highly constrained accounts of democracy. Within these narratives, it is easy enough to interpret these particular events as yet another variation on the struggle between popular sovereignty and state sovereignty within the context of a modernizing state seeking to catch up with the status of a powerful and fully legitimate actor in an international order while managing the stresses and strains of social and economic transformations required for modernization. The great unknown concerns the degree to which this pattern, the kind of quasi-democracy enabled and limited by a nation-state engaged in highly centralized forms of modernization and development from above, is likely to be seriously disrupted by some other kind of democratic practice rooted in the energies of the young, the urban, the technologically savvy, the environmentally aware, or even just a new middle class.

Moments later, something very similar but more sustained seemed to be signalled by a sudden eruption of widespread protest in Brazil, where I happen to be struggling to make sense of what it now means to make claims about democracy in Europe. In Brazil, too, the tradition of modernization from above has been deeply entrenched. Many of the achievements of democracy here have rested on the negotiation of shifts from highly centralized forms of military rule to still highly centralized forms of civilian rule. As in Turkey and elsewhere, however, it is not clear either that this is sufficient or that the pattern is likely to change in any significant way. Contradictions are palpable, but contained. The centralization of power that expresses this particular form of democracy is at odds with the highly diverse geography and culture of the country. The construction of a cohesively national politics despite the scale and diversity of the place has required all the usual strategies of modern nationalist politics inspired by French, German and other models of nation-building by a modernizing state. At this point, it is not easy to identify any significant social, political or cultural movement in Brazil that is not supported and shaped by the state. The most obvious, and even startling feature of the recent protests is the presence of national colours and flags, of solidarity with a very strong nationalist identity. The possibility that democracy might be reconstituted through the kind of creative antagonism of civil society and the state, of the kind that were once celebrated in the democratization movements of Eastern Europe, for example, seems quite remote.

Still, in Brazil as elsewhere, centralization of authority and nationalist mythology, or even the highly monolithic media, cannot completely obscure radical differences within the national *demos*. The top-down model of modernization has lost some of its legitimacy. Many people are troubled by the convergence between political interests acting in the name of centralized state power with various forms of corporate and international capital that has so obviously led to a preference for profitable megaprojects like sports stadiums rather than education, healthcare and other social services; though it is also the case that the many opportunities for specific corruptions by particular groups and individuals easily deflects attention from the much more worrying degrees of complicity between state structures and huge multinational conglomerates and the distortion of developmental priorities this has brought. The media are unlikely to redirect attention in ways that give citizens the kind of knowledge necessary to make informed judgments about the national/ international and transnational structures of power shaping their lives. Levels of inequality are notoriously extreme despite many impressive achievements. As in Turkey, it is thus unsurprising that the specific grievance triggering mass protests quickly morphed into much broader and diffuse demands. But it is one thing to force a retrenchment of an increase in bus-fares, the initial trigger in this case, and something else entirely to engage with the state-corporatist organization of Brazilian transportation more generally which, among other things, is replacing public spaces with spaces for private cars and aggressive ostentation.

It is thus equally unsurprising that the specialists in instant interpretation have been forced to admit considerable uncertainty about the significance of it all. Uncertainty is undoubtedly the right response. What is nevertheless fairly clear is that two different dynamics are in motion in both contexts. The better known dynamic is shaped within more or less well-known parameters: along a continuum running from some form of authoritarianism towards a form of statist democracy that is nevertheless largely under the control of a single ruling order, a party, an elite, a political class: corporatism, cronyism and all the rest. The less obvious dynamic is shaped by struggles against these well-known parameters. As in many other places, much attention has been focused on new tactics of mobilization, on the role of new communication technologies, social networking, social learning (not least about the reach of corruption and the extent of social deprivation), and the occupation of specific and mainly urban spaces. The multiplication of substantive demands points in exactly the opposite direction to the old Leninist or even Gramscian concern with capturing centralized power, whether of party or state. Established politicians and political institutions have been broadly delegitimized, but any single alternative understanding of political life is hard to identify.

For some commentators, this shows that the protests lack serious political purpose. For others, there are signs that democracy is being enacted through different rules. After all, one does not expect to get very far when the rules of the game are set by those one seeks to challenge, and it is no longer obvious that seriousness of purpose can be defined by nostalgic desires to capture centres of power and authority. There is certainly at least some sense that new understandings of basic political principles – those questions that are sometimes even more difficult than the question of democracy itself – are being articulated in some settings: new conceptions of freedom, probably; new conceptions of equality, perhaps; new understandings of citizenship, almost certainly, perhaps mainly in relation to the narrowly but increasingly functional middle class or perhaps as an expression of new forms of civil society, or a shift to the city as the primary site of political life, or even new forms of republicanism. Still, new forms of reactionary politics cannot be discounted either.

So in both cases, much of the interpretive terrain is familiar enough, but there is also sufficient scope to imagine that something more interesting is at stake. There may be grounds for pessimism, for fears that unrest may bring some kind of authoritarian backlash or just that the diversity of demands can lead only into unfocused and ultimately futile agitation. There may be grounds for optimism, for a few more concessions, perhaps, but also for hopes that new energies and values will stimulate alternatives to the highly centralized and tightly controlled forms of democracy shaped by the dynamics of modernization from above. Much remains unpredictable. It remains unpredictable not least in relation to the degree to which the *polis* expressed in the claims of statist law remains consistent with the *polis* shaped by the demands of emerging forms of economic value. Even on familiar nationalist terms, the possibilities for democracy hinge on struggles to define which and what kind of *demos* can sustain which kind of democracy, and on which kind of democracy can constitute and sustain what kind of *demos*, especially in relation to the twin gods of modern political life. In principle, state law remains paramount. In practice, other sovereignties are in play. Law is one thing, but legitimacy is quite another, and a widening gap between legitimacy and law invariably spells trouble. Europe has considerable experience of this respect.

In the different but related events centred in the USA, a single whistleblower has added yet more information to our still hazy but deeply disturbing knowledge of the capacity of various intelligence and security services, in still uncertain degrees of alliance with many small companies as well as with large corporations, to enlarge their presumed right to detailed information about citizens and foreigners alike. The word treason has been mentioned, even by relatively progressive politicians, and thus the relation between legality and legitimacy has also begun to open up with some virulence but in a rather different way.

This capacity for unprecedented knowledge/power rests partly on the legitimacy of a claim that it is justified by the need for security, as well as by claims that the relevant procedures are covered by appropriate legal safeguards. It also rests partly on massive advances in technological capacities for surveillance of many kinds: for data-mining, for computer simulation, for the tapping of transmission lines, for making judgments about 'persons of interest' through probabilistic generalizations, worst-case scenarios, and so on. The extraordinary scale and reach of the technical systems in question and the complex institutional apparatus that is somehow supposed to be in control of it all has given rise to horrified comparisons with other famous historical cases of Big Brother politics, from the Nazis, to the Soviets, to J Edgar Hoover's FBI, to the Stasi to any number of terrifying police states in many places. The scale of operations alone may well warrant such comparisons even if these specific cases may be profoundly misleading on other fronts.

These twin foundations have extensive historical roots. It is not exactly news that states spy on their citizens, or on the citizens of other states. And the claim that fundamental political principles, especially liberty, must reach some limitation when trumped by threats of insecurity is hardly novel either. A version of it is found in Hobbes's famous account of liberty under law. Another version is found in Carl Schmitt's account of sovereignty as a capacity to decide on the exception to established norms. Both are echoed in the familiar claim that democracy must stop at the edge of the apparatus guaranteeing national security. That edge, of course, was the boundary of the state itself, the place where territorial limit and the limit of sovereign law must coincide, at least in principle. But the scale, scope and reach of contemporary surveillance operations points to a very different kind of political order, although precisely what kind of political order this may be is far from clear. Mapping networks is not the same as mapping the territorial limits of sovereign states.

Much of the immediate critical commentary on the capacities for surveillance that have been revealed so far arise from a concern for the erosion of privacy. Privacy is undoubtedly one of the key values embodied in the more overtly liberal forms of democratic politics. It is one of the characteristic expressions of a political culture grounded in citizens being able to be subjects for themselves rather than the subjects of others. It speaks to the many traditions in which freedom of conscience and the most basic ideas about what it means to be a person, about how one might reconcile one's citizenship with one's humanity, about personhood, have been expressed through the possibilities of democratic politics.

Laws may or may not prevent the spying machines from snooping on the substantive content of phone calls and electronic correspondence, but there seems to be relatively little safeguard against the collection of so-called metadata, aggregate information that treats people once again as mere objects, made subject to external rule rather than self-rule, and to ever mutating forms of what various recent literatures seek to understand as governmentality, bio-politics and the manipulation of paranoia rather than anything resembling a democratic society. Democrats, especially liberal democrats, have ample reason to be angry and afraid. As Hobbes himself also saw very clearly, the sovereign power promising to bring subjects a more secure form of liberty could well be the very same power that destroys subjects in the name of the security of subjects. From this angle, it is not silly to suspect that the scale of the contemporary capacity for surveillance has the capacity to destroy much of what we have come to name as democracy.[3]

---

3   For exemplary topical discussions, see Didier Bigo et al, 'Open Season for Data Fishing on the Web: The Challenges of the US PRISM System for the EU' *CEPS Policy Brief*, No 293 (Brussels, June 18 2013); Jennifer Stisa Granick and Christopher Jon Sprigman, 'The Criminal N.S.A.' *International Herald Tribune* (June 29–30 2013) 8.

But privacy, subjectivity and liberalism are not the only principles at stake here. At the heart of the matter, as it has been for the dozen or so years of the supposed 'war on terror', is what we are supposed to make of the relationship between principles of liberty and the demands of security. In the present context, many military figures have been deployed in order to make claims about the degree to which surveillance has prevented many acts of terror. The loss of liberty, the explicit argument goes, is simply the price to be paid for security under contemporary conditions. The implicit argument, of course, is that these are exceptional conditions, conditions under which the cost in liberty is worth the price we are asked to pay. Between them, the explicit and the implicit capture an enormous terrain of competing political principles. The same can be said for the constant appeal to the figure of a 'balance' between liberty and security, the apparent choice, as if in a supermarket, between competing commodities purchasable with the same currency.[4]

President Obama elegantly expressed the underlying premise of a homogeneous but scalar order at work here when he said that 'You cannot have 100 per cent security and then have 100 per cent privacy and zero inconvenience'.[5] He went on to remark: 'You know, we're going to have to make some choices as a society'.[6] A *demos* is invoked. A choice is going to have to be made, by someone. A line must be drawn, at some point along the scale. The question of the relation between sovereign authority and the *demos*, between the sovereignty of a people and the sovereignty of a state – the relation upon which all claims about modern forms of democracy, and law, and legitimacy, are grounded – is broached. But this question has already been depoliticized by the framing of the problem as a choice between two equal values on a continuum, a choice framed in relation to what amounts to a normal curve of distribution, the bell curve on which the relative price of competing but equal principles can be calculated at a point of balance somewhere along the curve, or at the point at which two such curves meet.

Balance is such a seductive concept, perhaps one of the most seductive of all political concepts. In this particular context, and with the insertion of a logic of markets into the logic of state law, it is entirely misleading. Liberty and security are simply not competing values of equal status. These do not constitute a pairing like liberty and equality, which at least nominally have equal status among the highest principles of modern politics, even if their relationship is better understood as aporetic rather than as a choice to be made along a curve of rational distribution. Security names the condition of possibility under which the relation between

---

4   In relation to the European context, especially, see Didier Bigo, Elspeth Guild, Sergio Carrera and RBJ Walker (eds), *Europe's 21st Century Challenge: Delivering Liberty* (Ashgate 2010); Didier Bigo and Anastasia Tsoukala (eds), *Terror, Insecurity and Liberty: Illiberal Practices of Liberal Regimes After 9/11* (Routledge 2008). For a more generalized formulation see RBJ Walker, *After the Globe, Before the World* (Routledge 2010) 246ff.

5   Barack Obama, quoted in *The International Herald Tribune* (8–9 June 2013) 5.

6   Obama (n 5).

liberty and equality might be negotiated, not least through democratic procedures. Security is the name we give to a limit condition, to the edge of the curve, to the exception to the normal rule, to the point at which it becomes legitimate to suspend the law, to invoke the necessity for secrecy, for surveillance, for sovereign decision. This is partly why we remember Hobbes, and Schmitt, and why we fear the manipulation of fear and paranoia; it is why the illiberal character of modern liberal societies is becoming so insidious.

When Obama invokes a 'we' that must make choices, he coolly avoids the central question of which sovereign authority is supposed to be in play, effectively passing responsibility onto society, onto a social negotiation over exchangeable norms while legitimizing a sovereign decision of the state to suspend norms. When he treats the spatiotemporally expansive apparatus of surveillance that has been revealed over the past few years as just another moment in a normalized routine in a spatially contained statist politics of norms and exceptions that is then masked by rhetorics of balance and consumer choice, he simply reveals the enormous gap between legality and legitimacy that is now opening up in so many situations in so many places. The relative autonomy and the public/private and globally networked character of contemporary intelligence agencies undermines the regulative ideal of a sovereign state acting to secure the liberty of its citizens. The whistleblower has been named as a traitor, but if the accusation is deemed to be plausible in law it remains to be seen whether it is an accusation that is grounded in legitimate authority, or in relation to which *polis* we are supposed to identify either the law or the authority.

In this case, the relation between democracy and *demos* opens up in especially confusing ways, as long-established tensions between sovereignty expressed in state law and sovereignty expressed in economic value converge with tensions between the sovereignty we know from the history of states and the international system and the kind of sovereignty, or anti-sovereignty, we vaguely remember from systems of empire. Empire, we might recall, is precisely the form of rule against which the modern state struggled, against theologies and emperors to affirm a new basis for political possibility, eventually enabling the possibilities of democracy within a singular *demos*. Which democracy for which *demos* are we talking about in this particular context? After all, some of the most startling revelations about the scale of contemporary forms of surveillance have been made in relation to Europe – at least if the UK is taken to be part of Europe, and especially if this part of Europe is engaged in snooping into the lives of citizens throughout Europe, or into European institutions within the USA.

Laws of *imperium* are officially obsolete, having been replaced by the modern double of state and international law. Laws of economic value are officially subordinate to state law and international law. Such regulative ideals have been increasingly implausible guides to empirical practices for a long time. They nevertheless remain powerful guides for the ways in which we think about democracy and its possibilities. In some places, these ideals still have purchase. In some they seem increasingly perverse.

As all these situations mentioned here flow along, as they will, one notices many other stories about events that seem to have little to do with democracy but probably have a lot to do both with the concept of democracy and with the prospects for democracies everywhere. One is probably the observation that at least three-quarters of the arctic ice has disappeared over the past 35 years or so. A lot of other observations refer to dynamics working on a similarly enormous scale. At the very least, we might say, the kind of modernization project, whether from above, from below, from inside, or from outside, that has shaped what it means to engage in democratic aspirations at least since Kant's gamble on a providential teleology taking humans, as citizens, towards greater freedom, with greater and greater scope for self-determination, is in very deep trouble.

III

The specific questions asked in the discussions of the CoE Foundations of European Law and Polity were 'how does the European Polity meet the challenge of its European democratic, legal and cultural heritage?' This is, to say the least, a loaded question; so loaded, in fact, that it is a question to which it may be impossible to give any plausible or even coherent answer at all. The question that is posed in the title of this paper specifies my initial response to it. My very brief discussion of a few recent cases that are not conventionally situated in Europe specifies a way of thinking about what is at stake in the terms presupposed in the question that was initially asked. Although it is largely unanswerable as formulated, it is nonetheless an instructive question. Its very formulation tells us a lot about how we can and cannot think about many of the most pressing problems of our time, including the status of the concept of democracy when put into conjunction with a place called Europe.

Stated so boldly, it is obviously a question that takes far too much for granted. To begin with, it refers to a singular heritage, one that can be understood simultaneously to be democratic, legal and cultural, though not, perhaps, social, or economic, or even political. Yet there is clearly no singular democratic, legal and cultural heritage that can be identified as European, in the singular. To put it politely, pluralism rules, and attempts to insist on a unifying narrative express various political agendas more than they do any concern with scholarly procedure. Among the plurality of democratic, legal and cultural forms that might be described as part of some European heritage, some (notions of civil society, perhaps, or of republican virtuosities, or the rule of law) may deserve praise, but the record is, shall we say, mixed. It is mixed not least where, for example, plebiscitary and elite theories of democracy slide into various forms of authoritarian rule or practices of representation enable various arts and techniques of governance and governmentality. In any case, many concepts that are readily said to be European are scarcely only European, that singular name for many things that neither originated in nor are limited to a place or identity we call Europe.

Moreover, there is no European polity, but again a plurality of polities; not only of Member States and the various formal jurisdictions through which the European Union has been constituted but also of many other forms of polity that have been largely ignored by much of the industry of European Studies that doggedly imagined the conceptual and normative opposition between states and a singular Europe to be the necessary ground for thinking about politics in this part of the world. Europe has its regions, its east and its west, its norths and its souths, its cities, its transatlantic alliances, its entanglements that may or may not usefully described as global. It may even be that insofar as there is an identifiable European polity, it is one that exists by virtue of multifaceted debates about what it means to be a European polity and even about how polities that attract some other categorization – as urban, or transnational, or imperial, or diasporic, or migrant, or cosmopolitan, or planetary – fit within or themselves encapsulate a European polity.

Furthermore, Europe is not where it is supposed to be, as I have put it in a different context.[7] Events in Turkey are related to the conflicting dynamic shaping formal decisions about whether or not Turkey is or is not to be counted as European. Brazil is significantly shaped by European accounts of what Brazil must be, and not only in the relation to the effects of planning for the upcoming World Cup. The line between Europe and the USA is very hard to draw in relation to emerging regimes of surveillance. The kind of modernization from above that has shaped political life in so many other places has been a central part of European experiences and resistance to those experiences has shaped much of the attempt to create a Europe that is precisely not that kind of Europe. Many Europeans, like many Americans, have fond hopes for the universalization of what it means to be civilized, and democratic. Europe is subject to many of the same forces that are at work well beyond European territorial borders and legal limits. And so on.

So, constructions of what counts as Europe, whether in historical or contemporary terms, are clearly contestable, and strongly contested. There is much that might be said about the complexity and contestation on both counts, as well as about the ways in which narratives about singularity maintain their purchase on both scholarly and popular debate. Europe is not alone in this respect. Still there is something distinctive about the ways in which Europe has been framed as a presumed singularity, both spatially and temporally. Insofar as one might be able to get a grip on a thematic that seeks to put claims about some specific heritage together with claims about a European polity, we would need to have some understanding of what it means to speak about a polity, and a politics, that somehow has historical and contemporary presence as well as future possibility.

Thus, put simply, many contemporary claims about democracy, law and culture work to affirm that we know what we are talking about when we refer to something as a polity. I doubt that this is the case. Claims about democracy are conventionally grounded in claims about a *demos*, a people, or community,

---

7   RBJ Walker, 'Europe is Not Where it is Supposed to Be' in M Kelstrup and M Williams (eds), *International Relations and the Politics of European Integration* (Routledge 2000) 14.

or population, or jurisdiction, or a place within which democracy might be envisaged. Most conventions identify this collectivity as the modern, sovereign nation-state. This was always a dubious convention, not least because the modernity, sovereignty and nationality of states is conditional upon the presence of external formations, sometimes more or less imperial and sometimes more or less international. As I have argued fairly extensively elsewhere, the obsessive focus of political and social theory on the internal claims of states, and the sharp distinction of these internal claims with theories of an international has more or less crippled thinking about many fundamental political principles, not least when claims about democracy, law and culture have been at stake.[8]

Alternatively, references to a European polity are often deployed precisely so as to resist the supposed parochialisms of statist political and social theory, but also to resist supposedly old-fashioned obsessions with an international. As we all supposedly know, we live in a moment of probably quite profound structural and historical change. As with claims about changes in planetary climate, we probably tend to underestimate the degree and significance of such change even while we overestimate our capacity to interpret it. To ask about the degree to which a polity, any polity, meets the challenge of its heritage, may be to ask whether it lives up to established principles that are worth defending, which I take to be at least part of the positive intention behind the specific question to which I am struggling to respond, but it is also to risk a defence of established even if contested principles in a moment in which such principles may seem increasingly nostalgic. The watchword here has been 'integration', and the measure of 'progress' has been extended along an historical line projected from a dangerous plurality, and principles of national/statist self-determination, to a more consensual universality, and principles of common rights, legal jurisdiction, and cultural aspiration.

In this context, references to a European polity express a fundamental ambivalence, not to say contradiction, and not just between a claim to a singular European polity and claims about a multiplicity of polities. On the one hand, they lay claim to a polity that finds its place in yet another form of an international order, the world of the new multipolarity that many Europeans, along with the BRICS countries, now champion as a welcome change from the unipolar moment of recent memory, with Europe in the role of what used to be called a 'great power'. On the other hand, they lay claim to a polity that claims to have left the international behind in an ascent to a higher reason and a new hierarchical order. This is the narrative that would not know what to say if the word 'level' were not available to organize the categories of modern politics in a vertical rather than a horizontal direction.

This ambivalence speaks to the continuing grip of a profound puzzle that has provoked and shaped modern conceptions of politics since the early-modern period. Machiavelli formulated one version of this puzzle as a rupture between an ethics of salvation and thus virtue, and an ethics more attuned to the salvation of the city,

---

8   RBJ Walker, *Inside/Outside: International Relations as Political Theory* (Cambridge University Press 1993).

and thus *virtù*. Others soon understood the centrality of a fundamental rift between the claims of citizenship in the secular *polis* or city and claims about the priority of humanity in general. This rift has shaped modern – and European – conceptions of polity for a very long time. Insofar as one can speak about a singular European political heritage, this problem would be difficult to ignore. Indeed, insofar as one can identify anything resembling a European political heritage, it would have to be first and foremost some kind of problem: of scepticism rather than some mythologized Enlightenment; of the very possibility of liberty in a condition of finitude rather than the various creeds proclaiming liberty to be achieved condition; the even trickier possibility that liberty and equality might be achieved at the same place and the same time despite their profound incompatibility in many situations; the at least equally tricky possibility that principles of liberty might be reconciled (but not balanced) with principles of security; and so on. The antagonistic character of claims about citizenship and claims about humanity that have shaped so many accounts of what it means to be political falls into this familiar pattern. Claims about a European polity are often used to give the impression that this particular antagonism has been resolved in favour of a higher citizenship, one that is closer to humanity, and indeed might sometimes speak as if its conception of citizenship should simply be taken, universally, as the proper conception of humanity – with entirely predictable consequences.

The idea that we can speak of a European polity, in the singular, is the outcome of that famously determined philosophy of history which insists on the necessity for or evidence of a progressive teleology through which European nation-states, or state-nations, get their act together to constitute a common – integrated – Europe. Indeed we might say that more than most other places on Earth, Europe has often seemed to know what it means to speak about change. In this sense, Europe is itself not only a geographical space but also a spatialized temporality, one in which change is officially read as a movement from plurality and fragmentation to universality and integration. Hopes embedded in this understanding of a European polity may have been frustrated in various ways, but the overall aspiration has been difficult to dislodge. This aspiration encourages the idea that the heritage remembered from the old world of fragmented nation states might or should be reproduced in the new world of an integrated polity. The key assumption, of course, is that the term polity, and the term *demos*, means much the same thing in the old Europe as in the new: that the difference is largely one of scale, so that the shift from old to new, from fragmentation to integration, is envisaged as a move up a scale from lower to higher. This is a striking way of thinking about novelty given that much of what is now celebrated as the heritage of Europe involved a profound struggle to move down much the same scale: from the City of God to the City of Man, from divine right and natural law to a politics of subjectivity, self-determination and the rule of a man-made law.

The much more likely probability is that Europe will not become new in the way predicted by this very specific and conceptually dubious understanding of change. Not only is it possible that we tend to underestimate the character and significance of change in contemporary political life, but we tend to get rather nervous at suggestions that what we mean by change is probably not what the standard clichés of a teleological modernization tell us it must be. It does not take much to appreciate that such a possibility has disturbing implications for the way we think about both traditions and contemporary practices of democracy, law and culture. Most fundamentally, it implies that it makes little sense to think about either of these concepts without putting concepts of polity and *demos* into some fairly serious questioning – and without automatically assuming that this involves grandiose claims about the demise of the state or the rise of some all-encompassing globalization.

IV

The different contemporary cases that I have sketched earlier are all deeply implicated in any possible account of the status and potential of democracy in Europe. The model of statist modernization from above is inseparable from the European experiences in the twentieth century. That model in turn is inseparable from the principles of freedom as autonomy, as self-determination, as an emancipatory challenge to practices of dependence, that promised the capacity for thinking for oneself, as Kant had it. Claims about democracy in Europe are caught up in both the more uplifting and the more depressing moments of this ambition: depressing both in relation to the internal formation of authoritarian and fascist tendencies and to the external experience of war between self-determining nation states. Europe has both celebrated this heritage – a still to be realized ambition, some say – and has come to define itself against it, to overcome the traumas of the twentieth century by constructing a different kind of polity, a European rather than an international order, all the while seeking to build upon principles of self-determination. This is a tough ambition, in principle as well as in practice. It is not surprising that eyes have been lifted upwards, to try to solve the problems of a politics articulated in a horizontal plane by appealing to a vertical hierarchy, an integrated order of subsidiary authorities. Not surprisingly, contemporary Europe has turned out to be a much messier, untidy and fragile affair.

Europe celebrates its achievement of many of the aspirations for democracy, for the rule of law, and so on, that could be ascribed to events in Turkey, Brazil and elsewhere. But the celebration must be tempered by the degree to which in Europe too one needs to speak about media monopolies, about structural and personal corruptions, about the possibilities and limits of civil society, about multiple threats to principles of liberty and equality, and so on. Europe, too, encompasses practices of surveillance. Moreover, Europe is deeply implicated in the problems of democracy elsewhere.

Still, what seems especially clear from the European case, for all its specificities and for all its complexity, is that it shares in the two great tensions that are intensifying questions about our capacity to speak about democracy anywhere:

the tension between state (and international) law as the ultimate ground of political possibility and the 'laws' of (capitalist) market as the ultimate ground of economic possibility; and the tension between state/international law and the hierarchical claims of imperium, both internally as the construction of a different kind of Europe and externally as the implication of Europe within much wider networks of power and rule whose contours we have barely begun to understand.

Much of the upside of democracy in contemporary Europe, I would say, comes from forces struggling to adapt the rule of law to contemporary developments; from, for example, those trying to resist the erosion of liberties through especially promiscuous claims about security, or to affirm the rights of migrants and re-imagine the possibilities of citizenship. Much of the downside has come from forces affirming an economistic understanding of the relevant *demos* on the one hand and an imperious understanding of security on the other. The privileging of banking and financial systems may be compatible with – indeed part of a revival of older forms of – those old elite theories of democracy, but the Europe that has come to think of itself as a beacon of light in a darkening world is nothing if not a principled repudiation of that inheritance. We may live in a world of many terrors, terrorists among them, but the apparatus of intelligence, security and systematic fear-mongering that is being normalized on a transnational scale challenges many of the most basic assumptions about what it means to be a human being; these assumptions go to the heart of what Europe has come to mean, in principle even if not always in practice. It may be that the days of that understanding of humanity are numbered, and in any case may be challengeable on many grounds. But it is also the case that the potential for new (and perhaps very different) forms of authoritarianism and/or populisms that mock democracy has not been erased anywhere, and Europe is certainly not an exception.

The regulative ideals of state law, as of international law, are easily encompassed on a Gauss (or bell) curve of normal distribution that I have mentioned already. This is what gives all the rhetoric about balancing liberty with security its seductive plausibility. It is what gives us our prevailing sense of a realm of normality and its margins, of laws and its exceptions, of the promise of equalitarian distribution, liberty and justice bounded by regulative borders and limits. The Gauss curve, we might say, is a pervasive formalization of the forms within which modern forms of democracy have been imagined. Its characteristic indicator of trouble is its sharp edge, the zone where the curve flares out like a bell into a very short tail. This is where it is easy to imagine the official limits of the state, the sharp point distinguishing law and its necessary derogations. The form may be a misleading guide to empirical practice of course, not least when claims about liberty meet claims about security not at the edge of the curve but somewhere nearer the middle, somewhere closer to a point of an imagined balance. Still it symbolizes an idealization of the limits within which democracy may be thought: the ideal in which a politics of friends and enemies may be expected, or overcome, between statist polities.

The alternative curve, celebrated by the older elite theorists of democracy and contemporary neoliberals alike, is the one named after Pareto, one of those elite theorists of democracy. Gauss (or 50/50) distributions may symbolize a politics in which equalitarianism is a plausible ideal. Pareto (or 80/20) distributions affirm the greater value of a minority over a majority. It is the curve favoured by proponents of capitalist markets. Trouble here also occurs on the edge, but in this case the tail on the side of the majority is long. It is not a curve suggesting a politics of friends and enemies, nor of equalitarian norms. Its norms are specifically elitist, but its margins are not precipitous; they tail away slowly. The point of distinction is less determinate, more a matter of indifference, one might say. Distinctions between norms and exceptions require no obvious sovereign, just the hidden hand of market forces, statistical probabilities or bureaucratic processing. It signals not a world of always potential friends and enemies but a world in which it might become ever easier to distinguish between human beings who may well think of themselves as citizens of the world in some sense and others who effectively live in some other place, in some other time.

If it is indeed the case that questions about democracy in Europe, as elsewhere, are especially difficult because it is becoming ever more unclear which *demos* we should be talking about, then it is probably the case that we should be worrying rather more about the implications of the Pareto distribution. It speaks both to recent attempts to read political necessities through a logic of capitalist markets and attempts to act in the name of some new imperium. In both cases, many of the details and most of the technologies seem to affirm claims about radical novelty, but the underlying dynamics have been around for a while. Both are legacies of Europe: legacies to which we all need to find some alternatives very quickly.

Bibliography

Bigo D et al, 'Open Season for Data Fishing on the Web: The Challenges of the US PRISM System for the EU' (Centre for European Policy Studies, 293 CEPS Policy Brief, Brussels 18 June 2013)

Bigo D, Guild E, Carrera S and Walker RBJ (eds), *Europe's 21st Century Challenge: Delivering Liberty* (Ashgate 2010)

Bigo D and Tsoukala A (eds), *Terror, Insecurity and Liberty: Illiberal Practices of Liberal Regimes After* 9/11 (Routledge 2008)

Granick JS and Sprigman CJ, 'The Criminal N.S.A.' *International Herald Tribune* (29–30 June, 2013) 8

Nancy J-L, 'Finite and Infinite Democracy' in G Agamben et al (eds), *Democracy in What State?* (Columbia University Press 2010) 58

Walker RBJ, *After the Globe, Before the World* (Routledge 2010) 246ff

—— 'Europe is Not Where it is Supposed to Be' in Morten Kelstrup and Michael Williams (eds) *International Relations and the Politics of European Integration* (Routledge 2000) 14–32

—— *Inside/Outside: International Relations as Political Theory* (Cambridge University Press 1993)

Chapter 8

Law, Community and *ultima ratio* in Transnational Law[1]

Massimo Fichera

Introduction

This chapter aims to examine how the principle of *ultima ratio* (last resort) can operate in the context of transnational law. It warns against the risk that contemporary legal developments turn into the imposition of standards, criteria and categories formulated at a level which is too detached from regional and sub-regional areas, without ensuring adequate forms of 'bottom-up' democracy (especially in terms of transparency and responsibility/accountability in decision-making). The chapter is divided into three parts.

To begin with, the chapter looks briefly at the concept of transnational law as elaborated by academic work, starting from the 1950s. It aims to show how this concept has acquired relative autonomy and is currently employed alongside or as an alternative to more traditional concepts, such as international and national law. One of the assumptions of this work is that European Union (EU) law represents a significant example of transnational law, due to the high level of overlap between legal systems. Indeed, many theories have been elaborated in the last few decades to describe the nature of the relationship between the Member States' and the EU legal systems. The majority of these theories (for example constitutional pluralism, societal constitutionalism, the 'many constitutions' approach) emphasise the non-hierarchical structure of transnational legal processes. This mind frame is the expression of an effort to conceptualise law beyond the State by employing new paradigms that do not fit with conventional images, starting from classic theories of international law. The global financial crisis has highlighted precisely the relevance of transnational legal processes for the current and future development of the EU as a polity.

Second, the chapter focuses on a general discussion on whether the market can be considered an integral part of a transnational community and the extent to which principles and ideas having a criminal and constitutional law origin can contribute to a community-oriented approach.

---

1 An earlier version of this work was published in the *Oñati Institute Socio-legal Series* [online], 1 (3), 62–80. See <http://opo.iisj.net/index.php/osls/article/viewFile/226/95> accessed 23 June 2014.

Third, this chapter inquires into the possibility of employing the principle of *ultima ratio* as an expression of the above-mentioned community-oriented approach. Recent events, including the expansion of anti-money laundering legislation and measures enacted following the economic crisis, will be mentioned as emblematic cases illustrating the development of transnational law and its impact on society.

The Concept of Transnational Law

Criteria for Identification of Transnational Law

Law is very hard to classify. Both its nature and content tend to change. They can vary depending on the object of our analysis but also on the eye of the observer. This means not only that ideological, cultural or scientific assumptions affect our statements about what, say, a piece of legislation should look like. For example, the application of a general principle or enforcement of a contract will have to be adapted to the context which they refer to and their impact will be different; interpretation is not a mechanical hair-splitting device, but a social activity supported, wittingly or unwittingly, by a great variety of agendas. Another indication of the changeable nature of law is its permeability to temporal and systemic factors.[2] The idea of law in the nineteenth century is not identical with the idea that prevailed in the thirteenth century.[3] For a variety of reasons that cannot be examined here further, law is one of those 'essentially contested concepts' that spur debate and critical approaches.[4]

It has been noted however that some characteristics of law are much more resistant to change because they belong to deeper layers and require a longer period before being subject to significant modifications.[5] Still, what appears on the surface is what is more easily visible in the daily practice of lawyers and ordinary people. The phenomenon of *transnational* law as it has emerged from this practice has increasingly attracted the interest of specialists precisely because it challenges our common perceptions and inherited view of law.

Not surprisingly, however, transnational law is a controversial concept. First of all, doubts have been raised due to the difficulty of identifying its main

---

2   By 'systemic' factors I mean those elements of law that have been identified by systems theory. See for example Niklas Luhmann, 'Law as a social system' (1989) 83 *Northwestern University Law Review* 136.

3   Manlio Bellomo, *The Common Legal Past of Europe, 1000–1800* (The Catholic University of America Press 1995).

4   See Walter G Gallie, 'Essentially contested concepts' (1956) 56 *Proceedings of the Aristotelian Society* 167; Walter G Gallie, 'Art as an essentially contested concept' (1956) 6 *The Philosophical Quarterly* 97; Walter G Gallie, *Philosophy and the Historical Understanding* (2nd edn, Schocken Books 1968).

5   Kaarlo Tuori, *Critical Legal Positivism* (Ashgate 2002) 150.

features. Criticism has thus been levelled at it both negatively and positively. Negatively, it has been argued that it is impossible to distinguish transnational from both international and national law. Positively, it has been observed that any attempt to define it is doomed to fail because of its inherent ambiguity. Indeed, a considerable number of works have provided a variety of very different broad or narrow definitions of transnational law.[6]

The main point of contention is the distinction (or lack thereof) between transnational, national and international law. In the following pages we may try to sketch, rather schematically, how this distinction is commonly viewed. It will be submitted that current developments are blurring that distinction, due to increasing overlapping and cross-fertilisation of legal systems.

The prevailing configuration of international law nowadays owes much to the positivistic approaches and classical liberal theories adopted between the sixteenth and nineteenth centuries. The reason why the term '*inter*-national law' was coined and replaced the 'law of nations' is that it seems to convey more convincingly the idea of 'mutual transactions between sovereigns'[7] unrestrained by a superior authority. Reliance upon some more or less explicit form of voluntarism can be detected in the first works theorising on international law.[8] In line with the spirit of their time, these works emphasised the moral qualities of free will and self-fulfilment. Individual forces were to be left free to compete: war, diplomacy and the market were the most typical grounds where the struggle for self-assertion could take place. International law as we know it is therefore law between independent equals, which act according to their own self-guiding principles and

---

6   As a small sample, see Philip Jessup, *Transnational Law* (Yale University Press 1956); Eric Stein, 'Lawyers, Judges, and the Making of a Transnational Constitution' (1981) 75 *American Journal of International Law* 1; Harold H Koh, 'Transnational Legal Process' (1996) 75 *Nebraska Law Review* 181; Harold H Koh, 'Why Do Nations Obey International Law' (1997) 106 *Yale Law Journal* 2599; Anne-Marie Slaughter, 'A Liberal Theory of International Law' (2000) 94 *American Society of International Law Proceedings* 240; Oona A Hathaway, 'Between Power and Principle: An Integrated Theory of International Law' (2005) 72 *University of Chicago Law Review* 469; Terence C Halliday and Pavel Osinsky, 'Globalization of Law' (2006) 32 *Annual Review of Sociology* 447; Peer Zumbansen, 'Transnational Law' in J Smits (ed.) *Encyclopedia of Comparative Law* (Edward Elgar 2006) 738; Reza Dibadj, 'Panglossian Transnationalism' (2008) 44 *Stanford Journal of International Law* 253; Craig Scott, 'Transnational Law as Proto-Concept: Three Conceptions' (2009) 10 *German Law Journal* 859; Peer Zumbansen, 'Transnational Legal Pluralism' (2010) *Transnational Legal Theory* 1.

7   Jeremy Bentham, *Introduction to the Principles of Morals and Legislation*, Chapter XIX section XXV in J Bowring (ed.) *The Works of Jeremy Bentham* Vol. I (1843 Edinburgh: William Tait, orig. 1780).

8   See for example. Hugo Grotius, *On the Law of War and Peace* (2001 Batoche Books, trans. AC Campbell, orig. 1625); Emer de Vattel, *The Law of Nations, or the Principles of National Law applied to the Conduct and to the Affairs of Nations and Sovereigns* (1916 Carnegie Institution of Washington, trans. CG Fenwick, orig. 1758).

internal morality. They have no right to interfere in each other's activities and may recognise each other, as long as the commonly accepted criteria for statehood are met. The relationship between these sovereign entities was governed by a set of rules which reflected an established order, a *nomos* whose internal ordering would consist in a regulated space corresponding to the European region.[9] Only those entities which showed they deserved statehood were admitted to this highly selective club. Obviously, universalistic aspirations inspired by natural-law rationalistic models have always been present and have operated as background assumptions which may (or may not) be interpreted as condensations of hegemonic ideals.[10] Universality, certainly until the end of the twentieth century and arguably even afterwards, is a non-intruding, behind-the-scenes concept that appears and disappears like a karst river.

The so-called Westphalian system, relying on a carefully designed balance of sovereign wills, acquired progressively more complex features when the ideas of nation state, culture, collective or general will and, as a result, self-determination of peoples and nationality were elaborated and refined across the centuries. Sovereignty as an indivisible attribute of States has been traditionally understood as either internal or external. In reality, formal equality has always been associated with the capacity of the most powerful nations to influence directly or indirectly the behaviour of the least powerful ones.[11] Modern international law is thus characterised by a strong reliance upon reciprocity and formal equality, a 'thin' notion of universality and a sharp distinction between public and private authority as well as the internal and the external sphere of States.

The concept of transnational law does not fit with this conventional account. While this section does not intend to provide an exhaustive definition of the concept, it aims to focus on a few elements that may help in the analysis of new forms of law beyond the State. The following analysis proceeds on the assumption that State sovereignty is no longer an absolute principle and, as a result, some of the most prominent features of international law should be reconsidered, to the extent that, as will be seen, the need to draw a line between international and domestic law may be disputed.

A first peculiar element is the tendency of these new forms of law beyond the State to operate regardless of the existence of national borders. For example, ever more frequently domestic courts enforce and implement decisions taken by foreign and international courts.[12] It is also not uncommon for courts to cite

---

9   Carl Schmitt, *The Nomos of the Earth* (Telos Press 2003) 140.

10   Martti Koskenniemi, *From Apology to Utopia* (3rd edn, Cambridge University Press 2009).

11   The classic historical examples are the Concert of Europe (1815) and the Conference of Yalta (1945).

12   See for example the International Convention on the Settlement of Investment Disputes Between States and Nationals of Other States (ICSID) (1965), 17 U.S.T. 1270, 575 U.N.T.S. 159, whose Art. 54(1) requires State Parties to enforce judgments of international

judgments adopted by international courts or influential courts of other countries.[13] Cross-fertilisation is an integral component of transboundary interaction and it is increasingly advocated as a tool of constitutional interpretation.[14] This process is not developing only at the judicial level: it involves international organisations, domestic legislative bodies, academics and governments. In a sense the EU qualifies as a form of transnational law: the amount of legislation developed by the EU institutions is capable of penetrating Member States' legal systems very effectively in many ways, for example through the so-called direct effect doctrine and the activity of the Court of Justice of the European Union (CJEU). This implies that the boundaries between domestic and EU systems are very thin: in that light many theories consider the relationship between the CJEU and domestic courts through a heterarchical, rather than a hierarchical scheme.[15]

The recent EU financial crisis not only vividly demonstrates how the legal, social and economic realities of the Member States are intertwined and deeply affect each other. It also indicates how the EU as a transnational entity is linked with other transnational bodies and entities across the globe. In the following pages some examples of this connection will be mentioned. It should be borne in mind that overlapping and interdependence have decreased the capacity of the national level to satisfy sufficiently high standards of 'input-legitimacy'. Accountability becomes a central issue of contemporary law beyond the State.[16]

The second element of the transnationalisation of law is the blurring of relevant distinctions that are normally identified within the discipline of international law. For example, transboundary relations can be regulated not only by so-called 'hard law'

---

arbitral tribunals established according to the Convention itself; in the United States, 19 U.S.C. § 1516a(g)(7)(A) (2000) authorizes bi-national panels set up according to the North American Free Trade Agreement to direct US agencies to take action not inconsistent with the decisions of the panel.

13   See for example *State v. Makwanyane*, 1995 (3) SALR 391 (CC) (S. Afr.), in which the South African Constitutional Court, in its analysis of the death penalty issue, took into account decisions adopted by other domestic and international courts, including the ECtHR and the UN Human Rights Committee; *Lawrence e.a. v. Texas*, 539 U.S. 558, 575 (2003) 41 S. W. 3d 349 (also referring to the ECtHR).

14   See for example Harold H Koh, 'International Law As Part of Our Law' (2004) 98 *The American Journal Of International Law* 43.

15   Among the most popular approaches, see for example Neil Walker, 'The Idea of Constitutional Pluralism' (2002) 65 *Modern Law Review* 317; Mattias Kumm, 'The Jurisprudence of Constitutional Conflict: Constitutional Supremacy in Europe before and after the Constitutional Treaty' (2005) 11 *European Law Journal* 262; Ingolf Pernice, 'The Treaty of Lisbon: Multilevel Constitutionalism in Action' (2009) 15 *Columbia Journal of European Law* 349; Kaarlo Tuori and Suvi Sankari (eds) *The Many Constitutions of Europe* (Ashgate 2010); Gunther Teubner, *Constitutional Fragments – Societal Constitutionalism and Globalisation* (OUP 2012).

16   See for example Arthur Benz, Carol Harlow and Yannis Papadopoulos, 'Introduction' (2007) 13 *European Law Journal* 441 and related articles of that special issue.

measures, but also by non-binding instruments spanning between standard-setting, recommendations, experts' advice and legal opinions ('soft law'). Nowadays, the normative relevance of a wide range of sources of law has rapidly increased and this has made distinctions between public and private as well as between domestic (or internal) and international (or external) matters less significant than in the past. Legal rules capable of producing cross-border effects are being elaborated by organisations such as the International Monetary Fund (IMF), the World Bank (WB), the Basel Committee on Banking Supervision, the International Labour Organisation (ILO), the World Trade Organisation (WTO), the Codex Alimentarius Commission, the International Civil Aviation Organisation (ICAO), the International Standardisation Organisation (ISO), the Internet Corporation for Assigned Names and Numbers (ICANN), bond-rating agencies such as Standard and Poor's, committees of experts and so on.[17] Moreover, standard-setting and self-regulation originate from multinational corporations as well.[18] As a result, law tends to cover situations and behaviours that increasingly involve non-State, including private, actors.

A third element of the phenomenon under examination is the fact that a remarkable percentage of the normative rules embraced by it have an economic nature, although they reach beyond the scope of the so-called *lex mercatoria*.[19]

We may easily deduce from the previous pages that a traditional international law approach struggles to categorise transnational legal events and this also explains the temptation to understate their relevance. Next to the classic, positivist setting of the Westphalian order a relatively broad normative space possessing a regulatory or quasi-regulatory nature has been developing its own claims and rationalities.

The second reason why transnational law is deeply contested is that it can be associated with global governance and it therefore generates concerns related to lack of democratic mechanisms and structures, particularly in terms of legitimacy and accountability.[20]

Can the transnational law project claim to have ecumenical ambitions and in this perspective replace international law? Can arguments from hegemony be made

---

17   See for example Christian Joerges and Jürgen Neyer, 'From Intergovernmental Bargaining to Deliberative Political Processes: The Constitutionalisation of Comitology' (1997) *European Law Journal* 273; <www.bis.org> (website of the Bank for International Settlements, which the Basel Committee belongs to); <www.icann.org>; <www.codexalimentarius.net>; <www.iso.org>; <www.standardandpoors.com> all accessed 23 June 2014

18   Paul S Berman, 'A Pluralist Approach to International Law' (2007) 32 *Yale Journal of International Law* 301, 312.

19   Joel P Trachtman, 'The International Economic Law Revolution' (1996) 17 *University of Pennsylvania Journal of International Economic Law* 33; David Zaring, 'International Law by Other Means: The Twilight Existence of International Financial Regulatory Organizations' (1998) 33 *Texas International Law Journal* 281; Zumbansen, 'Transnational Law' (n 6).

20   See for example Neil Walker and Gráinne de Búrca, 'Reconceiving Law and New Governance' (2007) 13 *Columbia Journal of European Law* 519; Joshua Cohen and Charles Sabel, 'Directly-Deliberative Polyarchy' (1997) 3 *European Law Journal* 313.

in the same way as they are made in relation to the international law project, which, as mentioned earlier, has been characterised *both* as advancing claims of formal equality stemming from paradigms of universal reason *and* as an instrument for the stabilisation of power and dominance?[21] Or, to put it in other words, is the development of transnational law the translation of a peculiar balance of powers or is it, instead, a sign of the unsettling of those powers? It has been argued that more flexible forms of law better suit the strategic moves of dominant States.[22] On this view, hegemonic or dominant States would only seek to regulate those areas which correspond more closely with their interests, as is the case with the United States-sponsored free trade and market-enhancing legislation.[23] The recent financial crises have prompted a great many proposals in favour of a better discipline of market forces. Would this discipline simply mirror the United States agenda? The legal and political landscape seems more nuanced than an answer in the positive would suggest. Interests and agendas cannot always be discerned easily. First, the trend towards decentralised, less formal legal rules coincides with the gradual weakening of the position of the United States as a monopolistic hegemon, as it had emerged at the end of the Cold War, and the strengthening of other States or clusters of States.

Second, institutionalist and constructivist theories should not be dismissed too easily. International law is not merely a reflection of instrumental rationality: it simultaneously generates constraints through bilateral and multilateral frameworks that are shaped by specific interests and agendas but are also capable in turn of influencing actors' behaviour and policies. The institutional setting in which international law-making takes place aims to increase predictability and coherence.[24] It thus produces a type of legitimacy that is socially constructed by way of prevailing normative expectations at any given time. In this sense, interactions will not be based simply on rational calculus, but also on a minimum degree of mutual trust deriving from past episodes and consolidated practice.[25]

To be sure, the capillary diffusion of informal rules and standards set by private, public and semi-public bodies might be interpreted as a means of implementing policies and enforcing values which belong to the most powerful nations or entities operating on their behalf. It thus becomes important to qualify the type of interaction that takes place within the transnational sphere.

---

21   Koskenniemi (n 10).

22   Kenneth W Abbott and Duncan Snidal, 'Hard and Soft Law in International Governance' in JL Goldstein et al (eds) *Legalization and World Politics* (2005 MIT Press) 37, 63–5.

23   Frederick Abbott, 'NAFTA and the Legalization of World Politics: A Case Study' in JL Goldstein et al (eds) (n 22) 135.

24   Robert Keohane, *International Institutions and State Power* (Westview 1989) 10.

25   Friedrich V Kratochwil, *Rules, Norms and Decisions: On the Conditions of Practical and Legal Reasoning in International Relations and Domestic Affairs* (CUP 1989); Jutta Brunnée and Stephen J Toope, 'International Law and Constructivism: Elements of an Interactional Theory of International Law' (2000) 39 *Columbia Journal of Transnational Law* 19.

Theoretical approaches on transnational law and governance have oscillated between at least three strands of thought, which can roughly be labelled as 'community-oriented', 'liberal' and 'functional'. Some authors conceive of 'pluralistic' and diversified communities based on stable and continuous interaction fed by virtuous trust-enhancing practices as conceptual tools to explore the overlapping of transnational normative orders.[26] The risk in this case is that any move towards an even minimal substantive understanding of the common good may smack of nineteenth-century-style universalism. In the view of some others, functionally differentiated regimes and societal rationalities are irreducible to one another: no overarching authority emerges and this results in the impossibility of identifying a meta-rationality that would operate as an instance of last resort (*ultima ratio*).[27] This view runs the opposite risk of denying any space for meaningful convergence and facing the 'absence of any intersubjectively shared values, norms and processes of understanding'.[28] The liberal approach attempts instead to emphasise the role of individual emancipation and self-fulfilment, but sometimes fails to give enough importance to the benefits that may derive from commonality.

However, regardless of the differences between the approaches mentioned above, the discussion on the relevance of community values for international law has been going on for a long time. For example, de Vattel emphasised international law's purpose of having a 'society of nations', which, although free and independent, have a duty to contribute to the happiness and perfection of all other nations by way of mutual assistance.[29] It should therefore come as no surprise that similar issues may be addressed in contemporary debates focusing on transnational law. This chapter aims at showing that some principles – and, in this particular case, the principle of *ultima ratio* – may play an important role in promoting a community-oriented approach, at least if one takes the perspective of a *thin* community of values and principles. In order to do so, it is necessary to illustrate the significance of the notions of 'network' and 'conflict' for the development of transnational law.

The Multifarious Nature of Transnational Law

Transnational legal processes are entrenched within the Westphalian order. They revolve around two fundamental hallmarks: the notions of 'network'[30] and

---

26   See for example Roger Cotterrell, 'A Legal Concept of Community' (1997) 12 *Canadian Journal of Law and Society* 75; Jan A Scholte, 'Reconstructing Contemporary Democracy' (2008) 15 *Indiana Journal of Global Legal Studies* 305.

27   Andreas Fischer-Lescano and Gunther Teubner, 'Regime-Collisions: The Vain Search for Legal Unity in the Fragmentation of Global Law' (2004) *Michigan Journal of International Law* 999.

28   Jürgen Habermas, *The Postnational Costellation* (Polity Press 2001) 142.

29   de Vattel (n 8) 33–7.

30   Andreas Hamann and Helen R Fabri, 'Transnational networks and constitutionalism' (2008) 3 & 4 *ICON* 481.

conflict. While the second notion will be dealt with more extensively in the second section of this chapter, this section will address some of the most significant issues stemming from the development of networks.

'Networks' are understood in this work as associated with decentralisation and deformalisation, as opposed to 'hierarchy', which is associated with centralisation. They are composed of cellular entities, mostly committees, expert groups, think-tanks, boards, governmental and non-governmental organisations, corporations, consultancies, agencies and so on that may or may not interact with each other and may or not be aware of each other's existence. The activities performed in this network space and the actors involved in them may overlap and stretch across a wide range of policy areas such as corporate accountability (for example, for violation of human rights in a third country), trade, environment, financial stability, internet regulation, welfare policies, sport and leisure, culture and education. The normative claims made within this network space may exist alongside the normative claims made within the sovereignty-based pluralistic system that has been developed in past centuries. Their scope of action does not even need to be legal. Indeed, the idea of 'network' has been used to define certain types of organised criminal groups, terrorist entities and business firms.[31] At the same time, the term can easily apply to the institutional and operational structures that deal most closely with them.[32]

Several branches of law are affected by this phenomenon either simultaneously or separately. Prominent examples are private law and economic law, criminal law and human rights. What is interesting about them is, first, that each conveys a distinct conception of what 'public goods' ought to be classified, produced and distributed. They can be identified with specific rationalities distinct from each other.

Second, the line between private and public law, as already suggested, is blurring (much like the line between national and international law). This was already evident in the work of Jessup, who was one of the first to employ the concept of transnational law. He characterised this form of law as 'all law which regulates actions or events that transcend national frontiers', thus embracing national and international law, public and private law.[33]

---

31   See for example Paul Williams, 'Organising Transnational Crime: Networks, Markets and Hierarchies' in P Williams and D Vlassis (eds), 'Combating Transnational Crime: Concepts, Activities and Responses' (1998) 4 *Transnational Organised Crime* 57, 73; 1998 Europol Organised Crime Situation Report and 2007 Europol Organised Crime Threat Assessment (OCTA) at www.europol.org.

32   See for example Resolution of the Council and of the Representatives of the Governments of the Member States, meeting within the Council, on the establishment of a Network for legislative cooperation between the Ministries of Justice of the European Union OJ C 326 20.12.2008; Council Decision 2008/976/JHA of 16 December 2008 on the European Judicial Network, OJ L 348.

33   Jessup (n 6).

The representation of a private and public legal sphere corresponds to different modalities of power and interpenetration of social and legal rules. Traditionally, public law is said to regulate relations between the State and the individual, while private law would pertain to relations between individuals. This mind frame somehow suggests that the 'private' reflects individual interests as opposed to the 'public', which would instead be associated with the idea of 'community'. However, this representation is largely fictitious and historically determined.[34] The reality is that neither can the public be automatically identified with the 'socially useful', nor can the private be dubbed socially irrelevant.[35] In fact, the emergence of a public and private authority in their modern interpretation is linked to changes in the social and political context and the resulting emergence of a 'self-regulating' market in the nineteenth century (although this trend has always faced competing protectionist forces opposing it).[36] Moreover, the role of the State as a *super partes* entity committed to the common good was essential for elaboration of the ordoliberal approach, which aimed at carving out a domain of unfettered action for the private.[37] In international law, it has been suggested that separation of the private and public fields is a derivation of the positivist emphasis on territorial sovereignty and the growing diversity of national legal systems.[38] On this view, identifying private international law with domestic law, rather than as a branch of public international law, was part of a move towards development of a global market economy, aiming to free private transactions from the operation of State law.[39] Nowadays, the decline of the division between the public and the private would be emblematic of a shift in the balance of power in the form of an 'expansion of capitalism through the promotion of private regulatory authority' and increased legitimacy of the private as a source of authority.[40]

-----

34   See, among many, Duncan Kennedy, 'The Stages of the Decline of the Public/ Private Distinction' (1982) 130 *University of Pennsylvania Law Review* 1349; Morton Horwitz, 'The History of the Public/Private Distinction' (1982) 130 *University of Pennsylvania Law Review* 1423.

35   John Dewey, *The Public and its Problems* (Ohio University Press 1954) 12–17. He warned against 'identifying the community and its interests with the state or the politically organized community'.

36   Karl Polanyi, *The Great Transformation: The Political and Economic Origins of Our Time* (Beacon Hill Press 1944) 68.

37   See for example David J Gerber, 'Constitutionalising the Economy: German Neo-liberalism, Competition Law and the "New" Europe' (1994) 42 *The American Journal of Comparative Law* 25.

38   Alex Mills, 'The Private History of International Law' (2006) 55 *International and Comparative Law Quarterly* 1, 23 and 41.

39   Mills (n 38) 44. See also A Claire Cutler, 'Artifice, Ideology and Paradox: The Public/Private Distinction in International Law' (1997) 4 *Review of International Political Economy* 261, 279.

40   Cutler (n 39) 279.

There are thus many reasons to believe that the public–private division is a remnant of the establishment of the nation State as a modern reference point. That reference point is currently deeply contested from a variety of perspectives. This implies that there might be a need to re-define ideas of community or communities through legal pluralist lenses.[41] In light of what has been said earlier, one may wonder in what terms the relationship between market values and community values operates at the transnational law level. After all, suggestions have been made in the sense that, for example, investment law can also serve the purpose of protecting peace and security, the environment, human rights and good governance.[42] On the one hand, the appearance and strengthening of a global market may lead to processes of empowerment and disentanglement of corporate interests. The market may emerge as an 'open space' where the individual unleashes their ambitions of self-fulfilment. Transnational law seems to offer an ideal terrain for such developments, precisely because it suggests new ways of conceiving the relationship between individual freedom and authority. In this sense, while advancing ideas of a cosmopolitan *Gemeinschaft* may look like an unrealistic or even dystopian proposition, the notion of 'community' may be adapted to a prismatic, ever-changing transnational reality. One may consider whether it is worthwhile to employ concepts such as 'networks of communities' (as modalities of social interaction operating outside State borders)[43] or 'rough consensus and running code' (as a form of spontaneous law-making based on a minimum shared understanding of transnational actors and not dissimilar from customary international law).[44] Transnational law may thus be reassessed as a powerful instrument for emancipating the individual agent in the context of a pluralistic and fragmented society.

However, on the other hand, enhancing private autonomy may still carry the risk of facilitating the diffusion of ideological discourses which, even if decoupled from specific State interests, have the potential of undermining input, throughput or output democracy.

Considering transnational law as an instrument for emancipating the individual agent in separate transnational regimes ought to go hand in hand with promoting the idea of *civic* membership and related rules on responsibility and transparency. This

---

41   Cotterrell (n 26).

42   Christoph Schreuer and Ursula Kriebaum, 'From Individual to Community Interests in International Investment Law' in U Fastenrath et al, *From Bilateralism to Community Interests: Essays in Honour of Judge Bruno Simma* (OUP 2011) 1079. The authors, however, concede that there are no empirical data supporting the view that the protection of foreign investments may indirectly promote economic growth and, as a result, enhance the quality of the rule of law of the host State: ibid 1088.

43   Roger Cotterrell, 'Transnational Communities and the Concept of Law' (2008) 21 *Ratio Juris* 1, 12.

44   Gralf-Peter Calliess and Peer Zumbansen, *Rough Consensus and Running Code: A Theory of Transnational Private Law* (Hart 2010) esp. 134.

would require a shift from market citizenship to a participative type of citizenship which, while taking into account the virtues of communicative rationality, is also aware of its limits and attempts to go a step forward in the search for sustainable and constructive forms of interaction in the transnational sphere.

It is argued here that principles drawn from general criminal and constitutional law can perhaps help forge a community-oriented dimension of transnational law.[45] There should be more reflection on the possibility of constructing a form of civic community at the transnational level that not only relies on shared values and a common moral ground, but also enables individual emancipation through the tools provided by human rights.[46] In order for this to happen, criminal law ought to be conceived not in functional or utilitarian terms,[47] but as a Kantian-style project focused on respect for the individual as an autonomous moral agent. Any attempt to build or represent a community postulates a shared commitment to specific values by its members, as well as their conviction that they are part of the same community and are therefore responsible towards each other.[48] This implies that punishment at the transnational law level, just as it is argued at the national level, ought to be able to communicate censure of those that breach community values, and enable them to reconcile themselves with the other members of the community and be re-admitted to the community.[49] The following section will examine one of these principles, *ultima ratio*. Its aim is to indicate how the essence of this principle, seen as a tool of conflict resolution, may be a starting point for elaborating forms of responsibility at the transnational level.

Ultima ratio and 'Glocalisation'

Transnational conflicts can occur along a vertical line and along a horizontal line, between different branches of law, or different policy areas. Depending on which rationality they rely on and the jurisdictional context within which they operate, courts tend to provide different answers.

Human rights can be an example of this. The European Court of Human Rights (ECtHR) often manages conflicts through the margin of appreciation mechanism,[50]

---

45   See also Massimo Fichera, 'Criminal Law Beyond the State: The European Model' (2013) 19 *European Law Journal* 174.

46   See for example Brun-Otto Bryde, 'Transnational Democracy' in U Fastenrath et al (n 42) 211, 213.

47   See the classic approach in Herbert LA Hart, 'Prolegomenon to the Principles of Punishment' (1959–60) 60 *Proceedings of the Aristotelian Society* 1; Herbert LA Hart, *Punishment and Responsibility* (OUP 2008).

48   Anthony Duff, *Punishment, Communication and Community* (OUP 2001) 43.

49   Duff (n 48) 201.

50   Yuval Shany, 'Toward a General Margin of Appreciation Doctrine in International Law?' (2005) 16 *European Journal of International Law* 907; Yutaka Arai-Takahashi, *The Margin of Appreciation Doctrine and the Principle of Proportionality in the Jurisprudence*

which uses 'fuzzy logic' reasoning rather than traditional binary reasoning (legal/illegal, true/false).[51] Conflicts require transparent devices of resolution. This, in turn, demands a high degree of accountability. Mireille Delmas-Marty has observed that for this to happen there would have to be

> a more precise definition of common interests which, by reference to human rights and global public goods, could provide the basis for the concept of international crime; a pluralist application adapted to the practical conditions specific to each national and regional normative level; and favouring a process of interaction and harmonisation. This implicitly includes the concept of a national margin of appreciation, which preserves pluralism while ordering it.[52]

She advocates forms of ordering based on hybridisation and flexibility. One may wonder whether the principle of *ultima ratio* may also be useful in this enterprise. After all, both *ultima ratio* and the margin of appreciation evoke the need for measure, balance, control. They can therefore serve as tools to resolve the conflictual character of the legal pluralistic world. In this light, can *ultima ratio* perform a normative function in transnational law?

One of the main challenges of transnational legal theory is the fact that law is faced with its 'other', with non-law,[53] the un-regulated, and the un-defined. Law sprouts in an area with no borders, no ups and downs, and no public sphere. Communication is broken, except some fragments that circulate now and then between legal systems. Inevitably, when faced with its 'other', law's nature is affected. The very confrontation with the 'other' means a form of recognition which is also a partial incorporation. When law and non-law come together, they may overlap and interpenetrate. Moreover, law is sometimes said to operate in a normative sense: it proclaims what it ought to be but is not (yet). In its very statements, law challenges its 'other' and tries to colonise it.

Ultima ratio can operate in connection with this relationship between law and its 'other'. Here we are not faced with a conceptualisation of *ultima ratio* as an overarching rule, but rather as a principle (in the Dworkinian sense)[54] or meta-principle which does not necessarily assume the possibility of systematising different sources.

In criminal law, last resort is a guideline for criminalisation and its purpose is to limit a State's intrusive power of punishment to those cases in which punishment

---

of the ECHR (Intersentia 2002) 233; Michael R Hutchinson, 'The Margin of Appreciation Doctrine in the European Court of Human Rights' (1999) 48 *International and Comparative Law Quarterly* 638, 645.

51 Mireille Delmas-Marty, *Ordering Pluralism: A Conceptual Framework for Understanding the Transnational Legal World* (Hart 2009) 57.

52 Delmas-Marty (n 51) 114.

53 Calliess and Zumbansen (n 44) 31–2.

54 Ronald Dworkin, *Taking Rights Seriously* (Duckworth 2005) 24 ff.

is the last available means to produce the desired effect.[55] Normally, conduct will be criminalised only when there are very important reasons to do so, for example because the legal response is proportionate to the blameworthiness of the conduct itself. When there are elements leading to the conviction that other tools should be employed, then criminal law should simply step back. These tools can belong to a variety of disciplines, including private law or administrative law. In a certain sense, law shows an attitude to flexibility here: it does not intervene to radically alter the external socio-political environment, but tries to shape it gradually, so that law itself becomes an integral part of this environment, rather than an external splinter that has been spatchcocked into it.

The principle of *ultima ratio* thus reflects a certain way of conceiving the relationship between the public and the private. The former ought to interfere in the domain of the latter as little as possible and with the least possible intrusive means. When it does interfere, this should occur in accordance with some general clearly defined criteria. It is also a manifestation of a common good-oriented rationality:[56] criminalisation and, more in general, enforcement measures need to be justified in light of some general interest, for example because they protect values that rank high in the constitutional system.

In transnational law, *ultima ratio* as a general principle applied in connection with the notion of community would be interpreted in the sense that flexible legislation, rather than classic instruments of State law, should be the preferred tool of action and both 'soft' and 'hard' legal measures would be adopted only when they are strictly necessary or a more efficient way of addressing a particular issue which is important for the common good. Necessarily, *ultima ratio* goes along with subsidiarity and proportionality: for example, transnational legislative measures would interfere in the domestic sphere only when measures at the local level seem inadequate or insufficient for safeguarding community values. This suggests that many, diverse communities can co-exist at different levels. These communities are not necessarily defined according to criteria of territorialisation. They should instead be conceived of as entities or groups consisting of those people that are affected by a particular decision and whose boundaries may overlap or shift. For example, measures adopted at the transnational level and deeply affecting local communities would have to go through a democratic process of incorporation into the specific legal and cultural context which they are addressed to. We can call this process 'glocalisation'. This would be particularly important when it comes to devising forms of responsibility in private law, criminal law or human rights schemes. 'Glocalisation' implies that forms of bottom-up legitimisation should be preferred to top-down schemes. In the same way that a marketed product is

---

55   See among many Andrew Ashworth, 'Is the Criminal Law a Lost Cause' (2000) 116 *Law Quarterly Review* 225; Douglas Husak, 'The Criminal Law as Last Resort' (2004) 24 *Oxford Journal of Legal Studies* 207; Nils Jareborg, 'Criminalization as Last Resort (Ultima Ratio)' (2005) 5 *Ohio State Journal of Criminal Law* 521.

56   See for example Jareborg (n 55) 522.

modified to suit the needs of a regional or sub-regional area, so a transnational legal product should take into account the cultural and social context which it applies to. This means enhancing transparency and accountability.

Moreover, a 'glocalised' perspective takes into account the fact that in contemporary stratified societies, individuals still show strong allegiance more to local or small-size communities so that any discussion on the emergence of an 'international community' is inappropriate.[57] This implies the recognition of legal and cultural diversity and is therefore not far from the idea of 'demoicracy'.[58]

However, there are risks associated with the introduction of a general *ultima ratio* mentality. These derive mainly from three hurdles. The first is the difficulty in applying this principle to transnational legal processes, characterised by 'dispersed' responsibility, that is a form of responsibility that is more difficult to detect. In particular, it is difficult to sanction specific behaviours through coercive mechanisms when not only proving but also detecting the causal link between commission of an act and the agent leads to uncertain results. The second hurdle is a certain degree of unease in defining community values and forms of shared understanding, as has been pointed out in much of the recent and classic works on the idea of community. As has been noted in the previous section, one could rely, for example, on an instrumental perspective, focusing on contractual relations converging towards a common aim; on commitment to certain types of value, for example constitutional; or on affective or cultural bonds. No conceptualisation of community can be easily adapted to the transnational dimension. The third hurdle derives from the general trend towards securitisation of law.[59] This difficulty is connected with the prevalence of discursive practices in our society that tend to emphasise forms of decisionism in times of emergency either outside the legal framework set by contemporary democracies or within them but at odds with their fundamental principles. One should always bear in mind the limits of so-called 'danger-averting' rationality, which has been frequently observed in criminal law in recent times but has expanded in other branches of law as well. Danger-averting rationality encourages forms of legislation that: (a) do not respond to a particular need in the present, but instead to a potential risk that *might* occur in the future but is not clearly defined or (b) react to a threat that is not evident, or that has been

---

57 Nico Krisch, *Beyond Constitutionalism: The Pluralist Structure of Postnational Law* (OUP 2010) 59–60.

58 Kalypso Nicolaïdis, 'We the Peoples of Europe' (2004) 83 *Foreign Affairs* 97; Samantha Besson, 'Deliberative Democracy in the European Union: Towards the Deterritorialisation of Democracy' in S Besson and JL Martí (eds), *Deliberative Democracy and its Discontents* (Ashgate 2006); Kalypso Nicolaïdis, 'The Idea of European Demoicracy' in J Dickson, P Eleftheriadis (eds), *Philosophical Foundations of European Union Law* (OUP 2012).

59 See for example Massimo Fichera, 'Security Issues as an Existential Threat to the Community' in M Fichera and J Kremer (eds), *Law and security in Europe: Reconsidering the Security Constitution* (Intersentia 2013).

constructed as such without appropriate debate in a public forum on what it really consists of.

The area of financial regulation, banking and investment is emblematic of what has been observed earlier. Financial and banking activities occur at remarkable speed across the world and are able to involve several countries simultaneously. 'Market forces' determine movements of capital and other material or immaterial goods and it is not always easy to understand their internal mechanisms. Various forms of transnational legislation have been devised precisely with a view to adapting to this complex reality. As a result, it is possible to observe types of law which would not be classified as such under the classic positivist formula. They are characterised by enhanced flexibility, non-bindingness and blurring of the line between public and private law.

For example, soft law is a common way of regulating the financial sector. Despite the lack of binding enforcement mechanisms and sanctions, it has been employed with relative success in the context of money laundering and financing of terrorism.[60] It has been observed that the features of soft law allow it to achieve a lower and less demanding level of consensus than that associated with hard law.[61] Money laundering has expanded considerably in recent decades and the Recommendations elaborated by the Financial Action Task Force (FATF), a special body that operates under the auspices of the Organisation for Economic Cooperation and Development (OECD), are a good example of *transnational* criminal law (in the narrow or phenomenological sense, that is that type of criminal law that concerns cross-border crime). Unsurprisingly, identifying this discipline is by no means uncontroversial. Some authors argue that employing such a wide definition would leave aside the complexity of cross-border offences and their local and national characteristics.[62] Others include within it only those activities that have actual or potential cross-border elements.[63] These activities would often involve private individual conduct and affect private interests[64] as well as those acts

    60   Navin Beekarry, 'The International Anti-Money Laundering and Combating the Financing of Terrorism Regulatory Strategy: A Critical Analysis of Compliance Determinants in International Law' (2011) 31 *Northwestern Journal of International Law and Business* 137; Ross S Delston and Stephen C Walls, 'Reaching Beyond Banks: How to Target Trade-based Money Laundering and Terrorist Financing Outside the Financial Sector' (2009) 41 *Case Western Reserve Journal of International Law* 85; Valsamis Mitsilegas and Bill Gilmore, 'The EU Legislative Framework Against Money Laundering and Terrorist Finance: A Critical Analysis in the Light of Evolving Global Standards' (2007) 56 *International and Comparative Law Quarterly* 119.

    61   Delston and Walls (n 60) 90.

    62   Cyrille Fijnaut, 'Transnational Crime and the Role of the United Nations' (2000) 8 *European Journal of Crime, Criminal Law and Criminal Justice* 119, 120.

    63   Neil Boister, 'Transnational Criminal Law' (2003) 14 *European Journal of International Law* 953, 955. He refers, for example, to conventions against drug trafficking, corruption or financing terrorism, that is merely positive law.

    64   Boister (n 63) 966.

that are normatively (instead of phenomenologically) transnational in the sense that, even when they only occur within national borders, they constitute a threat to shared national interests or cosmopolitan values but a threat which is nevertheless not considered sufficiently serious to rank them as 'international' in the proper sense (for example, torture).[65] Although only treaties and conventions have been mentioned by most commentators, there are no serious reasons to exclude the FATF Recommendations from transnational criminal law.[66] These Recommendations call upon States to perform specific actions, such as criminalising money laundering and financing terrorism, supervising financial institutions and reporting suspicious transactions. They have a certain degree of intrusiveness into the domestic sphere, as they require States to adopt 'effective, proportionate and dissuasive' sanctions, whether criminal, civil or administrative.[67] They can also be addressed to private agents, such as banks or lawyers and prescribe specific behaviour that is judged necessary to assist in identifying evidence and other information. Moreover, mutual evaluation and 'name and shame' practices seem to be effective.[68]

A second example is the set of measures adopted during the recent financial crisis. A large variety of statements and agreements at the EU level, for example concerning the Eurozone,[69] has been accompanied at the domestic level by legislative measures whose constitutionality has sometimes been questioned by domestic courts.[70] One of the main issues has been that of 'shadow banking', also known as 'market-based financing', that is 'the system of credit intermediation that involves entities and activities outside the regular banking system'.[71] The Financial Stability Board

---

65   Boister (n 63) 967, 968.

66   See the recently revised 2012 FATF Mandate and Recommendations, <www.fatf-gafi. org/media/fatf/documents/FINAL%20FATF%20MANDATE%202012–2020.pdf> and <www. fatf-gafi.org/media/fatf/documents/recommendations/pdfs/FATF%20Recommendations%20 approved%20February%202012%20reprint%20March%202012.pdf> accessed 5 October 2013.

67   2012 FATF Recommendations, *supra* point 35.

68   Michael Levi and Peter Reuter, 'Money Laundering' (2006) 34 *Crime and Justice* 289, 306.

69   See for example European Council Euro Summit Statement, Brussels, 26 October 2011, at <www.consilium.europa.eu/uedocs/cms_data/docs/pressdata/en/ec/125644.pdf> accessed 5 October 2013; Statement of the members of the European Council *Towards Growth-friendly Consolidation and Job-friendly Growth*, Brussels, 30 January 2012 at <www.consilium.europa.eu/uedocs/cms_data/docs/pressdata/en/ec/127599.pdf> accessed 5 October 2013; Report of the President of the European Council *Towards a Genuine Economic and Monetary Union*, Brussels, 26 June 2012 EUCO 120/12 Presse 296, at <http://ec.europa.eu/economy_finance/focuson/crisis/documents/131201_en.pdf> accessed 5 October 2013.

70   See for example 'Portugal court rules public sector pay cut unconstitutional' *BBC News* (6 July 2012) <www.bbc.co.uk/news/world-europe-18732184> accessed 23 June 2014.

71   Financial Stability Board Report on 'Shadow Banking: Strengthening Oversight and Regulation', 27 October 2011, at <www.financialstabilityboard.org/publications/ r_111027a.pdf> accessed 5 October 2013; G20 Leaders' Summit Communiqué, Cannes,

(FSB), in particular, was established in April 2009 as an upgrade of its predecessor, the Financial Stability Forum (FSF) and was tasked with implementing regulatory and supervisory policies in the financial sector. It brings together representatives of several international financial institutions and its Secretariat is hosted by the Bank for International Settlements in Basel, Switzerland.[72] Since the beginning of the financial crisis it has published reports containing recommendations and guidelines concerning standard-setting, codes of good practice and the monitoring of transparency, effectiveness and financial stability. These recommendations, directed towards State and non-State entities, concern *inter alia* making financial markets and products more transparent and strengthening standards for governance, risk management, capital and liquidity. They are part of a global effort to curb the negative effects of the crisis and have also been debated and elaborated within the EU institutions. The debate has focused not only on how to regulate the financial sector, but also, for example, on whether economic measures should be growth-oriented (including measures that bring European States' borrowing costs down) or whether austerity measures are sufficient.[73]

One of the most important achievements in the EU following the financial crisis has been the adoption of legislative measures that seek to regulate forms of aid and other support mechanisms for those States that need it. An example of this is the European Stability Mechanism (ESM), in force as of June 2013 to replace the existing European Financial Stabilisation Mechanism (EFSM).[74] It is interesting to observe that the new mechanism will involve the private sector. For example, in some situations negotiations between a Member State and private creditors will be carried out according to a plan in compliance with the principles of proportionality, transparency and fairness, amongst others.[75] In this context, it has been argued that Member States' activity in supporting other Member States is not sufficiently justified by the emergency and should not breach relevant provisions of the Treaty on the Functioning of the European Union (TFEU).[76]

November 2011, par. 30 at <http://www.g20.org/en> accessed 5 October 2013; European Commission Green Paper on 'Shadow Banking', Brussels, 19 March 2012 COM (2012) 102 final 3.

72   <www.financialstabilityboard.org> accessed 23 June 2014.

73   See for example Paul Krugman, 'The Crash of the Bumblebee' *The New York Times* (29 July 2012); Rosa Lastra, 'Legal and Regulatory Responses to the Financial Crisis', *Queen Mary University of London, School of Law Legal Studies Research Paper* 100/2012, at <http://papers.ssrn.com/sol3/papers.cfm?abstract_id=2020553> accessed 5 October 2013; Steven Schwarcz, 'The Global Financial Crisis and Systemic Risk', *Leverhulme Lecture, 9 November 2010, Faculty of Law, Oxford University.*

74   Council Decision No. 2011/199/EU of 25 March 2011 on the European Stability Mechanism, OJ 2011 L 91/1; Council Regulation No. 407/2010 of 11 May 2010 on the European Financial Stabilisation Mechanism, OJ 2010 L 118/1.

75   Matthias Ruffert, 'The European Debt Crisis and European Union Law' (2011) 48 *Common Market Law Review* 1777, 1784.

76   Ruffert (n 75) 1785–8.

In both cases mentioned above, the principle of *ultima ratio* can allow adoption of 'hard' and 'soft' legislative measures only when they possess a sufficient degree of legitimacy and transparency and are important for the protection of values judged fundamental for the community. However, 'soft' measures should generally be preferred when the degree of consensus over adoption of specific measures (for example, rules on the responsibility of individuals for damage to the general interest of the community) is not very high. In other words, the transnationalisation of law can increase, rather than reduce, the probability of conflict. An example of tension between different levels of transnational law is the rather unconventional expression of value judgments by private actors as regards the constitutional and political systems of Southern European States.[77]

Conclusion

This chapter has attempted to offer a brief account of recent developments in transnational law as a concept which is not merely different from international law and domestic law but which somehow embraces them and makes any traditional distinction between them meaningless. These developments are closely linked to the decline of State sovereignty and the emergence of new sites of authority and forms of law-making. There has already been some debate concerning the possibility of applying a community-oriented approach to transnational law. It is argued here that criminal law can provide some guidelines in this direction, not only concerning elaboration of forms of responsibility that take into account the general interests of the community and the need to protect them, but also in terms of promotion of individual autonomy. In particular, the principle of *ultima ratio* may serve this purpose, in the sense that transnational legal processes should not be intrusive and should be justified through the principles of subsidiarity and proportionality. Significant examples, as far as the EU is concerned, can be found in the areas of financial legislation and anti-money laundering legislation, in which soft law has proved to be rather effective.

Some problems may however be detected. They originate from the fact that in transnational law it is not always possible to sanction specific conduct through coercive mechanisms, due to evidence-gathering difficulties. Moreover, any attempt to refer to community values and forms of shared understanding faces the challenge of defining what these values are and how consensus should be built around them. Finally, this chapter has pointed out that security-oriented discursive

---

77 J.P. Morgan Report, 'The Euro area adjustment: about halfway there', Europe Economic Research, 28 May 2013 <http://dailystorm.it/wp-content/uploads/2013/06/JPM-the-euro-area-adjustment-about-halfway-there.pdf> accessed 5 October 2013, especially at 12–13, arguing that the 'political systems in the periphery' show a 'strong socialist influence' and have thus been only partially successful in coping with the crisis. This would make it necessary to 'engage in meaningful political reform'.

practices present some difficulties when they spread beyond the criminal law sector. In other words, they may lead to the emergence of forms of decisionism in times of emergency either outside the legal framework set by contemporary democracies or within them but at odds with their fundamental principles. Danger-averting rationality encourages forms of legislation that are enacted even when the existence of a risk or threat to common values has been declared without appropriate discussion in a public forum.

Bibliography

Abbott F, 'NAFTA and the Legalization of World Politics: A Case Study' in JL Goldstein et al (eds), *Legalization and World Politics* (MIT Press 2005)

Abbott KW and Snidal D, 'Hard and Soft Law in International Governance' in JL Goldstein et al (eds), *Legalization and World Politics* (MIT Press 2005)

Arai-Takahashi Y, *The Margin of Appreciation Doctrine and the Principle of Proportionality in the Jurisprudence of the ECHR* (Intersentia 2002)

Ashworth A, 'Is the Criminal Law a Lost Cause' (2000) 116 *Law Quarterly Review* 225

Beekarry N, 'The International Anti-Money Laundering and Combating the Financing of Terrorism Regulatory Strategy: A Critical Analysis of Compliance Determinants in International Law' (2011) 31 *Northwestern Journal of International Law and Business* 137

Bellomo M, *The Common Legal Past of Europe, 1000–1800* (The Catholic University of America Press 1995)

Bentham J, *Introduction to the Principles of Morals and Legislation*, Chapter XIX section XXV in J Bowring (ed.) *The Works of Jeremy Bentham* Vol. I (1843 Edinburgh: William Tait, orig. 1780)

Benz A, Harlow C and Papadopoulos Y, 'Introduction' (2007) 13 *European Law Journal* 441

Berman PS, 'A Pluralist Approach to International Law' (2007) 32 *Yale Journal of International Law* 301

Besson S, 'Deliberative Democracy in the European Union: Towards the Deterritorialisation of Democracy' in S Besson and JL Martí (eds), *Deliberative Democracy and its Discontents* (Ashgate 2006)

Boister N, 'Transnational Criminal Law' (2003) 14 *European Journal of International Law* 953

Bryde B-O, 'Transnational Democracy' in U Fastenrath et al, *From Bilateralism to Community Interest – Essays in Honour of Judge Bruno Simma* (OUP 2011) 211

Brunnée J and Toope SJ, 'International Law and Constructivism: Elements of an Interactional Theory of International Law' (2000) 39 *Columbia Journal of Transnational Law* 19

Calliess G-P and Zumbansen P, *Rough Consensus and Running Code: A Theory of Transnational Private Law* (Hart 2010)

Cohen J and Sabel C, 'Directly-Deliberative Polyarchy' (1997) 3 *European Law Journal* 313

Cotterrell R, 'Transnational Communities and the Concept of Law' (2008) 21 *Ratio Juris* 1

——— 'A Legal Concept of Community' (1997) 12 *Canadian Journal of Law and Society* 75

Cutler AC, 'Artifice, Ideology and Paradox: The Public/Private Distinction in International Law' (1997) 4 *Review of International Political Economy* 261

Delmas-Marty M, *Ordering Pluralism: A Conceptual Framework for Understanding the Transnational Legal World* (Hart 2009)

Delston RS and Walls SC, 'Reaching Beyond Banks: How to Target Trade-based Money Laundering and Terrorist Financing Outside the Financial Sector' (2009) 41 *Case Western Reserve Journal of International Law* 85

Dewey J, *The Public and its Problems* (Ohio University Press 1954)

Dibadj R, 'Panglossian Transnationalism' (2008) 44 *Stanford Journal of International Law* 253

Duff A, *Punishment, Communication and Community* (OUP 2001)

Dworkin R, *Taking rights seriously* (Duckworth 2005)

Fichera M, 'Security Issues as an Existential Threat to the Community' in M Fichera and J Kremer (eds), *Law and security in Europe: Reconsidering the Security Constitution* (Intersentia 2013)

——— 'Criminal Law Beyond the State: the European Model' (2013) 19 *European Law Journal* 174

Fijnaut C, 'Transnational Crime and the Role of the United Nations' (2000) 8 *European Journal of Crime, Criminal Law and Criminal Justice* 119

Fischer-Lescano A and Teubner G, 'Regime-Collisions: The Vain Search for Legal Unity in the Fragmentation of Global Law' (2004) *Michigan Journal of International Law* 999

Gallie WG, *Philosophy and the Historical Understanding* (2nd edn, Schocken Books 1968)

——— 'Essentially Contested Concepts' (1956) 56 *Proceedings of the Aristotelian Society* 167

——— 'Art as an Essentially Contested Concept' (1956) 6 *The Philosophical Quarterly* 97

Gerber DJ, 'Constitutionalising the Economy: German Neo-liberalism, Competition Law and the "New" Europe' (1994) 42 *The American Journal of Comparative Law* 25

Grotius H, *On the Law of War and Peace* (2001 Batoche Books, trans. AC Campbell, orig. 1625)

Habermas J, *The Postnational Costellation* (Polity Press 2001)

Halliday TC and Osinsky P, 'Globalization of Law' (2006) 32 *Annual Review of Sociology* 447

Hamann A and Fabri HR, 'Transnational Networks and Constitutionalism' (2008) 3 & 4 *ICON* 481

Hart HLA, *Punishment and Responsibility* (OUP 2008)

—— 'Prolegomenon to the Principles of Punishment' (1959–60) 60 *Proceedings of the Aristotelian Society* 1

Hathaway OA, 'Between Power and principle: An Integrated Theory of International Law' (2005) 72 *University of Chicago Law Review* 469

Horwitz MJ, 'The History of the Public/Private Distinction' (1982) 130 *University of Pennsylvania Law Review* 1423

Husak D, 'The Criminal Law as Last Resort' (2004) 24 *Oxford Journal of Legal Studies* 207

Hutchinson MR, 'The Margin of Appreciation Doctrine in the European Court of Human Rights' (1999) 48 *International and Comparative Law Quarterly* 638

Jareborg N, 'Criminalization as Last Resort (*Ultima Ratio*)' (2005) 5 *Ohio State Journal of Criminal Law* 521

Jessup P, *Transnational Law* (Yale University Press 1956)

Joerges C and Neyer J, 'From Intergovernmental Bargaining to Deliberative Political Processes: The Constitutionalisation of Comitology' (1997) *European Law Journal* 273

Kennedy D, 'The Stages of the Decline of the Public/Private Distinction' (1982) 130 *University of Pennsylvania Law Review* 1349

Keohane R, *International Institutions and State Power* (Westview 1989)

Koh HH, 'International Law as Part of Our Law' (2004) 98 *The American Journal Of International Law* 43

—— 'Transnational Legal Process' (1996) 75 *Nebraska Law Review* 181

—— 'Why Do Nations Obey International Law' (1997) 106 *Yale Law Journal* 2599

Koskenniemi M, *From Apology to Utopia* (3rd ed. Cambridge University Press 2009)

Kratochwil FV, *Rules, Norms and Decisions: On the Conditions of Practical and Legal Reasoning in International Relations and Domestic Affairs* (CUP 1989)

Krisch N, *Beyond Constitutionalism: The Pluralist Structure of Postnational Law* (OUP 2010)

Kumm M, 'The Jurisprudence of Constitutional Conflict: Constitutional Supremacy in Europe before and after the Constitutional Treaty' (2005) 11 *European Law Journal* 262

Lastra R, 'Legal and Regulatory Responses to the Financial Crisis', *Queen Mary University of London, School of Law Legal Studies Research Paper* 100/2012, at http://papers.ssrn.com/sol3/papers.cfm?abstract_id=2020553 accessed 5 October 2013

Levi M and Reuter P, 'Money Laundering' (2006) 34 *Crime and Justice* 289

Luhmann N, 'Law as a Social System' (1989) 83 *Northwestern University Law Review* 136

Mills A, 'The Private History of International Law' (2006) 55 *International and Comparative Law Quarterly* 1

Mitsilegas V and Gilmore B, 'The EU Legislative Framework Against Money Laundering and Terrorist Finance: A Critical Analysis in the Light of

Evolving Global Standards' (2007) 56 *International and Comparative Law Quarterly* 119

Nicolaïdis K, 'The Idea of European Demoicracy' in J Dickson and P Eleftheriadis (eds), *Philosophical Foundations of European Union Law* (OUP 2012)

—— 'We the Peoples of Europe' (2004) 83 *Foreign Affairs* 97

Pernice I, 'The Treaty of Lisbon: Multilevel Constitutionalism in Action' (2009) 15 *Columbia Journal of European Law* 349

Polanyi K, *The Great Transformation: the political and economic origins of our time* (Beacon Hill Press 1944)

Ruffert M, 'The European Debt Crisis and European Union Law' (2011) 48 *Common Market Law Review* 1777

Scott C, 'Transnational Law as Proto-Concept: Three Conceptions' (2009) 10 *German Law Journal* 859

Schmitt C, *The Nomos of the Earth* (Telos Press 2003)

Scholte JA, 'Reconstructing Contemporary Democracy' (2008) 15 *Indiana Journal of Global Legal Studies* 305

Schreuer C and Kriebaum U, 'From Individual to Community Interests in International Investment Law' in U Fastenrath et al, *From Bilateralism to Community Interests: Essays in Honour of Judge Bruno Simma* (OUP 2011) 1079

Schwarcz S, 'The Global Financial Crisis and Systemic Risk', *Leverhulme Lecture, 9 November 2010, Faculty of Law, Oxford University*

Shany Y, 'Toward a General Margin of Appreciation Doctrine in International Law?' (2005) 16 *European Journal of International Law* 907

Slaughter AM, 'A Liberal Theory of International Law' (2000) 94 *American Society of International Law Proceedings* 240

Stein E, 'Lawyers, Judges, and the Making of a Transnational Constitution' (1981) 75 *American Journal of International Law* 1

Teubner G, *Constitutional Fragments- Societal Constitutionalism and Globalisation* (OUP 2012)

Trachtman JP, 'The International Economic Law Revolution' (1996) 17 *University of Pennsylvania Journal of International Economic Law* 33

Tuori K, *Critical Legal Positivism* (Ashgate 2002)

—— and Sankari S (eds), *The Many Constitutions of Europe* (Ashgate 2010)

Walker N, 'The Idea of Constitutional Pluralism' (2002) 65 *Modern Law Review* 317

—— and de Búrca G, 'Reconceiving Law and New Governance' (2007) 13 *Columbia Journal of European Law* 519

Williams P, 'Organising Transnational Crime: Networks, Markets and Hierarchies' in P Williams and D Vlassis (eds), 'Combating Transnational Crime: Concepts, Activities and Responses' 4 *Transnational Organised Crime* (1998) 57

Vattel E de, *The Law of Nations, or the Principles of National Law applied to the Conduct and to the Affairs of Nations and Sovereigns* (1916 Carnegie Institution of Washington, trans. CG Fenwick, orig. 1758)

Zaring D, 'International Law by Other Means: The Twilight Existence of International Financial Regulatory Organizations' (1998) 33 *Texas International Law Journal* 281

Zumbansen P, 'Transnational Legal Pluralism' (2010) *Transnational Legal Theory* 1

—— 'Transnational Law' in J Smits (ed.) *Encyclopedia of Comparative Law* (Edward Elgar 2006) 738

Legislation

Council Decision 2008/976/JHA of 16 December 2008 on the European Judicial Network, OJ L 348

Council Decision No. 2011/199/EU of 25 March 2011 on the European Stability Mechanism, OJ 2011 L 91/1

Council Regulation No. 407/2010 of 11 May 2010 on the European Financial Stabilisation Mechanism, OJ 2010 L 118/1

International Convention on the Settlement of Investment Disputes Between States and Nationals of Other States (ICSID) (1965), 17 U.S.T. 1270, 575 U.N.T.S. 159

Resolution of the Council and of the Representatives of the Governments of the Member States, meeting within the Council, on the establishment of a Network for legislative cooperation between the Ministries of Justice of the European Union OJ C 326 20.12.2008

United States, 19 U.S.C. § 1516a(g)(7)(A) (2000)

Case Law

(South Africa) *State v. Makwanyane*, 1995 (3) SALR 391 (CC) (S. Afr.)

(United States) *Lawrence e.a. v. Texas*, 539 U.S. 558, 575 (2003) 41 S. W. 3d 349

Official Documents

1998 Europol Organised Crime Situation Report at <www.europol.org> accessed 5 October 2013

2007 Europol Organised Crime Threat Assessment (OCTA) at <www.europol.org> accessed 5 October 2013

2012 FATF Mandate and Recommendations, www.fatf-gafi.org/media/fatf/documents/FINAL%20FATF%20MANDATE%202012–2020.pdf accessed 5 October 2013

European Commission Green Paper on 'Shadow Banking', Brussels, 19 March 2012 COM (2012) 102 final

European Council Euro Summit Statement, Brussels, 26 October 2011, at <www.consilium.europa.eu/uedocs/cms_data/docs/pressdata/en/ec/125644.pdf> accessed 5 October 2013

Financial Stability Board Report on 'Shadow Banking: Strengthening Oversight and Regulation', 27 October 2011, at <www.financialstabilityboard.org/publications/r_111027a.pdf> accessed 5 October 2013

G20 Leaders' Summit Communiqué, Cannes, November 2011 at <http://www.g20.org/en> accessed 5 October 2013

J.P. Morgan Report, 'The Euro area adjustment: about halfway there', Europe Economic Research, 28 May 2013 <http://dailystorm.it/wp-content/uploads/2013/06/JPM-the-euro-area-adjustment-about-halfway-there.pdf> accessed 5 October 2013

Report of the President of the European Council *Towards a Genuine Economic and Monetary Union*, Brussels, 26 June 2012 EUCO 120/12 Presse 296, at <http://ec.europa.eu/economy_finance/focuson/crisis/documents/131201_en.pdf> accessed 5 October 2013

Statement of the members of the European Council *Towards Growth-friendly Consolidation and Job-friendly Growth*, Brussels, 30 January 2012 at <www.consilium.europa.eu/uedocs/cms_data/docs/pressdata/en/ec/127599.pdf> accessed 5 October 2013

Newspaper Articles

'Portugal court rules public sector pay cut unconstitutional' *BBC News* (6 July 2012) <www.bbc.co.uk/news/world-europe-18732184> accessed 23 June 2014

Krugman P, 'The Crash of the Bumblebee' *The New York Times* (29 July 2012)

PART III
Europe as a Post-National Polity?

Chapter 9

Nordic Democracy Facing the EU: Traditions, Myths and Challenges

Pia Letto-Vanamo

Introduction: The Nordic 'Family'

When analysing characteristics of law, it is quite typical to put the Nordic countries together as one legal group or at least as a subfamily of the so-called civil law family. In particular, the 1990s witnessed a boom of seminars on 'Nordic identity' and its future. The main reason for this was the upcoming or recently achieved Finnish and Swedish membership in the European Union. In seminars the Nordic countries and their legal systems were compared with other European (European Union) countries. It was typical to point out similarities of the Nordic legal systems on the one hand, and differences between them and other Western European countries on the other hand, and to try to foresee whether and what kind of 'convergence' would happen through EU membership.

Since Swedish and Finnish accession in 1995 it was Europe not *Norden* that was the focus of scholarly and political debates. Today, the situation has changed: it is again the EU, foremost its economic-political crisis, that has actualized discussions on the North and South but also on the future of the so-called Nordic model with welfare as a key element. At the same time, new openings for cooperation between the Nordic countries – even a proposal for a Nordic Federal State – have been launched.[1]

It is true that many similarities exist between the Nordic countries, not least for historical reasons. And many of them are well known. One can speak of small, quite homogeneous, even egalitarian societies, where big cities and their bourgeoisie were lacking. Thus, social and legal culture has been characterized as peasant or rural, as distinct from urban culture. Henrik Stenius has written of one-norm societies that provided fruitful soil for modern, universal practices of Nordic welfare states. More than in the rest of Western Europe, the Reformation in the North brought worldly (Royal) and spiritual (Church) power to an organic whole in which worldly and spiritual officialdoms were two dimensions of one

---

1   See for instance, Johan Strang, *Nordiska Gemenskaper. En vision för samarbetet* (Nord 2012) 9. For Gunnar Wetterberg's proposal for a Nordic federal state see G Wetterberg, *The United Nordic Federation* (TemaNord 2010) 583. Available at <http://www.norden. org/en/publications/publikationer/2010-583> accessed 16 June 2014.

body of authority.[2] Nor were one-norm ideals destroyed by modern democracy and parliamentarism.

These countries and their law were modernized relatively recently, generally speaking during the nineteenth century, with the first wave of industrialization. Here, too, at least some reasons exist for the dominance of the Nordic idea of a 'good' state, and for implementation of the idea of the social state as well. In addition, the Nordic countries used to be characterized by expressions such as 'countries with a lacking or weak civil society', and 'paternalistic' – actually, the concepts of state and society seem to be interchangeable – but also 'transparent' and 'democratic'.

Nordicness can also be found in the late professionalization of legal culture. And more generally, for a long time one could speak of non-expert or lay-dominated cultures. This again explains at least partly why Nordic legal culture is even today characterized by the term pragmatic.[3] At the same time, one can perceive a tension between conservatism and dynamism, at least when reforms of societal and legal institutions are concerned.

In this chapter I will discuss meaning(s) of democracy in the Nordic countries. My interest is mainly in legal history but I will also touch on present issues. Foremost I will argue for interdependence between the Nordic traditions of defining or understanding democracy and attitudes towards socio-legal changes, including EU integration and its future.

Norden as a Historical Construct

In comparative analysis peculiarities of the development of the Nordic legal system(s) are explained mainly by referring to a historical 'delay'. There is no early wave of Roman legal influence (that of the *ius commune*). Since the seventeenth century it had been possible to study law at university in the North, but a university-trained legal profession and legal science are phenomena of the nineteenth century. Additionally, modern civil law codifications such as the French *code civil* (1804) or the German BGB (1900) are missing in all the Nordic countries: civil law issues, such as contract or tort law, have been regulated by more or less independent acts. However, when national legal scholarship emerged in the Nordic countries during the nineteenth century, this happened mostly by adapting German legal ideas, quite often also by translating texts by German legal authors.[4]

---

2   Henrik Stenius, 'A Nordic Conceptual Universe. Multi-layered Historicity of the Present. Approaches to Social Science History' in Heidi Haggren, Johanna Rainio-Niemi and Jussi Vauhkonen (eds), *Publications of the Department of Political and Economic Studies* 8 (2013) 93–104; 95.

3   See Konrad Zweigert and Hein Kötz, *An Introduction to Comparative Law*, (3rd edn, Oxford University Press 1998) 276–85.

4   Robert Montgomery's book *Handbok i Finlands allmänna privaträtt I* (Helsinki 1889) was based on Bernhard Windscheid, *Lehrbuch des Pandektenrechts I* (Düsseldorf 1862).

These were also channels for the influence of Roman Law-based terminology and systematization. At the same time, they are links between Nordic law and the so-called civil law family. Moreover, ideas of German legal scholarship and state theory played an important role in the development of public law in the Nordic countries.

However, more detailed studies in legal institutions, legal education or (professional and non-professional) legal thinking reveal not only similarities but also differences between the Nordic countries. For instance, administrative courts exist in Sweden and Finland but not in other Nordic countries, while Scandinavian Realism, which also plays a role in discussions on (Nordic) democracy, was mostly a Swedish and Danish phenomenon. For socio-political reasons Finnish legal history has some peculiarities, of which some, linked with democracy, will be discussed later in this paper.

In both legal and political debates within the Nordic countries, the North (*Norden*) exists as a construct[5] based mainly on history. At the same time, the main elements of the construct are nation states. A common Nordic past has been referred to, and even ideas of a Nordic community of destiny have been pronounced, but the Nordic element has never lastingly gone beyond national frameworks. Again, in other countries, Scandinavia and *Norden* have played a role in contemporary political debates, either as a model worth striving for or as a warning example. During the Cold War Scandinavia was looked upon as the middle way between Western democratic capitalism and East European communism.[6]

It can be said that *Nordism* (Nordic ideology) has been above all a reinforcing element of national identities, with the Nordic peasant and the welfare state as predominating components, while peasants and welfare state were Nordic and Danish in Denmark or Nordic and Swedish in Sweden.[7] At the same time, the Nordic element was less conspicuous in Norway and Finland. In Finnish legal-political debates, however, the Nordic tradition or the Nordic example has referred foremost to Sweden.[8] In the Cold War context, historical and cultural dimensions attached to Nordic democracy were used when Finnish politicians and intellectuals

---

5   The construction of a Nordic model can be seen as a myth in the sense that much in social coherence and community is symbolically and mythically based.

6   See for example Marquis Childs, *Sweden: the Middle Way* (Yale University Press 1961[1936]). Actually, a Scandinavian or Nordic Model is a post-World War II phenomenon, even if interest in Sweden as a middle way society started during the New Deal controversy in the USA. Øystein Sørensen and Bo Stråth, 'Introduction: The Cultural Construction of Norden' in Øystein Sørensen and Bo Stråth (eds), *The Cultural Construction of Norden* (Scandinavian University Press 1997) 1–24; 21.

7   Sørensen and Stråth (n 6) 22–3.

8   In spite of language strife and a wave of right-wing extremism, Finland was hesitantly included in the group of Nordic democracies. This happened because of its former status as a part of Sweden with a political tradition of freedom and political participation, the (Swedish) legal system and Lutheran state religion; see more Jussi Kurunmäki, 'Nordic Democracy in 1935. On the Finnish and Swedish Rhetoric of Democracy' in

tried to navigate in a polarized world by making effective use of Finland's Nordic democratic heritage. References to the Nordic connection and Nordic democracy were important for arguing that Finland did not belong to the Eastern Bloc. However, in all Nordic countries *Norden* has functioned as a demarcation from 'Europe'. It is democratic, Protestant, progressive and egalitarian while (the continental) Europe is Catholic, conservative and capitalistic.[9]

Since the 1990s this old identity-related demarcation between *Norden* and Europe started to become defensive and confused. *Norden* was no longer the 'natural' basis of the community-of-destiny myth. Many, even traditional, political parties including Social Democrats, put their confidence in Europe or in the European market so that Nordic ideology – at least partly – lost credibility. In political debates 'Nordicness' became quite invisible. Instead, a new concept, the Northern Dimension (ND) saw daylight. The concept refers to a joint policy, initiated in 1999 and renewed in 2006, between the EU and Russia, Norway, and Iceland. Today, confidence in Europe has decreased, even been questioned, in the Nordic countries. There are new proposals for cooperation between these countries but also tendencies towards nationalism (national exclusiveness), which have been seen especially in the rhetoric of Nordic populist parties since the beginning of the last decade.

From Nordic Democracy to (Defence of) the Nordic Welfare State

In a recent analysis of meanings of Nordic democracy, three waves of rhetoric on Nordic democracy were discussed.[10] The first wave belongs to the context of the crisis of democracy in the 1930s–1940s and to the goal of a general acceptance of democracy within the Nordic countries. This rhetoric also contained a philosophical-theoretical dimension, first and foremost that of so-called Scandinavian Realism,[11] and the importance of democracy was often pointed out with cultural arguments. During this era, the idea of Nordic democracy became closely connected to social democracy. According to the Danish social democrat – and scholar in ancient philology – Hartvik Frisch, political democracy and parliamentarism created by the Nordic peasant was the foundation on which the labour movement was able to build social democracy.[12] This link between peasant freedom, legality, parliamentary institutions and the social democratic agenda of the labour movement in the context of rising totalitarianism was also

---

Jussi Kurunmäki and Johan Strang (eds), *Rhetorics of Nordic Democracy* (Finnish Literature Society 2011) 37–81.

9   Sørensen and Stråth (n 6) 22.
10   Kurunmäki and Strang (n 8).
11   See for example Alf Ross, *Hvorfor demokrati?* (Munksgaard 1946).
12   Hartvik Frisch, *Pest over Europa – Bolschevisme, Fascisme og Nazisme* (Henrik Koppels Forlag 1933).

characteristic of the celebration of the Day of Nordic Democracy in Malmö in August 1935.[13]

In the aftermath of the Second World War, however, there was an attempt at de-ideologizing democracy by placing it above everyday politics.[14] During the second wave of discussions on Nordic democracy of the 1940s and 1950s, the concept was used beyond party lines in order to signify features of the Nordic countries as a whole. Democracy[15] was depoliticized while participation and formal and procedural aspects of democracy (for example the majority principle) were stressed. Even earlier, a kind of enlightenment and education had become main features of the democratic way of life.[16] Especially in Finland, the concept of education (in Swedish *bildning*, in Finnish *sivistys*) remained a key political concept.[17] During the third wave of the 1960s and 1970s, Nordic democracy was giving way to emerging use of Nordic society, the welfare state and the Nordic model.

In the book *Nordic Democracy* published in 1981 – now also including Finland and Iceland – one can find a multidimensional description of exemplary and firmly established welfare societies. More and more, social policy and sociology issues were pointed out.[18] Actually, Nordic democracy was understood as virtually synonymous with the Nordic welfare state. Democracy was seen as not only a form of government but also comprising social and economic democracy, as well as the democratic principles underlying fundamental justice, education and culture, etc. Hence, Nordic democracy was something more than formal and procedural – and should be based on support by the people as a whole.[19]

Towards the end of the twentieth century optimism connected to Nordic democracy, mainly linked to or understood as the Nordic welfare model, came to be replaced by protectionism, even a kind of sentimentality.[20] In debates on EU membership, sceptics also tried to play 'the Nordic card' as a more democratic form of international cooperation, while the European integration process was seen as a threat to the future of the welfare state. In 2005, however, the authors

---

13   Organized by Swedish Social Democratic Youth and Socialist Youth International.

14   With Sweden as the model.

15   See for example Hal Koch and Alf Ross (eds), *Nordisk Demokrati* (Westermann et al 1949).

16   Interestingly, the Nordic countries were portrayed in Spain as a democratic heaven, that is with equal voting rights granted to women in Finland in 1906. See further Peter Stadius, 'Visiting Nordic Modernity around 1900' in Kurunmäki and Strang (n 8) 194–207.

17   Even the radicalism of the 1960s was in the Nordic Countries, especially in Finland, a process of prolonged enlightenment that effectively resisted post-modern pluralistic challenges, Stenius (n 2) 101–3.

18   Erik Allardt et al (eds), *Nordic Democracy. Ideas, Issues, Institutions in Politics, Economy, Education, Social and Cultural Affairs of Denmark, Finland, Iceland, Norway, and Sweden* (Det Danske Selskab 1981).

19   KB Andersen, Foreword in *Nordic Democracy* (n 18) i–ii.

20   See Lauri Karvonen and Elisabet Ljungberg (eds), *Nordisk Demokrati i förändring* (Demokratiinstitutet 1999).

(politicians and researchers) of the report *Demokrati i Norden*[21] argued that the Nordic countries were facing challenges which simultaneously deepened and counteracted the development of Nordic democracy: new types of popular initiative and referendums as well as welfare problems connected to the EU. Thus, the domestic and Nordic tradition of democracy /welfare had to be defended in the face of external threats.

Ancient Tradition with Peasant Participation

In Nordic legal history literature democracy is closely connected with the question of popular participation but also linked to the (one-dimensional and consensual) idea of the common good. Simultaneously, the importance of legislation as the dominant legal source and the central role of the legislator – from ancient assembly to modern parliament – are pointed out. Thus, medieval laws, such as Swedish or Danish provincial laws (from the thirteenth and fourteenth centuries) with the statements '*Med lag skal land byggas*' – '*Med lov ska land bygges*' (in English, The land shall be built upon the law),[22] are often referred to as examples of a long Nordic tradition with (stated) law. Again, the Rules of Judges drafted by the Swedish clergyman and contributor to the Protestant Reformation Olaus Petri (in the 1530s) and still published in the first pages of the Finnish and Swedish law codes are witness to the idea of law for the good of the common man. Interesting references to democracy, democratic participation, or 'democratization' can be found especially where the history of the court system and procedural law is concerned.

Often, democratization has been connected to the term modernization: (legal) modernization of the Nordic countries should happen with the help of legislation[23] but also with the participation of the people – including the participation of laymen in dispute resolution in the courts. Thus, in Sweden, procedural law and court reforms were initiated during the nineteenth century 'in order to change the aristocratic model of the judiciary, and to implement modern procedural principles such as orality and so on'. During the 1920s–1930s 'democratization

---

21   Democracy Committee of the Nordic Council of Ministers 2005. The Report with an English summary can be found at <http://www.norden.org/en/publications/publikationer/2005-701> accessed 16 June 2014.

22   However, the idea can be found in Gratian and in Liber extra: the king is protector of *pax et justitia*, and bound by law, as well.

23   After the Second World War in the Swedish doctrine of legal sources preparatory work for laws (legislation) was pointed out. This means that almost all theoretical and systematic legal discussions focused on or around legislative work (by the legislator) and by secretaries of the state committee drafting so-called 'statliga utredningar' (SOU). At the same time, Marxist theories and critical legal studies (CLS) in law were missing. See in detail Kjell Åke Modéer, *Juristernas nära förflutna* (Santérus Förlag 2011) 312–13.

of the judicial system' was one of the main goals of Swedish Social democratic legal policy.[24] Still, the court system and legal procedure were reformed in the country as late as 1948. In Norway and Denmark this had happened some years earlier but in Finland reform took place as late as during the 1990s, although the 'democratization' process had started two decades earlier.

A long tradition of political democracy, often connected with transparency, or 'Nordic Openness', based upon a high degree of popular participation, has characterized political and scholarly literature on Nordic democracy.[25] Nordic democracy has been anchored to the idea of an ancient democratic tradition with representative assemblies of local communities (*tings*, parish and community meetings), freedom of the peasant and with a consensual and egalitarian political culture. This narrative usually goes back to the Viking Age[26] without any rhetorical link to Athenian democracy or to the Roman Republic.[27] The five Nordic countries have both similarities and differences where democracy is concerned, but what they seem to have in common is the 'ancient background': the early democratic tradition constitutes an important factor in the development and characterization of modern Nordic democracy, while democracy and national identity have been brought together through narratives on the history of democracy. Thus, democracy in Denmark, for instance, is of Nordic origin.[28] In this narrative the peasant is a central figure.

The peasant has been seen as the mythical incarnation of freedom and equality. The free and equal Nordic peasant represents a progressive historical force much more than does the bourgeoisie in the Western European societal and legal tradition. The role of the peasant in the modernization of Nordic societies has been underlined especially in nineteenth-century historiography. This emphasis has a point of departure in the fact that the peasants in Sweden and Finland had constituted a separate Diet estate since the fifteenth century. Although this was not the case in Denmark-Norway, the peasant's role in local government was considerable, especially in Norway, but to a certain degree also in Denmark.

In this narrative, special focus is directed towards the organizational form of assemblies, often the *ting*, to develop specific democratic aspects of political

---

24 Kjell Åke Modéer, 'Den stora reformen: rättegångbalkens förebilder och förverkligande' (1999) *Svensk juristtidning* 400.

25 Other elements of Nordicness – based on development since the last century – include a high standard of living and social equality. See Niels Finn Christensen and Pirjo Markkula, 'Introduction' in Niels Finn Christensen et al (eds), *The Nordic Model of Welfare – A Historical Reappraisal* (Museum Tusculanum Press 2006) 9–29; 10–11.

26 In Sweden the Age of Liberty also plays a role. On the ancient idea of Nordic Democracy see Sigurd Lindahl, 'Early Democratic Tradition in the Nordic Countries' in Allardt et al (n 18) 15–43.

27 At the same time, Nordic democracy – as a Nordic model – refers to (historically rooted) shared values. It is culturally shaped, a way of life and mentality.

28 Uffe Jakobsen, 'The Conception of "Nordic Democracy" and European Judicial Democracy' (2009) *Nordisk tidsskrift for menniskerettigheter* 221–41; 227–8.

life.[29] Even the early *ting* sessions or the common meetings of the assemblies in the Viking Age are seen as legislative bodies even if they also, and perhaps primarily, were courts, arbitrators of disputes, and electors of kings. Although the forms and procedures of these assemblies were admittedly different from today's parliaments, they are presented as democratic. Thus, the concept of Nordic democracy equals an assembly of free men that came together to make decisions and to pass judgments for the sake of the common good.

In addition, Nordic democratic political culture has been linked to a specific kind of 'enlightenment'.[30] According to Peter Aronsson, education (in German *Bildung*, in Swedish *bildning*) was a key instrument of emancipation and self-realization. The negotiating peasant was not Utopian but pragmatic. His *bildning* was the basis of politics, and politics was based on disputes and quarrels at the *ting*, at the parish assembly, and at the Diet. The peasantry's communication skills developed in early meetings, and later paved the way for communication between social democracy and liberalism with a social rather than an economic emphasis.[31]

Power of Tradition: Popular Participation and Courts

This peasant myth based on the idea of peasants as bearers of freedom, equality and education was crucial in the construction of a national community in the North of Europe. And, in Finland, for instance, this peasant tradition has played an important role as an ideological argument when reforms of legal institutions have been discussed. In particular, comments on and attitudes towards the Finnish court system and local (first instance) dispute resolution have stressed the importance of holding on to national customs and the 'Nordic peasant tradition'. Even in the 1970s, proposed reforms for modernization (democratization) of the court procedure were not markedly based on international – except Swedish – examples, while in contrast, in the 1990s and later many reforms could be justified by reference to international developments, especially obligations to 'Europeanize' the domestic system.[32]

---

29   Historical developments in the Viking Age are seen as a democratic heritage of post Second World War Nordic Countries. The Viking Age assemblies are constructed as anchor-points of Nordic democracy. The most important aspect of this heritage is the survival of assemblies in different forms as antecedents of modern parliamentary bodies, Jakobsen (n 28) 229. See also Bernd Hennigsen, 'The Swedish Construction of Nordic Identity' in Sørensen and Stråth (n 6) 91–120.

30   Actually, the inherent tension between freedom and equality in political culture was controlled by means of the peasant myth; the peasant was an increasingly active participant in economic and political processes, Jakobsen (n 28) 229.

31   Peter Aronsson, 'Local Politics – The Invisible Political Culture' in Sørensen and Stråth (n 6) 172–205.

32   See further Timo Honkanen and Pia Letto-Vanamo, *Lain nojalla kansan tuella. Moments of Finnish Justice in the 1970s* (Edita 2005).

Finnish legal history is characterized by the exceptionally slow disappearance of ancient, say peasant, forms of adjudication. Elsewhere in Europe, procedural rules had already been reformed in the nineteenth century or early twentieth century, as was the case in the other Nordic countries. As late as the 1970s – in a century of democratization – legal policy debates gave rise to procedural reforms that took effect over the following two decades. Until this, a system of special court buildings was also lacking. In the countryside, the local *ting* moved from the earliest sessions in farmhouses to parish halls, community halls, fire stations etc., but even in improvised premises the atmosphere in sessions was often devout and dignified, with the community spirit apparent. In contrast, today's court system, only 40 years younger, is just another set of cogs in the administrative machinery. The modern courtroom is marked by the offices and roles of those working there. Legal disputes have become more complex, and the parties almost always speak through experts, that is, their attorneys.

For a very long time the legitimacy of justice and judgments arose from the conviction, or at least the assumption, that the courts obeyed the law (laws) and that the law was an expression of the will of the people. Popular control and a common sense of justice were brought into the proceedings by the participation of the panel of laymen (in Swedish *nämnd*). In today's late modern society, however, the legitimacy of legal decisions is increasingly often sought elsewhere, *inter alia* from alternatives to traditional dispute resolution in court.[33]

There is good reason to state that the reforms of the 1970s were driven by the President of the Republic, Dr Urho Kaleva Kekkonen.[34] One of his main theses was that adjudication in the courts was a continuation of the legislative work of the Parliament. For this reason, the societal and political preferences of the judiciary were relevant – and with the judiciary being a 'monolith of conservatism', there was reason to intervene in the system of appointing judges. Thus, the most significant, and the most novel, of the legal policy ideas discussed in the 1970s was the linking of judicial decision-making to the exercise of political power. In some part at least, this was a paradigm shift in jurisprudence, casting doubt on the processes of mechanical application of the law and the possibility of only a single correct solution existing. Considering the other Nordic countries, this was nothing new. However, for historical reasons, faith in the law(s) and in the courts as the (quite mechanical) interpreters of law had remained strong in Finland.[35]

The framers of the new legislation did not consider adjudication to be merely use of 'professional technical skills', but noted that it often involved exercise of discretion. Accordingly, it was proposed that decision-making by the courts should

---

33   Moreover, the procedure in the court of first instance was a blend of judicial interventionism and folksy informality.

34   He outlined his views of the court system in a 70th birthday interview (actually drafted by Finnish social democratic legal intellectuals) in the learned journal *Lakimies* in 1970 and in a radio interview in 1971.

35   See further Honkanen and Letto-Vanamo (n 32).

proceed along the same lines of democratic process as any other form of exercise of political power. Then, participation of trusted laymen constituted a level of control over decision-makers. In order to ensure that control could in fact be exercised, the proceedings had to be open and transparent, and decisions accompanied by detailed reasons. Again, the express reasons for the reforms of the 1990s were already somewhat distanced from political considerations. Increasingly often, reforms were justified by reference to promptness and efficiency.

From Popular Control to Trust in Experts

The ancient, communal way of conflict resolution (in rural areas) was of course also in use elsewhere in Europe. In other European countries, however, the main rule was that a judiciary with an academic education gradually came to supersede earlier modes of dispute resolution. It was only in the nineteenth century that laymen were again accepted as court members; this was mostly a result of the French Revolution of 1789 and the democratization of Western European societies, courts included. The same process also took place in Norway and Denmark, but not in Finland or Sweden. In the latter countries, participation of laymen in the administration of justice continued uninterrupted. In part, this was a result of the late modernization of those societies, but also of the overall slow rate of change in the court system. Some reasons were ideological: it was important to safeguard the idea of a folksy and equal character of the court procedure, but in Finland finances also played a part. A system composed of a few circuit judges 'sitting *ting*' (and partly paying administrative costs by themselves) with lay panels placed little demand on the public purse.

In every case, justifications for lay participation changed from time to time. References to local knowledge became fewer, while popular control and democracy gained currency. In the debates in Sweden of the first half of the twentieth century and in Finland of the 1960s–70s, the prevailing arguments pertained precisely to the democracy of justice and to popular control over the judiciary. Then in 2003 the Finnish Commission for Development of the Court System, which emphasized the need for judicial specialization and expert competence, proposed that the use of laymen be severely curtailed on the basis that lay participation could only be justified at all by reference to its very long tradition. Now, 10 years later, abolition of the use of laymen seems very probable.

People, State and the EU

The link between democracy and popular participation, or the people, has been introduced. Similarly, the interdependence between the (mythical) narrative of the Nordic ancient peasant tradition of democracy and the nation building process has been pointed out, and the role of social democracy and importance of the idea of the Nordic welfare state mentioned. There are, however, differences between the Nordic countries especially as to how people, nation and state have been conceptualized and linked together. These again cause at least some variations in attitude towards the European Union and its future development.[36]

In all Nordic countries people and nation became[37] focal concepts of political thinking, giving regimes a new kind of legitimacy and a new content for the concept of the state. The concepts were bendable and mouldable, accommodating a tension that marks the political culture of the Nordic countries. At the same time, the holistic morale of the concepts was a demand for action in accordance with the interests of the whole. This announced a political competition as to who had the right to define what was in accordance with the interests of the whole. But concepts could also be loaded with a democratic moral: by referring to the will of the people, one could force the political public to interpret the moral demand to ask the people what they wanted. In addition, the democratic principle in the meaning of an equal relationship between the state and every inhabitant of a national polity was launched with a strong national moral. It was pointed out that citizenship consisted not only of rights but also of obligations.

The Norwegian or Danish nation was foremost a cultural conception to which the concept of *folket*, the people, belonged. The people were installed as a key referent of the nation. This romantic nationalist position became hegemonic especially in Norway.[38] In Denmark the later dominant construct of the nation also drew on cultural traits; in this context especially the name of N.F.S. Grundtvig (1783–1872) shall be mentioned. The nation was linked to 'the people' who had the potential to be articulated in opposition to the 'elite'. This constellation has played a role also in debates on the EU. In Norway and Denmark the people's anti-elite attitude has been quite successfully mobilized by the anti-EU side. One explanation for this is that it has been quite difficult to conceptualize the EU without nation state terms, and the EU has usually been held up as a federalist – not a political or cultural – project.[39] At the same time any political construct at the 'European level' can be seen as a threat to the nation.

In Sweden, too, the concept of the people (*folk/et*) has been key in politics. At the same time, the state and the people have been linked. The people's home was *folkstat* or *folkhemmet*.[40] Since the 1930s the Social Democratic ideology has changed and the entire national community (the people, *folket*) replaced the working

---

36　See further Lene Hansen and Ole Waever (eds), *European Integration and National Identity. The Challenge of the Nordic States* (Routledge 2002).

37　Ca. 1800–1860; see further Stenius (n 2) 100–101.

38　See further Iver B Neumann, 'This Little Piggy Stayed at Home. Why Norway is Not a Member of the EU' in Hansen and Waever (n 36) 88–129.

39　Lene Hansen, 'Conclusion' in Hansen and Waever (n 36) 214–25; 216–18.

40　This development was tied to the hegemonic position of the Social Democratic Party; on Swedish development see Lars Trägårdh, 'Sweden and the EU: Welfare state nationalism and the spectre of "Europe"' *European Integration* (n 38) 130–81.

class as the focal group of social reforms. But it was much later when *folkhemmet* became popular, referring to Social Democratic welfare, actually looking at the lost Golden Age of welfare.[41] In every case, the *Folkhemmet* (people's home) has presented a harmonious link between state and people but could become threatened via European integration. In all three countries the 'people' is a central concept but the distinct anti-elite and potential anti-state attitudes in Norway and Denmark have not been found to the same extent in Sweden. The Swedish constellation is the tightest and least flexible of the four countries.

Finland, again, is a kind of exception. Finland lacks the accentuation of the people as an anti-elite construction typical of Denmark and Norway. Finland is an exception also with regard to the relative ease with which the country joined the EU and the active, almost enthusiastic, role the Finnish state representatives played during the first years of EU membership. This has been seen[42] as a consequence of a certain duality of the Finnish concept of nation. There is a cultural nation and a state nation (*Kulturnation/Staatsnation*), and this duality allowed a rethinking of nation and state on separate levels once Finland was faced with European economic integration.

Actually, the first phase of formation of this constellation was Finland's period as an autonomous part of the Russian Empire (1809–1917). The transfer from Sweden to Russia facilitated the creation of 'Finland' as an entity with both a certain amount of political autonomy at administrative level and a cultural national identity. Independence was an almost unthinkable project, which led the nation to provide space for Finland's subjectivity as a cultural entity – and to do so without fusing into a state. When Finland gained independence in 1917 it was a by-product of the Russian defeat in the First World War and the subsequent revolution. At this point, a Hegelian understanding of the nation, and its relationship to the state, had gained force. The Hegelian understanding implied that the nation was fused to the state and that the state should be strong and powerful. At the same time the state was the ultimate objective of the citizenry. The outcome was not a complete reversal of the so-called Herderian[43] past, but flexibility in terms of which the concept of the nation prevailed.

This flexibility has allowed Finns to conceive of the cultural nation and the 'state nation' separately. Thus, the cultural can exist comfortably inside the EU as long as the EU is not trying to enforce a common cultural European identity.[44] Until the first years of this millennium, this conclusion had been quite easy to

---

41   See further Nils Edling, 'The Primacy of Welfare Politics. Notes on the language of Swedish Social Democrats and their adversaries in the 1930s' in Heidi Haggrén, Johanna Rainio-Niemi, Jussi Vauhkonen (eds), *Multi-layered Historicity of the Present: Approaches to social science history* (University of Helsinki Press 2013) 125–50.

42   Pentti Joenniemi, 'Finland in the New Europe: a Herderian or Hegelian project?' in Hansen and Waever (n 36) 182–213.

43   Referring to ideas of Johann Gottfried von Herder.

44   Joenniemi (n 42) 207–9.

reach, while today the political-economic crisis of the EU and the decreasing popularity of the 'True Finns' populist party with their slogan 'where the EU exists there are problems' are challenging our analysis of the EU–Finland relationship.

Challenges of Legal Scholarship

Not only are Nordic variations of the concept of democracy (here focused mainly on popular participation) and of the meaning of the people interesting when democracy and its future are discussed. For an understanding of the development of law and legal institutions the position and role of different legal actors should be noticed as well. The idea of a democratic legislator and of legislation as the primary source of law, as well as questions on the judiciary and its popular control, have been discussed. In the following, the history and current tasks of (Finnish) legal scholarship will be dealt with briefly.

The status of Finnish legal scholarship and the quite theoretical nature of legal education and legal writing have explanations mainly in the legal history of the country. Even the 'brand-new' legal science of the nineteenth century received a central function in legal development. In spite of the autonomous position of Finland within the Russian Empire (1809–1917), the role of the Parliament (Estates) was either non-existent (1809–1863) or weak. Many legal reforms necessary for industrialization were realized by the judiciary, through the legal practice of the courts of appeal (in Swedish, *hovrätt*). In addition, because of lack of democracy and constitutional guarantees, legalistic thinking and constitutional legal doctrine became important, too.[45] The first professorship in the Nordic countries solely for administrative law was founded at the University of Helsinki in 1907. Central topics of the discipline were the principle of the rule of law and its interpretations. An important model for Finnish doctrine was the German literature discussing the concept of *Rechtsstaat* and the principle of legality. In other fields of law, too, an orientation towards Germany was common.[46]

German legal literature inspired legal professionals in many other European countries, as well, but the Finnish phenomenon is that this influence was both long lasting and quite one-dimensional. It can be said that the German influence remained alive in Finland longer than elsewhere, and this influence was not free from the old conceptual characteristics although legal science in Germany changed partly as a result of the ideas of the so-called Free Law School (*Freirechtsschule*).

45   Lars Björne, *Den konstruktiva riktningen. Den nordiska rättsvetenskapens historia III* (Rättshistoriska institutet 2002) 169.

46   As mentioned, early civil law doctrine (for example by Robert Montgomery) was influenced by German pandect literature while the founding father of Finnish procedural law, Rabbe Axel Wrede, adopted ideas mainly from the Germans Oskar Bülow and Adolf Wach. However, interest in German legal science was not only a Finnish phenomenon.

It is quite common to maintain that conceptual jurisprudence (*Begriffsjurisprudenz*) with the idea of autonomous legal science was the most influential doctrine in Finland until the 1950s. According to Lars Björne, conceptual jurisprudence with its 'apolitical' nature and its self-referential notion of legal science fitted very well with the political and social climate in Finland – first with the Era of Autonomy's orientation towards legalistic thinking, and then with the politically sensitive circumstances after the Civil War of 1918. There, in the extra-legal law-external world, we can also find reasons for the position of Scandinavian Realism in Finland, where it is much weaker than in the other Nordic countries. The first critical remarks against 'constructivist orientation' in Sweden are from the first decades of the twentieth century. In this context especially, names such as Axel Hägerström, Vilhelm Lundstedt, Carl Olivecrona and the so-called Uppsala School should be mentioned, while the Danish Alf Ross and his 'Realistic doctrine of legal sources' cannot be omitted.[47]

The idea of law as an instrument of social engineering was a crucial element of Scandinavian Realism, while the role of the judiciary was pointed out, too. '*Reella överväganden*' (real considerations) formed part of the basis of the Swedish doctrine of legal sources.[48] The realistic approach, together with general democratization tendencies, led for instance to reforms of legal procedure and the Swedish court system in 1948[49] while similar reforms in Finland were realized as late as the 1990s, as noted above. The dominance of *Begriffsjurisprudenz* diminished in Finland above all through influences from the Analytic School of law.[50] 'Analytic' criticism focused mainly against 'conclusions from concepts'. But concepts were not neglected. They played a heuristic role – they were necessary for clarifying and classifying legal problems.

As already mentioned, the most important changes in Finnish society can be dated to as late as the 1970s. After that it became possible to speak of a welfare (social) state. The decade was characterized by various democratization and modernization procedures: for instance the school system, university education, and part of the court system were reformed.[51] Approximation of legal science to other social sciences was required when legal education in universities was discussed. Moreover, trends in legal research changed, as can be seen for instance

---

47   See further Lars Björne, *Realism och skandinavisk realism. Den nordiska rättsvetenskapens historia IV* (Rättshistoriska institutet 2007).

48   On Swedish pragmatism see for example Claes Sandgren, 'Den konstruktiva riktningen Juridikavhandlingarna vid Stockholms universitet 1957–2006' in Claes Peterson (ed.), *Juridiska fakulteten 1907–2007: Minneskrift* (Stockholms universitet Juridiska fakulteten 2007) 440–85.

49   See further Modéer (n 24) 400–427.

50   These were closely connected to Finnish philosophy of the 1960s and 1970s (for example GH von Wright and Jaakko Hintikka), which was strongly influenced by Anglo-American analytic philosophy.

51   See further Honkanen and Letto-Vanamo, (n 32).

in dissertations and other academic works where the 'social dimension' of the law was pointed out. Additionally, texts inspired by Marxist theory and the Italian School such as '*L'uso alternativo del diritto*' by Lars D Eriksson can be mentioned here.

Regardless of criticism, the Analytic School (as Analytic Positivism) preserved its importance. Today, however, legal principles have become important but concepts are still in use: they prepare the way for principles-based legal argumentation. Still, even 'critical' Finnish legal scholars share the view of three equally powerful legal actors, and the *ethos* of the active role of legal science as a means of changing law and society. This can also be seen among scholars interested in EU law studies. Legal scholarship, at least in the meaning of legal dogmatics, is understood as one – but just one – of the legal practices that continuously produce and reproduce the legal order. According to Kaarlo Tuori, legal scholarship contributes to the development of the legal order through its very results, such as systematizations of law. For instance, the law's divisions into different branches (family law, criminal law) are not determined by the legislator or decided by judges but proposed by legal scholars. But after the scholars' proposals have found general acceptance, systematic divisions, once established, form an integral part of 'legal-cultural pre-understanding' and also unfurl their heuristic effects in other legal practices such as law-making and adjudication.[52]

Conclusion

It is possible to argue that the concept of democracy in Nordic political debates and in theoretical discussions includes universal or at least common European elements, such as the idea of popular participation. At the same time, there are historically determined variations of 'Nordic democracy' varying from a cultural to a more economic understanding with the welfare state as a key concept. In every case, the most popular narrative of democracy and its roots in the North goes back to the Viking Age, and includes the participation of free and equal peasants in political as well as legal decision-making. Still, many differences exist between the Nordic countries, and these differences can be seen in the roles and functions of national socio-legal institutions and actors, as observed in this paper.

The ideology of *Norden*, but also the way the Danish, Finnish and other nations and their relationship to 'the people' on the one hand and to the state on the other hand has been defined, are reflected in attitudes towards European integration. In general, Nordic attitudes to the European Union, with Finland as a weak exception, can be characterized as sceptical. In all countries, however, the democracy deficit and problems of transparency in the EU have been on the agenda. Today, the economic and financial crisis has also increased criticism of the EU in Finland.

---

52   See Kaarlo Tuori, *Ratio and Voluntas. The Tension Between Reason and Will in Law* (Ashgate 2011) 151–3.

At the same time, new proposals have been launched for Nordic cooperation. Still, they are more academic than political by nature.

The most interesting political feature in the Nordic countries at the moment is the rise of populist parties with ideas of national exclusiveness and of the good of the 'common man'. *Norden*, however, is not an issue. The parties have mobilized voters around an anti-elitist political agenda accusing the mainstream parties (especially the Social Democrats) of protecting the interests of the privileged 'political and cultural elite' and of neglecting the values and needs of the common people. The concept of the common people, however, does not refer to the Nordic peasants (farmers) or to traditional working class members. It refers to those from the 'heartland', but not to immigrants, with the tone of a kind of welfare chauvinism.

European integration, along with the economic and financial crises in the Eurozone, has also challenged EU scholarship. However, it is not so much democracy (in EU decision-making) but the legitimacy of EU integration and especially solidarity between the Member States that have been discussed. One of the main topics referring to political, economic, social and legal dimensions of EU integration among legal scholars has been European constitutionalism. Finnish legal scholars have developed the theory of the 'many constitutions of Europe'[53] providing a framework for understanding European integration as a multilayered and diversified process of constitutionalization in which the economic, juridical, social, political, and security dimensions of constitutions have emerged separately and evolved at a pace of their own. Even as a legal phenomenon, the constitution has been understood through the interrelationships that constitutional law maintains with constitutional objects, i.e. its objects of regulation. And even as a legal phenomenon the constitution is in multi-faceted ways linked to democracy.

Bibliography

Allardt E et al (eds), *Nordic Democracy. Ideas, Issues, Institutions in Politics, Economy, Education, Social and Cultural Affairs of Denmark, Finland, Iceland, Norway, and Sweden* (Det Danske Selskab 1981)

Aronsson P, 'Local Politics – The Invisible Political Culture' in Øystein Sørensen and Bo Stråth (eds), *The Cultural Construction of Norden* (Scandinavian University Press 1997)

Björne L, *Realism och skandinavisk realism. Den nordiska rättsvetenskapens historia IV* (Rättshistoriska institutet 2007)

—— *Den konstruktiva riktningen. Den nordiska rättsvetenskapens historia III* (Rättshistoriska institutet 2002)

Childs M, *Sweden: the Middle Way* (Yale University Press 1961[1936])

---

53   See for example Kaarlo Tuori and Suvi Sankari (eds), *The Many Consititutions of Europe* (Ashgate 2009).

Christensen NF and Markkula P, 'Introduction' in NF Christensen et al (eds), *The Nordic Model of Welfare – A Historical Reappraisal* (Museum Tusculanum Press 2006)

Edling N, 'The Primacy of Welfare Politics. Notes on the Language of Swedish Social Democrats and their Adversaries in the 1930s' in H Haggrén, J Rainio-Niemi and J Vauhkonen (eds), *Multi-layered Historicity of the Present: Approaches to Social Science History* (University of Helsinki Press 2013)

Frisch H, *Pest over Europa – Bolschevisme, Fascisme og Nazisme* (Henrik Koppels Forlag 1933)

Hansen L and Waever O (eds), *European Integration and National Identity. The Challenge of the Nordic States* (Routledge 2002)

Hennigsen B, 'The Swedish Construction of Nordic Identity' in Øystein Sørensen and Bo Stråth (eds), *The Cultural Construction of Norden* (Scandinavian University Press 1997)

Honkanen T and Letto-Vanamo P, *Lain nojalla kansan tuella. Moments of Finnish Justice in the 1970s* (Edita 2005)

Jakobsen U, 'The Conception of "Nordic Democracy" and European Judicial Democracy' (2009) Nordisk tidsskrift for menniskerettigheter

Joenniemi P, 'Finland in the New Europe: a Herderian or Hegelian project?' in L Hansen and O Waever (eds), *European Integration and National Identity. The Challenge of the Nordic States* (Routledge 2002)

Karvonen L and Ljungberg E (eds), *Nordisk Demokrati i förändring* (Demokratiinstitutet 1999)

Kurunmäki J, 'Nordic Democracy in 1935. On the Finnish and Swedish Rhetoric of Democracy' in J Kurunmäki and J Strang (eds), *Rhetorics of Nordic Democracy* (Finnish Literature Society 2011)

Koch H and Ross A (eds), *Nordisk Demokrati* (Westermann et al 1949)

Lindahl S, 'Early Democratic Tradition in the Nordic Countries' in E Allardt et al (eds), *Nordic Democracy. Ideas, Issues, Institutions in Politics, Economy, Education, Social and Cultural Affairs of Denmark, Finland, Iceland, Norway, and Sweden* (Det Danske Selskab 1981)

Modéer KA, *Juristernas nära förflutna* (Santérus Förlag 2011)

—— 'Den stora reformen: rättegångbalkens förebilder och förverkligande' (1999) *Svensk juristtidning*

Montgomery R, *Handbok i Finlands allmänna privaträtt I* (Helsinki 1889)

Neumann IB, 'This Little Piggy Stayed at Home. Why Norway is Not a Member of the EU' in L Hansen and O Waever (eds), *European Integration and National Identity. The Challenge of the Nordic States* (Routledge 2002)

Ross A, *Hvorfor demokrati?* (Munksgaard 1946)

Sandgren C, 'Den konstruktiva riktningen Juridikavhandlingarna vid Stockholms universitet 1957–2006' in C Peterson (ed.), *Juridiska fakulteten 1907–2007: Minneskrift* (Stockholms universitet Juridiska fakulteten 2007)

Stadius P, 'Visiting Nordic Modernity around 1900' in J Kurunmäki and J Strang (eds), *Nordic Rhetorics* (Finnish Literature Society 2010)

Stenius H, 'A Nordic Conceptual Universe. Multi-layered Historicity of the Present. Approaches to social science history' in H Haggren, J Rainio-Niemi and J Vauhkonen (eds), Publications of the Department of Political and Economic Studies 8 (2013)

Strang J, *Nordiska Gemenskaper. En vision för samarbetet* (Nord 2012)

Sørensen Ø and Stråth B, 'Introduction: The Cultural Construction of Norden' in Sørensen and Stråth (eds), *The Cultural Construction of Norden* (Scandinavian University Press 1997)

Trägårdh L, 'Sweden and the EU: Welfare state nationalism and the spectre of "Europe"' *European Integration* 130–81

Tuori K, *Ratio and Voluntas. The Tension Between Reason and Will in Law* (Ashgate 2011)

—— and Sankari S (eds), *The Many Constitutions of Europe* (Ashgate 2009)

Wetterberg G, *The United Nordic Federation* (TemaNord 2010) 583. Available at <http://www.norden.org/fi/julkaisut/julkaisut/2010–583> accessed 16 June 2014

Windscheid B, *Lehrbuch des Pandektenrechts I* (Düsseldorf 1862)

Zweigert K and Kötz H, *An Introduction to Comparative Law* (3rd edn, Oxford University Press 1998)

Chapter 10

Governance Networks as a Means to Enhance European Democracy

Eva Sørensen and Tore Vincents Olsen

Introduction

The Eurozone crisis has demonstrated how connected we are to each other across borders and boundaries in Europe. The popular discontent with Eurozone politics has emphasized the need to democratize political decisions at the European level. This has induced European politicians to discuss how to increase the democratic authorization of European-level decisions. The predominant thought among political elites is to include the popular elected representatives in the European Parliament in the decision-making procedures. As such, the political elites follow a rather conventional conception of democracy. This is not the only approach, however, to further democratization of the European Union (EU). This chapter aims to demonstrate that governance networks between different public and private actors across different levels in the EU can be an important contribution to EU democratization, despite the criticism levelled against governance networks and other interactive forms of governance. We suggest that networks can facilitate 'inter-demos' participation and deliberation not only to the benefit of the overall quality of European governance, but also to the level of participation and deliberation within each of the European demoi. In making this argument we extend some of the newest theories of democratic multi-level governance in the EU[1] and recent theories of European *demoi*cracy, the latter emphasizing the need to think democracy not in terms of the self-determination of a singular *demos* but as a necessary exchange and engagement between several *demoi*.[2]

Despite different views on the value of participation and deliberation, traditional theories of democracies stress that that all those affected by decisions should be given an equal political influence on them. However, traditional theories presuppose democracy relates to a singular demos. They have little

---

1 Beate Kohler-Koch and Berthold Rittberger, 'The Governance Turn' (2006) 44 *Journal of Common Market Studies* 27.

2 Francis Cheneval and Frank Schimmelfennig, 'The Case For Demoicracy In The European Union' (2013) 51 *Journal of Common Market Studies* 334; Kalypso Nicolaïdis, 'European Demoicracy and Its Crisis' (2013) 51 *Journal of Common Market Studies* 351–69.

to say about the affectedness that reaches across borders and boundaries. The simultaneous processes of globalization and decentralization have resulted in pluricentric political systems in which territorially or functionally defined demoi and governance units affect each other across borders and boundaries. The EU is an important case in point. Theories of democracy need to address the fact of pluricentric political systems not only to investigate their democratic problems[3] but also to explore their democratic potentials. This chapter focuses on the latter. It aims to show that governance networks making up an important part of pluricentric systems can trigger democratization by making democracy more inclusive, because they can help institutionalize inter-demoi governance. The particular value of governance networks is tied to the fact that they provide a specific kind of weak institutional tie between institutions that are constituted on strong ties.[4] As such, these networks provide some order, albeit a flexible and fragile order that destabilizes the closure and softens the patterns of inclusion and exclusion that are inherent to institutions and, thus, also to a demos. In short they can *function as a much needed means to facilitate democratic inter-demos participation and deliberation, and this kind of participation and deliberation has a positive impact on the quality of intra-demos participation and deliberation.* In making this argument, the chapter first demonstrates how traditional liberal theories of democracy have tended to focus on intra-demos participation and deliberation, while paying little or no attention to the democratic quality of the interplay between demoi. It then outlines the recent growth in pluricentric forms of governance in advanced liberal democracies and goes on to describe, evaluate, and criticize the strategies used to cope with the democratic implications of pluricentrism. Finally, we will show how governance networks can contribute to the development of a strong pluricentric democracy.

Traditional Theoretical Approaches to Participation and Deliberation

Traditional theories of liberal democracy share the view that participation and deliberation are core features of democracy. Some theories have celebrated the ability of these features to ensure public control with decision makers.[5]

---

3   Jon Pierre and B Guy Peters, *Governing Complex Societies: Trajectories and Scenarios.* (Palgrave Macmillan 2005); Arthur Benz and Ioannis Papadopoulos, *Governance and Democracy: Comparing National, European and International experiences* (Routledge 2006).

4   Mark Granovetter, 'The Strength of Weak Ties' (1973) 78 *American Journal of Sociology* 1360–80.

5   John Stuart Mill, *Considerations on Representative Government* (Prometheus Books 1991[1861]) 45; Jeremy Bentham, *An Introduction to the Principles of Morals and Legislation.* (Hafner 1948[1776]) 143; Robert Dahl, *Democracy and its Critics* (Yale University Press 1989) 113.

Others have highlighted their importance for the creation of shared identity and a strong communality between the members of the demos.[6] Democratic control exists when citizens deliberate in a free public debate and participate in general elections. A strong sense of communality is obtained by visualizing the interrelatedness between individual and collective interests and developing shared understandings, which are provided by participation and deliberation. This theoretical framework has produced different theoretical tensions, some of which are internal to the demos and others which relate to the relationship with other demoi. Table 10.1 summarizes these tensions.

When viewed from the perspective of traditional theories of liberal democracy, the tensions related to ensuring *democratic control* through participation and deliberation are inherently considered to be caused by a trade-off between democracy and effectiveness. *Internally*, it is a matter of ensuring that the control wielded by the members of a demos over the decision makers does not prevent necessary and wise decisions being made in the interest of the citizens. This dilemma is the subject matter of ongoing debates between democratic elite theorists[7] and theorists of participatory democracy.[8] *Externally*, the trade-off is apparent in relation to foreign policy,[9] where secrecy is considered necessary and acceptable, despite the lack of publicity, accountability, and open public debate about the form and content of the interaction between governments which reduces the citizens' ability to control those who represent them.

Table 10.1   Democratic tensions

	Internal to demos	**External relation to other demoi**
Democratic control	Effectiveness versus control	Effectiveness versus publicity
Democratic communality	Including all versus some	Membership versus affectedness

---

6   Mill (n 5) 254; Alexis de Tocqueville, *Democracy in America* (Fontana 1968[1835]) 25; Gabriel Almond and Sidney Verba, *The Civic Culture* (Princeton University Press 1963) 88–9; Carole Pateman, *Participation and Democratic Theory* (Cambridge University Press 1970) 105.

7   Joseph Schumpeter, *Capitalism, Socialism and Democracy* (Harper and Row 1942) 264; Giovanni Sartori, *The Theory of Democracy Revisited* (Volumes 1 and 2, Chatham House 1987) 162.

8   Pateman (n 6) 4; Benjamin Barber, *Strong Democracy. Participatory Politics for a New Age* (University of California Press 1984) 5ff.

9   William E Connolly, *The Ethos of Pluralization* (University of Minnesota Press 1995) 141.

The call for a *sense of communality* among the members of a demos also involves certain tensions. These tensions derive from a desire to both include and exclude actors and viewpoints from the democratic process. On one hand, democracy calls for the inclusion of all affected actors and viewpoints. On the other hand, the idea that a demos is constituted on communality sentiments makes it necessary to exclude those who do not subscribe to the prevailing understanding of the content of this communality. The excluded can be newcomers in a society, different subcultures or people who do not master or wish to adjust to dominating codes of conduct.[10] Furthermore, creating a strong 'we' unavoidably involves constructing an excluded outside; in other words, that which 'we' are not. *Internally*, the line is drawn between those who express and act in accordance with certain hegemonic communality sentiments and those who do not. This behavior can be a point of reference for including some members of the demos in participation and deliberation and excluding others. A case in point is the question of how to deal with those who speak against democracy or express racist viewpoints. Should such sentiments be allowed to advance through political participation and deliberation? *Externally*, the constitutive outside of the unitary community consists of those who do not belong to the community, regardless of whether they are affected by the decisions made by that community. A question that has been the subject of increasing discussion, not least in the wake of global warming and other cross-border policy problems, is how to deal with situations in which the impact of decisions made by a demos affects members of other demoi.

Clearly, traditional theories of democracy perceive democracy as a way of ensuring participation and deliberation within a governance unit. *This intra-demos perspective on democracy produces sharp demarcation lines between the inside and the outside of democracy. These lines exist between that which is to be democratically regulated and that which is not, as well as between those who are allowed to participate and deliberate and those who are not.*

From Neat Theory to Complex Institutional Models

There is a sizeable gap between the images of democracy offered by traditional liberal theories of democracy and the complexity of the institutional models of liberal democracy that have actually seen the light of the day in last 200 years. This gap is particularly evident in federal democracies that have experienced persistent difficulties in terms of theoretically conceptualizing and institutionalizing the relationship between the federal government and the states.[11] These conceptual difficulties have materialized in the ongoing battle between federalists and

10   Iris Marion Young, *Inclusion and Democracy* (Oxford University Press 2002) 6.

11   Robert Dahl, 'Power as the Control of Behavior' in Steven Lukes (ed), *Power* (Blackwell 1986) 114.

confederalists[12] as well as in theorizing about consociationalism[13] which seeks to deal with the question of intra-demos heterogeneity within multi-leveled and/or socially pillared societies.[14]

The distance between simple theories and complex models is also well known in unitary states, which usually involve a degree of autonomy for self-regulating communities and a degree of involvement in transnational political institutions. In other words, actual models of democracy usually consist of several interlinked demoi. In addition to the many territorial demoi at national, regional, and municipal levels, there is often a plurality of functional demoi, such as public schools governed by elected school boards and a variety of democratically organized committees, councils, and associations that enable intensely affected groups to have influence on particular governance issues.[15]

The European Union is the example *par excellence* of the complex institutional model containing and combining several territorially and functionally defined demoi which are sought to be balanced and engaged with one another.

Many still seem to be caught in rather conventional models of democracy when it comes to discussing European democracy. Two positions tend to stick with the main model viewing democracy as based on a singular demos ruling itself through democratic procedures and institutions established to structure intra-demos political processes. The first position sees proper democracy as anchored in the national representative institutions. European politics is indirectly legitimized by the fact that national governments have a democratic mandate to pursue the national interests in the negotiations at the European level. The second position envisions the emergence of a European demos and a federal structure to ensure that the political processes relating to the European demos can unfold democratically. The latter is a 'gradualist approach' to democracy beyond the nation state that in simple terms replicates an already known model at a higher level and seeks to establish new hierarchies between demoi and jurisdictions.[16]

A third group of scholars, however, have pointed out the need to engage further with the pluricentric forms of governance that we see in modern transnational societies in general and in the EU in particular. In this third group of scholars, some argue for conceiving the EU as a demoicracy emphasizing the need to create democratic engagement across the boundaries of demoi, predominantly

---

12   Peter DeLeon, *Democracy and the Political Sciences* (State University of New York Press 1997) 14ff.

13   Arendt Lijphart, *Democracy in Plural Societies: A Comparative Exploration* (Yale University Press 1977).

14   Bob Jessop, 'Multi-Level Governance and Multi-level Metagovernance' in I Bache and MV Flinders (eds) *Multi-level Governance* (Oxford University Press 2004) 57.

15   Dahl (n 5) 126.

16   See for example Erik Oddvar Eriksen and John Erik Fossum, 'Introduction: Reconfiguring European Democracy' in EO Eriksen and JE Fossum (eds), *Rethinking Democracy and the European Union* (Routledge 2011).

understood as territorially differentiated (that is national demoi).[17] Others have developed alternative views of European democracy in connection with and as an extension of the analysis of European governance.[18]

The theoretical ambition of this third group of scholars could be seen as an attempt to break with the otherwise hegemonic idea that politics is a matter for the sovereign state and to deal more head on with the heterogeneity that emerges as a result of the political and administrative globalization and decentralization. We shall argue that the governance approach in general and in the EU in particular has a valuable contribution in showing how democracy can be constituted anew under these heterogeneous conditions.

Towards Pluricentrism

While they might quarrel over the details, governance theorists agree that advanced liberal democracies are becoming increasingly pluricentric.[19] This pluricentrism is, among other things, a result of increased political globalization and administrative fragmentation. A gradually accelerated process of *political globalization* has intensified the level of governance processes that involve more than one demos. Governments are governing in unison, metropolitan cities are collaborating across borders, and stakeholder groups from different countries are joining forces. This development has intensified the need to set standards for ensuring democratic participation and deliberation in inter-demos governance processes. As part of this globalization process, new and old transnational political institutions, as well

---

17   See for example Nicolaïdis (n 2) 351–69; Cheneval and Schimmelfennig (n 2) 334–50; Richard Bellamy and Dario Castiglione, 'Three Models of Democracy, Political Community and Representation in the EU' (2013) 20 *Journal of European Public Policy* 206.

18   Kohler-Koch and Rittberger (n 1) 27–49; Joshua Cohen and Charles Sabel, 'Directly-Deliberative Polyarchy' (1997) 3 *European Law Journal* 313–42; James Bohman, *Democracy Across Borders – From Demos to Demoi* (MIT Press 2007).

19   Rod AW Rhodes, *Understanding Governance: Policy Networks, Governance, Reflexivity and Accountability* (Open University Press 1997) 15; Walter Kickert, Erik-Hans Klijn and Johannes Koppenjan (eds) *Managing Complex Networks* (Sage 1997) 2; Stephen Goldsmith and William D Eggers, *Governing by Network: The New Shape of the Public Sector* (Brookings Institution Press 2002) 7; Chris Ansell, 'The Networked Polity: Regional Development in Western Europe' (2000) 13 *Governance* 303; Donald Kettl, *The Transformation of Governance* (Johns Hopkins University Press 2002); Kees van Kersbergen and Frans van Warden, 'Governance as a Bridge Between Disciplines: Cross-Disciplinary Inspiration Regarding Shifts in Governance and Problems of Governability, Accountability and Legitimacy' (2004) 43 *European Journal of Political Research* 143; Pierre and Peters (n 3); Chris Skelcher, 'Jurisdictional Integrity, Polycentrism, and the Design of Democratic Governance' (2005) 18 *Governance* 89E n3)val and Schimmelfennig (n2)AUGUST Waever (n 36) ; Eva Sørensen and Jacob Torfing (eds) *Theories of Democratic Network Governance* (Palgrave Macmillan 2007).

as courts and organizations, have sought to gain status and momentum as strong transnational demoi capable of setting the rules of the game in the transnational governance arena. One of the central objectives is to define, hegemonize, and enforce transnational standards for how nation-states and other public authorities may treat each other and their populations.[20]

Simultaneously, a series of *administrative reforms* in many advanced liberal democracies have fragmented the political systems by dividing them into a plurality of self-regulating governance units: public agencies, partnerships, and private businesses on contract. The balance between the different kinds of self-regulating governance units varies from country to country. Such governance units count as demoi to the extent that they allow affected stakeholders to exert influence through exit- and voice-based forms of participation and deliberation. Governance units that rely exclusively on exit options do little to promote the formation of communality sentiments; these should therefore be regarded as weak demoi.[21] At the same time, the administrative reforms have changed the role of elected politicians from sovereign rulers to members of political 'Boards of Directors' who govern at a distance and leave the actual governing to public and private stakeholders.[22] Representative democracy has been pushed back.

The aggregated outcome of political globalization and administrative reform is a pluricentric political system that divides the capacity to govern between a plurality of multi-leveled and mutually overlapping territorially and functionally

---

20   Michael Greven, 'Can the European Union Finally Become a Democracy?' in M Greven and L Pauly (eds), *Democracy Beyond the State? The European Dilemma and the Emerging Global Order* (Rowman and Littlefield Publishers 2000); Ian Bache and Matthew Flinders, *Multi-level Governance* (Oxford University Press 2004) 7; Wendy Larner and William Walters (eds), *Global Governmentality: Governing International Spaces* (Routledge 2004); Oscar van Heffen, Walter Kickert and Jacques JA Thomassen (eds), *Governance in Modern Society: Effects Change and Formation of Government Institutions* (Kluwer 2000) 3.

21   Albert O Hirschman, *Exit, Voice and Loyalty: Responses to Decline in Firms, Organizations and States* (Harvard University Press 1970) 7; Eva Sørensen, 'Democracy and Empowerment' (1997) 75 *Public Administration* 553; Paul Hirst, *Associative Democracy: New Forms of Economic and Social Governance* (Polity Press 1994); Paul Hirst, 'Democracy and Governance' in J Pierre (ed), *Debating Governance.* (Oxford University Press 2000) 1.

22   H Brinton Milward and Keith Provan, 'The Hollow State: Private Provision of the Public Sector' in HM Ingram and SR Smith (eds), *Public Policy for Democracy* (Brookings Institutions 1993) 200ff; Rod AW Rhodes, 'Governance and Public Administration' in J Pierre (ed), *Debating Governance: Authority, Steering and Democracy* (Oxford University Press 2000) 345ff; Kettl (n 19) 119; Christopher Pollitt and Geert Bouckaert, *Public Management Reform: A Comparative Analysis* (Oxford University Press 2004) 175; Peter Bogason, 'Local Democratic Governance: Allocative, Integrative or Deliberative?' in P Bogason, S Kensen and HT Miller (eds), *Tampering with Tradition: The unrealized Authority of Democratic Agency* (Lexington Books 2004) 27f; Eva Sørensen, 'Metagovernance: The Changing Role of Politicians in Processes of Democratic Governance' (2006) 36 *American Review of Public Administration* 79.

demarcated units of governance. In a pluricentric political system, democracy is a result of the degree to which each of these individual units of governance is democratically regulated, and the extent to which the relationship and interaction between these demoi is democratically regulated. Traditional theories of democracy offer advice about how to ensure the former, but not the latter.

While most governance theorists agree on some version of the globalization and fragmentation diagnosis, there has been a great deal of debate about the consequences of pluricentrism on the role of the state. Some researchers have insisted that the position of the state has not really changed,[23] while others have claimed that the powers of the state have been reduced considerably.[24] A third group of governance theorists, with whom we agree, have argued that the role of the state has changed, insofar as it has become a metagovernor of interactive governance arenas rather than a sovereign ruler.[25] While sovereign rule is exercised through detailed bureaucratic control and regulation, both within and beyond the state apparatus, meta-governance is exercised by shaping and regulating self-regulating actors. As such, it can be seen as an extended and strategically facilitated form of delegation and decentralization, which functions by constructing capable autonomous governance units. The most powerful members of a pluricentric society are those that can metagovern other self-regulating actors. Although state actors tend to be in a strong position to do this, no single public authority, agency, or private organization can monopolize the role of metagovernor. In sum, the age of pluricentric governance has destabilized the image of public governance and politics as a unitary process in which a People make collective decisions and act on them and in which the state is an expression of this unity. What emerges instead is an image of a decentered governance process in which a variety of relatively autonomous territorially and functionally organized governance units seek to govern and metagovern themselves and others.

The European Union itself represents the development of a more globalized or supranational form of politics where legislation and coordination for and between member states take place. This has lifted a number of issues from 'domestic politics' and from intra-democratic processes to the European level where they have become the subject of procedures that tie different demoi together.

---

23   Paul Hirst and Grahame Thompson, *Globalization in Question* (Polity Press 1996); Kees van Kersbergen, Robert H Lieshout and Bruno Verbeek, 'Institutional Change in the Emerging European Polity' in van Heffen, Kickert and Thomassen (n 20).

24   John Rosenau, 'Governance, Order and Change in World Politics' in J Rosenau and EO Cziempel (eds), *Governance Without Government* (Cambridge University Press 1992); Milward and Provan (n 22); Rod AW Rhodes, 'Understanding Governance: Ten Years On' (2007) 28 *Organization Studies* 1260.

25   Bob Jessop, 'Governance and Meta-governance: On Reflexivity, Requisite Variety and requisite Irony' in HP Bang (ed), *Governance as Social and Political Communication* (Manchester University Press 2003); Jan Kooiman (ed), *Modern Governance. New Government-Society Interactions* (Sage 1993) 4; Jan Kooiman, *Governing as Governance* (Sage 2003) 8; Sørensen and Torfing (n 19) ch 7.

At the European level, the European Council, the Council of Ministers, the European Parliament and, arguably, the European Commission each represent different constituencies which by the respective institutions' involvement in the decision-making procedures ensure that these constituencies, or demoi, are involved in the decision making. At the national level national parliaments have to varying degrees been involved in mandating their national governments' position in the European Council and the Council. With the Lisbon Treaty, national parliaments formally have become a part of the European-level institutional structure with their role in the subsidiarity procedure (Article 12 TEU).

Similarly, the Lisbon Treaty included Article 11 TEU from the Constitutional Treaty concerning 'participatory democracy' in the European Union. The article stipulates that the European institutions facilitate open, transparent and regular interaction between and with different civil society actors.[26] This relates to the discussion of European governance, very consciously pursued in connection with the Commission's *White Paper on Governance* (2001). The White Paper was criticized for having too much focus on steering and ensuring compliance and less on democratic participation and input,[27] but the treaty articles still contain the potential of active civil society engagement.

The Committee of Regions and the Economic and Social Committee are, along with the various committees in the Comitology, examples of the participation of multi-level governance networks involving both public and private actors with varying degrees of participation and formal standing in EU policy creation and implementation.

Finally, the EU has consciously shifted from old style 'governance' using the 'community method' and legislative acts and replaced it with softer new governance modes in areas such as Occupational Health and Safety,[28] while having introduced new governance methods, notably the Open Method of Coordination (OMC) in areas which partly fall outside the purview of regular EU competences such as employment, social inclusion, healthcare, education, immigration and integration.[29] Also here the intention is to involve civil society actors in the formulation of targets and mechanisms to solve problems relating to these areas.

---

26   Stijn Smismans, 'The Constitutional Labeling of "The Democratic Life of the EU": Representative and Participatory Democracy' in L Dobson and A Føllesdal (eds), *Political Theory and the European Constitution* (Routledge 2004).

27   Smismans (n 26); Stijn Smismans, 'European Civil Society: Shaped By Discourses and Institutional Interests' (2003) 9 *European Law Journal* 482; Andreas Føllesdal, 'The Political Theory of the White Paper on Governance: Hidden and Fascinating' (2003) 9 *European Public Law* 73.

28   Stijn Smismans, 'New Modes of Governance and the Participatory Myth' (2008) 31 *West European Politics* 874; Adrienne Heritier and Dirk Lehmkuhl, 'New Modes of Governance and Democratic Accountability' (2011) 46 *Government and Opposition* 126.

29   Luc Tholoniat, 'The Career Of The Open Method Of Coordination: Lessons From A "Soft" EU Instrument' (2010) 33 *West European Politics* 93.

De-politicization as a Response to Pluricentrism

When viewed from a traditional perspective on democracy, pluricentrism deepens the above-mentioned tensions related to balancing effectiveness against control and communality versus heterogeneity. The strategies that are available for dealing with these tensions are problematic because they tend to relocate the boundary between the inside and the outside of democracy in ways that diminish the democratic realm.

Political globalization deepens the tension between effectiveness and control because it produces more 'foreign policy', while administrative reforms leave governance tasks in the hands of stakeholders rather than citizens. The partly intergovernmental or consociational nature of the EU has some inbuilt tendencies towards de-politicization[30] and the experience with European governance, including the OMC, does not involve a high level of democratic participation of citizens and civil society organizations.[31]

Traditional theories of democracy have responded to these tensions by inspiring two de-politicization strategies. The first strategy proposes establishing a world government and court of law that regulates governments as well as intergovernmental affairs by referring to a constitution that determines certain 'rules of the game'.[32] This strategy is problematic, partly because the chances of establishing such a world government appear slim, and partly because it reduces the regulatory ambitions to a set of constitutive rules. The second strategy consists in defining a large part of the transnational and de-centered governance processes out of the realm of democratic regulation. This de-politicization strategy is pursued by those who claim that it is either desirable or only plausible that the EU deals with regulatory issues and/or low politically salient issues and not with (re-)distributive and more politically salient issues.[33] The strategy is advocated in the New Public Management reform

---

30 Yannis Papadopoulos and Paul Magnette, 'On the Politicisation of the European Union: Lessons from Consociational National Polities' (2010) 33 *West European Politics* 711.

31 Smismans (n 28) 874; Dawid Friedrich, 'Policy Process, Governance and Democracy in The EU: The Case Of Open Method Of Coordination On Social Inclusion In Germany' (2006) 34 *Policy and Politics* 367; Sandra Kröger, 'The Open Method of Coordination: Underconceptualisation, Overdetermination, Depoliticisation and Beyond' in S Kröger (ed), *What We Have Learnt: Advances, Pitfalls and Remaining Questions in OMC Research*, Special Issue 1 EioP (Volume 13, Article 5). Available at <http://eiop.or.at/eiop/texte/2009–005a.htm> accessed 11 June 2013.

32 David Held, 'Democracy: From City States to Cosmopolitan Order' in D Held (ed), *Prospects for Democracy* (Polity Press 1993) 40.

33 Giandomenico Majone, 'Europe's Democratic Deficit: The Question of Standards' (1998) 4 *European Law Journal* 5; Robert Dahl, 'Can International Organizations be Democratic?' in I Shapiro and C Hacker-Cordón (eds), *Democracy's Edges* (Cambridge University Press 1999); Fritz Wilhelm Scharpf, 'Notes Towards a Theory of Multilevel Governing in Europe' (2001) 24 *Scandinavian Political Studies* 1; Andrew Moravscik, 'Is there a "Democratic Deficit" in World Politics? A Framework for Analysis' (2004) 39 *Government and Opposition* 336.

program which defines the considerable amount of governance performed by actors other than politicians as production in relation to preset uncontroversial goals which should stay at arm's length from political intervention.[34]

Pluricentrism is also viewed as problematic for democracy because it increases the heterogeneities that must be overcome in order to promote the sense of communality that constitutes a strong democracy. Hence, political globalization and institutional fragmentation cause growth in the governance processes that involve actors with different territorially and functionally defined 'we' identities. Again, two strategies are available. The first strategy involves canonizing a universal sense of communality that can serve as a common point of identification for all demoi. An example is the current efforts to give this pre-political status to a set of human rights and to consolidate international courts that can enforce them.[35] This strategy is insufficient for solving the inter-demos problem because it tends to presume that such universal rights can be established as a pre-political fact and because it says little about how to provide the necessary degree of communality to govern policy issues that are largely unrelated to human rights.[36] For the European Union the creation of a common political identity and European demos on the basis of either cultural values or a shared political culture has long been seen as a necessary requirement for a genuine European democracy.[37] Another strategy is to insist that democratic communality sentiments are, by definition, territorial in orientation because functionally founded communalities engage in governance from a particularistic perspective rather than a communal perspective.[38] Consequently, functionally organized governance units should be considered to be outside the realm of democratic politics and kept at a safe distance from the political participation and deliberation that takes place at different levels in territorially defined demoi. The problem with this strategy is that it overlooks the fact that all references to a 'we', regardless of whether they are territorially or functionally oriented, are particularistic in the sense that they are an outcome of political power games and are likely to produce exclusions.[39]

---

34   Pollitt and Bouckaert (n 22); Christopher Hood, 'A Public Management for All Seasons?' (1991) 69 *Public Administration* 1.

35   David Held, *Democracy and the Global Order: From the Nation State to Cosmopolitan Governance* (Polity Press 1995) 231ff; Jürgen Habermas, *The Post-national Constellation* (MIT Press 2001).

36   James Bohman, 'From Demos to Demoi: Democracy across Borders' (2005) 18 *Ratio Juris* 293.

37   Mette Jolly, 'A Demos For The European Union' (2005) 25 *Politics* 12; Valeria Camia, 'Normative Discussions on European Identity: A Puzzle For Social Science' (2010) 11 *Perspectives On European Politics And Society* 109–18.

38   Allan Dreyer Hansen, 'Governance Networks and Participation' in Sørensen and Torfing (n 25).

39   John S Dryzek, 'Networks and Democratic Ideals: Equality, Freedom and Communication' in Sørensen and Torfing (n 25); Arash Abizadeh, 'Does Collective Identity Presuppose an Other' (2005) 99 *American Political Science Review* 45–60.

Rather than excluding forms of participation and deliberation from the democratic realm, efforts should be made to set standards for the democratic interaction and institutionalization of the interaction between different types of communality sentiments.

Governance Networks as Providers of Weak Ties

The above-mentioned strategies for ensuring democracy in a pluricentric political system are unsatisfactory. They all, in their own particular way, depoliticize significant parts of the governance processes that form their members' lives, and, thereby, legitimize the fact that these processes are not democratically regulated. A better option is to recognize the political character of this interaction and find ways to democratically regulate inter-demoi governance. When addressing these issues, it is essential to look for forms of participation and deliberation other than those suggested by traditional theories of liberal democracy.

The search for inter-demoi forms of participation and deliberation is complicated. No single institutional mechanism can do the job, so what is needed is a mixture of new and old forms of democratic regulation. Rather than attempting to comment on the nature of this mix,[40] the present chapter focuses exclusively on *the role that governance networks might play in enhancing democratic participation and deliberation in a pluricentric political system*. The purpose is to show that governance networks provide a promising institutional framework for inter-demos participation and deliberation between the many territorially and functionally demarcated demoi involved in pluricentric governance. The specific contribution of governance networks is that they are different from institutions and organizations. While institutions and organizations provide what Mark Granovetter describe as 'strong ties' within a group of actors, governance networks establish 'weak ties' between such groups.[41]

This kind of democratic tie is needed for governance processes that involve more than one demos. So what, then, is a governance network? Governance networks are not institutions or organizations. Although they do provide some sort of temporal order and pattern of action between different actors, their temporal, situated, and fragile character makes it more appropriate to view them as institutionalizations. The temporality, situatedness, and fragility of governance networks are related to the fact that they rely on interdependence between the involved actors. The extensive literature on the subject has defined governance networks as (1) relatively stable articulations of interdependent, but operationally autonomous actors who (2) interact with one another through negotiations, which (3) take place within a regulative, normative, cognitive, and imaginary framework

---

40   See Eva Sørensen and Jacob Torfing, 'The Democratic Anchorage of Governance Networks' (2005) 28 *Scandinavian Political Studies* 195

41   Granovetter (n 4) 1360–80.

that is (4) self-regulating within limits set by external forces, and (5) contributes to the production of public purpose.[42]

Governance network theorists argue that the growth in governance networks can be explained by the ability of those networks to provide inter-organizational coordination, which is essential for the production of efficient and effective public governance under pluricentric conditions.[43] As Jan Kooiman argues, the fragmented and differentiated nature of pluricentric societies (or, as Kooiman calls them, sociopolitical systems of governance) produces long cross-organizational lines of interdependency. This is because efforts to solve concrete governance problems usually demand cross-organizational coordination, cooperation, and communication.[44] Governance networks provide an institutional framework for enhancing negotiated coordination between such 'long lines' of interdependent but operationally autonomous actors.

Empirical studies have found that governance networks take many forms. Some are loose, inclusive, and short-lived, while others are tight, exclusive, and long-lived.[45] Some governance networks are ambitious and target positive coordination by formulating shared objectives, while others are less ambitious and settle for negative coordination; that is, seeking to avoid externalities.[46] Finally, some governance networks seek to enhance vertical coordination between actors at different levels of governance, while others target horizontal coordination between different governance units placed at the same level of governance.[47]

With these differences in mind, governance networks do generally establish control and communality ties that are 'weaker' than those that characterize governance institutions and organizations, such as governments and agencies. Issue networks establish weaker ties than policy communities.[48] The ties that bind network actors together can be characterized as weak because they are driven by temporal and situated interdependencies rather than codified rules and procedures. This makes them shorter and less repetitive and sedimented than intra-organizational

---

42   Sørensen and Torfing (n 25) 8.

43   H Brinton Milward and Keith Provan, 'Do Networks Really Work? A Framework for Evaluating Public-Sector Organizational Networks' (2000) 61 *Public Administration Review* 601; Jacob Torfing, B Guy Peters, Jon Pierre and Eva Sørensen, *Interactive Governance: Advancing the Paradigm* (Oxford University Press 2012) ch 9; Sørensen and Torfing (n 25)15ff .

44   Jan Kooiman, 'Societal Governance: Level, Modes and Orders of Social-Political Interaction' in J Pierre (ed), *Debating Governance. Authority, Steering and Democracy* (Oxford University Press 2000) 139.

45   Rod AW Rhodes and David March, 'New Directions in the Study of Policy Networks' (1992) 21 *European Journal of Political Research* 181.

46   Fritz Wilhelm Scharpf, 'Games Real Actors Could Play: Positive and Negative Coordination in Embedded Negotiations' (1994) 6 *Journal of Theoretical Politics* 27.

47   Martin Markussen and Jacob Torfing (eds), *Democratic Network Governance in Europe* (Palgrave Macmillan 2007) 3.

48   Rhodes and March (n 45).

ties. However, as Granovetter argues, this weakness does not make the network ties less valuable than strong ties.[49] On the contrary, weak ties are important because they provide patterns of interaction and communication that reach beyond the narrow confines of a group bound together by strong ties. Although Granovetter is interested more in effectiveness than democracy, the 'strength of weak ties' argument is just as relevant for considerations of the relationship between patterns of control and communality within a demos and between different demoi.

This raises the question of the specific contribution that weak ties make in relation to democracy. According to Granovetter, the presence of weak ties between groups bound together by strong ties is crucial for ensuring effective governance. This is because weak ties stimulate an effective diffusion of influence and information and a certain level of social cohesion in contexts that are characterized by differentiation. From a democratic perspective, this is interesting because the kind of democratic control and communality sentiments that democratic participation and deliberation are meant to produce is basically a function of the level of diffusion of political influence and information in society and the presence of some degree of social cohesion. Diffusion of political influence between demoi can help ensure that everyone affected by a political decision has access to influence that decision. Diffusion of information across demoi can help prevent the kind of secrecy that makes it difficult to hold decision makers to account and produce the kind of disturbance of sedimented political positions and beliefs that trigger a vibrant public debate. The promotion of a certain level of social cohesion between demoi can pave the way for developing political identities that can participate and deliberate with actors that belong to other demoi. In this context, weak ties provide a level of democratization of inter-demos governance processes, and they also reduce exclusionary tendencies within the individual demos.

Enhancing Democratic Control and Communality by Means of Inter-demos Governance Networks

Having argued that weak ties are important for democracy and that governance networks provide such ties, the next step is to consider how governance networks can promote democratic participation and deliberation in ways that enhance inter-demos control and communality. This is achieved by first discussing the role of governance networks in providing inter-demos control, and then analyzing their possible contribution to inter-demos communality.

Enhancing Democratic Control

In a pluricentric context, the fact that governance processes often involve more than one demos makes it insufficient to view democratic control as an intra-demos affair.

---

49   Granovetter (n 4).

It is uncontroversial to argue that ensuring democratic control calls for the institutionalization of both vertical and horizontal control mechanisms. Vertical control mechanisms provide the affected actors with the information and sanctioning powers they need to hold the decision makers to account. Horizontal control mechanisms that separate powers between different political elites enable different elites to hold each other to account.[50] Inter-demoi governance networks can help enforce both forms of control by establishing weak ties between demoi. Vertical patterns of accountability within a demos are enforced when other demoi diffuse information about the content and consequences of intra-demos decision making. Horizontal accountability is further strengthened when elites hold each other to account in an attempt to ensure that none of them oversteps their democratically sanctioned authorization, not only within the individual demos but also from different demoi. Following Charles Montesquieu's line of thinking,[51] Eva Ezioni-Halevy argues that an extension of the separation of powers between political elites and sub-elites, like the one accommodated by pluricentrism, is positive for democracy.[52] This is because pluricentrism accommodates an intensive political competition and contestation between a plurality of political actors, both within and beyond the individual demos. The separation of powers and influence channels available to ordinary citizens and stakeholders within the individual demos guarantees some level of democratic control and political contestation. Nevertheless, the contestation provided by other functionally and territorially demarcated demoi can upgrade this control because it produces an independent and informed opposition. The opposition is more independent than it would be within a demos because of the weak ties, while the opposition is more informed than the larger public because it includes different political elites, sub-elites, and mini-publics with specialized knowledge about the territorial or functional implications of various policy decisions.

However, the activation of inter-demoi control mechanisms calls for the institutionalization of governance arenas and publics in which autonomous political elites and sub-elites can hold each other to account and negotiate.[53] This is where governance networks enter the stage as an important instrument for ensuring an ongoing situated contestation and negotiated cooperation between democratically

50   Guillermo O'Donnell, 'Horizontal Accountability in New Democracies' (1998) 9 *Journal of Democracy* 112; CD Kenney, 'Reflections on Horizontal Accountability: Democratic Legitimacy, Majority Parties and Democratic Stability in Latin America'. (Conference on Institutions, Accountability and Democratic Governance in Latin America University of Notre Dame, May 8–9 2000).

51   Charles de Montesquieu, *The Spirit of Law* (Willing Benton 1952[1793]).

52   Eva Etzioni-Halevy, 'Network Governance as a Challenge to Democratic Elite Theory' (Conference on Democratic Network Governance, Roskilde, 2003).

53   Lijphart (n 13) ch 6; Andreas Føllesdal and Simon Hix, 'Why there is a Democratic Deficit in the EU: A Response to Majone and Moravcsik' (2006) 44(3) *Journal of Common Market Studies* 533.

authorized demoi.[54] Networks fit this task so well because they provide weak ties that are dynamic and short-lived enough that they do not ossify in ways that reduce their capacity to keep political debates open and vibrant, while also constructing temporal interdependencies that motivate interaction and negotiated co-governance.[55]

Enhancing Inter-demos Communality

As well as promoting democratic control, inter-demos governance networks also institutionalize patterns of political participation and deliberation that promote communality sentiments that can deal with heterogeneity without producing systematic exclusions of affected actors. In seeking to make democracy more inclusive, the promotion of strong unitary communality sentiments within the individual demos should be pursued with caution. Although such communality sentiments are an important motor for shared decision making, they can be problematic if they become so sedimented and narrow that they cause the systematic exclusion of affected actors. Affectedness often cuts across institutional borderlines and patterns of affectedness change over time. Accordingly, it is crucial to pursue the development of communality sentiments that do not block inter-demos decision making or the dynamic reconstruction of communalities in light of shifting patterns of affectedness. The first task is to ensure that the outside of a demos is not perceived as an outside to democracy as such. This can be done by developing a cross-demos communality based on agonist communality sentiments that set out democratic conducts for inter-demos decision making.[56] The next task is to highlight the contingent and overlapping character of demoi and to pursue the construction of political identities that are capable of identifying with shifting communalities. As Michael Sandel put it:

> The civic virtue distinctive to our time is the capacity to negotiate our way
> among sometimes overlapping, sometimes conflicting obligations that claim us,
> and to live with the tension to which multiple loyalties give rise. This capacity

---

54   Anders Esmark, 'At forvalte Europa – Den Danske Centraladministrations Omstilling til det Europæiske Samarbejde' (PhD thesis, University of Copenhagen 2002); Anders Esmark, 'Democratic Accountability and Network Governance – Problems and Potentials' in Sørensen and Torfing (n 25).

55   Archon Fung and Erik Olin Wright, *Deepening Democracy. Institutional Innovations in Empowered Participatory Governance* (Verso 2003) 23.

56   Connolly (n 9); Chantal Mouffe, *The Return of the Political* (Verso 1993); James Tully, 'The Politics of Recognition' (2000) *Working Paper Series, Department of Political Science*, University of Essex.

is difficult to sustain, for it is easier to live with the plurality between persons than within them.[57]

In a pluricentric political system, democratic communality sentiments involve dealing with heterogeneity and difference and multiple belongings rather than being loyal to one overarching and stable political 'we'.

Recognizing the open and contingent character of political communities is important because it promotes accepting difference as something that is to be dealt with within the realm of democratic decision making rather than through internal and/or external exclusions. Exclusions are intrinsically political and must, therefore, be outcomes of democratically regulated decisions. This leads to the question of how to produce agonist *sentiments between demoi and political identities that can relate to multiple communalities.* The answer is through shaping arenas for political decision making that involve actors from more than one demos. By spurring political debate and communication between demoi, such arenas encourage the perception of members of other demoi not as enemies, but as adversaries with legitimate democratic rights to their own opinions that can be pursued in political contestations.[58] This idea is along the same lines as Robert Putnam's claim that networks provide societal trust by establishing bridges between groups that bond.[59]

Governance networks present themselves as arenas for this kind of debate and communication because they institutionalize weak ties between participants rather than strong ones. In doing so, they pave the way for the construction of a sense of communality that is driven by stories of interdependency and is weak in the sense that it does not aim to remove difference but to exploit it. In doing so, governance networks not only promote the construction of agonistic sentiments, but they also contribute to developing pluricentric political identities that view the ability to identify with multiple and shifting communities as a democratic virtue. In this way, governance networks contribute to the development of a more inclusive pluricentric democracy, both externally and internally.

Metagoverning Inter-demoi Governance Networks

Governance networks offer themselves essentially as a promising institutional frame for inter-demos governance, although there is no guarantee that they will serve this democratic function in practice. As several empirical studies have

---

57   Michael J Sandel, *Democracy's Discontent – America in Search of a Public Philosophy* (Harvard University Press 1996) 350.

58   Mouffe (n 56) 1.

59   Robert D Putnam (ed), *Democracies in Flux: The Evolution of Social Capital in Contemporary Society* (Oxford University Press 2002).

shown,[60] many inter-demoi governance networks operate in seclusion. Although these networks might serve as arenas for political contestation and for promoting a sense of inter-demos communality between participants, their opacity makes it difficult for the larger group of affected constituencies to hold them to account and to develop the same kind of dynamic and cross-cutting political identities. As mentioned, the experience with European government and governance does not unequivocally demonstrate a high level of participation and critical engagement across a number of territorially and functionally defined demoi.

However, the European Union has the potential of being constituted on the basis of something other than a European demos, namely weaker links between the various (in this case territorially defined) demoi.[61] Moreover, studies of 'politicization of European issues' reveal that it does not necessarily lead to the reinforcement of exclusionary national identities[62] but can open up space for discussion about the European interest and different views on the future direction of the European project.[63] Indeed new communalities are likely to be created through political engagement.[64]

For European governance networks more specifically, studies demonstrate that more is required to structure the inclusion, transparency and critical engagement between demoi in order to ensure accountability and tap into the democratic potential that European governance networks could deliver.[65] This may mean that governance networks would have to be nested within the more encompassing institutional framework of representative democracy.[66]

---

60   Frank Hendricks and Juliet Musso, 'Making Local Democracy Work: Neighborhood-Oriented Reform in Los Angeles and Dutch Randstadt' in Bogason, Kensen and Miller (n 22); Peter Bogason and Mette Zølner, *Methods in Democratic Network Governance* (Palgrave Macmillan 2007); Markussen and Torfing (n 47); N Aarsather et al., 'Interactive accountability – Evaluating the democratic accountability of governance networks' (2009) 35 *Local Government Studies* 577.

61   Tobias Theiler, 'Does The European Union Need To Become A Community' (2012) 50 Journal of Common Market Studies 783.

62   Liesbet Hooghe and Gary Marks, 'A Postfunctionalist Theory of European Integration: From Permissive Consensus to Constraining Dissensus' (2009) 39 *British Journal Of Political Science* 1.

63   Paul Statham and Hans-Jörg Trenz, *The Politicization of Europe – Contesting The Constitution In The Mass Media* (Routledge 2012) 1–19; Ulrike Liebert, 'Civil Society, Public Sphere and Democracy in the EU' in Eriksen and Fossum (n 16) 112.

64   Magdalena Gora, Zdzislaw Mach and Hans-Jörg Trenz, 'Situating The Demos Of A European Democracy' in Eriksen and Fossum (n 16) ; Føllesdal and Hix (n 53).

65   Smismans (n 31); Heritier and Lehmkuhl (n 28) 126; Yannis Papadopoulos, 'Accountability and Multi-Level Governance: More Accountability, Less Democracy' (2010) 33 *West European Politics* 1030.

66   Andreas Føllesdal, 'The Legitimacy Challenges For New Modes Of Governance: Trustworthy Responsiveness' (2011) 46 *Government and Opposition* 81–100.

In general, inter-demos governance networks must be metagoverned if they are to add to the development of a strong pluricentric democracy, rather than move political decision making out of the realm of democratic regulation.[67]

Within this context, one of the most important tasks for metagovernors is to bring inter-demos governance networks into the open as political arenas that must legitimize their actions in the eyes of the affected constituencies. The objective of these metagovernors is to change the hegemonic perception of inter-demos governance as apolitical regulatory arenas, and then to push for the development of a plurality of inter-demoi publics. The public of each inter-demos governance network keeps a close eye on the behavior of the various political elites and sub-elites that participate in governance networks. In some cases, the issues at stake in a governance network are such that the internal network proceedings call for some level of privacy.[68] The task of a network public in such cases is to hold the networks collectively accountable for the governance outcomes they produce.

Although there are many problems related to holding inter-demos governance networks accountable, this is possible if many actors attempt to metagovern them using some of the new forms of democratic participation and deliberation. Hence, efforts to establish network publics can come from many directions. They can be initiated from the 'top down' by political authorities at higher levels of governance through various legal, political, institutional, and financial regulatory measures; they can come from the 'outside in' from other governance networks through acts of contestation or infiltration; and they can come from the 'bottom up', from affected citizens through the activation of the many new internet enabled media. The metagoverning powers of these new media have already proved to be effective means of shaping ad hoc publics around shifting inter-demos governance networks.

Conclusion

As the attempts to solve the Eurozone crisis have elucidated, political decision making in the EU is both an intra-demos and an inter-demos activity. The EU epitomizes the development of pluricentric political systems that has resulted from political globalization and administrative fragmentation. Pluricentric political systems in general and the EU in particular have spurred the need to develop theories of democracy that move beyond a purely intra-demos perspective on democracy to a perspective that directly addresses the institutionalization of inter-demos political processes. In line with recent theoretical discussions about *demoicracy* and multi-level governance in Europe, we have argued that with the right meta-governance counteracting de-politicization, governance networks offer themselves as an important institutional frame for promoting inter-demos participation and deliberation, because networks provide the kind of weak ties

---

67   Sørensen and Torfing (n 40).
68   Torfing et al (n 43).

between demoi constituted on strong ties that are needed to develop a strong pluricentric democracy.

Governance networks have been seen as problematic because they offer a weaker form of control and communality than that provided by traditional political institutions and organizations. However, the potential value of governance networks is that the forms of control and communality they provide represent an important supplement to institutions and organizations. The linkages between strong and weak ties ensure a strong pluricentric democracy because they mutually enforce one another. The individual demoi have an important role to play in metagoverning inter-demos governance networks, and these networks have an important role to play in making democracy more inclusive (partly by reducing tendencies to intra-demos closure) and in providing arenas for inter-demos participation and deliberation. Although inter-demos governance networks are no democratic panacea, neither generally speaking or in the current EU crisis, they do represent a promising contribution to the development of a pluricentric democracy.

Bibliography

Aarsather N et al, 'Interactive Accountability – Evaluating the Democratic Accountability of Governance Networks' (2009) 35 *Local Government Studies* 577–94

Abizadeh A, 'Does Collective Identity Presuppose an Other' (2005) 99 *American Political Science Review* 45–60

Almond G and Verba S, *The Civic Culture* (Princeton University Press 1963)

Ansell C, 'The Networked Polity: Regional Development in Western Europe' (2000) 13 *Governance* 303–33

Bache I and Flinders M, *Multi-level Governance* (Oxford University Press 2004)

Barber B, *Strong Democracy. Participatory Politics for a New Age* (University of California Press 1984)

Bellamy R and Castiglione D, 'Three Models of Democracy, Political Community and Representation in the EU' (2013) 20 *Journal of European Public Policy* 206–23

Bentham J, *An Introduction to the Principles of Morals and Legislation* (Hafner 1948[1776])

Benz A and Papadopoulos I, *Governance and Democracy: Comparing National, European and International experiences* (Routledge 2006)

Bogason P, 'Local Democratic Governance: Allocative, Integrative or Deliberative?' in P Bogason, S Kensen and HT Miller (eds), *Tampering with Tradition: The Unrealized Authority of Democratic Agency* (Lexington Books 2004) 23–8

—— and Zølner M, *Methods in Democratic Network Governance* (Palgrave Macmillan 2007)

Bohman J, 'From Demos to Demoi: Democracy across Borders' (2005) 18 *Ratio Juris* 293–314

—— *Democracy across Borders – From Demos to Demoi* (MIT Press 2007)

Camia V, 'Normative Discussions on European Identity: A Puzzle For Social Science' (2010) 11 *Perspectives On European Politics And Society* 109–18

Cheneval F and Schimmelfennig F, 'The Case For Demoicracy In The European Union' (2013) 51 *Journal of Common Market Series* 334–50

Cohen J and Sabel C, 'Directly-Deliberative Polyarchy' (1997) 3 *European Law Journal* 313–42

Connolly WE, *The Ethos of Pluralization* (University of Minnesota Press 1995)

Dahl R, *Democracy and its Critics* (Yale University Press 1987)

—— 'Can International Organizations be Democratic?' in I Shapiro and C Hacker-Cordón (eds), *Democracy's Edges* (Cambridge University Press 1999)

—— 'Power as the Control of Behavior' in S Lukes (ed), *Power* (Blackwell 1986)

—— *Who Governs?* (Yale University Press 1961)

DeLeon P, *Democracy and the Political Sciences* (State University of New York Press 1997)

Dryzek JS, 'Networks and Democratic Ideals: Equality, Freedom and Communication' in E Sørensen and J Torfing (eds), *Theories of Democratic Network Governance* (Palgrave Macmillan 2007)

Eriksen EO and Fossum JE, 'Introduction: Reconfiguring European Democracy' in EO Eriksen and JE Fossum (eds), *Rethinking Democracy and the European Union* (Routledge 2011)

Esmark A, 'At forvalte Europa – Den Danske Centraladministrations Omstilling til det Europæiske Samarbejde' (PhD thesis, University of Copenhagen 2002)

—— 'Democratic Accountability and Network Governance – Problems and Potentials' in E Sørensen and J Torfing (eds), *Theories of Democratic Network Governance* (Palgrave Macmillan 2007)

Etzioni-Halevy E, *The Elite Connection: Problems and Potential of Western Democracy* (Polity Press 1993)

—— 'Network Governance as a Challenge to Democratic Elite Theory' (Conference on Democratic Network Governance, Roskilde, 2003)

Friedrich D, 'Policy Process, Governance and Democracy in The EU: The Case Of Open Method Of Coordination On Social Inclusion In Germany' (2006) 34 *Policy and Politics* 367–83

Fung A and Wright EO, *Deepening Democracy. Institutional Innovations in Empowered Participatory Governance* (Verso 2003)

Føllesdal A, 'The Political Theory of the White Paper on Governance: Hidden and Fascinating' (2003) 9 *European Public Law* 73–86

—— 'The Legitimacy Challenges For New Modes of Governance: Trustworthy Responsiveness' (2011) 46 *Government and Opposition* 81–100

—— and Simon Hix, 'Why there is a Democratic Deficit in the EU: A Response to Majone and Moravcsik' (2006) 44 *Journal of Common Market Studies* 533–62

Goldsmith S and Eggers WD, *Governing by Network: The New Shape of the Public Sector* (Brookings Institution Press 2002)

Gora M, Mach Z and Trenz H-J, 'Situating The Demos Of A European Democracy' in EO Eriksen and JE Fossum (eds), *Rethinking Democracy and the European Union* (Routledge 2011)

Granovetter M, 'The Strength of Weak Ties' (1973) 78 *American Journal of Sociology* 1360–80

Greven M, 'Can the European Union Finally Become a Democracy?' in M Greven and L Pauly (eds), *Democracy Beyond the State? The European Dilemma and the Emerging Global Order* (Rowman and Littlefield Publishers 2000)

—— and Pauly L (eds), *Democracy Beyond the State? The European Dilemma and the Emerging Global Order* (Rowman and Littlefield Publishers 2000)

Habermas J, *The Post-national Constellation* (MIT Press 2001)

Hansen AD, 'Governance Networks and Participation' in E Sørensen and J Torfing (eds), *Theories of Democratic Network Governance* (Palgrave Macmillan 2007)

Held D, *Models of Democracy* (Polity Press 1987)

—— 'Democracy: From City States to Cosmopolitan Order' in D Held (ed.), *Prospects for Democracy* (Polity Press 1993)

—— *Democracy and the Global Order: From the Nation State to Cosmopolitan Governance* (Polity Press 1995)

Hendricks F and Musso J, 'Making Local Democracy Work: Neighborhood-Oriented Reform in Los Angeles and Dutch Randstadt' in P Bogason, S Kensen and HT Miller (eds), *Tampering with Tradition: The Unrealized Authority of Democratic Agency* (Lexington Books 2005)

Héritier A and Lehmkuhl D, 'New Modes of Governance and Democratic Accountability' (2011) 46 *Government and Opposition* 126–44

Hirschman AO, *Exit, Voice and Loyalty: Responses to Decline in Firms, Organizations and States* (Harvard University Press 1970)

Hirst P, *Associative Democracy: New Forms of Economic and Social Governance* (Polity Press 1994)

—— 'Democracy and Governance' in J Pierre (ed.), *Debating Governance* (Oxford University Press 2000)

—— and Thompson G, *Globalization in Question* (Polity Press 1996)

Hood C, 'A Public Management for All Seasons?' (1991) 69 *Public Administration* 1–19

Hooghe L and Marks G, 'A Postfunctionalist Theory of European Integration: From Permissive Consensus to Constraining Dissensus' (2009) 39 *British Journal Of Political Science* 1–23

Jessop B, 'Governance and Meta-governance: On Reflexivity, Requisite Variety and requisite Irony' in HP Bang (ed.), *Governance as Social and Political Communication* (Manchester University Press 2003)

—— 'Multi-Level Governance and Multi-level Metagovernance' in I Bache and MV Flinders (eds), *Multi-level Governance* (Oxford University Press 2004)

Jolly M, 'A Demos For The European Union' (2005) 25 *Politics* 12–8

Kenney CD, 'Reflections on Horizontal Accountability: Democratic Legitimacy, Majority Parties and Democratic Stability in Latin America'. (Conference on Institutions, Acountability and Democratic Governance in Latin America University of Notre Dame, 8–9 May 2000)

Kersbergen K van and Warden F van, 'Governance as a Bridge Between Disciplines: Cross-Disciplinary Inspiration Regarding Shifts in Governance and Problems of Governability, Accountability and Legitimacy' (2004) 43 *European Journal of Political Research* 143–71

Kersbergen K van, Lieshout RH and Verbeek B, 'Institutional Change in the Emerging European Polity' in O van Heffen, WM Kickert and JJA Thomassen (eds), *Governance in Modern Society* (Kluwer 2000)

Kettl D, *The Transformation of Governance.* (Johns Hopkins University Press 2002).

Kickert W, Klijn E-H and Koppenjan J (eds), *Managing Complex Networks* (Sage 1997)

Kohler-Koch B and Rittberger B, 'The Governance Turn' 44 *Journal of Common Market Studies* 27–49

Kooiman J, 'Societal Governance: Level, Modes and Orders of Social- Political Interaction' in J Pierre (ed.), *Debating Governance. Authority, Steering and Democracy* (Oxford University Press 2000)

—— *Governing as Governance* (Sage 2003)

—— (ed.), *Modern Governance. New Government-Society Interactions* (Sage 1993)

Kröger S, 'The Open Method of Coordination: Underconceptualisation, overdetermination, depoliticisation and beyond' in S Kröger (ed.), *What We Have Learnt: Advances, Pitfalls and Remaining Questions in OMC Research*, Special Issue 1 EioP (Volume 13, Article 5). Available at <http://eiop.or.at/eiop/texte/2009–005a.htm> accessed 11 June 2013

Larner W and Walters W (eds), *Global Governmentality: Governing International Spaces* (Routledge 2004)

Liebert U, 'Civil Society, Public Sphere and Democracy in the EU' in EO Eriksen and JE Fossum (eds), *Rethinking Democracy and the European Union* (Routledge 2012)

Lijphart A, *Democracy in plural societies: A comparative Exploration* (Yale University Press 1977)

Majone G, 'Europe's Democratic Deficit: The Question of Standards' 4 *European Law Journal* 5–28

Markussen M and Torfing J (eds), *Democratic Network Governance in Europe* (Palgrave Macmillan 2007)

Mill JS, *Considerations on Representative Government* (Prometheus Books 1991[1961])

—— *An Essay on Government* (E. Barker 1937[1820])

Milward HB and Provan K, 'The Hollow state: Private Provision of the Public Sector' in HM Ingram and SR Smith (eds), *Public Policy for Democracy* (Brookings Institutions 1993)

—— 'Do Networks Really Work? A Framework for Evaluating Public-Sector Organizational Networks' 61 *Public Administration Review* 601–13

Montesquieu C, *The Spirit of Law* (Willing Benton 1952[1793]).

Moravscik A, 'Is there a "Democratic Deficit" in World Politics? A Framework for Analysis' (2004) 39(2) *Government and Opposition* 336–63

Mouffe C, *The Return of the Political* (Verso 1993)

Nicolaidis K, 'European Demoicracy and Its Crisis' (2013) 51 *Journal of Common Market Studies* 351–69

O'Donnell G, 'Horizontal Accountability in New Democracies' (1998) 9 *Journal of Democracy* 112–26

Papadopoulos Y, 'Accountability and Multi-Level Governance: More Accountability, Less Democracy' (2010) 33 *West European Politics* 1030–49

—— and Magnette P, 'On the Politicisation of the European Union: Lessons from Consociational National Polities' (2010) 33 *West European Politics* 711–29

Pateman C, *Participation and Democratic Theory* (Cambridge University Press 1970)

Pierre J and Peters BG, *Governance, Politics and the State* (Palgrave Macmillan 2000)

—— *Governing Complex Societies: Trajectories and Scenarios.* (Palgrave Macmillan 2005)

Pollitt C and Bouckaert G, *Public Management Reform: A Comparative Analysis* (Oxford University Press 2004)

Putnam RD (ed.), *Democracies in Flux: The Evolution of Social Capital in Contemporary Society* (Oxford University Press 2002)

Rhodes RAW, *Understanding Governance: Policy Networks, Governance, Reflexivity and Accountability* (Open University Press 1997)

—— 'Governance and Public Administration' in Jon Pierre (ed.), *Debating Governance: Authority, Steering and Democracy* (Oxford University Press 2000)

—— 'Understanding Governance: Ten Years On' (2007) 28 *Organization Studies* 1243–64

—— and David March, 'New Directions in the Study of Policy Networks' (1992) 21 *European Journal of Political Research* 181–205

Rosenau J, 'Governance, Order and Change in World Politics' in J Rosenau and EO Cziempel (eds), *Governance Without Government* (Cambridge University Press 1992)

Sandel MJ, *Democracy's Discontent – America in Search of a Public Philosophy* (Harvard University Press 1996)

Sartori G, *The Theory of Democracy Revisited* (Volumes 1 and 2, Chatham House 1987)

Scharpf FW, 'Notes Towards a Theory of Multilevel Governing in Europe' (2001) 24 *Scandinavian Political Studies* 1–26

—— 'Games Real Actors Could Play: Positive and Negative Coordination in Embedded Negotiations' (1994) 6 *Journal of Theoretical Politics* 27–53

Schumpeter J, *Capitalism, Socialism and Democracy* (Harper and Row 1942)

Skelcher C, 'Jurisdictional Integrity, Polycentrism, and the Design of Democratic Governance' (2005) 18 *Governance* 89–110

Smismans S, 'European Civil Society: Shaped By Discourses and Institutional Interests' (2003) 9 *European Law Journal* 482–504

—— 'The Constitutional Labeling of 'The Democratic Life of the EU': Representative and Participatory Democracy' in L Dobson and A Føllesdal (eds), *Political Theory and the European Constitution* (Routledge 2004)

—— 'New Modes of Governance and the Participatory Myth' (2008) 31 *West European Politics* 874–95

Statham P and Trenz HJ, *The Politicization of Europe – Contesting The Constitution In The Mass Media* (Routledge 2012)

Sørensen E, 'Democracy and Empowerment' (1997) 75 *Public Administration* 553–67

—— 'Metagovernance: The Changing Role of Politicians in Processes of Democratic Governance' (2006) 36 *American Review of Public Administration* 79–97

—— and Jacob Torfing, 'The Democratic Anchorage of Governance Networks' (2005) 28 *Scandinavian Political Studies* 195–218

—— (eds), *Theories of Democratic Network Governance* (Palgrave Macmillan 2007)

Theiler T, 'Does The European Union Need To Become A Community' (2012) 50 *Journal of Common Market Studies* 783–800

Tholoniat L, 'The Career Of The Open Method Of Coordination: Lessons From A "Soft" EU Instrument' (2010) 33 *West European Politics* 93–117

Tocqueville A de, *Democracy in America* (Fontana 1968[1835])

Torfing J, 'Governance Network Theory: Towards a Second Generation' (2005) 44 *European Political Studies* 305–15

——, Peters BG, Pierre J and Sørensen E, *Interactive Governance: Advancing the Paradigm* (Oxford University Press 2012)

Tully J, 'The Politics of Recognition' (2000) Working Paper Series, Department of Political Science, University of Essex

van Heffen O, Kickert W and Thomassen JJA (eds), *Governance in Modern Society: Effects Change and Formation of Government Institutions* (Kluwer 2000)

Young IM, *Inclusion and Democracy* (Oxford University Press 2002)

Chapter 11

Patterns of Post-National Europe: The Future of Integration after the Crisis of Monetary Union[*]

Giandomenico Majone

1. The Rhetoric of European Integration

In classical rhetoric synecdoche is a figure of speech in which a part represents the whole, as in the expressions 'hired hands' for workers, 'good brains' for intelligent people, or 'Brussels' for EU institutions, whether or not the institutions are actually located in the Belgian capital. A synecdoche provides understanding by picking out from the many parts that can stand for the whole the one that best illuminates a particular aspect or dimension of the whole. It can also be badly misleading, however, if it induces people to confuse or identify the part with the whole. Since autumn 2011, if not before, chancellor Angela Merkel has been repeating that 'if the euro fails then Europe fails'. Europe is larger than the EU and there are many other problems besides the euro crisis, but presumably the phrase is meant to call attention to the broader implications of a possible collapse of the common currency by focusing attention on this particular problem. Still, the synecdoche is misleading, if not plainly wrong, for there are important European bodies, such as the Council of Europe, whose fate is not linked in any obvious way to the fate of EU monetary union. The Council of Europe has more than 40 member countries and may concern itself with all political, economic, and social matters of general European interest. Thus, the Council has an even broader mandate than the European Union. With the creation of the European Court of Human Rights, the European Convention for the Protection of Human Rights and Fundamental Freedoms provides an enforcement structure which subjects the states to a 'European' supervision of their compliance with the provisions of the Convention. For this reason, it has been argued that the ECHR constitutes a first expression of supranationalism in the European integration process.[1] Despite the non-binding character of the norms, levels of compliance with the ECHR and with

---

[*] Paper presented at the Conference on Democracy and Law in Europe organized by the CoE Foundations, Helsinki, 27–28 September 2012
1 Koen Lenaerts and Piet Van Nuffel, *Constitutional Law of the European Union* (Sweet and Maxwell 1999).

the decisions of the Strasbourg Court do not appear to be at all lower than levels of compliance with European Union (EU) law.[2]

But probably the German chancellor uses 'Europe' as shorthand for the approach to European integration followed since the 1950s, and which has in the so-called Community method – and its variants, for example, in the case of monetary union – its most distinctive expression. What is plainly wrong in this case is the identification of the traditional ('Monnet') approach to integration with integration 'tout court'. As I wrote some years ago

> it is wrong to reduce the history of European integration after World War II to one particular approach, and wrongheaded to insist that the EU should be the main, if not the only, forum for close European cooperation. Neither geographically nor functionally or culturally the 'Europe of Brussels' coincides with, or represents, the entire continent. Actually, the variety of modes of integration and interstate cooperation is one of the distinguishing features of European history. As Eric Jones (1987) has stressed, for most of its history Europe formed a cultural, economic, even a political unity. Of course, it was a special type of unity that did not exclude frequent, if limited, wars. Not the unity of the Chinese or Ottoman empires; rather, unity in diversity, embodied in a system of states competing and cooperating with each other. Such a system realized the benefits of competitive decision-making and the economies of scale of the centralized empire, giving Europe some of the best of both worlds.[3]

One explanation of the tendency to reduce the recent history of European integration to one particular approach may be found in the conviction of many past and present integrationist leaders that the process started with the establishment of the Coal and Steel Community and continued with the EEC can only lead to something closely akin to a European federation – a traditional territorial state 'writ large'. Of course, even the most ardent advocates of 'More Europe' deny that their goal is anything like a United States of Europe. However, the fact that the same integrationist leaders seem to be unable to specify their goal, reduces the credibility of their denials – and the political appeal of their ideas. Long ago Edward Carr gave the best possible explanation of the inadequacy of such open-ended commitments as 'ever closer union': 'The conception of politics as an infinite process seems in the long run uncongenial or incomprehensible to the human mind. Every political thinker who wishes to make an appeal to his contemporaries is consciously or unconsciously led to posit a finite goal'.[4]

---

2   Neil MacCormick, *Questioning Sovereignty: Law, State, and Nation in the European Commonwealth* (Oxford University Press 1999).

3   G.iandomenico Majone, *Europe As The Would-Be World Power: The EU At Fifty* (Cambridge University Press 2009) 206.

4   Edward H Carr, *The Twenty Years' Crisis, 1919–1939* (Harper & Row 1964[1939]) 89.

Also the symbolism used by integrationist leaders, and by their academic and bureaucratic supporters, casts serious doubts on the denials of any aspiration to statehood. Already in the 1960s some German legal scholars were claiming that the institutions of the European Communities had been designed with the idea of replicating the model of the Federal Republic. The Council of Ministers was said to correspond to the German *Bundesrat*; the European Commission, the body responsible for implementing the Council's decisions and would-be kernel of the future government of a united Europe, was the analogue of the federal executive; finally, the European Court of Justice was simply the Constitutional Court of the future federation. In an early, highly original presentation of European law, Hans Peter Ipsen warned about the risk of taking such analogies too seriously.[5] Nevertheless, the habit of using state-like terminology persists. The failed Constitutional Treaty introduced, in addition to 'President of the European Council', the title of 'Foreign Minister' of the EU – changed into the less state-like title of 'High Representative for Foreign Affairs and Security Policy' by the Lisbon Treaty. Other important symbols of statehood are the directly elected European Parliament, and the independent ECB; the supremacy of European law; the EU Court of Justice's assertion of its own *Kompetenz-Kompetenz*, despite the refusal of national constitutional courts to accept this position; and the sort of 'federal pre-emption' represented by total harmonization.

Monetary union may be seen as the latest and most advanced version of total harmonization, presenting many of the same pathologies of other applications of the traditional one-size-fits-all philosophy of European governance.[6] The main normative justification for EMU saw monetary union as a necessary step towards a politically integrated Europe. But recently this rhetorical argument has been reversed: now a more or less complete political union is said to be necessary in order to rescue monetary union. In this perspective the debt crisis of the Eurozone is even seen as a blessing in disguise – a unique opportunity to complete with political and economic union the process started with monetary union. In the words of the German finance minister, Wolfgang Schäuble, as reported by the *International Herald Tribune* of 3 October 2011: 'In recent months it has become clear: the answer to the crisis can only mean more Europe ... Without ... further steps toward stronger European institutions, eventually Europe will lose its effectiveness. We have to look beyond the national state'.

Other members of the Berlin government, including the chancellor, seem to share the view that the crisis could, paradoxically, bring the EU much closer to a political union. The crisis, they argue, cannot be resolved without a much tighter coordination of the fiscal and social policies of the members of the Eurozone, even if this implies additional limits on national sovereignty. Also the leader of the opposition Social Democratic Party, Sigmar Gabriel, is of the opinion

---

5 Hans Peter Ipsen, *Europäisches Gemeinschaftsrecht* (J.C.B. Mohr/Paul Siebeck 1972) 190–91.

6 Majone (n 3).

that the crisis calls for political union. Thinking of the EU as an actor on the international scene, Commission President Barroso, in an article in the *Observer* of 13 November 2011 wrote that the crisis confronts Europeans with the choice: 'either unite or face irrelevance'. The status quo will not do and the EU must 'move on to something new and better'. What Barroso suggests with his dilemma of union or irrelevance is stated explicitly by high level practitioners of European law and by noted scholars:

> At the scale of the world individual member states are geographically small, economically fragile, and demographically in a declining and ageing trend. In the future they will need the help of the EU to meet these problems. The EU must be able to help, but with its present institutions and procedures the EU is slow, heavy, and not flexible enough.[7]

> The peoples of Europe must learn that they can only preserve their welfare-state model of society and the diversity of their nation-state cultures by joining forces and working together. They must pool their resources if they want to exert any kind of influence on the international political agenda and the solution of global problems. To abandon European unification now would be to quit the world stage for good.[8]

That political, as well as economic, union is necessary if Europe is to count more in the world is one of the oldest, but also one of the most fallacious, arguments of the rhetoric of European integration. Already in the 1930s Ortega y Gasset in his *Rebellion of the Masses* had asked 'who rules the world?'. His answer was that only a United States of Europe would make it possible for the Old Continent to play again a commanding role in the world. The Spanish philosopher gave no indication of how that ambitious aim was to be achieved, however. The ambitions of contemporary writers are more modest, but they too fail to provide any indication of how the political union of Europe is to be achieved. Monetary union was supposed to be the royal road to political union but instead it has produced a level of division and conflict never experienced before within the EU. Moreover, it is fallacious to assume that size is needed to play a significant international role. Switzerland, the Scandinavian countries, not to mention Luxembourg, have achieved much better results, both domestically and internationally, than other, far larger, European countries. Tiny Switzerland, for example, in addition to being the home of some of the most important international organizations, is the home base for international leaders in a number of industries, including pharmaceuticals,

---

7   Jean Claude Piris, 'It is Time for the Euro Area to Develop Further Closer Cooperation Among its Members' *Jean Monnet Working Paper 05/11*, NYU Institute on the Park (2011).

8   Peter Bofinger, Jürgen Habermas and Julian Nida-Rümelin, 'Einspruch gegen die Fassandendemokratie' *Frankfurter Allgemeine Zeitung* (4 August 2012).

finance, and food. What counts is not size but social and cultural cohesion, political stability, shared objectives, and great flexibility – precisely the qualities lacking in the present EU. The proof of this is the fact that the members of the EU have made the least progress in unification precisely in those areas where size and abundant resources would count most: foreign and security policy.

2. Monetary Union: Public Good or Club Good?

Before the present crisis the more or less official position was that the degree of integration reached in the EU was sufficient to guarantee the long-term survival of the monetary union: the EU did not have to become anything like a federal state. Monetary policy was viewed as something more similar to a microeconomic policy like anti-trust than to fiscal policy, and as such its design and implementation could be safely delegated to a 'non-majoritarian' institution with a clear and exclusive statutory mandate: price stability. 'Even were there to be a trade-off between price stability and employment', Otmar Issing wrote shortly before the beginning of the euro crisis, 'the ECB could not under any circumstances give it the slightest consideration'.[9] The crisis has made evident the socioeconomic embeddedness of monetary policy. The question today is whether we need a transfer of competences in all major policy areas – so that the EU does in fact become a sort of superstate – or whether this transfer can be selective. Something else, never openly discussed in the past despite its obvious importance, has now become clear: for the Eurozone to survive the member states must continue to perceive that the benefits of monetary union still exceed the costs. Even today there is a good deal of opposition, at least at the official level, to such a utilitarian view of EMU. Hence the ECB's favoured slogan 'the euro is forever', and the attempt by some political leaders to make the future of European integration depend on the survival of the common currency.

The view of monetary union as an obligation is particularly clear in the case of the new member states, which must join the Eurozone, as soon as they satisfy the requisite criteria, as part of their acceptance of the *acquis communautaire*. At least, this is the theory. In practice, the political willingness in favour of significant enlargement of the Eurozone to include the new member states has declined. As a result, it is likely that the Maastricht convergence criteria will be used as an instrument to postpone this entry.[10] But the new member states are also starting to have second thoughts about the net benefits of membership in an exclusive but expensive club. One of the earliest and clearest expressions of these doubts has been given by Slawomir Skrzypek, the late president of the National Bank of Poland. Shortly before dying in the Smolensk air crash in which the President of Poland and numerous other personalities lost their life, Mr Skrzypek published

---

9   Otmar Issing, *The Birth of the Euro* (Cambridge University Press 2008) 63.

10   Paul De Grauwe, *Economics of Monetary Union* (Oxford University Press 2007) 161.

an article in the *Financial Times* of 13 April 2010, titled 'Poland should not rush to sign up to the euro'. In this article, the central banker pointed out that in 2010, when Europe was plagued by concerns over excessive public debt in Greece and elsewhere, the Polish economy was projected to grow 2.7 per cent, accelerating to 3 per cent in 2011. One important reason for this, he wrote,

> is that as a non-member of the euro, Poland has been able to profit from the flexibility of the zloty exchange rate in a way that has helped growth and lowered the current account deficit without importing inflation ... Because Poland's currency is not bound by the Exchange Rate Mechanism II, we have been able to adjust the value of the zloty in line with domestic requirements.[11]

The decade-long story of peripheral euro members drastically losing competitiveness, Mr Skrzypek added, has been a salutary lesson. The 'Greek imbroglio' (as he called it) shows that there is no substitute for countries' own efforts to improve competitiveness, boost fiscal discipline and increase labour and product market flexibility – whether or not they are in the Eurozone. This banker's advice to his fellow citizens:

> [W]e must temper the wish to adopt the euro with necessary prudence. We should not tie ourselves to timetables that may be counterproductive. Solid economic growth and sensible policies are possible both within and outside the euro zone. Nations in a hurry to join the euro may end up missing their overriding objectives.[12]

A cautious approach similar to the one suggested by Mr Skrzypek has been followed by Sweden since it joined the EU in 1995. This country, not a member of the EU when the Maastricht Treaty was ratified, could not obtain a *de jure* opt-out from EMU, like the United Kingdom and Denmark did. Sweden however asked, and was granted, a derogation – in practice, a *de facto* opt-out – when it became a member of the Union. Swedish leaders have decided that future membership of their country in the Eurozone shall depend, not on EU prescriptions but on the approval of the voters in a popular referendum. Since the beginning of the sovereign-debt crisis opinion polls show growing popular opposition to joining monetary union, so that the prospect of Swedish membership in EMU keeps receding into the future. According to a survey conducted in July 2010, 61 per cent of the Swedes were against joining monetary union; one year earlier the negative votes were only 44 per cent. One important reason for the growing opposition to the euro is the fact that Sweden, like Poland, has weathered the financial crisis rather well, also thanks to its independent monetary policy. The Swedish economy, which is heavily

---

11 Slawomir Skrzypek, 'Poland should not rush to sign up to the euro' *Financial Times* (13 April 2010) 11.

12 Skrzypek (n 11).

dependent on exports, has profited significantly from the weakness of the Krone. Recently, Sweden had the lowest budget deficit of all EU member states and one of the highest rates of economic growth, providing additional evidence in support of Mr Skrzypek's assessment of the advantages of an independent monetary policy.

It is quite possible that a number of countries from Central and Eastern Europe may decide to follow Mr Skrzypek's advice and join Sweden in the camp of the *de facto* opt-outs. The Czech Republic and Hungary have already linked their membership in the Eurozone to approval by popular referendum or by a supermajority in the national parliament. Moreover, in a greatly enlarged and increasingly heterogeneous monetary union even the original members of the Eurozone may conclude that the policies of the ECB no longer correspond to their national conditions as well as they did before the enlargement. This is because the original members will more often than today be outliers, in terms of inflation and output, compared to the average that the ECB will have to focus on. As a consequence, some older members may realize that the calculus of the benefits and costs of monetary union has become less favourable.[13]

One final point on the present situation of the Eurozone. Economic historians know that monetary unions that are not supported by sufficient political integration are fragile. What is perhaps less clearly recognized is that also the members of incomplete monetary unions, like the EMU, become fiscally fragile. This is because the members are no longer sovereign states or components of a federation. The big challenge for the Eurozone, wrote Martin Wolf in the *Financial Times* of 3 May 2011, is to resolve this contradiction. Given the state of public opinion throughout Europe, he notes, the federal solution is politically impossible. 'Does this mean that the members of the eurozone can resolve the contradiction only by recovering their sovereignty in the monetary field?' In the following pages I shall argue that this is not the only alternative, provided monetary union is no longer viewed as a legal and political obligation but as an option open to all countries which expect to benefit from it. In the language to be introduced in a later section, a common currency should be viewed as a 'club good', rather than as a public good. Before considering alternative models of integration, however, it is important to discuss another issue which is important for understanding the fragility, not only of the Eurozone but of the traditional integration method itself.

3. The Euro Crisis and the Problem of the Reluctant Hegemon

In his classic study of the 1929–1939 world depression Charles P Kindleberger writes: 'for the world economy to be stabilized, there has to be a stabilizer, one stabilizer'.[14] The explanation of the great depression proposed by the noted

---

13   De Grauwe (n 10) 97–101.

14   Charles Kindleberger, *The World in Depression* (University of California Press 1973) 305.

economist and economic historian is that the severity of the crisis was caused by the British inability and the United States unwillingness to do what was needed in a timely fashion. Britain had stabilized the world economic system in the nineteenth century and up to 1913. But in 1929 the British couldn't and the United States wouldn't do the same: because of domestic concerns the country able to provide leadership stood aside. In theory, a joint Anglo-American leadership in the economic affairs of the world would have been possible, but Kindleberger points out that according to most economists arrangements such as duopoly or bilateral monopoly are unstable, and the same seems to be true in politics. The reason: 'With a duumvirate, a troika, or slightly wider forms of collective responsibility, the buck has no place to stop'.[15] These observations served to lay the foundations of what came to be called the theory of hegemonic stability. The two central propositions of the theory are: (1) that order in world politics is typically created by a single dominant power and (2) that the maintenance of world order requires continued hegemony.[16] Hegemony is defined as preponderance of material resources: 'a situation wherein the products of a given core state are produced so efficiently that they are by and large competitive even in other core states, and therefore the given core state will be the primary beneficiary of a maximally free world market'.[17]

Kindleberger noted that 'leadership is a word with negative connotations in the 1970s when participation in decision-making is regarded as more aesthetic'. In those years the leadership of the United States was beginning to slip, and the American scholar was not sure that 'the rising strength of Europe in an enlarged European Economic Community will be accompanied by an assertion of leadership ... and assumption of responsibility for the stability of the world system'.[18] As we know, neither the EEC nor the EC or the EU even tried to assume responsibility for the stability of the world system. However, the crisis of monetary union has made clear that only Germany, within the present Union, could provide the needed leadership – not for the world system but at least for the old continent. The attempt to establish a sort of French-German duopoly – in the short *Merkozy* interlude – did not work, as Kindleberger would have predicted.

Germany is neither feeble like the UK in the inter-war period nor irresponsible like the USA in the same period. In spite of the (limited) leadership it has provided and is still providing in the present crisis, however, it is extremely reluctant to play the role of the hegemon – for very good reasons having to do with history but also with the ideology of the European integration project. A key element of that ideology is the basic equality and equal dignity of all the member states, from the smallest to the largest. This principle of formal and (to the extent possible) substantive equality has inspired all the European treaties and also day-to-day practice. It is reflected in the design and *modus operandi* of the European

---

15   Kindleberger (n 14) 299–300.
16   Robert O Keohane, *After Hegemony* (Princeton University Press 1984).
17   I Wallerstein, cited in Keohane (n 16) 33.
18   Kindleberger (n 14) 307–8.

institutions. Indeed, an important, if tacit, responsibility of the Commission is to ensure that the interests of the smaller member states are sufficiently taken into consideration – which explains why the strongest supporters of this particular European institution have always been the small countries. Clear evidence of the importance the smaller member states attach to membership in the Commission is the promise made by the European Council after the failure of the first Irish referendum on the Lisbon Treaty to abandon the planned reduction of the number of Commissioners in order to facilitate the success of the second referendum. The price of the concession is not negligible, however: as Piris points out, a Commission with 27 (or 28) members is hardly capable of taking decisions.[19]

Given this pervasive mutual mistrust, it is almost unimaginable that the members of the Union, large or small, would accept the necessity of a hegemon, even though Germany, *de facto,* already conditions the economies of the other member states in important respects. Thus Paul De Grauwe, a distinguished monetary economist, maintains that when the Federal Republic in the late 1990s dramatically improved its competitive position within the Eurozone, this was at the expense of other members which saw their competitive position deteriorate. It can be said, he adds, that Germany exported its problem of a lack of competitiveness to other member states. Since 1999 this country has followed a tight policy of wage moderation while the rest of the Eurozone maintained more or less constant wage increases of around 3 per cent per year. Thus, each year Germany tended to improve its competitive position *vis-à-vis* the rest of the Eurozone – a trend partly explained by the fact that the power of German labour unions has declined significantly, more so than in other Eurozone countries. Other countries with particularly close economic ties to Germany are forced to intensify their policies of wage moderation, inducing the leading country again to restrict wage increases. A vicious circle may result when everybody attempts to improve their competitiveness at the expense of others. As in the case of the so-called race to the bottom in environmental policy, the final outcome is that these countries will not have improved their competitive position, but will have adopted wage policies that do not correspond to the preferences of their citizens.[20] At the same time, the distance between the leading group and the other member states keeps growing. In fact, one of the unanticipated consequences of monetary union has been the extent to which the competitive positions of the members of the Eurozone have diverged. Italy, Spain, Portugal, Greece, and also France, have lost a significant amount of competitiveness. Germany, Austria and a few other northern countries have gained a significant amount of competitiveness.[21]

In a recent essay ('Deutschland muss fuehren oder aus dem Euro austreten', *Spiegel On Line* of 9 September 2012) the Hungarian-born American financier George Soros argued that in order to avoid a definitive split of the Eurozone into

19 Piris (n 7).
20 Majone (n 3) 135–6.
21 De Grauwe (n 10) 32–3.

creditor and debt countries, and thus a likely collapse of the EU itself, Germany must resolve a basic dilemma: either assume the role of the benevolent hegemon ('*wohlwollender Hegemon*') or else leave the Eurozone. If Germany were to choose the second alternative the euro would depreciate, and since all debts are denominated in the common currency, their weight, for the countries remaining in the Eurozone, would be reduced in real terms. The debtor countries would export more because of the reduced (real) price of their products, and import less; hence their competitiveness would be restored. Creditor countries, on the other hand, would suffer losses on their investments in the Eurozone and also on the credits accumulated within the euro-clearing system. The end result, according to Soros, would be the fulfilment of Keynes's dream of an international monetary system in which both creditors and debtors share responsibility for the stability of the system. At the same time Europe would escape a threatening economic depression. But Germany could achieve the same result at lower cost if it was willing to play the role of the benevolent hegemon. Such a role would entail two conditions: first, debtor and creditor countries should be able to refinance their debts on near equal terms; and, second, a nominal growth rate of up to five per cent should be aimed at. Through growth Europe could reduce the burden of its debts, but the level of inflation would probably exceed what the Bundesbank is prepared to accept. At any rate, both conditions could be satisfied only with significant progress on the road to a political EU in which Germany accepts the responsibilities implied by its role as the leader. Regardless of Germany's decision, both alternatives are preferable to the present approach, which can only lead to a long depression, to political and social conflicts, and finally to the breakdown not only of the euro but of the EU.

Soros concludes that if the members of the Eurozone cannot live together except by pushing the Union into a long-lasting depression, then a consensual separation of debtor and creditor countries seems preferable. Were a debtor country to leave the Eurozone, this could improve somewhat its competitiveness but the country would find it hard to service its euro-denominated debt, with incalculable consequences for the financial markets, especially in the case of large countries like Spain or Italy. If instead Germany were to give up the euro, leaving the Eurozone in the hands of the debtor countries, all problems that now appear to be insoluble, could be resolved through depreciation, improved competitiveness, and a new status of the ECB as lender of last resort. The common market would survive, but the relative position of Germany and of other creditor countries that might wish to leave the Eurozone would change from the winning to the losing side. They would be exposed to strong competition from the Eurozone, and would suffer significant losses from their euro-denominated assets and their credits under the Target-2 clearing system. After the initial shock, however, Europe would manage to get out of the present debt trap. Both groups of countries could avoid such problems if only Germany was willing to assume the role of the benevolent hegemon. As already mentioned, however, this would require the more or less equal treatment of debtor and creditor countries, and a much higher rate of growth, with consequent inflation. These may well be unacceptable conditions for the German leaders and, even more, for their voters. Thus it is unlikely that the EU will move towards a situation of hegemonic stability.

4. Differentiated Integration

With the worsening of the euro crisis and the growing diversity of EU membership many informed observers see some form of differentiated integration no longer as an option – as was the case with the 'enhanced cooperation' envisaged by the Amsterdam, Nice and Lisbon Treaties – but as a necessity. The deepening crisis is said to require closer fiscal and economic coordination by the members of the Eurozone. At the same time a still expanding membership is transforming the EU into an entirely new entity: Croatia, the latest member of the EU, is likely to be followed by most, if not all, other Western Balkan countries – Albania, Bosnia-Herzegovina, Kosovo, Macedonia, Montenegro, and Serbia – possibly also Georgia, Moldova, even Ukraine; though almost certainly not Turkey. 'Differentiated integration' is a generic and neutral term used 'to denote variations in the application of European policies or variations in the level and intensity of participation in European policy regimes'.[22] The label applies to several possible models such as 'multi-speed Europe', 'Europe à la carte', and 'variable geometry', to mention only the most important ones. The model of two-speed or multi-speed Europe assumes that all member states would do the same things but not necessarily at the same pace. On the other hand, integration à la carte presupposes some general rules accepted by everybody but grants freedom of choice to each member state on whether to participate in some policies. According to this model, there would be common European policies in areas where the member states have a common interest, but not otherwise. Thus integration à la carte diverges significantly from the philosophy of enhanced cooperation which allows voluntary associations of member states only to the extent that they 'further the objectives of the Union and of the Community, protect and serve their interests, and reinforce the integration process'.

Different meanings have been attached to the label 'variable geometry'. In the meaning most relevant to the present discussion the label refers to a situation where a subset of member states undertakes some project, for instance an industrial or technological project in which other members of the Union are not interested, or to which they are unable to make a positive contribution. Since, by assumption, not all member states are willing to participate in all EU programmes, this model combines the criterion of differentiation by country, as in multi-speed integration, and differentiation by function or project – as in integration *à la carte*. Still, all member states are supposed to respect a core of binding rules, but no broader

---

22   Helen Wallace, 'Differentiated Integration' in Desmond Dinan (ed), *Encyclopedia of the European Union* (Lynne Rienner Publishers 1998) 137.

commitments than those implied by the rules. Monetary union (with the British and Danish *de jure* opt-outs) and the Schengen Agreement (with the British and Irish opt-outs, and Denmark's partial opt-out) are cited as concrete examples of variable geometry.

Unfortunately, the precise conditions under which a particular model applies are seldom spelled out. For example, it has been argued (for example, by the Belgian political leader Leo Tindemans) that the idea of multi-speed Europe has found application in the design of monetary union, but this interpretation only reflects the intention of the architects of EMU, namely that all member states should adopt the common currency, sooner or later. In fact, it is far from clear whether the countries which opted out of the monetary union, in particular the UK, intend to join the Eurozone in the foreseeable future, if ever. To speak in this case of multi-speed Europe is only to express a wish; 'variable geometry', or even integration à la carte, are the more appropriate labels. In this connection it is interesting to note that already in the 1970s Ralf Dahrendorf, while still a member of the European Commission, had severely criticized the European institution for their excessive reliance on the Community method, and had argued that integration à la carte, or something like it, should become the general rule rather than the exception if we wish to prevent continuous demands for special treatment, destroying in the long run the coherence of the entire system.[23]

The need for closer cooperation by the members of the Eurozone is explicitly acknowledged by Article 136 TFEU: 'In order to ensure the proper functioning of economic and monetary union ... the Council shall adopt measures specific to those Member States whose currency is the euro'. The Council will be able to take measures 'to strengthen the coordination and surveillance of their [members of the Eurozone] budgetary discipline' and 'to set out economic policy guidelines for them, while ensuring that they are compatible with those adopted for the whole of the Union and are kept under surveillance'. It should be noted that measures adopted on the basis of Article 136 TFEU in order to strengthen the coordination and surveillance of budgetary discipline, will become part of the *acquis* and thus will have to be applied to all future members of the Eurozone. On the other hand, only the full Council with its 27 members can take legally binding decisions, on the basis of proposals from the Commission. The ministers of the members of the Eurozone can only 'meet informally'. According to Article 138, however, it us up to the members of the Eurozone to decide to have a unified representation in all international institutions, including the International Monetary Fund and the World Bank. According to Piris, 'if euro countries decided to use fully the extensive potentialities offered by Articles 136 and 138 TFEU, this would entail a dramatic change of the EU ... the establishment of a "two-speed Europe" would not need any other legal text to become a reality'.[24] Presumably, it would be a two-speed Europe with the Eurozone as the 'hard core' group. Also other students

23   Majone (n 3) 216.
24   Piris (n 7) 39.

of European integration see the members of the Eurozone as the group which should cooperate more closely in different matters – but not on a case-by-case basis – in order to move faster than the other member states of the EU. Thus, Bofinger et al in a much cited article in the *Frankfurter Allgemeine Zeitung* write: 'If we wish to avoid both a return to monetary nationalism and a permanent euro crisis, then we need to do now what we failed to do at the time of the euro's launch: we need to begin the process of moving towards political union, beginning with the core Europe of the 17 EMU member countries'.[25]

This view of the present euro group as the spearhead of deeper integration raises several questions which so far have remained unanswered. To begin with, new institutions may have to be set up since it is not clear how the EP and the Commission, whose composition includes the entire membership of the EU, could exercise their functions for a smaller group of states. Hence a new treaty would be required, but this additional treaty should not establish a new international organization but only new forms of cooperation among the participating members. For example, Jean-Claude Piris proposes a new 'European Parliamentary Organ' and a new 'Administrative Authority', but not a new Court. The Parliamentary Organ would be established by the national parliaments, rather than being directly elected, but would have something which the EP lacks: the power of legislative initiative. The major task of the Administrative Authority would be to control the correct application of all measures adopted on the basis of the additional treaty, and to bring infringement action against the participating states, if needed. On the other hand, this author is against the establishment of a new court because of the risk of conflicts with the Court of Justice of the EU. However it is not difficult to imagine that conflicts could also arise between the new institutions and the European Commission or the EP. On balance, it might be preferable to work out special arrangements so that the avant-garde group could still rely on the Commission and the EP, perhaps in a different configuration.

But these are technicalities. The real problem with the idea of the members of the Eurozone forming the avant-garde of a two-speed Europe is that the present members of the euro group are about as different – economically, politically and socially – as the entire membership of the EU. Also their reasons for joining EMU were quite different: most, if not all governments, supported the project not for the sake of more and deeper integration, but in the hope of getting help in solving their own domestic problems. Indeed, it could be argued that the euro crisis has made the heterogeneity within this assumed core group a good deal more evident that the diversity of the other members of the Union. The key principle holding together Piris's avant-garde group is that all participating states should be fully committed to participate in all areas of closer cooperation. The additional, legally binding, commitments could include: stricter budgetary rules, together with close examinations of draft national budgets by the other members of the group; an enforceable maximum level of budgetary deficits; and a commitment to

---

25   Bofinger, Habermas and Nida-Rümelin (n 8).

limit the level of public debt, preferably through an amendment in each national constitution, with controls by an independent body. Is it realistic to assume that all the members of the Eurozone would voluntarily agree on a set of policies in which they would accept such closer cooperation? Piris himself is not sure:

> Would Germany, the Netherlands or Finland agree with Greece, Ireland or Portugal on a common list of social, fiscal, and economic (legally binding) measures to be taken? Would Germany accept common endeavours in the military domain, or in EU penal legislation? The thrust of the problem is here.[26]

The available evidence indicates the difficulty of finding agreement even on a more limited list of potential common measures – as shown by the negative reactions to the 'Pact for Competitiveness' conceived by Germany in 2011 in an attempt to force all Eurozone members to adhere to sound fiscal and social policies. Biting criticism of the Pact came from across the EU: from long-time members of the Union and from the new members of Central and Eastern Europe; from small and large countries; from debt-ridden southern countries and fiscally virtuous northern countries; even from the head of the European Commission, who expressed concerns that the Competitiveness Pact would undermine the single market. It is true that because of the debt crisis countries like Greece, Portugal, Ireland and Spain adopted tough and legally binding measures of fiscal discipline, but such measures were forced on them, not freely agreed to, and as such were deeply resented. Indeed, one has to go back to the years immediately following the end of World War II to find such levels of mutual resentment between the publics of the southern and the northern members of the would-be core Europe – surely one of the most unintended and undesirable consequences of monetary union. Moreover, it should be kept in mind that monetary union is part of the *acquis*, which means that in the future the membership of the Eurozone will be even more heterogeneous than it is today.

5. Functional *vs.* Territorial Integration: A Post-National 'Europe of Clubs'

In other words, the severity of the monetary crisis should not make us forget that the integration project is facing another, potentially even more explosive, problem: the growing economic, social and political diversity of an EU whose membership is still growing. This is the mistake committed by those who, like Piris, Bofinger, or Habermas propose a two-speed Europe, with the members of the Eurozone forming the avant-garde. Not only is the present group heterogeneous enough; in the future it is bound to become even more diverse, unless the dogma of the *acquis* is given up – a possibility not even considered by these and other scholars. Thus, if we want to think constructively about the future after the crisis of monetary union, we must consider alternatives that are reasonably robust against the two main

---

26   Piris (n 7) 57.

problems the EU is facing today: excessive centralization in some key domains, and a level of internal diversity that is changing the very nature of the enterprise. Piris saw the problem clearly even though his proposal of a two-speed Europe does not adequately reflect his insight:

> Although the EU includes 27 Member States at very different levels of socioeconomic development, the current decision-making system is still largely based on the principle of 'one-decision-fits-all' inherited from the time when the aim was to establish a uniform common market among the Six rather homogeneous founding countries.[27]

From this perspective, the model of integration à la carte looks certainly more flexible, hence more robust, than the two- or multi-speed alternative. As already mentioned, for Dahrendorf, writing in the 1970s, integration à la carte meant that there would be common European policies in areas where the member states have a common interest, but not otherwise. This, he said, must become the general rule rather than the exception if we wish to prevent continuous demands for special treatment, destroying in the long run the coherence of the entire system – a prescient anticipation of the present practice of moving ahead by granting opt-outs from treaty obligations. Unfortunately, none of the forms of differentiated integration discussed by Dahrendorf, Tindemans, and other writers in the 1970s were based on, or inspired by, any formal social-scientific theory.

All concepts of differentiated integration were worked out and presented as *ad hoc* responses to concerns raised by the growing number and diversity of the members of the European Community, and then of the EU. In preparation for the 'big bang' enlargement at the beginning of the new century no serious attempt was made to reduce or compensate the risks entailed by a high and growing level of heterogeneity among the member states. The more optimistic Euro-leaders – among whom figured prominent members of the German government and of the European Commission – claimed that geographical widening and policy deepening were not just compatible, but mutually reinforcing aspects of the integration process. Other European leaders who neither shared this simplistic view, nor wished to follow the eurosceptics in supporting enlargement as a way of preventing further 'deepening', tended to view enlargement primarily as an organizational or managerial problem, to be solved by better institutional design and more effective decision-making procedures. What all leaders were reluctant to admit, at least in public, was that each enlargement of the EU necessarily changes the calculus of the benefits and the costs of integration for all the member states – the reduction of transaction costs made possible by harmonized rules, on the one hand, and the welfare losses entailed by rules that are less adequately tuned to the resources and preferences of each member state, on the other.[28]

---

27 Piris (n 7) 6.
28 Majone (n 3) 215–16.

Concerning the benefits and costs of policy harmonization the economic theory of clubs, originally developed by James Buchanan (1965), has been applied by Alessandra Casella (1996) to study the interaction between expanding markets and the provision of standards. She argues, *inter alia*, that if we think of standards as being developed by communities of users, then 'opening trade will modify not only the standards but also the coalitions that express them. As markets ... expand and become more heterogeneous, different coalitions will form across national borders, and their number will rise'.[29] The relevance of these arguments extends well beyond the narrow area of standard-setting. In fact, Casella's emphasis on heterogeneity among traders as the main force against harmonization and for the multiplication of 'clubs' suggests an attractive theoretical basis for the study of differentiated integration in the EU. For this we need to recall a few definitions and key concepts of the theory.

Pure public goods, such as national defence or environmental quality, are characterized by two properties: first, it does not cost anything – leaving aside eventual congestion costs – for an additional individual to enjoy the benefits of the public goods, once they are produced (*joint-supply property*); and, second, it is difficult or impossible to exclude individuals from the enjoyment of such goods (*non-excludability*). A '*club good*' is a public good from whose benefits individuals may be (or may wish to be) excluded – only the joint-supply property holds. An association established to provide excludable public goods is a *club*. Two elements determine the optimal size of a club. One is the cost of producing the club good – in a large club this cost is shared over more members. The second element is the cost to each club member of the good not meeting precisely his or her individual needs or preferences. The latter cost is likely to increase with the size of the club. The optimal size is determined by the point where the marginal benefit from the addition of one new member, that is the reduction in the per capita cost of producing the good, equals the marginal cost caused by a mismatch between the characteristics of the good and the preferences of the individual club members. If the preferences and the technologies for the provision of club goods are such that the number of clubs that can be formed in a society of given size is large, then an efficient allocation of such excludable public goods through the voluntary association of individuals into clubs is possible. With many alternative clubs available each individual can guarantee herself a satisfactory balance of benefits and costs, since any attempt to discriminate against her would induce her exit into a competing club – or the creation of a new one. The important question is: what happens as the complexity of the society increases, perhaps as the result of the integration of previously separate markets? It has been shown that under plausible hypotheses the number of clubs tends to increase as well, since the greater diversity of needs and preferences makes it efficient to produce a broader range of club goods, for instance, product standards. The two main forces driving the results of Casella's model are heterogeneity among the economic agents,

---

29   Majone (n 3) 149.

and transaction costs – the costs of trading under different standards. Harmonization is the optimal strategy when transaction costs are high enough, relative to gross returns, to prevent a partition of the community of users into two clubs that reflect their needs more precisely. Hence harmonization occurs in response to market integration, but possibly only for an intermediate range of productivity in the production of standards, and when heterogeneity is not too great.

Think now of a society composed not of individuals, but of independent states. Associations of independent states (alliances, leagues, confederations) are typically voluntary, and their members are exclusively entitled to enjoy certain benefits produced by the association, so that the economic theory of clubs is applicable to this situation. In fact, since excludability is more easily enforced in the context envisaged here, many goods that are purely public at the national level become club goods at the international level.[30] The club goods in question could be collective security, policy coordination, common technical standards – or a common currency. In these and many other cases, countries unwilling to share the costs are usually excluded from the benefits of inter-state cooperation. Now, as an association of states expands, becoming more diverse in its preferences, the cost of uniformity in the provision of such goods – harmonization – can escalate dramatically. The theory predicts an increase in the number of voluntary associations to meet the increased demand of club goods more precisely tailored to the different requirements of various subsets of more homogeneous states. Of the integration models mentioned above, integration *à la carte* and 'variable geometry' come closest to the situation modelled by the theory of clubs.

Both integration models refer to situations where a subset of member states undertakes some project, for instance an industrial or technological project in which other members of the Union are not interested, or to which they are unable to make a positive contribution. Basically, all these models are updated versions of the functional (rather than territorial) approach to international governance advocated by David Mitrany in the 1940s. A territorial union, he argued, 'would bind together some interests which are not of common concern to the group, while it inevitably cut asunder some interests of common concern to the group and those outside it'. To avoid such 'twice-arbitrary surgery' it is necessary to proceed by 'binding together those interests which are common, where they are common, and to the extent to which they are common'. Thus the essential principle of a functional organization of international activities 'is that activities would be selected specifically and organized separately, each according to its nature, to the conditions under which it has to operate, and to the needs of the moment'.[31] A comparison of Mitrany's functionalism with the neo-functionalism of Ernst Haas and Jean Monnet is outside the scope of this paper. I will only point out that while

---

30 Giandomenico Majone, *Dilemmas of European Integration* (Oxford University Press 2005) 20–21.

31 Citations in Mette Eilstrup-Sangiovanni, *Debates On European Integration* (Palgrave 2006) 57–8.

the aim of neo-functionalism was to achieve political integration by functional (economic) means, Mitrany was sceptical about the advantages of political union. His first objection to schemes for continental unions was that 'the closer the union the more inevitable would it be dominated by the more powerful member'.[32] This is a point which neither Haas nor Monnet seems to have considered at all, but which is directly linked to our previous discussion of Germany as a potential hegemon.

A 'Europe of Clubs' certainly does not exclude the possibility of large projects supported by all the member states – as long as there is clear evidence (by referendum, supermajorities in national parliaments, etc.) of sufficient popular support. This is precisely what Dahrendorf meant when he said that in his model of integration à la carte there would be common European policies in areas where the member states have a common interest, but not otherwise. The Single Market project, for example, seems to enjoy broad support even in so-called euro-sceptic countries. Hence, this would be a natural starting point from which to assess the extent of democratic acceptance of further movement towards closer integration. Once decisions about the extent of integration are no longer taken *in camera* but are submitted to the decision of the voters, however, the provision of correct information about expected benefits and costs, about successes and failures, becomes truly indispensable. Even in cases of a project like the Single Market, the general public should know that the promise of reaching that goal by 1992 is still far from being fulfilled. The aim of the internal market project was to open the internal borders of the EU to the free movement of goods, services, capital, and workers, as within a nation state. This aim, writes Piris:

> is presented as having been more or less achieved, but the truth is that it is not complete, especially in the services sector. In many areas the Single Market exists in the books but, in practice, multiple barriers and regulatory obstacles fragment the intra-EU trade and hamper economic initiative and innovation.[33]

In fact, Piris points out, 'the development of a single market in services' was still one of the proposals made by Mario Monti in 2010 in a report commissioned by the president of the Commission. But what the member states of the EU need today is not more top-down, one-size-fits-all harmonization, but more flexibility and inter-state competition. This is particularly true of those countries which experienced severe losses of competitiveness after joining EMU, see Section 2.

6. Competitive Governments

In his path-breaking study of *Competitive Governments* the Canadian economist Albert Breton criticizes the EU for what he calls its excessive policy harmonization:

---

32   Eilstrup-Sangiovanni (n 31) 47.
33   Piris (n 7) 15.

> I believe that the European Union is quite stable but that the stability has been acquired by the virtual suppression of intercountry competition through excessive policy harmonization … To prevent the occurrence of instability, competition is minimized through the excessive harmonization of a substantial fraction of social, economic, and other policies … If one compares the degree of harmonization in Europe with that in Canada, the United States, and other federations, one is impressed by the extent to which it is greater in Europe than in the federations.[34]

Today we know that even 'excessive' policy harmonization has not been sufficient to ensure the stability of the EU. Indeed, one could argue that excessive harmonization has been the immediate cause of the present instability. Monetary union is, after all, an example of total harmonization if with this terminology we denote measures designed to regulate exhaustively a given problem to the exclusion of previously existing national measures.[35] In this sense, total harmonization corresponds to what in the language of US public law is referred to as federal pre-emption, and for a long time the ECJ supported total harmonization as a foundation stone in the building of the common market. This is not to say that no attempts were made to reduce the dependency on harmonization as the main tool of integration. The principle of mutual recognition was indeed supposed to reduce the need of ex ante, bureaucratic harmonization, and to facilitate regulatory competition among the member states. Supposedly a cornerstone of the Single Market programme, mutual recognition requires member states to recognize regulations drawn by other EU members as being essentially equivalent to their own, allowing activities that are lawful in one member state to be freely pursued throughout the Union. In this way, a virtuous circle of regulatory competition would be stimulated, which should raise the quality of all regulation, and drive out rules offering protection that consumers do not, in fact, require. The end result would be ex post harmonization, achieved through competitive processes rather than by administrative measures. However, the high hopes raised by the *Cassis de Dijon* judgment and by what appeared to be the Commission's enthusiastic endorsement of the Court's doctrine were largely disappointed. For political, ideological, and bureaucratic reasons, ex post, market-driven harmonization was never allowed to seriously challenge the dominant position of the centralized, top-down version. While the *Cassis de Dijon* doctrine was greeted enthusiastically at a time when the priority was to meet the deadlines of the Single Market ('Europe 92') project, institutional and political interests militate against wholehearted support of mutual recognition and regulatory competition. Instead of viewing competition as a discovery procedure (Hayek), the tendency has always been to

---

34 Albert Breton, *Competitive Governments* (Cambridge University Press 1998) 275–6.

35 Stephen Weatherill, *Law and Integration in the European Union* (Clarendon Press 1995).

assert that integration can be only one way if one wants to prevent a 'Europe of Bits and Pieces'.[36]

It is true that rules on market competition are a constituent part of the EU economy, but I have argued that the reason for the importance attached to them by the founding fathers was utilitarian, rather than a commitment to a genuine free-market philosophy.[37] What is at any rate clear is that inter-jurisdictional competition – competition between different national approaches to economic and social regulation, or between national currencies, for example – has played no role in the integration process. Indeed, well-known EU lawyers like Stephen Weatherill maintain that competition among regulators is incompatible with the notion of undistorted competition in the internal European market to which reference is made in Article 3(g) of the EC Treaty. Hence the UK – the member state which has most consistently defended the benefits of inter-state competition – has been accused of subordinating individual rights and social protection to a free-market philosophy incompatible with the basic aspirations of the European Community/Union: 'Competition between regulators on this perspective is simply incompatible with the EC's historical mission'.[38] Widespread opposition to inter-jurisdictional competition explains why the principle of mutual recognition has played a more limited role in the process of European integration than originally expected.

Thus, it is not surprising that Albert Breton came to the conclusion that in the EU inter-country competition has been virtually suppressed through excessive policy harmonization. He also suggested that part of the widespread opposition to the idea that governments, national and international agencies, clubs, vertical and horizontal networks, and so on, should compete among themselves derives from the notion that competition is incompatible with, even antithetical to, cooperation. Breton cogently argues that this perception is mistaken. Excluding the case of collusion, cooperation and competition can and generally do coexist, so that the presence of one is no indication of the absence of the other. In particular, the observation of cooperation and coordination does not per se disprove that the underlying determining force may be competition. If one thinks of competition not as the *state* of affairs neoclassical theory calls 'perfect competition', but as an *activity* – à la Schumpeter, Hayek, and other Austrian economists who developed the model of *entrepreneurial competition* – then it becomes plain that 'the entrepreneurial innovation that sets the competitive process in motion, the imitation that follows, and the Creative Destruction that they generate are not inconsistent with cooperative behaviour and the coordination of activities'.[39] Given the appropriate competitive stimuli, political entrepreneurs, like their business

---

36   Deirdre Curtin, 'The Constitutional Structure of the Union: A Europe of Bits and Pieces' (1993) 30 *Common Market Law Review* 17.

37   Majone (n 3) 79–87.

38   Weatherill (n 35)180.

39   Breton (n 34) 33.

counterparts, will consult with colleagues at home and abroad, collaborate with them on certain projects, harmonize various activities, and in extreme cases integrate some operations – all actions corresponding to what is generally meant by cooperation and coordination.

In some governmental systems the potential movement of citizens from one jurisdiction to another offering comparable services at lower cost may act as a stimulus to intergovernmental competition. According to the so-called Tiebout hypothesis, inter-jurisdictional competition results in communities supplying the goods and services individuals demand, and producing them in an efficient manner.[40] This hypothesis may be extended to apply to governmental systems where Tiebout's potential entry and exit mechanisms do not work effectively, for instance because mobility is limited by language and/or cultural and social cleavages, as in the EU. The extension consists in assuming that the citizens of a jurisdiction can use information about the goods and services supplied in other jurisdictions as a benchmark to evaluate the performance of their own government. This is of course the idea underlying the Open Method of Coordination, but the results so far have been disappointing for several reasons. The excessive bureaucratization of the approach is one problem; another problem is that the OMC is under the complete control of the national executives. The crucial point, however, is that citizens are unable in practice to use information about the performance of other member states to induce their government to improve its own – the reason being that national parliaments are largely excluded from the OMC process. Thus, the stimulus to intergovernmental competition which is assumed by the proposed extension of the Tiebout hypothesis, is missing. Generally speaking, opposition to intergovernmental competition – for instance, in the area of regulatory policies, as in the above quote from Weatherill – can be traced to the persistence of state-centred thinking even among people who see the EU as the model of post-national Europe, see Section 1.

Such state-centred thinking pervades all attempts to solve the euro crisis by extending the centralization of policy competences in key areas, such as fiscal and social policy, still under the control of the national governments. This may turn out to be a serious mistake, fed in part by the notion that in a globalized world the nation state is becoming increasingly irrelevant.

7. Concluding Remarks on Globalization, the Nation State and Federalism

It is almost a commonplace of much pro-integration literature that the nation-states of Europe are too small to meet the challenges of globalization. Recall, from Section 1, Piris's lament about the smallness and fragility of the individual member states of the EU, and the warning of Bofinger, Habermas and Nida-Ruemelin that the peoples of Europe must pool their resources if they want to exert any kind of influence on the international political agenda. The conclusion is always that

---

40   Joseph E Stiglitz, *Economics of the Public Sector* (2nd edn, W.W. Norton 1988).

the European nation state can survive only by giving up most of the features that made possible the 'European Miracle' of the seventeenth and eighteenth centuries, and even the 'Concert of Europe' of the nineteenth century.[41] The standard recipe is 'More Europe', along the lines that have been followed for more than half a century: 'To abandon European unification now would be to quit the world stage for good'. As I suggested above, these scholars, like most other integrationist scholars and political leaders, attach too much importance to size and quantity and not enough to flexibility, to the benefits of institutions and policies tailored to specific national needs, to shared values and common traditions. They fail to perceive the deeper roots of 'The Competitive Advantage of Nations', to use the title of an important book by Michael Porter, well-known professor at the Harvard Business School and management consultant. In a globalized world, he writes:

> [t]he role of the home nation seems to be as strong as or stronger than ever. While globalization of competition might appear to make the nation less important, instead it seems to make it more important ... the home nation takes on growing significance because it is the source of the skills and technology that underpin competitive advantage.[42]

Again,

> As globalization of competition has intensified, some have begun to argue a diminished role for nations. Instead, internationalization and the removal of protection and other distortions to competition arguably make nations, if anything, more important. National differences in character and culture, far from being threatened by global competition, prove integral to success in it. Understanding the new and different role of nations in competition will be a task which occupies much of what follows.[43]

And with specific reference to European integration:

> Efforts at European unification are raising questions about whether the influence of nations on competition will diminish. Instead, freer trade will arguably make them more important. While the effective locus of competitive advantage may sometimes encompass regions that cross national borders ... Europe is unlikely to become a 'nation' from a competitive perspective. National differences in demand, factor creation, and other determinants will persist, and rivalry within nations will remain vital.[44]

---

41   Eric L Jones, *The European Miracle: Environments, Economies and Geopolitics in the History of Europe and Asia* (2nd edn, Cambridge University Press 1987).

42   Michael E Porter, *The Competitive Advantage of Nations* (The Free Press 1990).

43   Porter (n 42) 30.

44   Porter (n 42) 158–9.

Thus, the adjective 'post-national' which appears in the title of this chapter is not meant to suggest the end of the European nation state, but rather its reconstruction on the ruins of political and economic nationalism. The old nation state had to be subjected to a strict discipline in order to correct the mistakes of the past, and the Treaty of Rome provided that discipline, at least in the economic domain. Hence the importance of such Articles as 12–17 (elimination of customs duties); 30–37 (elimination of quantitative restrictions to intra-Community trade); 48–73 (free movement of persons, services, and capital); and 85–94 (rules against distortion of competition). These are key rules of negative integration. More recently, however, positive integration has often been identified with positive values like social protection and the correction of market failures, negative integration with deregulation and the narrow interests of traders. In fact, economic and other special interests may find it convenient to support measures of positive integration, while fundamental rights and the diffuse interests of consumers are often better protected by measures of negative integration.[45]

Following this line of reasoning one can also distinguish between positive and negative federalism: the former attempts to reproduce the traditional state at the supranational level; the latter is perfectly compatible with the negative law contained in Treaty of Rome. A political system is federal if (a) there is a hierarchy of governments, each level of government with a delineated scope of authority, and autonomous in its own; and (b) the autonomy of each government is institutionalized in a manner that makes federalism's restrictions self-enforcing. If we add three more conditions we have what I called negative federalism, and Barry Weingast calls, more descriptively, market-preserving federalism. The additional conditions are (c) member states (*nota bene*: not the higher level of government) have primary regulatory responsibility over the economy; (d) a common market is ensured, preventing the member states from using their regulatory authority to erect trade barriers against goods and services from other members; finally, (e) the member states face a hard budget constraint, that is, they have neither the ability to print money nor access to unlimited credit – the federal government cannot bail out a member state which faces fiscal problems.[46] The last condition was not present in the Rome Treaty but was introduced by the Maastricht Treaty. Condition (c), on the other hand, has been repeatedly violated since the Single European Act, and the various measures proposed to solve the euro crisis amount to an almost complete reversal of roles, with the higher-level government assuming the major responsibility over the economy of the Eurozone.

To conclude: there are different models of federalism as there are different modes of territorial and functional integration, and a great variety of forms of inter-state cooperation and of policy coordination. The great challenge for all students

---

45   Majone (n 30) 145–61.

46   Barry R Weingast, 'The Economic Role of Political Institutions: Market-Preserving Federalism and Economic Development' (1995) VII *The Journal of Law, Economics, & Organization* 1, 4–6.

of European integration – whether from a legal, an economic, or a political science perspective – is to devote more attention to this wealth of possibilities, and to the constraints which may restrict the range of possible choices at a particular moment in history. A unilinear approach to European integration is too simplistic to provide reliable guidance in the complex situation we are facing today.

Bibliography

Bofinger P, 'Dem Euro-Raum eine Chance' *Wirtschafts Woche* (22 May 2010) 40

Bofinger P, Habermas J and Nida-Rümelin J, 'Einspruch gegen die Fassandendemokratie' *Frankfurter Allgemeine Zeitung* (4 August 2012)

Breton A, *Competitive Governments* (Cambridge University Press 1998)

Buchanan JM 'An Economic Theory of Clubs' (1965) 32 *Economica* 1

Carr EH, *The Twenty Years' Crisis, 1919–1939* (Harper & Row 1964[1939])

Casella A, 'Free Trade and Evolving Standards' in JN Bhagwati, and RE Hudec (eds), *Fair Trade and Harmonization* (MIT Press 1996) 119

Curtin D, 'The Constitutional Structure of the Union: A Europe of Bits and Pieces' (1993) 30 *Common Market Law Review* 17

De Grauwe P, *Economics of Monetary Union* (Oxford University Press 2007)

Eilstrup-Sangiovanni M, *Debates On European Integration* (Palgrave 2006)

Ipsen HP, *Europäisches Gemeinschaftsrecht* (J.C.B. Mohr/Paul Siebeck 1972)

Issing O, *The Birth of the Euro* (Cambridge University Press 2008)

Jones EL, *The European Miracle: Environments, Economies and Geopolitics in the History of Europe and Asia* (2nd edn, Cambridge University Press 1987)

Keohane R, *After Hegemony* (Princeton University Press 1984)

Kindleberger C, *The World in Depression* (University of California Press 1973)

Lenaerts K and Van Nuffel P, *Constitutional Law of the European Union* (Sweet and Maxwell 1999)

MacCormick N, *Questioning Sovereignty: Law, State, and Nation in the European Commonwealth* (Oxford University Press 1999)

Majone G, *Dilemmas of European Integration* (Oxford University Press 2005)

—— *Europe As The Would-Be World Power: The EU At Fifty* (Cambridge University Press 2009)

Mueller H, 'Dann wird die Eurozone explodieren' *Spiegel Online* (20 December 2006) <www.spiegel.de/wirtschaft/us-staroekonom-dann-wird-die-eurozone-explodieren-a-455705.html> accessed 25 May 2013

Piris JC, 'It is Time for the Euro Area to Develop Further Closer Cooperation Among its Members' *Jean Monnet Working Paper 05/11*, NYU Institute on the Park (2011)

Porter ME, *The Competitive Advantage of Nations* (The Free Press 1990)

Rodrik D, *The Globalization Paradox* (Oxford University Press 2011)

Skrzypek S, 'Poland Should not Rush to Sign up to the Euro' *Financial Times* (New York 13 April 2010) 11

Stiglitz JE, *Economics of the Public Sector* (2nd edn, W.W. Norton 1988)

Tsoukalis L, *The New European Economy* (2nd revised edn, Oxford University Press 1993)

Wallace H, 'Differentiated Integration' in Desmond Dinan (ed), *Encyclopedia of the European Union* (Lynne Rienner Publishers 1998) 137–140

Weatherill S, *Law and Integration in the European Union* (Clarendon Press 1995)

Weingast BR, 'The Economic Role of Political Institutions: Market-Preserving Federalism and Economic Development' (1995) VII *The Journal of Law, Economics, & Organization* 1

Chapter 12

Sovereignty, Organized Hypocrisy, the Paradox of Post-9/11 International Relations

Patricia Springborg

Introduction

Stephen Krasner wrote his book, *Sovereignty, Organized Hypocrisy* (1999), well in advance of two developments which have conspired to make it true. One was the post-9/11 Bush Doctrine, which claimed for the 'West' the right to impose its values on the 'Rest'. The second was the sovereign debt crisis, which opens up multiple sites of struggle: between the EU as a confederation and the sovereign rights of its member states; and between the rule of financial experts and the democratic rights of citizens. There was always an implicit paradox between the exigencies of policy and the neutrality of the Westphalian system of states as a pluralistic system which 'provides a structure of coexistence, built on the mutual recognition of states as independent ... members of society, on the unavoidable reliance on self-preservation ... and on freedom to promote their own ends subject to minimal constraint'.[1] But the Bush Doctrine with respect to the 'War against Terror' and the subsequent Transatlantic Alliance based on 'regime and value change', which see the substitution of 'selective sovereignty', make it explicit. Has this change in the concept of sovereignty to bring it into line with policy simply remedied a naiveté in our thinking? Are we content to abandon the equality of membership in a pluralistic system for the high moral terrain of human rights and universal values that must, if necessary, be imposed from without? And would we be happy to be the recipients of regime and value change as well as the perpetrators, were the shoe on the other foot? In the case of the sovereign debt crisis, are we required to seek the preservation of the EU confederation as a higher good that may override the interests of national publics and their representatives in democratic parliaments?

Sovereignty as Organized Hypocrisy

For decades political scientists have been debating the conflicting jurisdictions of finance capital and the nation state, but with the Eurozone crisis we face it squarely.

---

1   Kai Alderson and Andrew Hurrell, *Hedley Bull on International Society* (Macmillan Press 2000) 18.

If 'organized hypocrisy – the presence of long-standing norms that are frequently violated'[2] – is true of sovereignty, it is also true of financial institutions that are 'too big to fail'. Suddenly we exit the sunlight of legally enforceable rules into the twilight zone of contested jurisdictions. If this were not a problem already, we have the additional complication of traditional ideas of sovereignty, cemented in constitutional law and overlaid by centuries of national sentiment and patriotism that have real impact at the ballot box. The way the crisis has played itself out, Germany is in the cockpit with the power to enforce austerity measures on the debtor members of the EU. This policy may be heedless of the economic wisdom learned from the Great Depression, that growth and not austerity is the way out. But in a Federal Republic in which all the Lands have the right to vote on the matter, national sentiment in terms of the frugal northerners bailing out the spendthrift southerners plays an important role, as do constitutionally guaranteed notions of national sovereignty.

The evolution of the European Union from the Coal and Steel Community involved incremental delegations of sovereignty which the public more or less accepted over time. Full delegation of sovereignty to an economic and fiscal union was envisioned by some, but never widely canvassed until the crisis talks of 2012. The incrementalism of European integration, theorized in terms of 'spill-over',[3] disguised the fact that the EU developed in response to a specific set of problems: first, the demilitarization of the Ruhr in the wake of the Second World War; and second, the reconciliation of France and Germany as the basis for a new post-war Europe. Spill-over worked, and for 50 years the concept of a united Europe gained more and more adherents who joined willingly, although uninvolved in the original problem-solving exercise. Again it was hoped that the cumulative effect of integration in specific areas would spill over to the point of bringing about full integration in an economic and fiscal union by incremental means. In retrospect such a hope was wildly optimistic; 'spill-over' is a concept reminiscent of Adam Smith's 'hidden hand' and eighteenth-century notions of 'spontaneous order' that seriously underestimate the complexity of historical process.[4]

---

2   Stephen Krasner, *Sovereignty: Organized Hypocrisy* (Princeton University Press 1999). Krasner owes the concept of organized hypocrisy to Nils Brunsson, developed in a different context: *The Organization of Hypocrisy. Talk, Decisions and Actions in Organisations* (John Wiley 1989).

3   On spillover as a concept in economics to account for the cross-infection from one sector to another of economic growth, see Avinash K Dixit and Joseph E Stiglitz, 'Monopolistic Competition and Optimum Product Variety' (1977) 67 *American Economic Review* 297. On spillover as a political concept to account for the cumulative effects of integration such that at a certain point it becomes self-propelling, see David Mitrany, 'The Prospect of European Integration: Federal or Functional?' (1965) 4 *Journal of Common Market Studies* 119 and David Mitrany, *The Functional Theory of Politics* (St Martin's Press 1976); John McCormick, *The European Union* (Westview 1999) 13–14.

4   Lisa Hill, 'The Invisible Hand of Adam Ferguson' (1998) 3 *European Legacy* 42 and 'The Hidden Theology of Adam Smith' (2001) 8 *European Journal of the History of Economic Thought* 1.

The seed of European integration was initially sown on very fertile ground. Under post-war conditions and promoted by leaders like Jean Monnet, Robert Schuman and Konrad Adenauer, intent on solving the immediate problems of French-German relations and the peaceful reindustrialization of Europe's heartland, and supported by the US, it bore immediate fruit. Monnet promoted his dream of a united Europe on the model of the US confederation with high rhetoric. Thus on 5 August 1943, as a member of the National Liberation Committee of the French government in exile, he declared:

> There will be no peace in Europe if the states are reconstituted on the basis of national sovereignty … The countries of Europe are too small to guarantee their peoples the necessary prosperity and social development. The European states must constitute themselves into a federation[5]

And on 9 May 1950, with the agreement of Chancellor Konrad Adenauer, French Minister of Foreign Affairs, Robert Schuman, in a declaration prepared by Monnet, proposed integration of the French and German coal and steel industries under joint control, a so-called High Authority, open to the other countries of Europe.

> Through the consolidation of basic production and the institution of a new High Authority, whose decisions will bind France, Germany and the other countries that join, this proposal represents the first concrete step towards a European federation, imperative for the preservation of peace.[6]

But when indeed the rhetoric took wing and neighbouring states joined the bandwagon not only for the ideal, but also for their own practical purposes (for instance to piggy-back on the economic success of Germany and its low interest rate regime), complexities were introduced that were bound to work themselves out over the long run.

It is my thesis that the Eurozone crisis is the outcome of organized hypocrisy on at least two fronts: both in terms of the norms of sovereignty and in terms of the behaviour of financial institutions. Although 'breaking the rule to save the rule' is typical of human behaviour, it is constitutive of bailouts in a special way, precisely because to stipulate the rule behind the rule would be to structure incentives the wrong way. By this I mean, and as we shall see, history demonstrates, the lender of last resort has to be prepared both to bail out banks, and to deny that it is prepared to bail out banks. In an analogous way, sovereignty was always a concept with overstretch, such that in many cases it could not live up to its own claims, as Stephen Krasner has so cleverly demonstrated. The most fundamental principle of the Westphalian Peace, the non-interference in the internal affairs of sovereign

5   <http://www.historiasiglo20.org/europe/monnet.htm> accessed 6 June 2014.
6   <http://www.historiasiglo20.org/europe/monnet.htm> accessed 6 June 2014.

states, was already violated at its inception, in order to guarantee the freedom of religious minorities. In the same way, within months of passage of the British Bank Charter Act 1844, which stipulated no-bailouts, bailouts took place, but always on the pretext that this was an exception to the rule.

We might say that 'organized hypocrisy' is due to the socially constructed nature of sovereignty, a notion that Krasner, although a realist, plays with,[7] and to the similarly socially constructed nature of financial institutions and their governing norms. But this does not tell us much and it is not a line I will pursue, except to note that to a social constructivist 'organized hypocrisy' does not come as a surprise! Sovereignty, as Krasner in an excellent overview suggests, is a concept that expands and contracts with the times. Bodin and Hobbes were advocates of absolute sovereignty in a period in which the fledgling nation state was weak and under threat from ecclesiastical institutions which had brought Europe to the point of civil war. So concerned were they with the problem of social order that they reduced to vanishing point those human rights, theorized over a long tradition from Roman to Natural law, and in Hobbes's own day by the late Scholastics. But Locke, Rousseau and Montesquieu sought to redress the balance between the rights of citizens and the needs of the state, mindful that imbalance in either direction threatened social order. That great turning point in the creation of the international society of states, the Treaty of Westphalia (1648), as Krasner rightly points out, enshrined 'organized hypocrisy' in the name of religious toleration, to the extent that it allowed minority confessions the right to practise their own religion, in violation of the general principle established by the Peace of Augsburg (1555) that the people must follow the Prince: 'cuius regio eius religio' ('the religion is his who has the region').[8] Thus 'organized hypocrisy' was from the beginning part of the game, justified by the need for rhetorical overstretch in the name of state-security, but a relaxation of the rules in specific instances in the name of human rights. The long history of toleration and the struggle for human rights against *raison d'état* continues, a struggle that we have witnessed all over Africa and in the Arab Spring, and that has no foreseeable end.

The Organized Hypocrisy of Financial Institutions

'Organized hypocrisy' entails a paradox, and somehow challenges us to address it. The term is particularly alluring because it presents itself as a virtue disguised as a vice. Hypocrisy is not, in general, a very commendable trait. But in the case of 'organized hypocrisy' the opposite is a kind of fundamentalism that is more dangerous, and this is part of the charm of the paradox. So, for instance, a sovereignty which at all times and in all places lived up to the broad ambit of its claims would be absolute, which is not what we want. That sovereignty so early

---

7   Krasner (n 2) 44–9.
8   Krasner (n 2) 77–81.

broke its own rule to accommodate religious toleration we can only think highly commendable. In the same way, prohibitions against bailouts by the lender of last resort would be overly rigid if they could not accommodate relief in genuine cases of distressed banks which might threaten the stability of the entire financial system. This was the case, one could argue, with the failure of Lehman Brothers in 2008, where a newly elected President, Barack Obama, and the Chairman of the Federal Reserve, Ben Bernanke, were taken by surprise by a crisis that at the time was generally underestimated, but that was to have fundamental consequences in precipitating the world financial crisis. It was less a case of the lender of last resort refusing to bail out a distressed bank on principle, than a simple instance of miscalculation.[9] The Fed's first instinct was that it had insufficient funds to bail out both Lehman Brothers and AIG, as if the lender of last resort had an inelastic budget, and had to choose, based on which case presented the greatest threat to the international financial system. It was a position that Bernanke was later to reverse with his notion of 'fiat money', when he claimed that the government uniquely owned the means of creating money as the cure for deflation, and that, to this end, 'the U.S. government has a technology, called a printing press (or, today, its electronic equivalent), that allows it to produce as many U.S. dollars as it wishes at essentially no cost'.[10] In fact, as it turned out, the finances of the Investment Banks and their Reinsurers were so intertwined that allowing either of them to fail was perilous, and to have printed money to save them both at that stage, might have reduced the necessity for money-printing down the line.

Obama and Bernanke were quick to learn from their mistake, however, and Bernanke's special expertise on the Great Depression placed him well to deal with economic crisis.[11] The reigning wisdom on the Great Depression, postulated

---

9   See the Bloomberg report <www.bloomberg.com/news/2013-01-18/most-fed-officials-saw-economy-weathering-subprime-crisis.html> (New York, 18 January 2013), which notes that in transcripts of the Federal Open Market Committee meetings released that day in Washington, most members underestimated the sub-prime crisis of August 2007:

The transcripts show the committee's slow grasp of the enormity of contagion that was to spread throughout global markets as a result of billions of dollars in low-quality housing assets that had been securitized into bonds and sold to banks and investors worldwide. Several FOMC participants such as then San Francisco Fed President Janet Yellen sounded alarms in the first half of 2007. Still, the FOMC focused on the economy's performance and showed reluctance to alter policy until August. 'The odds are that the market will stabilize', Bernanke told the committee in August 2007, according to the transcripts from that year. 'This restrictive effect could come in various magnitudes. It could be moderate, or it could be more severe, and we are just going to have to monitor how it adjusts over time'.

10   Ben Bernanke, 'Deflation: Making Sure 'It' Doesn't Happen Here' (Remarks Before the National Economists Club, Washington, DC, November 21 2002) <www.federalreserve. gov/boardDocs/speeches/2002/20021121/default.htm> accessed 6 June 2014.

11   See Ben Bernanke, 'Nonmonetary effects of the financial crisis in the propagation of the great depression' (1983) 73 *American Economic Review* 257. See also 'The Macroeconomics of the Great Depression: A Comparative Approach' (1995) *Journal of*

both by Milton Friedman and Anna Schwarz, and further theorized by Charles Kindleberger, laid the blame at the door of the Federal Reserve for having tightened money supply in reaction to the Wall Street crash, and exacerbated the crisis.[12] This Bernanke had already admitted at a speech celebrating Milton Friedman's 90th birthday, 8 November 2002, where he closed by remarking: 'Let me end my talk by abusing slightly my status as an official representative of the Federal Reserve. I would like to say to Milton and Anna: Regarding the Great Depression. You're right, we did it. We're very sorry. But thanks to you, we won't do it again'.[13]

Bernanke's analysis of monetary policy in the wake of the 1929 crash has caused him to theorize a 'financial accelerator', whereby shocks to the real economy and tightening of financial markets have a mutually reinforcing effect, precipitating financial and macroeconomic downturn.[14] His determination, as Chairman of the Federal Reserve, appointed first under George W. Bush in 2006 and renewed under Obama in 2010, 'not to do it again' has caused what is viewed in the eyes of some as an over-reaction, in terms of relaxing the money supply. A footnote to a speech, where he made reference to Milton Friedman's concept of a 'helicopter drop' of money into the economy to fight deflation, has earned him the nick-name 'Helicopter Ben' and his critics refer to his 'helicopter printing press', in response to which Bernanke has noted that 'people know that inflation erodes the real value of the government's debt and, therefore, that it is in the interest of the government to create some inflation'.[15]

As the crisis has unwound observers add to the fear of another Great Depression the frightening prospect that history might repeat itself in the form of the Weimar Republic and its aftermath. Germany has an understandable phobia about hyperinflation, but that very phobia could bring about the condition it most fears. Paralysis on the part of the Eurozone, which lacking a fiscal union also lacks the superstructure to deal with such a crisis, has left Eurozone countries in the jaws of

---

Money, Credit, and Banking 1; Ben Bernanke and Kevin Carey, 'Nominal Wage Stickiness and Aggregate Supply in the Great Depression' (1996) *Quarterly Journal of Economic* 853; Ben Bernanke and Harold James, 'The Gold Standard, Deflation, and Financial Crisis in the Great Depression: An International Comparison' in R Glenn Hubbard (ed), *Financial Markets and Financial Crises* (University of Chicago Press for NBER 1991).

12   Milton Friedman and Anna J Schwartz, *A Monetary History of the United States, 1863–1960* (Princeton University Press 1963) 300; C Kindleberger, *The World in Depression 1929–1939* (University of California Press 1986).

13   Ben Bernanke, speech at the Conference to Honor Milton Friedman (University of Chicago, Chicago, Illinois, 8 November 2002) <www.federalreserve.gov/BOARDDOCS/SPEECHES/2002/20021108/> accessed 9 May 2013.

14   See Bernanke (n 11) 257; See also Ben Bernanke, Mark Gertler and Simon Gilchrist, 'The financial accelerator and flight to quality' (1996) 78 *Review of Economics and Statistics* 1.

15   'A money-financed tax cut is essentially equivalent to Milton Friedman's famous 'helicopter drop' of money': <www.federalreserve.gov/BOARDDOCS/.../2002/20021121/default.htm> accessed 6 June 2014.

conflicting demands: those of their constituencies who demand more transparency and the curbing of reckless financial institutions, and the demands of leadership to compensate the deficiencies of Eurozone financial institutions. These conflicting demands pose irresolvable dilemmas, first due to the immediate constraints of electoral politics, so that constituency demands come first; second, because there is a wide variation in the tolerance for more EU bureaucracy among the players. While the UK has always been highly sensitive to the leakage of sovereignty to Brussels, to the point that a majority of Tories polled now want to exit the EU, Wolfgang Schäuble, Germany's CDU Finance Minister has long supported economic and fiscal union, although he is among the few consistent supporters of this project.

This variance in enthusiasm for closer union is also a product of the differential effect of closer integration of EU member economies. The UK is a special case for three reasons. First, the role of the city of London as the world's leading centre of international finance; second, and related, London's status as a Global City, equal only to New York on the ATKearney Global Cities rankings, along with megacities like Hong Kong, Singapore, New Delhi and Mumbai, where English is predominant;[16] and third, the pull of Transatlantic and Commonwealth affiliation between kindred global cities like Sydney and Melbourne, Toronto, Montreal, and Johannesburg, enjoying similar Common Law and financial cultures.

In terms of the current financial crisis and the consequent Eurozone crisis of sovereignty, Weimar may, frighteningly, be the most salient precedent. The coincidence of hyperinflation and economic collapse with a liberal constitutionalist regime that was deemed too weak to deal with it caused a crisis of sovereignty, theorized by the architect of the juridical system of the Third Reich, Carl Schmitt in the context of emergency powers granted in the Weimar Constitution under Article 48.[17] A satisfactory solution to the use of those emergency powers could conceivably have broken the deadlock. This was a case where 'organized hypocrisy' was called for, breaking the rule to save the rule, which was the spirit in which the Roman Republican institution of 'dictator' has been created. But it was not the path that Schmidt took, instead opting for a permanent, rather than a temporary, dictatorship. As recent European elections have demonstrated, right wing parties, such as Marine Le Pen's Front National in France and the Golden Dawn in Greece, and Euro-sceptics, such as UKIP in the UK and the Five Star Movement in Italy, are gaining electoral success as a result of the austerity measures enforced in the wake of the current financial crisis. We can only hope that history will not mock us with a replay of the 1930s.

---

16   A. T. Kearney Global Cities Index and Emerging Cities Outlook (New York 2012) <http://www.atkearney.it/documents/10192/dfedfc4c-8a62-4162-90e5-2a3f14f0da3a> accessed 9 May 2013.

17   The text of the Article was vague in terms of conditions and implementation, but because it expressly stipulated that the Reichstag had the power to revoke this emergency power by simple majority vote, it was implied that its terms might impinge on the Reichstag's own constitutional functions.

Organized Hypocrisy and Bail-Outs

A better understanding of 'organized hypocrisy', both in terms of sovereignty and in the world of financial institutions, might help us find a way out. In both cases we are dealing with institutions where the rules seem to be set in stone. In the case of sovereignty we have legal edifices engineered over time in which state powers are constitutionally guaranteed but are not designed to respond to immediate shocks or challenges. The security apparatuses that surround financial institutions necessary to guarantee the economic order are not more daunting. And yet, in fact, we have a long history of 'organised hypocrisy', that is to say, of cases in which the rule is broken to uphold the rule that has worked in both cases. Set in this context the fluctuating positions and about-turns of important players in the current Eurozone crisis can be seen to represent a seriousness about problem-solving in the face of obdurate obstacles that is entirely commendable. This we see if we take seriously the history of financial institutions as a case of 'organised hypocrisy'. It was long recognized in the case of the Bank of England that breaking the rule to save the rule was the only way to solve the problem of moral hazard for the lender of last resort. Sir Francis Baring, co-founder in 1762 of Barings, London's oldest merchant bank which was brought to its knees in 1995 by a rogue trader who lost the bank £827 million, had as early as 1797 drawn attention to the problem, specifically in relation to the lender of last resort. It was a warning repeated in Henry Thornton's *Enquiry into the Paper Credit of Great Britain* of 1802, which explored the problem in relation to Bank of England policy towards country banks, and in Walter Bagehot's *Lombard Street* of 1873.[18] And here 'practice preceded theory'.

From at least the eighteenth century, when the Bank of England became aware of its role as lender of last resort and the moral hazard it involved, it set preventative ground rules which Kindleberger has described as follows: 'Capital outflows were not to be feared. Money should not be held artificially low to encourage speculation and intensify crises. When crises occurred, however, the Bank should feed commercial transactions by providing abundant and cheap discounts to moderate the intensity of the crisis and shorten its duration'.[19] The problem of moral hazard for the lender of last resort is an exquisite form of the 'prisoner's dilemma' with a predictable outcome, Kindleberger concludes: 'Central banks should act one way (lending freely) to halt the panic, but another (leaving the market to its own devices) to improve the chances of future panics. Actuality inevitably dominates contingency. Today wins over tomorrow'.[20]

In this respect the financial crisis of 2008 is no different from its predecessors, and nor in substance is the panacea. In the history of the British Bank Act of

---

18   Charles Kindleberger, *Manias, Panics, and Crashes: A History of Financial Crises* (Wiley 1996) 147.

19   Kindleberger (n 18).

20   Kindleberger (n 18) 149.

1844 we see this dilemma and how the Bank of England coped with it, by setting a firm rule and then breaking it in times of crisis. Legislators, when the Bank Act was under debate, had even given thought to including emergency powers to suspend its official provisions, but rejected the idea, aware no doubt that to undermine the policy with such powers for exceptional cases would only increase the moral hazard that the presence of a lender of last resort already posed. Instead, after 1847 and 1857, 'when it proved necessary to suspend the act and provide the possibility of issuing more money as a last resort', they simply went ahead, prepared to face a parliamentary enquiry after the event.[21] 'The principle of having a rule but breaking it if one had to, was so widely acknowledged that after the suspension in 1866 there was no demand for a new investigation'.[22] Subsequent debate throughout the nineteenth century about 'rules for adjusting the discount rate of the Bank of England to the state of its reserves by mathematical formulas written into legislation' predictably failed, because of the logic of the prisoner's dilemma: 'Actuality inevitably dominates contingency. Today wins over tomorrow':

> It may be optimal to leave the matter in doubt, along with the question of whether, in fact, the marines will come to the rescue, or if they decide to come, will arrive in time. Thus, in Britain, there was no explicit provision for a lender of last resort and no fixed rule as to who would fill the role if there was one. In 1825 it was not the Exchequer. The job was given resolutely to the reluctant Bank, the acceptance of which was 'the sulky answer of driven men'.[23]

This position, it should be noted, did not go uncontested:

> When *The Economist* and Walter Bagehot thought it proper that the Bank of England, and not the banks themselves, should hold the necessary reserves to get the country through a panic, Mr. Hankey, a former governor of the Bank, called this 'the most mischievous doctrine ever broached in the monetary or banking world in this country; viz. that it is the proper function of the Bank of England to keep money available at all times to supply the demands of bankers who have rendered their own assets unavailable'. The public, however, sided with Bagehot and practice against Hankey and theory. If one cannot control expansion of credit in boom, one should at least try to halt contraction of credit in crisis.[24]

---

21 Kindleberger (n 18) 149.
22 Kindleberger (n 18) 149.
23 Kindleberger (n 18) 149–50. See also JH Clapham, *The Bank of England: A History* (Cambridge University Press, 2 volumes, 1945) 108.
24 Kindleberger (n 18) 149–50.

Organized Hypocrisy, National Autonomy and the Westphalian System of States

'Organized hypocrisy' entails a paradox, and somehow challenges us to address it, I have claimed. There was always an implicit paradox between the exigencies of policy and the neutrality of the Westphalian system of states as a pluralistic system. One of the temptations is to 'unmask' this hypocrisy by declaring national sovereignty dead. But this is not a solution that recognizes the salience of the paradox. In the case of sovereignty, the notion of 'organized hypocrisy' also means breaking the rule to save the rule, and abolishing the rule is not a solution, although this is in effect the policy that the Bush Doctrine adopted.

In the Eurozone we have the opposite problem, and much of the confusion can be ascribed to a refusal to acknowledge the concept of sovereignty as 'organized hypocrisy'. In other words, member states tend to forget that economic union necessarily came at a cost in terms of national sovereignty, as all forms of confederation do. Because of the incremental growth of this particular union and the properties of 'spillover' in terms of which it was legitimated, member states tended to see it as a sort of 'organic' development that could only be healthy, making no provision for conflict or break-down and demonstrating a corresponding reticence to impose political norms on their fellow members. But while EU member states staunchly maintain rights of national sovereignty when it comes to political policy, upholding the Westphalian ideal despite their confederated status, they are much less reticent about imposing economic norms on their fellows. This is in a sense the worst of all possible worlds. Legal and constitutional constraints forbid a formal solution to the problems of a joint fiscal policy in the absence of a fiscal union, which the Germans at least hope to solve behaviourally, by inducing the spendthrift southerners to emulate the thrifty northerners!

In the US by contrast, reticence to impose its political norms on others is lacking and quite the opposite seems to be the case, particularly since the launching of the 'war on terror' in Bush's second inaugural of 2005. According to the Bush Doctrine the exceptional becomes the norm. The fact that in a world of Realpolitik powerful hegemons have sometimes violated the principles of Westphalian sovereignty in terms of non-interference in the domestic affairs of states, 'breaking the rule to save the rule', is now taken to mean that national sovereignty and the Westphalian system of states are obsolete, or at least apply only in selected cases. The invasion of Iraq, on the mistaken grounds that it harboured weapons of mass destruction, was a perfect demonstration of the Bush Doctrine at work, and of its hazards. One of the most important provisions of the Bush Doctrine, formulated in the wake of 9/11, is that the US has an obligation to intervene in the internal affairs of sovereign states that do not uphold 'our' values, that is, those of the hegemon. The doctrine grew out of the convergence of two different types of theory. The first is Hegemonic Stability Theory, a theory of neo-imperialism developed by Realist international relations theorists at the height of the Cold War. And the second source is the notion of 'epochal wars' as creating new social orders, according to the constitutional historian and international lawyer, Philip Bobbitt, where the victor has not only the duty, but also the obligation to impose its values on the vanquished.

According to the stipulations of hegemonic stability theory, in which Stephen Krasner has also played a formative role, the international system can only escape the anarchy that realists postulate as endemic, by accepting the government of a hegemon.[25] Generated out of Kindleberger's analysis of the Great Depression, as having been first and foremost a policy failure due to the changeover from British to American superpower supremacy, hegemonic stability theory is a neo-Keynesian approach to international relations theory.[26] Writing in the aftermath of the collapse of Bretton Woods, Kindleberger addressed the problem of global regulatory regimes in terms of a succession of hegemons who must maintain open markets and underwrite the costs of the international system as a public good. By so doing they achieve global power and the financial and political muscle that accrues to the world's policeman, who sets the norms and values while reaping financial rewards as the holder of the reserve currency. But, by underwriting the costs of the world system as a public good, the hegemon necessarily permits the free rider effect, which allows new hegemons to rise on the largesse of the old. This theory also incorporates liberal-democratic assumptions in the stipulation that the hegemon must adopt a duty-worthy ideology (open markets and democracy) to attract further players and achieve the bandwagon effect. It follows then, that hegemonic stability theory, like the economic equilibrium theory on which it is parasitic, although explicitly denying the neoclassical doctrine of the self-equilibrating market, still suffers from undue mechanism and a failure to interrogate its own assumptions about the inevitability of progress in the form of deregulation, modernization, liberalization and democratization.

Philip Bobbitt, Texan nephew of Lyndon B. Johnson and constitutional lawyer, who served in three US administrations, under Bush Sr., Clinton and Bush Jr., and a sometime advisor to Tony Blair, is one of the chief architects of the Bush Doctrine. He wrote an Oxford D. Phil. Dissertation that became the book, *The Shield of Achilles*, [27] where he argues that epochal wars are constitutional watersheds, in the aftermath of which the victors impose a new world order in which they exercise the right, and the duty, to impose on the vanquished their own values. Following a long historical review of the epochal wars of the early modern period, Bobbitt turns to the twentieth century, in which the epochal

---

25   See Robert O Keohane, *After Hegemony: Cooperation and Discord in the World Political Economy* (Princeton University Press 1984); Robert Gilpin, *The Political Economy of International Relations* (Princeton University Press 1987); Michael C Webb and Stephen D Krasner, 'Hegemonic Stability Theory: An Empirical Assessment' (1989) 15 *Review of International Studies* 183.

26   Kindleberger (n 12).

27   Philip Bobbitt, *The Shield of Achilles: War, Peace, and the Course of History* (Alfred A. Knopf 2002).

war against fascism is deemed to have lasted from 1914 to 1989, finally being resoundingly won by the US. It is now up to the US, he argues, to impose its values on the vanquished.

What is perhaps most reprehensible about Bobbitt's theory is the frequent slippage from fact to value, from empirical observation to recommendation, the most important slippage being his move from the observation that victors of epochal wars *do in fact* establish as hegemonic their own goals and values, to the claim that they *have the right and duty* to do so. The upshot is the surreptitious conversion of hegemonic stability from an empirical theory to a normative doctrine, according to which the hegemon must at all costs maintain his supremacy. This means excluding prospective challengers, Japan, China and Western Europe from the decision-making circle – despite the fact that hegemonic stability theorists have always maintained that the rise of free riders on the hegemon's largesse as potential challengers is a feature of the system. So Bobbitt calls to our attention the 'great insight' of Josef Joffe, editor of the prestigious German weekly *Die Zeit*, who emphasizes the hegemon's function to provide free public goods – a feature of hegemonic stability theory – but in this case to block the rise of competitors:

> The United States must produce three types of collective goods. First, act as regional protector by underwriting the security of those potential rivals – Japan, China, Western Europe – who would otherwise have to produce security on their own by converting their economic strength into military assets; [s]econd, act as a regional pacifier; [t]hird, universalize the [security] architecture [by which the United States acts with various regional players in concert against regional threats].
>
> As long as the US provides precious collective goods the Europeans or Asians cannot or will not produce for themselves – building coalitions and acting universally through regional cooperation, implementing anti-missile, anti-proliferation, and proenvironmental regimes, organizing humanitarian intervention – there will remain an important demand for US leadership. [28]

Bobbitt has melded his thesis of the foundation of states in war, and war as the litmus test of state legitimacy, to Samuel P. Huntington's thesis about the 'clash of civilizations' [29] in a strikingly effective way. If it falls to the victors to define constitutional order and governing values in the wake of epochal wars, as Bobbitt maintains, it is easy to see the Transatlantic wars against terror targeting Islam in just these terms. And unsurprising, given that Huntington's thesis fell into the lap of Osama bin Laden like a ripe plum, and was immediately interpreted as a

28   Bobbitt (n 28)

29   Samuel P Huntington, 'The Clash of Civilizations?' *Foreign Affairs* 72, 3, Summer, 1993; and Samuel P Huntington, *The Clash of Civilizations and the Remaking of World Order* (Simon and Schuster 1996).

statement of US intentions. Reacting to Huntington as early as 1998, 'Osama bin Laden and Ayman Zawahiri declared war on the US, outlining a philosophy of the clash of civilizations which legitimised attacks on the West – both soldiers and civilians'.[30] Barely a month after the September 11 attacks, in fact, bin Laden, in an interview with al-Jazeera correspondent Taysir Alouni, embraced Huntington's theory as representing the US agenda to which Al Qaeda was responding.[31] By the same logic, on 10 August 2006 the CNN website reported Bush's remarks following the discovery of a plot to blow up planes landing in the US, under the headline 'Bush: U.S. at war with "Islamic fascists"': 'President Bush said Thursday that an uncovered British terror plot to blow up planes flying to the United States was further proof "that this nation is at war with Islamic fascists".'[32] 'This country is safer than it was prior to 9/11', Bush declared: 'We've taken a lot of measures to protect the American people. But obviously we still aren't completely safe, because there are people that still plot and people who want to harm us for what we believe in'.

This heady mix of Bobbitt and Huntington, righteousness and Realpolitik, the Bible and the gun, also found favour with UK Prime Minister Tony Blair, who in a ground-breaking speech on 1 August 2006 to the World Affairs Council in Los Angeles, declared, 'ever since September 11th, the US has embarked on a policy of intervention in order to protect its and our future security. Hence Afghanistan. Hence Iraq. Hence the broader Middle East initiative in support of moves towards democracy in the Arab world'.[33] The 'war against terror', Blair claimed, meant fighting a war 'not just against terrorism but about how the world should govern itself in the early 21st century, about global values', going on to insist that 'the point about these interventions, military and otherwise, is that they were not just about changing regimes but changing the values systems governing the nations concerned. The banner was not actually "regime change" it was "values change"'. Blair, like Bush defending the Israeli invasion of Lebanon in August 2010, once again justified military intervention in terms of 'value change': 'What is happening today out in the Middle East, in Afghanistan and beyond is an elemental struggle about the values that will shape our future'.[34]But as we now know, the false hope of value change and spontaneous democratization has bleak prospects. The Arab Spring has brought an Arab Winter of anarchy and/or repression, and millions have suffered mutilation and death as a consequence.

----

30   <www.aljazeera.com/programmes/aljazeeraworld/2011/10/201110207512 4103401.html > accessed 12 May 2013.

31   <http://islamicmiddleeast.nmhblogs.org/2010/11/20/osama-bin-laden-and-the-clash-of-civilizations/> accessed 12 May 2013.

32   CNN website 10 August 2006: <http://edition.cnn.com/2006/POLITICS/08/10/washington.terror.plot/> accessed 9 May 2013.

33   <http://news.bbc.co.uk/2/hi/uk_news/5236896.stm > accessed 12 May 2013.

34   <http://news.bbc.co.uk/2/hi/uk_news/5236896.stm> accessed 12 May 2013.

Hypocrisy Unmasked, the War against Terror and Unilateralism

While Barack Obama has officially disowned the Bush Doctrine, he has nevertheless acted as if it was still in place and the Westphalian system was long dead. There is no better example than the killing of Osama bin Laden on 2 May 2011, which required the invasion of Pakistani sovereign territory by US Special Forces. US policy claiming the right to conduct systematic drone attacks in Yemen and in Afghanistan is a further example. While French Unilateralism in the invasion of first Libya and second Mali, whether covered by the fig-leaf of allied support or not, and however commendable in stopping dictators and Islamic Fundamentalists in their tracks, makes a mockery of the EU confederation, not to speak of bypassing the UN Security Council and NATO.

Similarly the shift from the use of regular forces to 'unmanned aerial vehicles', or drones, in the 'war against terror', opens the possibility to wars officially undeclared and even publicly unannounced. Christina Lamb has noted, citing the US Congressional Research Service, that the fleet of drones at the disposal of the US military has grown from 10 in 2001 to 7,000 today, ranging from 'missile launching Predators and the larger Reapers to tiny prototypes shaped like humming birds'.[35] And the CIA has its own fleet. At the same time there are reports of Iranian drones being employed by government forces in Syria to isolate and target insurgents, probably some variant of the 'Ababil' 'Swallow', an unmanned craft developed by HESA (Iran Aircraft Manufacturing Industrial Company) as long ago as 1986 during Iran's war with Iraq; as of 2006–2007, 369 Ababils had already been produced.[36] We cannot therefore rule out that major players in all theatres of war will eventually have drones at their disposal, if they do not have them already, including Russia, China, India and Pakistan, all of whom are nuclear powers with regional disputes of their own to settle.

The exponential growth in 'unmanned aerial vehicles' in the US is such that, while from 2004 to 2008, George W Bush launched 42 drone strikes, all in Pakistan, Obama, up to May 2013, had already launched 314, and most of these were personally authorized by the President:

35   Christina Lamb, 'Drone Force One' *The Sunday Times* (3 June 2012) <www.thesundaytimes.co.uk/sto/news/focus/article1052281.ece> accessed 9 May 2013.

36   'Ababil', Global Security. 10–07–2008: <www.globalsecurity.org/military … ran/ababil.htm> accessed 12 May 2013. See L Devlin, 'Iran Expands UAV Capability' (2006) 11 *Unmanned Vehicles* 16; N. Hodge, 'U.S. Military Confirms It Shot Down Iranian Drone', Danger Room, Wired, 16 March 2009: <http://www.wired.com/2009/05/pentagon-joins-pakistan-drone-war-gives-islamabad-robo-control/ > accessed 12 May 2013. Peter La Franchi, London, reported on an 'Iranian-made Ababil-T Hezbollah UAV shot down by Israeli fighter in Lebanon crisis', Flight Global, 15 August 2006. Web: <www.flightglobal.com/news/articles/israel-fields-armed-uavs-in-lebanon-208315/> accessed 12 May 2013.

Decision days are known as Terror Tuesdays. Obama sits in the black swivel chair in the Oval Office with John Brennan, his counterterrorism czar, and General Martin Dempsey, his chief military adviser, and scrutinises photographs and sketchy biographies one official refers to with macabre humour as the 'J. Crew catalogue of Jihad'. Together they select who will be the next target of unmanned drones 7000 miles away in the mountains of Pakistan, the deserts of Yemen, or the streets of Somalia. Once Obama approves a killing, instructions are transmitted to an office block in northern Virginia. Inside are computer monitors, keyboards and maps. A person who looks like an office worker sits at a desk with a hand on a joy-stick and watches a live feed from a drone hovering over the tribal areas of Pakistan. When he sees a figure entering a vehicle, he presses the button and an explosion fills the screen. It might look like a video game but in the real world the button has launched a 5ft Hellfire missile at 1000 mph.[37]

As Lamb notes, 'most of the estimated 2,000 to 3,000 suspected militants or terrorists killed by the US outside the battlefield have died via drone attacks', and these were all authorized by the presidential 'Grim Reaper debating society'.[38] A substantial number of them have been innocent civilians, 42 killed in one day on 17 March 2011, in North Waziristan. Gregory Johnsen, a Yemen specialist at Princeton, believes not only that the drone attacks are counterproductive, but that they have been used as a 'recruiting tool' by Al Qaeda in the Arabian Peninsula, helping it to triple its membership since 2009 to more than 1,000. John Brennan, chief counterterrorism advisor to Obama, with the official title Deputy National Security Advisor for Homeland Security and Counterterrorism, and Assistant to the President, and now Director of the Central Intelligence Agency, openly insisted on the right to such a policy in international law, claiming in 2011: 'The United States takes the legal position that … we have the authority to take action against Al Qaeda and its associated forces'.

But as Lamb observes, not all international lawyers agree. Most tellingly, Colonel Morris Davis, formerly the chief prosecutor at Guantanamo has argued: [39]

> If we have a CIA drone programme that operates on the premise that the president can tell anyone to pull the trigger and kill someone anywhere at any time, then have we not undermined the Geneva conventions and the whole rationale behind international humanitarian law? Why have a military and the rules that go with it when the president can just pick and choose when and where the law applies?

A great step forward in the restoration of Afghan territorial sovereignty, hailed by CNN, for example, as a 'landmark deal' that 'affords Afghan authorities an effective veto over controversial special operations raids', was the official

---

37   Lamb (n 35).
38   Lamb (n 35) 15.
39   Lamb (n 35) 15.

handover to Afghanis of control over night raids formalized in a Memorandum of Understanding (MOU) to coincide with Obama's surprise visit to Afghanistan on the anniversary of Osama bin Laden's death on 3 May 2012.[40] But Obama's 'Enduring Strategic Partnership' agreement with Afghanistan and accompanying Memoranda of Understanding were misleading in terms of 'a transition to Afghan responsibility and an end to U.S. war', as the fine print reveals:

> The agreement was negotiated between the U.S. military command in Kabul and Afghan Ministry of Defence, and lawyers for the U.S. military introduced a key provision that fundamentally changed the significance of the rest of the text. In the first paragraph under the definition of terms, the MOU says, 'For the purpose of this Memorandum of Understanding (MOU), special operations are operations approved by the Afghan Operational Coordination Group (OCG) and conducted by Afghan Forces with support from U.S. Forces in accordance with Afghan laws'. That carefully crafted sentence means that the only night raids covered by the MOU are those that the SOF commander responsible for U.S. night raids decides to bring to the Afghan government. Those raids carried out by U.S. units without consultation with the Afghan government fall outside the MOU.[41]

In fact the terms of the agreement simply legitimize the status quo and 'the only substantive agreement reached between the U.S. and Afghanistan – well hidden in the agreements – has been to allow powerful U.S. Special Operations Forces (SOF)[42] to continue to carry out the unilateral night raids on private homes that are universally hated in the Pashtun zones of Afghanistan'. So, while President Hamid Karzai seemed to get what he wanted, control over the SOF night raids plus a US 10-year commitment of economic support, and Obama seemed to get what he wanted, the apparent winding down of the unpopular war in Afghanistan and withdrawal of American troops, in fact everything remained the same. The Obama administration's success at postponing the issue of how many US troops will remain in Afghanistan after 2014, until a yet-to-be-negotiated 'Bilateral Security Agreement', meant that it could adopt the election posture of appearing to be getting out of Afghanistan while delaying the critical question of long-term troop commitments until after the Presidential elections.

There may always have been an implicit paradox between the exigencies of policy and the neutrality of the Westphalian system of states, as a pluralistic system

---

40 Gareth Porter, '*New Pact Won't Stop the War – or the Special Forces Night Raids: Why Obama is Not Ending the War in Afghanistan*' *Tom Dispatch*, 3 May 2012: <www. informationclearinghouse.info/article31236.htm> accessed 12 May 2013

41 Porter (n 44).

42 Special Operations Forces (SOF) refers to the many special operations units of the US Army, Navy, Marine Corps and Air Force, formed for a specific, limited objective, and later disbanded, or reconstituted under a different name for reasons of security, like the Navy Seals, for instance, who carried out the killing of Osama bin Laden.

designed to promote international order while preserving national sovereignty within states. But only with the Bush Doctrine was Westphalia officially abandoned for the high moral terrain of human rights and universal values that must, if necessary, be imposed from without. The perpetrators of the Bush Doctrine have clearly forgotten that it was precisely to end the Thirty Years' War, a lethal conflict over values in their most categorical form, as religion, that the Westphalian Peace was concluded. Are we to accept this radical break with the spirit of Westphalia (so often broken in terms of the letter of the law)? To restate the questions with which this chapter began, would we be happy to be the recipients of regime and value change as well as the perpetrators, were the shoe on the other foot – in the case of a Chinese or Russian hegemon, for instance?

The sovereign debt crisis involves us in a similar, if less apocalyptic, dilemma. Again we have to ask, does it require us to seek the preservation of the EU confederation as a higher good that may override the interests of national publics and their representatives in democratic parliaments? Or, seen differently, does it require sacrifice by some in the interest of preserving the whole for the many? These are the moral hazards with which we must live and 'organized hypocrisy' is one way of dealing with them. It allows us to make exceptions, 'breaking the rule to save the rule' so that the entire system does not fall victim to the discrete crises it encounters on its way. But 'organized hypocrisy' sidesteps without resolving the moral dilemmas it masks and sometimes the stretch is too great. The Bush Doctrine, one might say, stretches the fiction beyond credibility. It represents not just hypocrisy but abandonment of Westphalia. As for the Eurozone crisis, since the journey that confederations take is in any event something of a leap of faith, depending ultimately on trust for the collaboration to work, it should be no surprise that there will be ups and downs, that burdens will fall differentially, as do benefits. We see in the innumerable meetings of the Eurozone members, EU summits, and meetings of the G8 and now the G20, daily testimony that politicians believe that persuading their publics that this is the case is a major part of their job. This is work in good faith that may bode well for the future of the confederation.

Bibliography

Alderson K and Hurrell A, *Hedley Bull on International Society* (Macmillan Press 2000)

Bernanke B, 'Nonmonetary effects of the financial crisis in the propagation of the great depression' (1983) 73 *American Economic Review* 257

—— 'The Macroeconomics of the Great Depression: A Comparative Approach' (1995) *Journal of Money, Credit, and Banking* 1

—— and Carey K, 'Nominal Wage Stickiness and Aggregate Supply in the Great Depression' (1996) *Quarterly Journal of Economics* 853

——, Gertler M and Gilchrist S, 'The financial accelerator and flight to quality' (1996) 78 *Review of Economics and Statistics* 1

—— and James H, 'The Gold Standard, Deflation, and Financial Crisis in the Great Depression: An International Comparison' in R Glenn Hubbard (ed), *Financial Markets and Financial Crises* (University of Chicago Press for NBER 1991)

Bobbitt P, *The Shield of Achilles: War, Peace, and the Course of History* (Alfred A. Knopf 2002)

Brunsson N, *The Organization of Hypocrisy. Talk, Decisions and Actions in Organisations* (John Wiley 1989).

Clapham JH, *The Bank of England: A History* (Cambridge University Press, 2 volumes, 1945)

Devlin L, 'Iran Expands UAV Capability' (2006) 11 *Unmanned Vehicles* 16

Dixit AK and Stiglitz JE, 'Monopolistic Competition and Optimum Product Variety' (1977) 67 *American Economic Review* 297

Friedman M and Schwartz AJ, *A Monetary History of the United States, 1863–1960* (Princeton University Press 1963)

Gilpin R, *The Political Economy of International Relations* (Princeton University Press 1987)

Hill L, 'The Invisible Hand of Adam Ferguson' (1998) 3 *European Legacy* 42

—— 'The Hidden Theology of Adam Smith' (2001) 8 *European Journal of the History of Economic Thought* 1

Huntington SP, 'The Clash of Civilizations?' Foreign Affairs 72/3 Summer, 1993

—— *The Clash of Civilizations and the Remaking of World Order* (Simon and Schuster 1996)

Keohane R, *After Hegemony: Cooperation and Discord in the World Political Economy* (Princeton University Press 1984)

Kindleberger C, *The World in Depression 1929–1939* (University of California Press 1986)

—— *Manias, Panics, and Crashes: A History of Financial Crises* (Wiley 1996)

Krasner S, *Sovereignty: Organized Hypocrisy* (Princeton University Press 1999)

Lamb C, 'Drone Force One' *The Sunday Times*, June 3 2012 15

McCormick J, *The European Union* (Westview 1999)

Mitrany D, 'The Prospect of European Integration: Federal or Functional?' (1965) 4(2) *Journal of Common Market Studies* 119

—— *The Functional Theory of Politics* (St Martin's Press 1976)

Porter G, *'New Pact Won't Stop the War--or the Special Forces Night Raids:* Why Obama is Not Ending the War in Afghanistan' *Tom Dispatch*, May 3 2012

Webb MC and Krasner SD, 'Hegemonic Stability Theory: An Empirical Assessment' (1989) 15 *Review of International Studies* 183

Index

Made in the USA
Las Vegas, NV
23 April 2022

47891909R00184